*Dissertations in*
*Hispanic Languages and Literatures*

# Dissertations in Hispanic Languages and Literatures

AN INDEX OF DISSERTATIONS COMPLETED

IN THE UNITED STATES AND CANADA

1876-1966

## James R. Chatham & Enrique Ruiz-Fornells

WITH THE COLLABORATION OF SARA MATTHEWS SCALES

*The University Press of Kentucky*

Standard Book Number 8131-1183-8
Library of Congress Catalog Card Number 70-80093

# Contents

# *Preface*

With the impressive increase in doctoral studies in Hispanic languages and literatures in North America during the past decade, the need for a bibliography of doctoral dissertations has become more urgent. The resources for such a compilation are numerous (see List of Published Works Consulted, pp. xi-xiv). We have found the Merrill bibliography to be remarkably accurate and comprehensive for the rather slow beginnings of doctoral studies in Romance languages and literatures, and we have been able to add only a few titles for these years. Several specialized articles and book-length bibliographies, of highly variable accuracy, have given partial coverage of the fields of Hispanic languages and literatures for shorter periods and have had the effect of scattering information rather than consolidating it. To these must be added the hundreds of volumes of published abstracts, summaries, registers, and lists of completed doctoral dissertations published by individual universities. These reference works, which usually appear in annual or periodic volumes and seldom cover the entire period of doctoral production in a given university, are quite often poorly indexed, if, in fact, they are indexed at all. The problem of avoiding duplication of research is compounded by the reluctance of libraries to lend such reference materials. Even in the unlikely event that the researcher had all known publications listing dissertations, numerous hours of searching would be required of him before he could be reasonably certain that his topic had not already been investigated. Our purpose in compiling this bibliography, then, is to fill the need for a cumulative classified list of dissertations in Hispanic languages and literatures from the first, which was accepted in 1876, through the year 1966.

The procedure followed in this compilation has been the collection, on cards, of data from all known sources. The checking of this information was very difficult in a number of instances, since some universities do not maintain systematic records of dissertations accepted. Our most helpful sources for this purpose were library card catalogues or official publications of abstracts, summaries, lists, and commencement programs. Even in these, dates are sometimes given for academic years rather than for calendar years. The matter of dates is further complicated by varying practices among universities. In some, the date is listed as the year of the conferral of the degree; in others, it is that of the final examination for the defense of the dissertation. A problem here is that dissertations are sometimes defended toward the end of a calendar year, with the granting of the degree following in January of the next year. We have listed the date of the conferral of the degree when it was known. Otherwise, the date given in our bibliography is that of the final examination or title page of the dissertation. We have found, too, that titles of unfinished dissertations are sometimes reported in listings with no clear indication that they are only in progress. Subsequent correction of titles and dates upon their completion has sometimes been haphazard, and, as a result, we have seen as many as three different titles and dates for the same dissertation in numerous cases. In the last stage of verification of our data, we have mailed lists to chairmen of departments granting doctorates in Hispanic languages and literatures or to libraries as a final check for omissions and errors. We have been favorably impressed by the response of most departments to our inquiries. Reference librarians have helped us on numerous occasions. Our sources of verification are indicated by raised numbers following the abbreviated names of degree-granting institutions in the table of Doctoral Production which follows.

We have included dissertations of obvious interest to researchers in Hispanic languages and literatures even when these have been completed in other departments. Departments of comparative literature and applied linguistics, for example, have produced several dissertations of interest to Hispanists. To a lesser degree, departments of speech-theater, library science, English, French, history, Italian, German, and applied mathematics have made contributions of importance to our area. We have also included two dissertations on the use of the computer in translation and linguistic analysis because of their interest to our field. Although we have omitted dissertations dealing entirely with the indigenous, non-Romance languages of the Iberian peninsula and Latin America, we have included a few which show some relationship with the Spanish and Portuguese languages. Likewise we have included two dissertations on Philippine topics because the Spanish language was in some way involved. We have eliminated all titles of dissertations on language teaching from our bibliography. We shall publish these data separately.

The dissertations are classified according to the system of the *PMLA International Bibliography* prior to the June, 1968, issue. The wording in titles has been our guide in classification. Categories have been based upon the usual terminology of literary history, criticism, and philology. In the interest of thorough classification, we have listed the same dissertation under each of the possible categories derived from its title. Two categories have been added to those of the *PMLA International Bibliography*: (1) comparative studies on the relations of Spanish and Spanish American literature with other literatures are included in Section II, General, and (2) general studies on the literature of individual nations of Spanish America are classified under the name of the countries in Section VII, Literature of Spanish America. Comparative studies for Portuguese and Brazilian literatures are listed at the end of Sections IX and X. The general index gives a thorough topical analysis of the entries under each of the categories, together with names of authors of dissertations and literary figures upon whose lives and works dissertations have been written. Since some writers' lives and literary production do not fit neatly within the rather arbitrary periods of Spanish literature, the use of the general index will facilitate the exact location of entries for these writers. The system of classification and index point out areas in which some duplication or concentration of research has occurred as well as areas in which little or no investigation has been pursued.

We have included, for the convenience of the user, information pertaining to publication in book, microfilm, abstract, or summary form which we have encountered during our pursuit of verification of titles and dates. This information should by no means be construed to be a definitive bibliography of publications resulting from doctoral research, and the user is advised to make full use of all available bibliographic materials, since we have made no systematic effort to include books which may have appeared following the publication of abstracts, summaries, or microfilmed copies of dissertations. We have found that quite often the published form of a dissertation differs in length, content, or title from that presented for the degree, and it is frequently difficult to ascertain whether or not a published book, article, or series of articles, for example, is part of a dissertation or an expansion of research begun as a requirement for the doctorate.

To indicate facts of publication for books, we have given the place and date of publication and the number of the card in the *Library of Congress Catalog* or the *National Union Catalog*. References to entries in these catalogues will facilitate the location of books in the collection of the Library of Congress, and since 1953, those held by libraries throughout the United States. Additional facts of publication not given in our bibliography, such as series titles and names of publishers, may be found in these catalogues. An asterisk placed immediately before the place of publication indicates that the title is similar but not identical to the title of the dissertation presented for the degree or that no dissertation note is found in the *Library of Congress Catalog* or the *National Union Catalog* entry. We include information on a few foreign publications which are not listed in these catalogues.

For abstracts and summaries published in series, we include the shortened title of the collection, volume or year, and the page number on which the abstracts or summaries begin. The practice of requiring publication of abstracts or summaries of dissertations has been highly variable over the years. Our experience has shown that few universities have insisted upon publication of dissertations or abstracts prior to the granting of the degree during the entire period of 1876-1966. Some universities have published annual or periodic volumes of abstracts or summaries of dissertations accepted during the given period; others, while requiring publication of abstracts, have not bound them in periodic volumes. Many of the latter type, bound separately, are included with a thesis note in the *Library of Congress Catalog* or the *National Union Catalog* listings and are assigned card numbers in the same manner as published books.

In recent years, most universities have become affiliated with University Microfilms for the purpose of microfilming and abstracting dissertations. Some permit the postponement of microfilming to allow the degree candidate the opportunity to publish the dissertation in some other form. In a few others, microfilming is done in the university's own library, and the authors and titles are usually reported to the *National Union Catalog*, in which case we have included this information with our entry. Several universities have systematically reported titles of unpublished dissertations to the *National Union Catalog*, but only since around 1963 have card numbers been assigned to unpublished dissertations. As a point of reference for possible interlibrary loan requests, we cite *National Union Catalog* numbers for unpublished dissertations reported in this manner. Finally, we have omitted citations of published programs of the final examinations in defense of dissertations, because these bear only brief statements, usually a paragraph, about the contents of the dissertations.

We are very grateful to Mississippi State University and to Dr. J. C. McKee, Jr., Vice President for Research and Dean of the Graduate School, for a travel grant with which we were able to check much of our information.

Three of our former students, Eli N. Lauderdale, Jr., Miss Nancy Goodwin, and George E. Odom, kindly assisted us in checking library records at the University of Texas, University of Illinois, and Indiana University, respectively. Miss Agnes N. Tysse, University of Michigan Library, Mrs. Barbara L. Bell, Yale University Library, Mrs. Ann T. Hinckley, University of California at Los Angeles Library, and Miss Ruth Walling, Emory University Library, helped us beyond the call of duty, and we are thankful for their assistance. For reading portions of the manuscript and offering valuable suggestions, we are grateful to Professor Victor R. B. Oelschläger, Florida State University, Mrs. Cynthia Ruiz-

Fornells, University of Alabama, and Professors Harold S. Snellgrove, Glover Moore, Oskar H. Zernickow, and Jerry M. Whitmire, Mississippi State University.

We have been unable to verify two or three entries which we have found in annual lists, and in these few cases, we have enclosed the entire entry in brackets. We have taken minor liberties in capitalization and the use of italics in titles for the sake of uniformity, and we follow the English alphabet in the arrangement of entries. We make no claim to absolute perfection in this bibliography. It is our hope, however, that the entries are as accurate as our sources of information.

## DOCTORAL PRODUCTION IN HISPANIC LANGUAGES AND LITERATURES, 1876-1966

| Abbreviated Name of Institution | Name of Institution | Date of First Doctorate[5] | Total Doctorates Conferred[6] | |
| --- | --- | --- | --- | --- |
| Alabama[1,2,3] | University of Alabama | 1966 | | 1 |
| Arizona[1,3] | University of Arizona | 1962 | | 5 |
| Boston College[2] | Boston College | 1939 | | 1 |
| Boston University[1,2,3] | Boston University | 1926 | | 12 |
| Brown[1,2,3] | Brown University | 1932 | | 16 |
| Bryn Mawr[1,2,3] | Bryn Mawr College | 1902 | | 14 |
| California[1] | University of California, Berkeley | 1915 | (2) | 92 |
| Catholic[1,2,3] | Catholic University of America | 1933 | (1) | 24 |
| Chicago[1,2,3] | University of Chicago | 1900 | | 66 |
| Cincinnati[1,3] | University of Cincinnati | 1959 | | 2 |
| Colorado[1,3] | University of Colorado | 1906 | | 20 |
| Columbia[1,2] | Columbia University | 1902 | (7) | 134 |
| Connecticut[1,3] | University of Connecticut | 1966 | | 2 |
| Cornell[1,2] | Cornell University | 1909 | | 28 |
| Denver[1,3] | University of Denver | 1955 | | 2 |
| Duke[1,3] | Duke University | 1941 | | 9 |
| East Texas State[1,3] | East Texas State University | 1966 | | 1 |
| Emory[1,3] | Emory University | 1964 | | 1 |
| Florida[1,3] | University of Florida | 1962 | | 9 |
| Florida State[1,3] | Florida State University | 1953 | | 15 |
| Fordham[1,3] | Fordham University | 1951 | | 2 |
| Georgetown[1,3] | Georgetown University | 1965 | | 6 |
| George Washington[1] | The George Washington University | 1958 | | 2 |
| Harvard[1,2,4] | Harvard University | 1876 | (8) | 102 |
| Illinois[1,2,3] | University of Illinois | 1925 | | 80 |
| Indiana[1,2,3] | Indiana University | 1922 | (3) | 25 |
| Iowa[1,3] | The State University of Iowa | 1928 | | 45 |
| Johns Hopkins[1,2,4] | Johns Hopkins University | 1881 | | 28 |
| Kansas[1,3] | University of Kansas | 1941 | | 20 |
| Kentucky[3] | University of Kentucky | 1955 | | 1 |
| Laval[1] | Université Laval | 1945 | | 2 |
| Louisiana State[1,2,3] | Louisiana State University | 1942 | | 7 |
| Loyola, Chicago[1] | Loyola University, Chicago | 1949 | | 1 |
| Maryland[1,3] | University of Maryland | 1952 | (1) | 15 |
| M.I.T.[1,2,3] | Massachusetts Institute of Technology | 1965 | | 1 |

## DOCTORAL PRODUCTION IN HISPANIC LANGUAGES
### AND LITERATURES (continued)

| Abbreviated Name of Institution | Name of Institution | Date of First Doctorate[5] | Total Doctorates Conferred[6] | |
|---|---|---|---|---|
| McGill[1] | McGill University | 1932 | | 1 |
| Michigan[1,2,3] | University of Michigan | 1918 | (3) | 72 |
| Michigan State[1,3] | Michigan State University | 1965 | | 1 |
| Middlebury[3] | Middlebury College | 1931 | | 14 |
| Minnesota[1] | University of Minnesota | 1900 | | 34 |
| Missouri[1,3] | University of Missouri | 1939 | | 19 |
| Nebraska[1,3] | University of Nebraska | 1955 | | 6 |
| New Mexico[1,3] | University of New Mexico | 1950 | (1) | 23 |
| New York[1,2] | New York University | 1899 | (2) | 50 |
| North Carolina[1,3] | University of North Carolina | 1930 | (5) | 76 |
| Northwestern[1,3] | Northwestern University | 1929 | (1) | 27 |
| Ohio State[1,3] | Ohio State University | 1930 | (1) | 42 |
| Oklahoma[1,3] | University of Oklahoma | 1964 | | 2 |
| Oregon[1,2,3] | University of Oregon | 1932 | | 6 |
| Peabody[3] | George Peabody College for Teachers | 1927 | | 3 |
| Pennsylvania[1,2,3] | University of Pennsylvania | 1902 | (13) | 63 |
| Pennsylvania State[1,3] | Pennsylvania State University | 1954 | | 2 |
| Pittsburgh[1] | University of Pittsburgh | 1925 | (1) | 21 |
| Princeton[1,2,3] | Princeton University | 1921 | (1) | 29 |
| Puerto Rico[3] | Universidad de Puerto Rico | 1966 | | 2 |
| Radcliffe[2,4] | Radcliffe College | 1914 | | 9 |
| Rutgers[1,3] | Rutgers—The State University | 1966 | | 2 |
| St. Louis[1,3] | St. Louis University | 1964 | (1) | 9 |
| Southern California[1] | University of Southern California | 1942 | | 37 |
| Stanford[1,3] | Stanford University | 1923 | (1) | 57 |
| Syracuse[1,2] | Syracuse University | 1950 | | 8 |
| Texas[1,2,3] | University of Texas | 1936 | (3) | 67 |
| Toronto[1,3] | University of Toronto | 1935 | | 11 |
| Tulane[1,3] | Tulane University of Louisiana | 1950 | | 27 |
| U.C.L.A.[1,3] | University of California at Los Angeles | 1950 | | 31 |
| Utah[1,3] | University of Utah | 1958 | | 1 |
| Virginia[1,2,3] | University of Virginia | 1930 | | 12 |
| Washington, St. Louis[1,3] | Washington University | 1951 | | 4 |
| Washington, Seattle[1,3] | University of Washington | 1938 | | 34 |
| Western Reserve[1,3] | Case-Western Reserve University | 1939 | | 9 |
| Wisconsin[1,2,3] | University of Wisconsin | 1907 | (8) | 121 |
| Yale[1,2,3] | Yale University | 1894 | (1) | 60 |
| | | TOTAL | (64) | 1,783 |

[1] Published abstracts, summaries, or lists of dissertation titles.

[2] Library records.

[3] Departmental lists.

[4] Commencement programs.

[5] These dates do not necessarily indicate that the first doctorate was produced in a language department.

[6] Numbers of dissertations on Portuguese-Brazilian topics are indicated in parentheses and included in the totals for each university.

# List of Published Works Consulted

American Council on Education. *A Guide to Graduate Study.* Programs Leading to the Ph.D. Degree. Ed. Jane Graham. 3rd ed. Washington, D.C., 1965.

Arizona, University of. *Abstracts of Theses for Higher Degrees, 1933, and Lists of All Theses for Higher Degrees as Catalogued in the University Library.* University of Arizona General Bulletin, No. 1. Tucson, 1933.

————. Graduate College. *Abstracts of Theses for Higher Degrees.* Tucson, 1934–1946.

Association of Research Libraries. *Doctoral Dissertations Accepted by American Universities.* Nos. 1–22 (1933-34–1954-55). New York, 1934–1955. Superseded by *Index to American Doctoral Dissertations.*

————. *Index to American Doctoral Dissertations.* Combined with *Dissertation Abstracts,* XVI, No. 13 (1955-56)–XXVI, No. 13 (1965-66). Ann Arbor, 1956–1967.

Baricevic, Elizabeth M. "American Doctoral Degrees Granted in the Field of Modern Languages," *Modern Language Journal,* LII (1968), 90–104.

Barrett, L. Lomas. "Theses Dealing with Hispano-American Language and Literature," *Hispania,* XXVIII (1945), 210; XXIX (1946), 220; XXX (1947), 200; XXXI (1948), 157; XXXII (1949), 148-151.

————. "Doctoral Theses in the Hispanic Languages and Literatures," *Hispania,* XXXIII (1950), 119-122; XXXIV (1951), 148–151.

Boston University. *Abstracts of Dissertations,* 1941–1956. Boston, 1945–1957.

Bushong, Allen S. "Doctoral Dissertations on Pan American Topics Accepted by U.S. and Canadian Colleges and Universities, 1961–1965. Bibliography and Analysis," *Latin American Research Review,* II, No. 2 (Spring 1967), 10-54.

California, University of. Graduate Division. *Record of Theses Submitted in Partial Fulfillment of the Requirements for the Degree of Doctor of Philosophy at the University of California, 1885–1926.* Berkeley, 1926.

————. *Supplement to Record for 1885–1926.* Berkeley, 1932.

————. *Second Supplement to Record for 1885–1926.* Berkeley, 1942.

————. *Programmes of the Final Examination for the Degree of Doctor of Philosophy.* Berkeley, 1942–1962.

Canada. *Canadian Graduate Theses in the Humanities and Social Sciences.* 1921–1946. Ottawa, 1951.

Castillo, Homero. "La literatura chilena en los Estados Unidos de América," *Anales de la Universidad de Chile,* No. 113 (1959), 83–128.

————. "La literatura hispanoamericana en las tesis doctorales de los Estados Unidos," *Anales de la Universidad de Chile,* No. 123 (1961), 131–141.

Chicago, University of. *Doctors of Philosophy.* June 1893–April 1931. University of Chicago Announcements, Vol. XXXI, No. 19. Chicago, 1931.

————. Humanistic Series. *Abstracts of Theses, 1922–1932.* 9 vols. Chicago, 1925–1934.

Colorado, University of. *Abstracts of Theses and Reports for Higher Degrees, 1929–1954.* Boulder, 1938–1955.

Columbia University. *List of Theses Submitted by Candidates for the Degree of Doctor of Philosophy in Columbia University, 1872–1910.* New York, 1910. Annual supplements published in the *University Bibliography,* 1911–1966.

Cornell University. *Abstracts of Theses Accepted in Partial Satisfaction of the Requirements for the Doctor's Degree.* Ithaca, 1938–1948.

*Directory of American Scholars.* Vol. III: Foreign Languages—Modern and Classical—Linguistics and Philology. 4th ed. New York, 1964.

*Dissertation Abstracts.* 17 vols. Ann Arbor, 1952–1968.

Doyle, Henry Grattan. "Doctors' Degrees in Modern Foreign Languages," *Modern Language Journal,* XI (1926–27), 38–40; XII (1927–28), 36–39; XIII (1928–29), 28–30; XIV (1929–30), 37–39; XX (1935–36), 37–41, 429–430; XXI (1936–37), 55–60, 279–282, 347–350; XXII (1937–38), 215–220, 297–300, 372–375, 456–459, 547; XXIII (1938–39), 53–58; XXIV (1939–40), 55–59; XXV (1940–41), 58–62, 804–812.

Fordham University. *Dissertations Accepted for Higher Degrees in the Graduate School of Arts and Sciences.* 32 vols. New York, 1935–1966.

George Washington University, The. *Summaries of Doctoral Theses,* 1925–1966. The George Washington University Bulletin. Washington, D.C., 1931–1966.

Gerig, John L., "Advanced Degrees and Doctoral Dissertations in the Romance Languages at the Johns Hopkins University: A Survey and Bibliography," *The Romanic Review*, VIII (1917), 328–340.

——————. "Doctoral Dissertations in the Romance Languages at Harvard University: A Survey and Bibliography," *The Romanic Review*, X (1919), 67–78.

——————. "Doctoral Dissertations in the Romance Languages at Yale University: A Survey and Bibliography," *The Romanic Review*, XI (1920), 70–75.

——————. "Doctoral Dissertations in the Romance Languages at Columbia University: A Survey and Bibliography," *The Romanic Review*, XII (1921), 73–79.

Harvard University. *Doctors of Philosophy and Doctors of Science at Harvard University, 1873–1926.* Official Register of Harvard University, XXIII, No. 39. Cambridge, 1926.

——————. Graduate School of Arts and Sciences. *Summaries of Theses Accepted in Partial Fulfilment of the Requirements for the Degree of Doctor of Philosophy.* 1925–1947. Cambridge, 1928–1947.

Hulet, Claude L. "Dissertations in the Hispanic Languages and Literatures," *Hispania*, XLVIII (1965), 284–287; XLIX (1966), 263–265; L (1967), 297–300.

Iowa, The State University of. *Theses and Dissertations Presented in the Graduate College of the State University of Iowa, 1900–1950.* Compiled by Sarah Scott Edwards. Iowa City, 1952.

——————. *Doctoral Dissertation Abstracts and References, 1900–1952.* 10 vols. Iowa City, 1937–1952.

——————. *Programs Announcing Candidates for Higher Degrees.* Iowa City, 1931–1934.

Johns Hopkins University. Library. *Dissertations Submitted in Conformity with the Requirements for the Degrees of Doctor of Philosophy, Doctor of Engineering, and Doctor of Science in Hygiene in the Johns Hopkins University, 1876–1926.* Baltimore, 1926.

Kansas, University of. *Graduate School Theses, 1888–1947.* Compiled by Bessie E. Wilder. University of Kansas Publications, Library Series, No. 2. Lawrence, 1949.

——————. *Graduate School Theses, 1948–1958.* University of Kansas Publications, Library Series, No. 12. Lawrence, 1961.

Kasten, Lloyd, and others. "Brazilian and Portuguese Studies in Progress in the United States and Canada," *Luso-Brazilian Review*, II, No. 2 (Winter 1965), 97–103; III, No. 2 (Winter 1966), 99–104.

Kidder, Frederick Elwyn, and Allen David Bushong. *Theses on Pan American Topics Prepared by Candidates for Doctoral Degrees in Universities and Colleges in the United States and Canada.* Columbus Memorial Library. Bibliographic Series, No. 5. Fourth edition. Washington, D.C., 1962.

La Du, Robert R., "American Doctoral Degrees Granted in the Field of Modern Languages," *Modern Language Journal*, XLVIII (1964), 227–232, 442–449; XLIX (1965), 492–500; LI (1967), 93–102.

Larson, Ross F., "La literatura hispanoamericana en las tesis doctorales de los Estados Unidos," *Anales de la Universidad de Chile*, No. 133 (1965), 157–170.

Leavitt, Sturgis E., "A Bibliography of Theses Dealing with Hispano-American Literature," *Hispania*, XVIII (1935), 169–182, 458.

——————. "Theses Dealing with Hispano-American Language and Literature," *Hispania*, XX (1937), 175; XXI (1938), 113; XXII (1939), 115; XXIII (1940), 93; XXIV (1941), 199–200; XXV (1942), 204; XXVI (1943), 180; XXVII (1944), 164.

Library of Congress. Catalogue Division. *A List of American Doctoral Dissertations Printed . . . , 1912–1938.* Washington, D.C., 1913–1939.

——————. *A Catalog of Books Represented by Printed Cards.* 167 vols. Ann Arbor, 1942–1946.

——————. *Supplement, 1942–1947.* 42 vols. Ann Arbor, 1948.

——————. *Supplement, 1948–1952.* 24 vols. Ann Arbor, 1953.

——————. *The National Union Catalog, 1953–1957.* 28 vols. Ann Arbor, 1958.

——————. *The National Union Catalog, 1958–1962.* 54 vols. New York, 1963.

——————. *The National Union Catalog.* Annual Supplements, 1963–1967.

——————. *1952–1955 Imprints.* 30 vols. Ann Arbor, 1961.

Louisiana State University. Graduate School. *Abstracts of Theses, 1942.* In Louisiana State University Bulletin, XXXV, No. 1. Baton Rouge, 1943.

Merrill, R. M. *American Doctoral Dissertations in the Romance Field, 1876–1926.* New York, 1927.

*Microfilm Abstracts.* 11 vols. Ann Arbor, 1938–1951. Superseded by *Dissertation Abstracts.*

Miller, William Marion. "American Doctoral Degrees Granted in the Field of Modern Languages," *Modern Language Journal*, XXXIII (1949), 624–629; XXXV (1951), 45–52, 567–574; XXXVII (1953), 152–158; XXXVIII (1954), 246–252; XXXIX (1955), 100–106; XL (1956), 145–149; XLI (1957), 194–200; XLII (1958), 142–146; XLIII (1959), 147–151; XLIV (1960), 130–135; XLV (1961), 132–136; XLVI (1962), 179–183; XLVII (1963), 127–132.

Minnesota, University of. *Register of Ph.D. Degrees, 1888–1938.* The University of Minnesota Bulletin, XLII, No. 31. Minneapolis, 1939.

——————. *Register of Ph.D. Degrees Conferred by the University of Minnesota 1938 Through June, 1956.* Minneapolis, 1957.

————. *Summaries of Ph.D. Theses, 1939–1942*. 5 vols. Minneapolis, 1939–1951.

Missouri, University of. *Graduate School Degrees Conferred, 1892–1948*. University of Missouri Bulletin, L, No. 22. Columbia, 1949.

Moser, Gerald M., "Contemporary Portuguese Scholarship in North America," *Luso-Brazilian Review*, I, No. 1 (Summer 1964), 19–42.

New York University. *University Bibliography*. New York University Bulletin, XXXII-LV. New York, 1930–1955.

North Carolina, University of. *The Graduate School Dissertations and Theses*. Ed. James L. Godfrey and others. Chapel Hill, 1947.

————. *First Supplement: 1946–1959*. University of North Carolina Library Studies, No. 3. Chapel Hill, 1960.

————. "Research in Progress," University of North Carolina *Record*, No. 268 (Oct. 1930)—No. 590 (Oct. 1958).

Northwestern University. *A List of Doctoral Dissertations Submitted at Northwestern University, 1896–1934*. Chicago-Evanston, 1935.

————. *Summaries of Doctoral Dissertations*. 20 vols. Evanston, 1933–1952.

"Notes and News," *Modern Language Journal*, VII (1922–23), 44–46; VIII (1923–24), 41–43; IX (1924–25), 52–54; X (1925–26), 45–47.

Ohio State University. *Abstracts of Dissertations Presented by Candidates for the Degree of Doctor of Philosophy*. Nos. 1–67. Columbus, 1929–1957.

Oregon State System of Higher Education. *Graduate Theses, 1932–42*. Eugene, 1946.

Pennsylvania, University of. *Doctors of Philosophy of the Graduate School, 1889–1927*. Philadelphia, 1927.

Pennsylvania State College [University since 1953]. *Abstracts of Doctoral Dissertations, 1938–1955*. 18 vols. College Park, Pennsylvania, 1938–1955.

Pittsburgh, University of. The Graduate School. *Abstracts of Dissertations for the Degree of Doctor of Philosophy with an Appendix upon the Graduate Activities of the University*. Pittsburgh, Pennsylvania, 1926–1954.

Poesse, Walter. "Disertaciones lopescas: una compilación," *Hispanófila*, VI, No. 18 (May 1963), 77–89; IX, No. 26 (January 1966), 1–6.

Radcliffe College. Graduate School of Arts and Sciences. *Summaries of Theses Accepted in Partial Fulfilment of the Requirements for the Degree of Doctor of Philosophy, 1931–1938*. Cambridge, 1935–1943.

Roberts, William H., "Brazilian and Portuguese Studies in Progress in the United States and Canada, 1963–1964," *Luso-Brazilian Review*, I, No. 2 (Winter 1964), 97–102.

St. John's University. *Abstracts of Dissertations*. 12 vols. New York, 1939–1963.

Sedwick, Frank. "Theses on Miguel de Unamuno at North American Universities (to February 1955)," *Kentucky Foreign Language Quarterly*, III, No. 4 (1956), 192–196.

Smither, William J. "Doctoral Theses in the Hispanic Languages and Literatures," *Hispania*, XXXV (1952), 173–175.

————. "Dissertations in the Hispanic Languages and Literatures," *Hispania*, XXXVI (1953), 164–166; XXXVII (1954), 171–182; XXXVIII (1955), 182–184; XXXIX (1956), 321–322; XL (1957), 196–197; XLI (1958), 195–197; XLII (1959), 215–216; XLIII (1960), 219–220; XLIV (1961), 285–287; XLV (1962), 269–271; XLVI (1963), 333–335; XLVII (1964), 327–329.

————. "Subject Index: Dissertations in the Hispanic Languages and Literatures," *Hispania*, XXXVII (1954), 185–202.

South Atlantic Modern Language Association. *Thesis Supplement, 1917–1937. South Atlantic Bulletin*, IV, No. 1s (April 1938); annual lists to date.

Southern California, University of. *Annotations of Theses and Dissertations Accepted by the University of Southern California, 1910–1935*. University Chronicles Series, No. 4. Los Angeles, 1936.

————. *Abstracts of Dissertations, 1936–1958*. Los Angeles, 1938–1959.

Stanford University. *Degrees and Theses, 1892–1924*. Stanford, California, n.d.

————. *Abstracts of Dissertations, 1924–1952*. Stanford, California, 1927–1953.

"Tesis doctorales sobre filología española," *Revista de filología española*, VI (1919), 312–313.

Tulane University of Louisiana. Graduate School. *Titles of Theses, 1885–1937*. New Orleans, 1939.

————. *Abstracts of Theses, 1938–1955*. New Orleans, 1938–1955.

Virginia, University of. Department of Graduate Studies. *Abstracts of Dissertations Accepted in Partial Fulfilment of the Requirements for the Degree of Doctor of Philosophy, 1931–1952*. Charlottesville, 1931–1952.

Washington, University of. *Digests of Theses, 1914–1931*. University of Washington Publications, I. Seattle, 1931.

————. *Abstracts of Theses and Faculty Bibliography, 1931–1946*. University of Washington Publications, II-VIII. Seattle, 1937–1947.

Western Reserve University. *Bibliography of Publications and Abstracts of Dissertations, 1950–1958*. Cleveland, 1952–1958.

Wisconsin, University of. *Abstracts of Theses Submitted*

*in Partial Fulfillment of the Requirements for the Degree of Doctor of Philosophy.* Madison, 1917.

————. *Summaries of Doctoral Dissertations, 1935–1955.* Madison, 1937–1955.

————. Annual Commencement Registers. Madison, 1912–1952.

Yale University. *Doctors of Philosophy of Yale University, with the Titles of Their Dissertations, 1861–1915.* New Haven, 1916.

————. *Doctors of Philosophy of Yale University, with the Titles of Their Dissertations, 1861–1927.* New Haven, 1927.

————. *Doctors of Philosophy, Supplement for the Years 1928–1930.* New Haven, 1931.

## ABBREVIATIONS AND SYMBOLS

| | |
|---|---|
| * | Indication that a published book has a variant title or no thesis note in the preface |
| *BRAE* | *Boletín de la Real Academia Española* |
| *DA* | *Dissertation Abstracts* |
| LC | *Library of Congress Catalog* |
| *MA* | *Microfilm Abstracts* |
| NUC | *National Union Catalog* |
| *RFE* | *Revista de filología española* |

# PART ONE

# *Spain and Spanish America*

### I. LINGUISTICS

#### 1. *Bibliography*

1.1.  Hall, Pauline Cook.  A Bibliography of Spanish Linguistics: Articles in Serial Publications, 1887-1947.  Iowa, 1949.  Baltimore, 1957.  NUC 57-1838.

1.2.  Rutherford, Phillip Roland.  Linguistic Research in American Universities: Dissertations and Influences from 1900 to 1964.  East Texas State, 1966.  *DA,* XXVII, 2517-A.

#### 2. *Miscellaneous*

2.1.  Andrade, Graciela.  Las expresiones del lenguaje familiar de Pérez Galdós en *Fortunata y Jacinta.*  Iowa, 1957.  *DA,* XVII, 3008.

2.2.  Barker, George Carpenter.  Pachuco, An American Spanish Argot and Its Social Functions in Tucson, Arizona.  Chicago, 1948.  Tucson, 1950.  LC 50-63360.

2.3.  Beym, Richard.  The Linguistic Category of Emphasis in Colloquial Spanish.  Illinois, 1952.  *DA,* XIV, 362.

2.4.  Bodensieck, Anne Marie.  The Linguistic Comic in Cervantes' *Don Quixote de la Mancha.*  Wisconsin, 1928.

2.5.  Bucklin, Lincoln Brice.  Liturgical Influence on Popular Spanish.  Johns Hopkins, 1952.

2.6.  Corley, Ames Haven.  A Study in the Word-Play in Cervantes' *Don Quixote.*  Yale, 1914.  New York, 1917.  LC 18-6681.

2.7.  Foster, Richard H.  The Spanish in the Cebuano Vocabulary of the Bible as a Partial Revelation of Spanish Cultural, Political and Economic Influence in the Philippine Islands.  California, 1947.

2.8.  Frank, Francine Harriet Wattman.  Taxemic Redundancy in Spanish.  Illinois, 1955.  *DA,* XV, 2195.

2.9.  Giuliano, Vincent Edward.  An Experimental Study of Automatic Language Translation.  Harvard, 1959.  Cambridge, Mass., 1959.  NUC 59-1111.

2.10.  Henisz, Bozena.  Derivation: Morphophonemic Alteration Patterns, Generative Formation Rules and System for Computer Processing.  Georgetown, 1965.  *DA,* XXVIII, 653-A.

2.11.  Kirby, Kenneth N.  Unamuno and Language.  Texas, 1953.

2.12.  Kyger, Minor Ellsworth, Jr.  Indo-European Words and Locutions for Danger (With Emphasis on Germanic and Romance Languages).  Catholic, 1955.  Washington, 1955.  NUC A55-8705.

2.13.  Lopes, Albert Richard.  Aspects of the Language of the Realistic Novel of the Seventeenth Century.  California, 1935.

2.14.  Mantinband, James H.  An Index of Tense-Stems and Formants in Cognate Verbs of Representative Indo-European Languages.  New York, 1953.

2.15.  Rodriguez Bou, Ismael.  A Study of the Parallelism of English and Spanish Vocabularies.  Texas, 1943.  Río Piedras, P. R., 1950.  LC 51-62289.

2.16.  Rubin, Joan.  National Bilingualism in Paraguay.  Yale, 1963.  *DA,* XXV, 751.

2.17.  Sand, Louise.  The Role of Federico Hanssen and Rodolfo Lenz in the Intellectual Life of Chile.  North Carolina, 1958.  *DA,* XIX, 1391.

2.18.  Tarr, Frederick Courtney.  Prepositional Complementary Clauses in Spanish, with Special Reference to the Works of Pérez Galdós.  Princeton, 1921.  New York-Paris, 1922.  LC 24-14623.

2.19.  Valencia, Pablo.  An Historical Study of Syllabic Structure in Spanish.  Michigan, 1966.  *DA,* XXVIII, 218-A.

#### 3. *Adjective*

3.1.  Brownell, George Griffin.  The Position of the Attributive Adjective in the *Don Quixote.*  Johns Hopkins, 1904.  Paris-New York, 1908.  LC 13-22980.

3.2.  Conway, [Sister] M. Ann C., S.N.J.M.  Order Classes of Adjectives in Spanish.  Texas, 1964.  *DA,* XXV, 6607.

3.3.  García-Girón, Edmundo.  The Adjective: A Contribution to the Study of Modernist Poetic Diction.  California, 1952.

3.4.  Harrison, Gordon W.  A Study of the Range and Frequency of Constructions Involving Pronouns and Pronominal Adjectives in Manuscript J-1, Biblioteca Nacional, of the *Gran conquista de Ultramar.*  Chicago, 1940.  Chicago, 1940.  LC 41-9655.

3.5.  Mills, Dorothy Hurst.  A Descriptive Analysis of the Morphology of the Diminutives *ito, illo, ico, uelo* and of Their Increments (Including Feminine and Plural Forms) as Used in Spanish America.  Southern California, 1955.  Southern California *Abstracts,* 1955, p. 99.

3. 6.　Ringo, Elbert W.　The Position of the Noun Modifier in Colloquial Mexican Spanish.　Illinois, 1950. Urbana, 1950.　LC A51-2090.

3. 7.　Solé, Carlos Alberto, Jr.　Los adjetivos españoles terminados en *-al, -ar, -ero, -ico* y *-oso*.　Georgetown, 1966.　*DA,* XXVII, 762-A.

3. 8.　Trager, George Leonard.　The Use of the Latin Demonstratives (Especially *ille* and *ipse*) up to 600 A.D., as the Source of the Romance Article.　Columbia, 1932.　New York, 1932.　LC 33-15894.

### 4.　*Adverb*

4. 1.　Gerrard, Allen George.　A Study of the Usage of the Spanish Locative Adverbs, *Aquí* and *Acá*.　Michigan, 1963.　*DA,* XXV, 462.

4. 2.　Haynes, Randolph Arnold.　Negation in *Don Quixote*.　Chicago, 1931.　Chicago, 1933.　LC 34-2463.

4. 3.　London, Gardiner H.　Conjunctive Adverbs in the Prose Texts of Alfonso X, the Learned.　Wisconsin, 1951.　Wisconsin *Summaries,* XII, 464.

4. 4.　McWilliams, Ralph D.　The Adverb in Colloquial Spanish.　Illinois, 1951.　See Kahane, Henry R. and Angelina Pietrangeli, eds., *Descriptive Studies in Spanish Grammar* (Urbana, 1954), 73-137.　NUC 53-5154.

### 5.　*Anglicism*

5. 1.　Kochman, Thomas Michael.　Analysis of Phonetic Modification of the Anglicism in Chilean Spanish. New York, 1966.　*DA,* XXVII, 760-A.

5. 2.　Kreidler, Charles W.　A Study of the Influence of English on the Spanish of Puerto Ricans in Jersey City, New Jersey.　Michigan, 1958.　*DA,* XIX, 527.

5. 3.　Tsuzaki, Stanley Mamoru.　English Influences in the Phonology and Morphology of the Spanish Spoken in the Mexican Colony in Detroit, Michigan. Michigan, 1963.　*DA,* XXIV, 2471.

5. 4.　Zúñiga-Tristán, Virginia.　El anglicismo en el habla costarricense.　Tulane, 1958.　*DA,* XIX, 2609.

### 6.　*Archaism*

6. 1.　Fjelstad, Ruth N.　Archaisms in *Amadís de Gaula*. Iowa, 1963.　*DA,* XXIV, 4687.

6. 2.　Jeffers, Coleman R.　Medievalisms in the Writings of the Spanish Romanticists.　Iowa, 1954.　*DA,* XIV, 1723.

6. 3.　Lapp, Donald.　Archaisms in Four Novels of Chivalry.　Iowa, 1964.　*DA,* XXV, 5270.

### 7.　*Catalan*

7. 1.　Flam, Bernard Paul.　A Concordance to the Works of Auzias March.　Wisconsin, 1962.　*DA,* XXIII, 2127.

7. 2.　Frost, Francis LeJau.　The *Art de contemplacio* of Ramón Lull, Published with an Introduction and a Study of the Language of the Author.　Johns Hopkins, 1901.　Baltimore, 1903.　LC 3-29045.

7. 3.　Hasegawa, Yothinosuke.　On the Catalan of Northern New York.　Columbia, 1880.

7. 4.　Heaton, Harry Clifton.　The *Gloria d'amor* of Fra Rocabertí, a Catalan Vision-Poem of the 15th Century.　Edited with Introduction, Notes and Glossary. Columbia, 1916.　New York, 1916.　LC 17-6377.

7. 5.　Neugaard, Edward Joseph.　A Critical Edition of a Portion of the 13th Century *Vides de Santz Rosselloneses* with Introduction, Notes, Table of Proper Names, and Glossary.　North Carolina, 1964.　*DA,* XXVI, 1048.

7. 6.　Ventura, Miguel.　Historical Catalan Phonetics. Cornell, 1909.

### 8.　*Clause*

8. 1.　Brend, Ruth Margaret.　A Tagmemic Analysis of Mexican Spanish Clauses.　Michigan, 1964.　*DA,* XXV, 2972.

8. 2.　Chatham, James R.　A Syntactical Study of the Indirect Interrogative in Old Spanish.　Florida State, 1960.　*DA,* XXI, 2284.

8. 3.　Chenery, Winthrop Holt.　Object Pronouns in Dependent Clauses: A Study in Old Spanish Word Order.　Harvard, 1904.

8. 4.　Cressey, William W.　A Transformational Analysis of the Relative Clause in Urban Mexican Spanish. Illinois, 1966.　*DA,* XXVII, 3857-A.

8. 5.　Paratore, Angela.　Spanish Verb Phrase and Clause Structure.　Cornell, 1950.

8. 6.　Tarr, Frederick Courtney.　Prepositional Complementary Clauses in Spanish, with Special Reference to the Works of Pérez Galdós.　Princeton, 1921. New York-Paris, 1922.　LC 24-14623.

### 9.　*Dialectology*

9. 1.　Bowen, Jean D.　The Spanish of San Antonio, New Mexico.　New Mexico, 1952.

9. 2.　Boyd-Bowman, Peter M.　A Linguistic Study of the Spanish of Guanajuato, Mexico.　Harvard, 1950. *Mexico, 1960.　NUC 60-46320.

9. 3.　Cárdenas, Daniel N.　The Spanish of Jalisco: A Contribution to Spanish-American Linguistic Geography.　Columbia, 1953.　*DA,* XIV, 137.

9. 4.　Cerezo de Ponce, Engracia.　La zona lingüística de Aguadilla.　Puerto Rico, 1966.

9. 5.　Cheskis, Joseph Israel.　Philological Studies in Judaeo-Spanish.　Harvard, 1917.

9. 6.　Cowles, Ella Nancy.　A Vocabulary of American Spanish Based on Glossaries Appended to Literary Works.　Michigan, 1952.　*DA,* XII, 294

9.7.   Doty, Edith Aultman. A Glossary of "Filipinismos" in the Spanish Language Found in the Philippine Publications of the Period 1890-1920. Michigan, 1958. *DA,* XIX, 530.

9.8.   Dunstan, Robert T. A Critical Edition of Fernández de Heredia's Translation into Aragonese of Guido Delle Colonne's *Crónica troyana.* Wisconsin, 1928.

9.9.   Espinosa, Aurelio Macedonio. Studies in New Mexican Spanish. Part 1, Phonology. Chicago, 1909. Chicago, 1909. LC A11-1172.

9.10.  Galván, Robert A. El dialecto español de San Antonio, Tejas. Tulane, 1954. Tulane *Abstracts,* Series 55, No. 14, p. 90.

9.11.  Griffin, David A. Elementos mozárabes del *Diccionario Latino-Arábigo* (Siglo XIII) atribuido a Ramón Martí. Chicago, 1956. Chicago, 1956. NUC Mic 58-6262.

9.12.  Gulsoy, Joseph. El *Diccionario valenciano-castellano* de Manuel Joaquín Sanelo: Edición, estudio de fuentes e investigación lexicológica. Chicago, 1961. Microfilmed, Chicago Library, 1961.

9.13.  Hejtmanek, Lillian. The Syntax of the Exclamation in Colloquial Mexican. Illinois, 1947. Urbana, 1948. LC A48-10160.

9.14.  Hills, Elijah Clarence. New-Mexican Spanish. Colorado, 1906. Baltimore, 1906. LC 16-21276.

9.15.  Hirsch, Ruth. A Study of Some Aspects of a Judeo-Spanish Dialect as Spoken by a New York Sephardic Family. Michigan, 1951. *MA,* XI, No. 3, p. 674.

9.16.  Holzapfel, Tamara O. The Antioquian Dialect of Tomás Carrasquilla. Iowa, 1964. *DA,* XXV, 5269.

9.17.  Hull, Adrian L. The Linguistic Accommodation of a Cultural Innovation as Illustrated by the Game of Baseball in the Spanish Language of Puerto Rico. Columbia, 1963. *DA,* XXV, 7256.

9.18.  Jaffé, Erwin. A Treatment of Certain Aspects of Galician as Found in the *Crónica troyana.* Harvard, 1939. Harvard *Summaries,* 1939, p. 268.

9.19.  Jones, Morgan Emory. A Phonological Study of the English as Spoken by Puerto Ricans Contrasted with Puerto Rican Spanish and American English. Michigan, 1962. *DA,* XXIII, 2127.

9.20.  Jungemann, Frederick H. The Substratum Theory and the Hispano-Romance and Gascon Dialects: A Functional-Structural Analysis of Some Phonological Problems. Columbia, 1952. *DA,* XIII, 399.

9.21.  Kasten, Lloyd August William. *Secreto de los secretos,* Translated by Juan Fernández de Heredia: An Edition of the Unique Aragonese Manuscript, with Literary Introduction and Glossary. Wisconsin, 1931.

9.22.  Kochman, Thomas Michael. Analysis of Phonetic Modification of the Anglicism in Chilean Spanish. New York, 1966. *DA,* XXVII, 760-A.

9.23.  Kreidler, Charles W. A Study of the Influence of English on the Spanish of Puerto Ricans in Jersey City, New Jersey. Michigan, 1958. *DA,* XIX, 527.

9.24.  Lévy, Isaac Jack. Prolegomena to a Study of the *Refranero sefardí.* Michigan, 1966. *DA,* XXVIII, 198-A.

9.25.  Lozano, Anthony G. A Study of Spoken Styles in Colombian Spanish. Texas, 1964. *DA,* XXV, 2973.

9.26.  Luria, Max Aaron. A Study of the Monastir Dialect of Judeo-Spanish Based on Oral Material Collected in Monastir, Yugo-Slavia. Columbia, 1930. New York-Paris, 1930. LC 31-8946.

9.27.  MacCurdy, Raymond R. The Spanish Dialect in St. Bernard Parish, Louisiana. North Carolina, 1948. Albuquerque, New Mexico, 1950. LC 50-63452.

9.28.  McCullough, Joe Thompson. The Spanish of Antioquian Oriente (Colombia). California, 1954.

9.29.  Marden, Charles Carroll. The Phonology of the Spanish Dialect of Mexico City. Johns Hopkins, 1894. Baltimore, 1896. LC 3-22020.

9.30.  Meikle, Herbert Galt. A Glossary of Colombian Colloquialisms; Based on the Speech of Colombian Males. Michigan, 1961. *DA,* XXI, 3776.

9.31.  Murphy, Spencer L. A Description of Noun Suffixes in Colloquial Mexican Spanish. Illinois, 1950. Urbana, 1950. LC A51-4253.

9.32.  Nykl, Alois Richard. *Rrekotamiento del rrey Alisandere,* An *Aljamiado* Text, with Introduction and Notes. Chicago, 1921. Chicago *Abstracts,* II, 347.

9.33.  Pardo, Aristóbulo V. Esquema morfológico del leonés antiguo en el *Fuero de Zamora.* Ohio State, 1966. *DA,* XXVII, 3031-A.

9.34.  Petersen, Phillip Burns. A Linguistic Study of the Old Leonese *Fuero de Ledesma.* California, 1955.

9.35.  Post, Anita Calneh. Southern Arizona Spanish. Stanford, 1932. *Tucson, 1934. LC 34-27911.

9.36.  Rael, Juan Bautista. A Study of the Phonology and Morphology of New Mexican Spanish Based on a Collection of 410 Folk-Tales. Stanford, 1937. Stanford *Abstracts,* 1936-37, p. 55.

9.37.  Ringo, Elbert W. The Position of the Noun Modifier in Colloquial Mexican Spanish. Illinois, 1950. Urbana, 1950. LC A51-2090.

9.38.  Robe, Stanley L. A Dialect and Folkloristic Study of Texts Recorded in Los Altos of Jalisco, Mexico. North Carolina, 1949. North Carolina *Record,* No. 478, p. 233.

9. 39. Sáez, Mercedes de los Angeles. Puerto-Rican English Phonotactics. Texas, 1962. *DA*, XXIII, 1013.

9. 40. Sawyer, Janet B. M. A Dialect Study of San Antonio, Texas: A Bilingual Community. Texas, 1957. *DA*, XVIII, 586.

9. 41. Sousa, Thomas Frederic. A Linguistic Analysis of a Portion of the Galician Translation of the *General estoria* by Alfonso X, el Sabio. Wisconsin, 1964. *DA*, XXIV, 5418.

9. 42. Spiegel, Irving. Old Judaeo-Spanish Evidence of Old Spanish Pronunciation. Minnesota, 1953. *DA*, XIII, 819.

9. 43. Stern, Charlotte Daniels. Studies on the *Sayagués* of Early Spanish Drama. Pennsylvania, 1960. *DA*, XXI, 1195.

9. 44. Tsuzaki, Stanley Mamoru. English Influences in the Phonology and Morphology of the Spanish Spoken in the Mexican Colony in Detroit, Michigan. Michigan, 1963. *DA*, XXIV, 2471.

9. 45. Umphrey, George Wallace. A Study of the Aragonese Dialect, Based on a Fourteenth Century Manuscript Now Edited for the First Time. Harvard, 1905. Seattle, 1913. LC 14-31182.

9. 46. Vaquero de Ramírez, María del T. Estudio lingüístico de Barranquitas. Puerto Rico, 1966.

9. 47. Vetrano, Anthony J. The Ecuadorian Indian and *Cholo* in the Novels of Jorge Icaza: Their Lot and Language. Syracuse, 1966. *DA*, XXVII, 4268-A.

9. 48. Villegas, Francisco. Glosario del argot costarricense. Michigan, 1953. *DA*, XIII, 383.

9. 49. Zúñiga-Tristán, Virginia. El anglicismo en el habla costarricense. Tulane, 1958. *DA*, XIX, 2609.

## 10. *Etymology*

10. 1. Bachmann, Ann Opalak. An Etymological and Partial Syntactical Analysis of the *Rimado de palaçio* of Pero López de Ayala. Florida State, 1958. *DA*, XIX, 526.

10. 2. DeLand, Graydon S. An Etymological Vocabulary to the Books of Exodus and Leviticus of the *General estoria* of Alfonso el Sabio. Wisconsin, 1935. Wisconsin *Summaries*, I, 335.

10. 3. DeMent, Russell Duke. An Etymological Lexicon of *El poema de Alfonso Onceno*. North Carolina, 1961. *DA*, XXII, 3653.

10. 4. Duncan, Robert M. An Etymological Vocabulary of Plant Names in the Works of Alfonso el Sabio. Wisconsin, 1936. Wisconsin *Summaries*, I, 333.

10. 5. Holmes, Henry Bert. An Etymological Vocabulary of *Calila y Dimna*. Wisconsin, 1935. Wisconsin *Summaries*, I, 338.

10. 6. McDowell, David Franklin. The Nature of Old Spanish Vocabulary as Determined by an Etymological and Semantic Analysis of the Verbs in the *Primera parte* of the *General estoria* of Alfonso el Sabio. North Carolina, 1943. North Carolina *Record*, No. 429, p. 231.

10. 7. Moseley, William Whatley. An Etymological Vocabulary of the Spanish in the Works of Gil Vicente. New Mexico, 1954. *DA*, XV, 119.

10. 8. Munro, Edwin C. An Etymological Vocabulary of Military Terms in the Works of Alfonso X. Wisconsin, 1950. Wisconsin *Summaries*, XI, 373.

10. 9. Owre, Jacob R. The *Poema de Fernán Gonçález*: A Paleographic Edition of the Escorial Manuscript IV-B-21, with Notes and Etymologic Vocabulary. Minnesota, 1934. Minnesota *Summaries*, I, 174.

10. 10. Pincus, Michael Stern. An Etymological Lexicon of *Ysopete hystoriado*. North Carolina, 1961. *DA*, XXII, 3671.

10. 11. Poston, Lawrence S., Jr. An Etymological Vocabulary to the *Celestina*, A-E. Chicago, 1938. Chicago, 1940. LC 42-2786.

10. 12. Prado, Miguel Angel. Estudio comparado de las derivaciones eruditas y populares del *Cantar de Don Sancho II de Castilla*. Stanford, 1942. Stanford *Abstracts*, 1941-42, p. 68.

10. 13. Romeo, Andrew L. An Etymological Vocabulary for Ms. S.34 of Don Juan Manuel's *Los enxiemplos del Conde Lucanor et de Patronio* Together with a Total Word-Frequency Concordance. Tulane, 1950. Tulane *Abstracts*, Series 51, No. 13, p. 63.

10. 14. Steiner, Mary Florence Fox. An Etymological Study of Old Spanish Personal Names. Northwestern, 1953. *DA*, XIII, 1205.

10. 15. Whitted, Joseph Willard. An Etymological Lexicon to the *Historia troyana*. North Carolina, 1963. *DA*, XXIV, 3346.

10. 16. Zahn, Louis J. An Etymological Lexicon of *El libro de los exenplos por a.b.c.* North Carolina, 1957. *Madrid, 1961. NUC 62-42136.

## 11. *Figurative Language*

11. 1. Fränkel, Hans Hermann. Figurative Language in the Serious Poetry of Quevedo: A Contribution to the Study of *Conceptismo*. California, 1942.

11. 2. McGarry, [Sister] Francis de Sales. The Allegorical and Metaphorical Language in the *Autos Sacramentales* of Calderón. Catholic, 1937. Washington, 1937. LC 38-7907.

## 12. *Galician*

12. 1. Jaffé, Erwin. A Treatment of Certain Aspects of Galician as Found in the *Crónica troyana*. Harvard, 1939. Harvard *Summaries*, 1939, p. 268.

12. 2. Parker, Kelvin M. A Classified Vocabulary of the *Crónica troyana*. Chicago, 1953. *Salamanca, 1958. NUC 60-26925.

12. 3. Sousa, Thomas Frederic. A Linguistic Analysis of a Portion of the Galician Translation of the *General estoria* by Alfonso X, el Sabio. Wisconsin, 1964. *DA,* XXIV, 5418.

### 13. *Gallicism*

13. 1. DeForest, John Bellows. Old French Borrowed Words in Old Spanish of the Twelfth and Thirteenth Centuries with Special Reference to the *Cid,* Berceo's Poems, the *Alexandre,* and *Fernán González.* Yale, 1915. New York, 1916. LC 19-16238.

13. 2. Hess, Steven. Gallicisms in Old Spanish of the Twelfth and Thirteenth Centuries. Harvard, 1966. See NUC 67-98397.

13. 3. Rubio, Antonio. La crítica del galicismo desde Feijóo hasta Mesonero (1726-1832). Chicago, 1934. *Mexico, 1937. LC 39-31646.

### 14. *Interrogative*

14. 1. Chatham, James R. A Syntactical Study of the Indirect Interrogative in Old Spanish. Florida State, 1960. *DA,* XXI, 2284.

14. 2. Farley, Rodger A. Interrogative Patterns of Sentence Units in Contemporary Castilian Dramatic Speech. Florida State, 1956. *DA,* XVI, 1451.

14. 3. Sapon, Stanley Martin. A Study of the Development of the Interrogative in Spanish from the Twelfth Through the Fifteenth Centuries. Columbia, 1949. Columbus, Ohio, 1951. LC A51-5120.

### 15. *Lexicology-Lexicography*

15. 1. Bayliss, Betty. Sebastián de Covarrubias' *Suplemento al Tesoro de la lengua castellana*: A Critical Edition of Selections from the Original Manuscript. Illinois, 1959. *DA,* XX, 3735.

15. 2. Bentley, Harold Woodmansee. A Dictionary of Spanish Terms in English. Columbia, 1932. New York, 1932. LC 33-4588.

15. 3. Brown, Leslie P. Some Romance Words of Arabic Origin. Southern California, 1935. *Los Angeles, 1938. LC 38-33359.

15. 4. Bulatkin, Eleanor Webster. The Expression of the Concept "Nuance" in Spanish, Italian, and French. Johns Hopkins, 1952.

15. 5. Causey, James Young. A Cultural Study of the Agricultural Terms in the Works of Alfonso el Sabio. Wisconsin, 1940. Wisconsin *Summaries,* VI, 321.

15. 6. Cowles, Ella Nancy. A Vocabulary of American Spanish Based on Glossaries Appended to Literary Works. Michigan, 1952. *DA,* XII, 294.

15. 7. Crowley, Cornelius Joseph. Persisting Latinisms in *El poema de Mío Cid* and Other Selected Old Spanish Literary Works. New York, 1951. Baltimore, 1952. NUC A53-1036.

15. 8. Davis, Jack Emory. Estudio lexicográfico de *El periquillo sarniento.* Tulane, 1956. *DA,* XVI, 1137.

15. 9. DeForest, John Bellows. Old French Borrowed Words in Old Spanish of the Twelfth and Thirteenth Centuries with Special Reference to the *Cid,* Berceo's Poems, the *Alexandre,* and *Fernán González.* Yale, 1915. New York, 1916. LC 19-16238.

15. 10. Delaney, John T. A Selective English-Old Spanish Glossary as a Basis for Studies in Old Spanish Onomatology and Synonymics. Catholic, 1966. Washington, 1966. NUC 67-91049.

15. 11. Doty, Edith Aultman. A Glossary of "Filipinismos" in the Spanish Language Found in the Philippine Publications of the Period 1890-1920. Michigan, 1958. *DA,* XIX, 530.

15. 12. Doblin, Helga B. Designations of Stringed Instruments in Romance Languages. Harvard, 1965.

15. 13. Edgerly, Clifton T. A Vocabulary of the *Siete partidas,* I and II, of Alfonso X. Yale, 1918.

15. 14. Edgerton, Mills Fox. Color Terms in Transitional Latin; A Method for the Diachronic Investigation of the Semantics of an Area of Vocabulary, Together with an Initial Study. Princeton, 1960. *DA,* XXI, 2285.

15. 15. Georges, Emanuel Spear. Studies in Romance Nouns Extracted from Past Participles. California, 1965. *DA,* XXVI, 1032.

15. 16. Glover, Bobby Ray. A History of Six Spanish Verbs Meaning "To Take, Seize, Grasp." Louisiana State, 1966. *DA,* XXVII, 203-A.

15. 17. Griffin, David A. Elementos mozárabes del *Diccionario Latino-Arábigo* (Siglo XIII) atribuido a Ramón Martí. Chicago, 1956. Chicago, 1956. NUC Mic 58-6262.

15. 18. Gulsoy, Joseph. El *Diccionario valenciano-castellano* de Manuel Joaquín Sanelo: Edición, estudio de fuentes e investigación lexicológica. Chicago, 1961. Microfilmed, Chicago Library, 1961.

15. 19. Heaton, Harry Clifton. The *Gloria d'amor* of Fra Rocabertí, a Catalan Vision-Poem of the 15th Century. Edited with Introduction, Notes and Glossary. Columbia, 1916. New York, 1916. LC 17-6377.

15. 20. Hess, Steven. Gallicisms in Old Spanish of the Twelfth and Thirteenth Centuries. Harvard, 1966. See NUC 67-98397.

15. 21. Hill, John M. A Contribution to Old Spanish Lexicography. Wisconsin, 1912.

15. 22. Holman, William Lee. An Edition and Glos-

sary of the *Crónica del Rey D. Enrique Segundo de Castilla* by Pero López de Ayala from Manuscript A-14 of the Academia de la Historia. Wisconsin, 1965. *DA,* XXVI, 5425.

15. 23. Honsa, Vladimír Jiří Jaroslav. *La gran conquista de Ultramar,* Book IV, Chapters 126-193: Critical Edition, Grammatical Analysis, and Glossary. Michigan, 1957. *DA,* XVIII, 1420.

15. 24. Johnston, Marjorie C. Cognate Relationships Between English and Spanish Vocabularies as a Basis for Instruction. Texas, 1939.

15. 25. Kasten, Lloyd August William. *Secreto de los secretos,* Translated by Juan Fernández de Heredia: An Edition of the Unique Aragonese Manuscript, with Literary Introduction and Glossary. Wisconsin, 1931.

15. 26. Knowlton, Edgar Colby, Jr. Words of Chinese, Japanese, and Korean Origin in the Romance Languages. Stanford, 1959. *DA,* XX, 665.

15. 27. Kochman, Thomas Michael. Analysis of Phonetic Modification of the Anglicism in Chilean Spanish. New York, 1966. *DA,* XXVII, 760-A.

15. 28. Kouvel, Audrey L. Pedro Espinosa: Desarrollo de su sintaxis, vocabulario, estructuras formales e imágenes. Harvard, 1965.

15. 29. Lavin, James Duncan. A Study of Spanish Firearms. Florida State, 1964. *DA,* XXV, 7218.

15. 30. Lihani, John. Glossary of the *Farsas y églogas* of Lucas Fernández. Texas, 1954.

15. 31. Lloyd, Paul M. A Linguistic Analysis of Old Spanish Occupational Terms. California, 1960.

15. 32. Lobo, Félix, S.J. A 10,000 Word Spanish Vocabulary Expanded from 3,000 English Cognates. Georgetown, 1966. *DA,* XXVII, 3030-A.

15. 33. Meikle, Herbert Galt. A Glossary of Colombian Colloquialisms; Based on the Speech of Colombian Males. Michigan, 1961. *DA,* XXI, 3776.

15. 34. Meyer, George Arthur. The Latin Suffix -*aticus* in Old French and in Spanish. A Study in Word Formation: The History and Function of the Suffix. Yale, 1934.

15. 35. Mocas, Christo T. Aspectos lexicográficos de *La lozana andaluza.* Tulane, 1954. Tulane *Abstracts,* Series 55, No. 14, p. 99.

15. 36. Moffett, Elizabeth Jean. A Glossary of the Spanish Inquisition. Illinois, 1966. *DA,* XXVII, 2141-A.

15. 37. Myers, Oliver T. Phonology, Morphology and Vocabulary in the Language of Juan del Encina. Columbia, 1961. *DA,* XXII, 569.

15. 38. Narváez, Richard August. A Descriptive Analysis of Word Formation in Old Spanish. Minnesota, 1959. *DA,* XX, 4103.

15. 39. Neugaard, Edward Joseph. A Critical Edition of a Portion of the 13th Century *Vides de Santz Rosselloneses* with Introduction, Notes, Table of Proper Names, and Glossary. North Carolina, 1964. *DA,* XXVI, 1048.

15. 40. Nunemaker, John Horace. Index of the Stones in the Lapidary of Alfonso X with Identifications in Other Lapidaries. Wisconsin, 1928.

15. 41. Oelschläger, Victor R. B. A Preliminary Spanish Word-List of First Appearances up to Berceo. Wisconsin, 1937. *Madison, 1940. LC 40-34779.

15. 42. Parker, Kelvin M. A Classified Vocabulary of the *Crónica troyana.* Chicago, 1953. *Salamanca, 1958. NUC 60-26925.

15. 43. Pérez, Raoul M. Vocabulario clasificado de *Kalila et Digna.* Chicago, 1942. Chicago, 1943. LC A44-1241.

15. 44. Piccus, Jules. Expressions for Color in Old-Spanish Poetry. Princeton, 1951. *DA,* XIII, 557.

15. 45. Poland, George W. *El poema de Alfonso Onceno,* a Critical Edition and Vocabulary. North Carolina, 1953. North Carolina *Record,* No. 534, p. 253.

15. 46. Prado, Miguel Angel. Estudio comparado de las derivaciones eruditas y populares del *Cantar de Don Sancho II de Castilla.* Stanford, 1942. Stanford *Abstracts,* 1941-42, p. 68.

15. 47. Redfield, John Howard. The Earliest Latin-Romance Loan Words in Basque and Their Bearing on the History of Basque and the Neighboring Romance Languages. Harvard, 1914.

15. 48. Rey, Agapito. Leomarte: *Sumas de historia troyana;* edición, prólogo, notas y vocabulario. Wisconsin, 1929. *RFE,* Anejo XV. Madrid, 1932. LC 33-5364.

15. 49. Richardson, Henry Brush. A Vocabulary to the *Libro de buen amor* of Juan Ruiz, Arcipreste de Hita. Yale, 1923. New Haven, 1930. LC 30-25445.

15. 50. Selbert, Louis. A Glossary of Juan Manuel's *El libro de los enxiemplos del Conde Lucanor et de Patronio.* Yale, 1916. *DA,* XXVIII, 1409-A. [*sic*]

15. 51. Smith, Harlie L., Jr. The Phonology of Arabic Loan-Words in Old Spanish. Minnesota, 1953. *DA,* XIII, 1205.

15. 52. Solé, Yolanda Antonia F. Russinovich. *Hacer:* Verbo funcional y lexical. Georgetown, 1966. *DA,* XXVII, 486-A.

15. 53. Stavrou, Christopher. Present Status and Present Problems of Spanish Monolingual Lexicography. Pennsylvania, 1965. *DA,* XXVI, 3321.

15. 54. Steiner, Roger Jacob. Two Centuries of Spanish and English Bilingual Lexicography (1590-1798). Pennsylvania, 1964. *DA,* XXV, 466.

15. 55. Tappan, Robert L. Estudio lexicográfico del *Poema de Fernán González* con un índice completo

de las frecuencias de los vocablos. Tulane, 1954. Tulane *Abstracts*, Series 55, No. 14, p. 103.

15. 56. Thomas, Bart E. A Concordance to the Works of Gonzalo de Berceo. Wisconsin, 1937. Wisconsin *Summaries*, II, 344.

15. 57. Tukey, Ann. Kinship Terminology in the Romance Languages. Michigan, 1962. *DA*, XXIII, 1014.

15. 58. Turner, Elbert D., Jr. The Vocabulary of Bernal Díaz del Castillo's *Historia verdadera de la conquista de la Nueva España*. North Carolina, 1949. North Carolina *Record*, No. 478, p. 234.

15. 59. Van Scoy, Herbert A. Spanish Words Defined in the Works of Alfonso X. Wisconsin, 1939. Wisconsin *Summaries*, IV, 263.

15. 60. Villegas, Francisco. Glosario del argot costarricense. Michigan, 1953. *DA*, XIII, 383.

15. 61. Willbern, Glen D. Vocabulary Elements in Thirteenth-Century Castilian. Chicago, 1940. Chicago, 1944. LC A44-1617.

15. 62. Woodbridge, Hensley C. Spanish Nautical Terms of the Age of Discovery. Illinois, 1950. Urbana, 1950. LC A51-4249.

15. 63. Zeitlin, Marion Albert. A Vocabulary to the *Rimado de palacio* of López de Ayala. California, 1931.

## 16. *Linguistic Analysis*

16. 1. Allen, John Jay. An Analysis of the Language and Style of Cervantes' *Las dos doncellas* and *El casamiento engañoso*. Wisconsin, 1960. *DA*, XXI, 618.

16. 2. Baird, Herbert Leroy, Jr. Un análisis lingüístico y filológico de *El cuento muy fermoso del enperador Otas de Roma*. Chicago, 1955. Microfilmed, Chicago Library, 1955.

16. 3. Brown, Anita Dolores. Linguistic Analysis of St. Paul's Epistle to the Romans and Prologues to the Epistles in MS. I. 1. 2 of the Library of the Escorial. Wisconsin, 1957. *DA*, XVII, 624.

16. 4. Compton, James Donald. A Linguistic Study of the *Libro del cavallero et del escudero* of Don Juan Manuel in Manuscript 6376 of the National Library of Madrid, Spain. Wisconsin, 1965. *DA*, XXV, 6620.

16. 5. Cooper, Louis. A Linguistic Study of the *Liber regum* of the *Cronicón villarense*. Chicago, 1952. *Zaragoza, 1960. See NUC, 1958-1962, p. 417.

16. 6. Cooper, Paul Joel. The Language of the *Forum judicum*. Columbia, 1953. *DA*, XIV, 138.

16. 7. Field, William Hugh. A Critical Edition of Part of the Works of Raimón Vidal de Basalú, with Linguistic and Literary Commentary. Chicago, 1965. See NUC 67-17704.

16. 8. Honsa, Vladimír Jiří Jaroslav. *La gran conquista de Ultramar*, Book IV, Chapters 126-193: Critical Edition, Grammatical Analysis, and Glossary. Michigan, 1957. *DA*, XVIII, 1420.

16. 9. Jennings, Augustus C. A Linguistic Study of the *Cartulario de San Vicente de Oviedo*. Columbia, 1940. New York, 1940. LC 41-1395.

16. 10. Kouvel, Audrey L. Pedro Espinosa: Desarrollo de su sintaxis, vocabulario, estructuras formales e imágenes. Harvard, 1965.

16. 11. Lloyd, Paul M. A Linguistic Analysis of Old Spanish Occupational Terms. California, 1960.

16. 12. Montgomery, Thomas Andrew. A Linguistic Study of the Book of Matthew in Manuscript I. I. 6 of the Escorial Library. Wisconsin, 1955. *DA*, XVI, 118.

16. 13. Nelson, Iver Nicholas. A Study of the Language of Fray Juan de Pineda's *Agricultura Christiana*. California, 1934.

16. 14. Petersen, Phillip Burns. A Linguistic Study of the Old Leonese *Fuero de Ledesma*. California, 1955.

16. 15. Sousa, Thomas Frederic. A Linguistic Analysis of a Portion of the Galician Translation of the *General estoria* by Alfonso X, el Sabio. Wisconsin, 1964. *DA*, XXIV, 5418.

16. 16. Strout, Clevy Lloyd. A Linguistic Study of the Journals of the Coronado Expedition. Colorado, 1958. *DA*, XIX, 2608.

16. 17. Uhrhan, Evelyn E. Linguistic Analysis of Góngora's Baroque Style. Illinois, 1950. Urbana, 1950. LC A52-365.

16. 18. Vaquero de Ramírez, María del T. Estudio lingüístico de Barranquitas. Puerto Rico, 1966.

## 17. *Linguistic Theory*

17. 1. Craven, Robert K. Auditory Equivalence in the Phonology of French and Spanish: A Critical Examination of Certain Linguistic Theories. Harvard, 1947.

17. 2. Jungemann, Frederick H. The Substratum Theory and the Hispano-Romance and Gascon Dialects: A Functional-Structural Analysis of Some Phonological Problems. Columbia, 1952. *DA*, XIII, 399.

17. 3. Zucker, George K. Linguistic Theory in the *Siglo de Oro*: An Evaluation. Iowa, 1964. *DA*, XXV, 6611.

## 18. *Morphology*

18. 1. Alexander, Luther Herbert. Participial Substantives of the *-ata* Type in the Romance Languages, with Special Reference to French. Columbia, 1911. New York, 1912. LC 12-5848.

18. 2. Brewer, William Benjamin. The Object Pro-

nouns *le* and *lo* in Alphonsine Prose. Tulane, 1966. *DA,* XXVII, 3447-A.

18. 3. Foley, James A., Jr. Spanish Morphology. M.I.T., 1965.

18. 4. Hatheway, Joel. An Historical Study of *Hubiera* and *Hubiese.* Boston University, 1926.

18. 5. Iannucci, James Emanuel. Lexical Number in Spanish Nouns with Reference to Their English Equivalents. Pennsylvania, 1951. Philadelphia, 1952. NUC 54-4140.

18. 6. Larkin, James Brian. A Morphological and Syntactical Study of Fifteenth-Century Spanish Prose. Stanford, 1966. *DA,* XXVII, 195-A.

18. 7. Leuschel, Donald Ardell. Spanish Verb Morphology. Indiana, 1960. *DA,* XXI, 2708.

18. 8. Mills, Dorothy Hurst. A Descriptive Analysis of the Morphology of the Diminutives *ito, illo, ico, uelo* and of Their Increments (Including Feminine and Plural Forms) as Used in Spanish America. Southern California, 1955. Southern California *Abstracts,* 1955, p. 99.

18. 9. Myers, Oliver T. Phonology, Morphology, and Vocabulary in the Language of Juan del Encina. Columbia, 1961. *DA,* XXII, 569.

18. 10. Pardo, Aristóbulo V. Esquema morfológico del leonés antiguo en el *Fuero de Zamora.* Ohio State, 1966. *DA,* XXVII, 3031-A.

18. 11. Rael, Juan Bautista. A Study of the Phonology and Morphology of New Mexican Spanish Based on a Collection of 410 Folk-Tales. Stanford, 1937. Stanford *Abstracts,* 1936-37, p. 55.

18. 12. Reiff, Donald Gene. A Characterization-Evaluation System for Theories of Spanish Verb Morphology. Michigan, 1963. *DA,* XXIV, 1608.

18. 13. Saporta, Sol. Morpheme Alternants in Spanish. Illinois, 1955. *DA,* XV, 1850.

18. 14. Seymour, Arthur Romeyn. The Development of the Latin Pluperfect Indicative in Spanish. Wisconsin, 1907.

18. 15. Solé, Carlos Alberto, Jr. Los adjetivos españoles terminados en *-al, -ar, -ero, -ico* y *-oso.* Georgetown, 1966. *DA,* XXVII, 762-A.

18. 16. Tsuzaki, Stanley Mamoru. English Influence in the Phonology and Morphology of the Spanish Spoken in the Mexican Colony in Detroit, Michigan. Michigan, 1963. *DA,* XXIV, 2471.

18. 17. Weaver, Billy Rupert. The Forms and Usage of the Personal Pronouns in *Castigos e documentos para bien vivir ordenados por el Rey don Sancho IV.* Wisconsin, 1964. *DA,* XXIV, 3743.

18. 18. Wolfe, David Lee. A Generative-Transformational Analysis of Spanish Verb Forms. Michigan, 1966. *DA,* XXVIII, 219-A.

18. 19. Woods, Perry Daniel. The *-ra* Verb Form in Spanish-American Writings. Oregon, 1932. Oregon *Theses,* p. 63.

18. 20. Wright, Leavitt Olds. A Study of the History of the *-ra* Verb-Form in Spain. California, 1929. *Berkeley, 1932. LC A32-1580.

19. *Noun.* (See also *Onomastics,* 20; *Suffix,* 28; *Toponymics,* 30.)

19. 1. Alexander, Luther Herbert. Participial Substantives of the *-ata* Type in the Romance Languages, with Special Reference to French. Columbia, 1911. New York, 1912. LC 12-5848.

19. 2. Doblin, Helga B. Designations of Stringed Instruments in Romance Languages. Harvard, 1965.

19. 3. Georges, Emanuel Spear. Studies in Romance Nouns Extracted from Past Participles. California, 1965. *DA,* XXVI, 1032.

19. 4. Iannucci, James Emanuel. Lexical Number in Spanish Nouns with Reference to Their English Equivalents. Pennsylvania, 1951. Philadelphia, 1952. NUC 54-4140.

19. 5. Mills, Dorothy Hurst. A Descriptive Analysis of the Morphology of the Diminutives *ito, illo, ico, uelo* and of Their Increments (Including Feminine and Plural Forms) as Used in Spanish America. Southern California, 1955. Southern California *Abstracts,* 1955, p. 99.

19. 6. Moorefield, Allen S. The Infinitive as Accusative in Modern Spanish. Southern California, 1958. Southern California *Abstracts,* 1958, p. 85.

19. 7. Tukey, Ann. Kinship Terminology in the Romance Languages. Michigan, 1962. *DA,* XXIII, 1014.

20. *Onomastics.* (See also *Toponymics,* 30.)

20. 1. Alvarez, Grace de Jesús. Topónimos en apellidos hispanos; un estudio onomástico. Southern California, 1962. *DA,* XXV, 2503.

20. 2. Chamberlain, Mary Helen. Contribución a la hidronimia de España. Georgetown, 1965. *DA,* XXVI, 3937.

20. 3. Chittenden, Jean Stahl. Los nombres de personajes en las comedias de Tirso de Molina. Texas, 1964. *DA,* XXV, 7263.

20. 4. Delaney, John T. A Selective English-Old Spanish Glossary as a Basis for Studies in Old Spanish Onomatology and Synonymics. Catholic, 1966. Washington, 1966. NUC 67-91049.

20. 5. Duncan, Robert M. An Etymological Vocabulary of Plant Names in the Works of Alfonso el Sabio. Wisconsin, 1936. Wisconsin *Summaries,* I, 333.

20. 6. Iventosch, Herman. Five Types of Onomastic Invention in Spanish Baroque Fiction, 1616-1657. Harvard, 1959.

20.7. Lloyd, Paul M. A Linguistic Analysis of Old Spanish Occupational Terms. California, 1960.

20.8. Newcomer, Charles A. Animal Names in the Works of Alfonso el Sabio. Wisconsin, 1937. Wisconsin *Summaries*, II, 339.

20.9. Steiner, Mary Florence Fox. An Etymological Study of Old Spanish Personal Names. Northwestern, 1953. *DA*, XIII, 1205.

## 21. *Orthography*

21.1. Douglass, Ralph Thomas. The Evolution of Spanish Orthography from 1475 to 1726. Pennsylvania, 1964. *DA*, XXV, 4143.

21.2. Newhard, Margaret Eleanor. Spanish Orthography in the Thirteenth Century. North Carolina, 1960. *DA*, XXI, 1951.

21.3. Walsh, James L. Some Aspects of Medieval Spanish Sibilants as Reflected in Ms.S. of the *Libro de buen amor*. Illinois, 1963. *DA*, XXIV, 4186.

## 22. *Parts of Speech*

22.1. Senior, Judith. The Concepts of Parts of Speech in the Early Grammars of the Spanish Language. Radcliffe, 1956.

## 23. *Phonetics-Phonology*

23.1. Ackerman, Ella Lauretta. Photographic Study of the Action of the Velum Palatinum as Related to the Velar Sounds (k) and (g). Ohio State, 1934. Ohio State *Abstracts*, No. 15, p. 1.

23.2. Anderson, James Maxwell. A Structural Account of the Evolution of Intervocalic Consonant Clusters in Spanish. Washington, Seattle, 1963. *DA*, XXV, 1204.

23.3. Arnold, Frederic K. The Use of Glide Sounds in Consonant Groups in the Romance Languages. Harvard, 1937. Harvard *Summaries*, 1937, p. 293.

23.4. Blaylock, William Curtis. Studies in Possible Osco-Umbrian Influence on Hispano-Romance Phonology. California, 1964. *DA*, XXV, 1899.

23.5. Buckingham, Lucius Henry. That the Romance Languages, in Deriving from the Latin, Followed Tendencies to Change, Which the Latin Already Exhibited, Is Illustrated by the Study of Romance Verbal Formations. Harvard, 1876.

23.6. Campbell, Richard Joe. Phonological Analyses of Spanish. Illinois, 1966. *DA*, XXVII, 2137-A.

23.7. Canfield, Delos L. Spanish Literature in Mexican Languages as a Source for the Study of Spanish Pronunciation. Columbia, 1934. New York, 1934. LC 34-41629.

23.8. Connell, Chester C. The Closing of Atonic Vowels in the Romance Languages. Harvard, 1936. Harvard *Summaries*, 1936, p. 374.

23.9. Craven, Robert K. Auditory Equivalence in the Phonology of French and Spanish: A Critical Examination of Certain Linguistic Theories. Harvard, 1947.

23.10. Cross, Ephraim. Syncope and Kindred Phenomena in Latin Inscriptions from the Parts of the Roman World Where Romance Speech Developed. Columbia, 1930. New York, 1930. LC 31-639.

23.11. Dato, Daniel Peter. A Historical Phonology of Castilian. Cornell, 1959. *DA*, XX, 3287.

23.12. Dykstra, Gerald. Spectrographic Analysis of Spanish Sibilants and Its Relation to Navarro's Physiological Phonetic Descriptions. Michigan, 1955. *DA*, XV, 1394.

23.13. English, James Henry. The Alternation of *h* and *f* in Old Spanish. Columbia, 1926. New York, 1926. LC 26-14512.

23.14. Espinosa, Aurelio Macedonio. Studies in New Mexican Spanish. Part 1, Phonology. Chicago, 1909. Chicago, 1909. LC A11-1172.

23.15. Everett, Paul E., Jr. The History of Nasal Consonants and of Vocalic Nasalization in the Romance Languages. Harvard, 1939. Harvard *Summaries*, 1939, p. 266.

23.16. Fischer, Milla. Verification of a Suggested Hierarchy of Problems Encountered by English Speakers Learning Spanish Phonology: Dialectical Case Studies. Georgetown, 1966. *DA*, XXVII, 758-A.

23.17. Ford, Jeremiah Denis Matthias. The Old Spanish Sibilants. Harvard, 1897. Boston, 1900. LC 6-38042.

23.18. Forsyth, John. The Phonemic Structure of Medieval Spanish as Reflected in the *Libro de buen amor*. New Mexico, 1961. *DA*, XXII, 2792.

23.19. Frey, Herschel Jerome. A Comparative Phonology of Medieval and Modern Spanish: *El libro de buen amor*. North Carolina, 1963. *DA*, XXIV, 3331.

23.20. Gurren, M. Louise. A Comparison on a Phonetic Basis of the Two Chief Languages of the Americas, English and Spanish. New York, 1955. *DA*, XV, 1849.

23.21. Hardigree, Cruz Aurelia Cancel Ferrer. Effects of Selected Phonetic Aspects in the Transmission of the Spanish Language. Ohio State, 1957. *DA*, XVII, 1547.

23.22. Jones, Morgan Emory. A Phonological Study of English as Spoken by Puerto Ricans Contrasted with Puerto Rican Spanish and American English. Michigan, 1962. *DA*, XXIII, 2127.

23.23. Jungemann, Frederick H. The Substratum Theory and the Hispano-Romance and Gascon Dialects: A Functional-Structural Analysis of Some Phonological Problems. Columbia, 1952. *DA*, XIII, 399.

23.24.　Knowles, Richard.　Phonetic Tendency in Romance Languages.　Harvard, 1931.　Harvard *Summaries*, 1931, p. 5.

23.25.　Kochman, Thomas Michael.　Analysis of Phonetic Modification of the Anglicism in Chilean Spanish.　New York, 1966.　*DA*, XXVII, 760-A.

23.26.　Marden, Charles Carroll.　The Phonology of the Spanish Dialect of Mexico City.　Johns Hopkins, 1894.　Baltimore, 1896.　LC 3-22020.

23.27.　Meadows, Gail Keith.　The Development of Vulgar Latin Hiatus Groups in the Romance Languages.　Harvard, 1944.　Harvard *Summaries*, 1943-45, p. 527.

23.28.　Myers, Oliver T.　Phonology, Morphology and Vocabulary in the Language of Juan del Encina.　Columbia, 1961.　*DA*, XXII, 569.

23.29.　Purczinsky, Julius O., Jr.　Historical Study of the Spanish Segmental Phoneme System.　Texas, 1957.　*DA*, XVIII, 585.

23.30.　Rael, Juan Bautista.　A Study of the Phonology and Morphology of New Mexican Spanish Based on a Collection of 410 Folk-Tales.　Stanford, 1937.　Stanford *Abstracts*, 1936-37, p. 55.

23.31.　Raggio, Andrew Paul.　A Treatment of the Development from Popular Latin to Spanish of Certain Consonant Groups Ending in *y*.　Harvard, 1904.

23.32.　Romeo, Luigi.　The Economy of Diphthongization in Early Romance.　Washington, Seattle, 1960.　*DA*, XXI, 3776.

23.33.　Skelton, Robert Beattie.　A Spectrographic Analysis of Spanish Vowel Sounds.　Michigan, 1950.　*MA*, X, No. 4, p. 205.

23.34.　Smith, Harlie L., Jr.　The Phonology of Arabic Loan-Words in Old Spanish.　Minnesota, 1953.　*DA*, XIII, 1205.

23.35.　Spiegel, Irving.　Old Judaeo-Spanish Evidence of Old Spanish Pronunciation.　Minnesota, 1953.　*DA*, XIII, 819.

23.36.　Tsuzaki, Stanley Mamoru.　English Influences in the Phonology and Morphology of the Spanish Spoken in the Mexican Colony in Detroit, Michigan.　Michigan, 1963.　*DA*, XXIV, 2471.

23.37.　Turner, Ronald C.　An Acoustic Study of Syllabication.　Harvard, 1966.　See NUC 67-62425.　[Part deals with Spanish.]

23.38.　Valencia, Pablo.　An Historical Study of Syllabic Structure in Spanish.　Michigan, 1966.　*DA*, XXVIII, 218-A.

23.39.　Walsh, James L.　Some Aspects of Medieval Spanish Sibilants as Reflected in Ms. S. of the *Libro de buen amor*.　Illinois, 1963.　*DA*, XXIV, 4186.

23.40.　Zipf, George Kingsley.　Relative Frequency as a Determinant of Phonetic Change.　Harvard, 1930.
*Cambridge, Mass., 1932.　LC 32-19392; Harvard *Summaries*, 1930, p. 9.　[Part deals with Spanish.]

### 24.　*Phrase*

24.1.　Blansitt, Edward L., Jr.　The Verb Phrase in Spanish: Classes and Relations.　Texas, 1963.　*DA*, XXIV, 2897.

24.2.　Feldman, David Morris.　The Historical Syntax of Modal Verb Phrases in Spanish.　Cornell, 1962.　*DA*, XXIII, 4682.

24.3.　Paratore, Angela.　Spanish Verb Phrase and Clause Structure.　Cornell, 1950.

### 25.　*Pronoun*

25.1.　Brewer, William Benjamin.　The Object Pronouns *le* and *lo* in Alphonsine Prose.　Tulane, 1966.　*DA*, XXVII, 3447-A.

25.2.　Chenery, Winthrop Holt.　Object Pronouns in Dependent Clauses: A Study in Old Spanish Word Order.　Harvard, 1904.

25.3.　Harrison, Gordon W.　A Study of the Range and Frequency of Constructions Involving Pronouns and Pronominal Adjectives in Manuscript J-1, Biblioteca Nacional, of the *Gran conquista de Ultramar*.　Chicago, 1940.　Chicago, 1940.　LC 41-9655.

25.4.　Kuersteiner, Albert Frederick.　The Use of the Relative Pronoun in the *Rimado de palacio*.　Johns Hopkins, 1904.　Paris, 1911.　LC 13-14242.

25.5.　Leavitt, Walter David.　The Position of the Object Pronouns in Old Spanish: A Contribution to Medieval Syntax.　Yale, 1954.

25.6.　Weaver, Billy Rupert.　The Forms and Usage of the Personal Pronouns in *Castigos e documentos para bien vivir ordenados por el Rey don Sancho IV*.　Wisconsin, 1964.　*DA*, XXIV, 3743.

### 26.　*Romance Languages, Comparative, General*

26.1.　Alexander, Luther Herbert.　Participial Substantives of the *-ata* Type in the Romance Languages, with Special Reference to French.　Columbia, 1911.　New York, 1912.　LC 12-5848.

26.2.　Arnold, Frederic K.　The Use of Glide Sounds in Consonant Groups in the Romance Languages.　Harvard, 1937.　Harvard *Summaries*, 1937, p. 293.

26.3.　Arnold, Harrison Heikes.　Romance Imperatives.　Harvard, 1926.

26.4.　Bowen, Benjamin Lester.　Contributions to Periphrasis in the Romance Languages.　Johns Hopkins, 1888.

26.5.　Brown, Leslie P.　Some Romance Words of Arabic Origin.　Southern California, 1935.　*Los Angeles, 1938.　LC 38-33359.

26.6.　Buckingham, Lucius Henry.　That the Romance Languages, in Deriving from the Latin, Followed

Tendencies to Change, Which the Latin Already Exhibited, Is Illustrated by the Study of Romance Verbal Formations. Harvard, 1876.

26. 7. Bulatkin, Eleanor Webster. The Expression of the Concept "Nuance" in Spanish, Italian, and French. Johns Hopkins, 1952.

26. 8. Chambers, Frank M. Uses of the Subjunctive Mood in the Romance Languages. Harvard, 1935. Harvard *Summaries,* 1935, p. 299.

26. 9. Connell, Chester C. The Closing of Atonic Vowels in the Romance Languages. Harvard, 1936. Harvard *Summaries,* 1936, p. 374.

26. 10. Crabb, Daniel M. A Comparative Study of Word Order in Old Spanish and Old French Prose Works. Catholic, 1955. Washington, 1955. NUC A55-4943.

26. 11. Craven, Robert K. Auditory Equivalence in the Phonology of French and Spanish: A Critical Examination of Certain Linguistic Theories. Harvard, 1947.

26. 12. Cross, Ephraim. Syncope and Kindred Phenomena in Latin Inscriptions from the Parts of the Roman World Where Romance Speech Developed. Columbia, 1930. New York, 1930. LC 31-639.

26. 13. Cryesky, Ralph H. A Semantic Study of Verbs of Thinking in the Romance Languages. Harvard, 1953.

26. 14. Doblin, Helga B. Designations of Stringed Instruments in Romance Languages. Harvard, 1965.

26. 15. Edgerton, Mills Fox. Color Terms in Transitional Latin; A Method for the Diachronic Investigation of the Semantics of an Area of Vocabulary, Together with an Initial Study. Princeton, 1960. *DA,* XXI, 2285.

26. 16. Everett, Paul E., Jr. The History of Nasal Consonants and of Vocalic Nasalization in the Romance Languages. Harvard, 1939. Harvard *Summaries,* 1939, p. 266.

26. 17. Fay, Edward Allen. On the Conditional Relations in the Romance Languages. Johns Hopkins, 1881.

26. 18. Ferrigno, James Moses. Linguistic Patterns of the Iberian Peninsula in Sicilian and Other Southern Italian Dialects. Boston University, 1951.

26. 19. Fontaine, Joseph Auguste. On the Auxiliary Verbs in the Romance Languages. Johns Hopkins, 1886. Lincoln, Nebraska, 1888. LC 4-2307.

26. 20. Garner, Samuel. The Gerundial Construction in the Romance Languages. Johns Hopkins, 1881.

26. 21. Georges, Emanuel Spear. Studies in Romance Nouns Extracted from Past Participles. California, 1965. *DA,* XXVI, 1032.

26. 22. [Gerig, John Lawrence. Romance Semantics. Nebraska, 1902. Not available in Nebraska library.]

26. 23. Gilcreast, Seaver Richmond. A Study of the Idea of Indefiniteness Behind *Some* and *Any* and Their Equivalents in the Romance Languages. Harvard, 1929. Harvard *Summaries,* 1929, p. 181.

26. 24. Jungemann, Frederick H. The Substratum Theory and the Hispano-Romance and Gascon Dialects: A Functional-Structural Analysis of Some Phonological Problems. Columbia, 1952. *DA,* XIII, 399.

26. 25. Keys, George Robert, Jr. The Present Tense in the Romance Languages with Special Reference to French and Italian. North Carolina, 1948. North Carolina *Record,* No. 464, p. 362.

26. 26. Knowles, Richard. Phonetic Tendency in Romance Languages. Harvard, 1931. Harvard *Summaries,* 1931, p. 5.

26. 27. Knowlton, Edgar Colby, Jr. Words of Chinese, Japanese, and Korean Origin in the Romance Languages. Stanford, 1959. *DA,* XX, 665.

26. 28. Meadows, Gail Keith. The Development of Vulgar Latin Hiatus Groups in the Romance Languages. Harvard, 1944. Harvard *Summaries,* 1943-45, p. 527.

26. 29. Meyer, Christine Louise. A Semantic Survey of Certain Verbs Indicating Departure and Arrival in the Romance Languages. Ohio State, 1941. Ohio State *Abstracts,* No. 35, p. 201.

26. 30. Meyer, George Arthur. The Latin Suffix *-aticus* in Old French and in Spanish. A Study in Word Formation: The History and Function of the Suffix. Yale, 1934.

26. 31. Moffatt, Lucius Gaston. A Physiological and Historical Study of Preconsonantal *L* in the Romance Languages. Harvard, 1929. Harvard *Summaries,* 1929, p. 191.

26. 32. Patiño, Carlos. The Development of Studies in Romance Syntax. Michigan, 1965. *DA,* XXVI, 7307.

26. 33. Redfield, John Howard. The Earliest Latin-Romance Loan-Words in Basque and Their Bearing on the History of Basque and the Neighboring Romance Languages. Harvard, 1914.

26. 34. Reid, James Richard. The Expression of Future Time: From Indo-European to Romance. Harvard, 1943. Harvard *Summaries,* 1943-45, p. 161.

26. 35. Richman, Stephen Herbert. A Comparative Study of Spanish and Portuguese. Pennsylvania, 1965. *DA,* XXVI, 3319.

26. 36. Romeo, Luigi. The Economy of Diphthongization in Early Romance. Washington, Seattle, 1960. *DA,* XXI, 3776.

26. 37. Scottron, Edith M. The Development of the Latin Passive Verb in the Romance Languages. Columbia, 1949. Wooster, Ohio, 1950. LC 50-3263.

26. 38. Siracusa, Joseph. A Comparative Study of Syntactical Redundancy in Spanish and Italian. Illinois, 1962. *DA,* XXIII, 2520.

26. 39. Taylor, George Benjamin. Verbal Aspect in Early Romance. Stanford, 1951. Stanford *Abstracts,* XXVII, 375.

26. 40. Trager, George Leonard. The Use of the Latin Demonstratives (Especially *ille* and *ipse*) up to 600 A.D., as the Source of the Romance Article. Columbia, 1932. New York, 1932. LC 33-15894.

26. 41. Tukey, Ann. Kinship Terminology in the Romance Languages. Michigan, 1962. *DA,* XXIII, 1014.

### 27. *Semantics*

27. 1. Bates, Margaret Jane. *Discreción* in the Works of Cervantes: A Semantic Study. Catholic, 1945. Washington, 1945. LC A45-4644.

27. 2. Bays, Robert Alexander. The Semantic Development of Tenses in Spanish. Yale, 1958. *DA,* XXVIII, 3165-A.

27. 3. Brosman, Margaret C. The Verbal Concept of Motion in Old Spanish. North Carolina, 1956. North Carolina *Record,* No. 576, p. 284.

27. 4. Cryesky, Ralph H. A Semantic Study of Verbs of Thinking in the Romance Languages. Harvard, 1953.

27. 5. Delaney, John T. A Selective English-Old Spanish Glossary as a Basis for Studies in Old Spanish Onomatology and Synonymics. Catholic, 1966. Washington, 1966. NUC 67-91049.

27. 6. Edgerton, Mills Fox. Color Terms in Transitional Latin; A Method for the Diachronic Investigation of the Semantics of an Area of Vocabulary, Together with an Initial Study. Princeton, 1960. *DA,* XXI, 2285.

27. 7. [Gerig, John Lawrence. Romance Semantics. Nebraska, 1902. Not available in Nebraska library.]

27. 8. Glover, Bobby Ray. A History of Six Spanish Verbs Meaning "To Take, Seize, Grasp." Louisiana State, 1966. *DA,* XXVII, 203-A.

27. 9. Kendrick, Edith J. A Semantic Study of Cognates in Spanish and English. Illinois, 1943. *MA,* VII, No. 2, p. 94.

27. 10. McCurdy, Joseph Alexander. The Development in Meaning of the Spanish Word *Romance.* Pittsburgh, 1925. Pittsburgh *Abstracts,* I, 31.

27. 11. McDowell, David Franklin. The Nature of Old Spanish Vocabulary as Determined by an Etymological and Semantic Analysis of the Verbs in the *Primera parte* of the *General estoria* of Alfonso el Sabio. North Carolina, 1943. North Carolina *Record,* No. 429, p. 231.

27. 12. Meyer, Christine Louise. A Semantic Survey of Certain Verbs Indicating Departure and Arrival in the Romance Languages. Ohio State, 1941. Ohio State *Abstracts,* No. 35, p. 201.

27. 13. Rossi, Pietro Carlo. Derivatives of Latin *FAC* in Italian, Spanish and French: A Study in Semantics. California, 1940.

### 28. *Suffix*

28. 1. Lasley, Marion M. Nominal Suffixes in Old Spanish. Columbia, 1953. *DA,* XIV, 140.

28. 2. Meyer, George Arthur. The Latin Suffix *-aticus* in Old French and in Spanish. A Study in Word Formation: The History and Function of the Suffix. Yale, 1934.

28. 3. Murphy, Spencer L. A Description of Noun Suffixes in Colloquial Mexican Spanish. Illinois, 1950. Urbana, 1950. LC A51-4253.

28. 4. Olson, Paul Richard. Nominal Suffixes in Sixteenth Century Spanish. Harvard, 1959.

### 29. *Syntax*

29. 1. Babcock, Sandra Scharff. The Syntax of Spanish Reflexive Verbs: The Parameters of the Middle Voice. Ohio State, 1965. *DA,* XXVI, 1640.

29. 2. Bachmann, Ann Opalak. An Etymological and Partial Syntactical Analysis of the *Rimado de palaçio* of Pero López de Ayala. Florida State, 1958. *DA,* XIX, 526.

29. 3. Beardsley, Wilfred A. Infinitive Constructions in Old Spanish. Columbia, 1917. New York, 1921. LC 21-9382.

29. 4. Beberfall, Lester. A History of the Partitive Indefinite Construction in the Spanish Language. Michigan, 1952. *DA,* XII, 416.

29. 5. Blansitt, Edward L., Jr. The Verb Phrase in Spanish: Classes and Relations. Texas, 1963. *DA,* XXIV, 2897.

29. 6. Brend, Ruth Margaret. A Tagmemic Analysis of Mexican Spanish Clauses. Michigan, 1964. *DA,* XXV, 2972.

29. 7. Brewer, William Benjamin. The Object Pronouns *le* and *lo* in Alphonsine Prose. Tulane, 1966. *DA,* XXVII, 3447-A.

29. 8. Brown, Charles Barrett. The Passive and Indefinite Reflexives in Old Spanish. Chicago, 1928. Chicago *Abstracts,* VI, 313.

29. 9. Chambers, Frank M. Uses of the Subjunctive Mood in the Romance Languages. Harvard, 1935. Harvard *Summaries,* 1935, p. 299.

29. 10. Chatham, James R. A Syntactical Study of the Indirect Interrogative in Old Spanish. Florida State, 1960. *DA,* XXI, 2284.

29. 11. Cressey, William W. A Transformational Analysis of the Relative Clause in Urban Mexican Spanish. Illinois, 1966. *DA,* XXVII, 3857-A.

29.12. Eyring, Edward. The Uses of the Accusative *a* in Certain Old Spanish Documents. California, 1933.

29.13. Fay, Edward Allen. On the Conditional Relations in the Romance Languages. Johns Hopkins, 1881.

29.14. Feldman, David Morris. The Historical Syntax of Modal Verb Phrases in Spanish. Cornell, 1962. *DA,* XXIII, 4682.

29.15. Fontaine, Joseph Auguste. On the Auxiliary Verbs in the Romance Languages. Johns Hopkins, 1886. Lincoln, Nebraska, 1888. LC 4-2307.

29.16. Frank, Francine Harriet Wattman. Taxemic Redundancy in Spanish. Illinois, 1955. *DA,* XV, 2195.

29.17. Gilbert, Donald Monroe. The Personal Accusative in the Works of Blasco Ibáñez. Wisconsin, 1920.

29.18. Gilcreast, Seaver Richmond. A Study of the Idea of Indefiniteness Behind *Some* and *Any* and Their Equivalents in the Romance Languages. Harvard, 1929. Harvard *Summaries,* 1929, p. 181.

29.19. Gminder, Albert Borden. A Study in Fourteenth-Century Spanish Syntax. North Carolina, 1959. *DA,* XX, 2792.

29.20. Gordon, Calvin Gustav. The Subjunctive Mood in Representative Spanish Works from the 12th to the 18th Century. Nebraska, 1964. *DA,* XXV, 4134.

29.21. Gould, William Elford. The Subjunctive Mood in *Don Quijote de la Mancha.* Johns Hopkins, 1903. Baltimore, 1905. LC 6-37895.

29.22. Harrison, Gordon W. A Study of the Range and Frequency of Constructions Involving Pronouns and Pronominal Adjectives in Manuscript J-1, Biblioteca Nacional, of the *Gran conquista de Ultramar.* Chicago, 1940. Chicago, 1940. LC 41-9655.

29.23. Hatheway, Joel. An Historical Study of *Hubiera* and *Hubiese.* Boston University, 1926.

29.24. Hejtmanek, Lillian. The Syntax of the Exclamation in Colloquial Mexican. Illinois, 1947. Urbana, 1948. LC A48-10160.

29.25. Javens, Charles. A Study of Old Spanish Syntax: The Fifteenth Century. North Carolina, 1965. *DA,* XXVI, 3924.

29.26. Kouvel, Audrey L. Pedro Espinosa: Desarrollo de su sintaxis, vocabulario, estructuras formales e imágenes. Harvard, 1965.

29.27. Kuersteiner, Albert Frederick. The Use of the Relative Pronoun in the *Rimado de palacio.* Johns Hopkins, 1904. Paris, 1911. LC 13-14242.

29.28. Larkin, James Brian. A Morphological and Syntactical Study of Fifteenth-Century Spanish Prose. Stanford, 1966. *DA,* XXVII, 195-A.

29.29. Leavitt, Walter David. The Position of the Object Pronouns in Old Spanish: A Contribution to Medieval Syntax. Yale, 1954.

29.30. Martin, John Watson. Objective Criteria of Syntax and the Determination of Authorship in Spanish Literature: A Study of the Method and Its Validity. Washington, Seattle, 1956. *DA,* XVII, 855.

29.31. Mendeloff, Henry. The Evolution of the Conditional Sentence Contrary to Fact in Old Spanish. Catholic, 1960. Washington, 1960. NUC 60-3957.

29.32. Moore, Clarence King. An Historical Study of the Spanish Preposition *á* with the Accusative Case. Harvard, 1906.

29.33. Moorefield, Allen S. The Infinitive as Accusative in Modern Spanish. Southern California, 1958. Southern California *Abstracts,* 1958, p. 85.

29.34. Paratore, Angela. Spanish Verb Phrase and Clause Structure. Cornell, 1950.

29.35. Patiño, Carlos. The Development of Studies in Romance Syntax. Michigan, 1965. *DA,* XXVI, 7307.

29.36. Reed, Frank Otis. The History of the Spanish Past Participle Compounded with *Haber.* Harvard, 1905.

29.37. Roldán, María de las Mercedes. Ordered Rules for Spanish. Selected Problems of Syntactic Structure. Indiana, 1965. *DA,* XXVI, 5427.

29.38. Seltzer, Harriett A. The Development of the Function Word System from Vulgar Latin to Modern Spanish. Illinois, 1950. Urbana, 1950. LC A51-2194.

29.39. Seymour, Arthur Romeyn. The Development of the Latin Pluperfect Indicative in Spanish. Wisconsin, 1907.

29.40. Siracusa, Joseph. A Comparative Study of Syntactical Redundancy in Spanish and Italian. Illinois, 1962. *DA,* XXIII, 2520.

29.41. Solé, Yolanda Antonia F. Russinovich. *Hacer:* Verbo funcional y lexical. Georgetown, 1966. *DA,* XXVII, 486-A.

29.42. Spaulding, Robert Kilburn. A Study of the History and Syntax of Progressive Constructions in Spanish. California, 1925. *Berkeley, 1926. LC 27-2367.

29.43. Strausbaugh, John Anthony. The Use of *auer a* and *auer de* as Auxiliary Verbs in Old Spanish from the Earliest Texts to the End of the Thirteenth Century. Chicago, 1933. Chicago, 1936. LC 36-9733.

29.44. Sturcken, Henry T., Jr. Studies in Thirteenth-Century Spanish Syntax. North Carolina, 1953. North Carolina *Record,* No. 534, p. 253.

29.45. Sublette, Edith B. The Locative Functions of *ser* and *estar* and Some Auxiliary Functions of *ser* and *haber.* Iowa, 1938. Iowa *Abstracts,* II, 238.

29. 46. Tarr, Frederick Courtney. Prepositional Complementary Clauses in Spanish, with Special Reference to the Works of Pérez Galdós. Princeton, 1921. New York-Paris, 1922. LC 24-14623.

29. 47. Weaver, Billy Rupert. The Forms and Usage of the Personal Pronouns in *Castigos e documentos para bien vivir ordenados por el Rey don Sancho IV*. Wisconsin, 1964. *DA*, XXIV, 3743.

29. 48. Winget, Lynn Warren. Auxiliary Verbs in the Prose Works of Alfonso X. Wisconsin, 1960. *DA*, XX, 4104.

29. 49. Wolfe, David Lee. A Generative-Transformational Analysis of Spanish Verb Forms. Michigan, 1966. *DA*, XXVIII, 219-A.

29. 50. Woods, Perry Daniel. The *-ra* Verb Form in Spanish-American Writings. Oregon, 1932. Oregon *Theses*, p. 63.

29. 51. Wright, Leavitt Olds. A Study of the History of the *-ra* Verb-Form in Spain. California, 1929. *Berkeley, 1932. LC A32-1580.

### 30. *Toponymics*

30. 1. Alvarez, Grace de Jesús. Topónimos en apellidos hispanos: un estudio onomástico. Southern California, 1962. *DA*, XXV, 2503.

30. 2. Núñez, Benjamín. Términos topográficos en la Argentina colonial (1516-1810). Columbia, 1957. *DA*, XVII, 1751.

30. 3. Reynolds, Jack Adolphe. Louisiana Place-Names of Romance Origin. Louisiana State, 1942. Louisiana State *Bulletin*, XXXV, No. 1, p. 9.

### 31. *Verb*

31. 1. Arnold, Harrison Heikes. Romance Imperatives. Harvard, 1926.

31. 2. Babcock, Sandra Scharff. The Syntax of Spanish Reflexive Verbs: The Parameters of the Middle Voice. Ohio State, 1965. *DA*, XXVI, 1640.

31. 3. Bays, Robert Alexander. The Semantic Development of Tenses in Spanish. Yale, 1958. *DA*, XXVIII, 3165-A.

31. 4. Beardsley, Wilfred A. Infinitive Constructions in Old Spanish. Columbia, 1917. New York, 1921. LC 21-8313.

31. 5. Blansitt, Edward L., Jr. The Verb Phrase in Spanish: Classes and Relations. Texas, 1963. *DA*, XXIV, 2897.

31. 6. Bowen, Benjamin Lester. Contributions to Periphrasis in the Romance Languages. Johns Hopkins, 1888.

31. 7. Brosman, Margaret C. The Verbal Concept of Motion in Old Spanish. North Carolina, 1956. North Carolina *Record*, No. 576, p. 284.

31. 8. Brown, Charles Barrett. The Passive and In-

definite Reflexives in Old Spanish. Chicago, 1928. Chicago *Abstracts*, VI, 313.

31. 9. Buckingham, Lucius Henry. That the Romance Languages, in Deriving from the Latin, Followed Tendencies to Change, Which the Latin Already Exhibited, Is Illustrated by the Study of Romance Verbal Formations. Harvard, 1876.

31. 10. Chambers, Frank M. Uses of the Subjunctive Mood in the Romance Languages. Harvard, 1935. Harvard *Summaries*, 1935, p. 299.

31. 11. Cryesky, Ralph H. A Semantic Study of Verbs of Thinking in the Romance Languages. Harvard, 1953.

31. 12. Feldman, David Morris. The Historical Syntax of Modal Verb Phrases in Spanish. Cornell, 1962. *DA*, XXIII, 4682.

31. 13. Fontaine, Joseph Auguste. On the Auxiliary Verbs in the Romance Languages. Johns Hopkins, 1886. Lincoln, Nebraska, 1888. LC 4-2307.

31. 14. Garner, Samuel. The Gerundial Construction in the Romance Languages. Johns Hopkins, 1881.

31. 15. Georges, Emanuel Spear. Studies in Romance Nouns Extracted from Past Participles. California, 1965. *DA*, XXVI, 1032.

31. 16. Glover, Bobby Ray. A History of Six Spanish Verbs Meaning "To Take, Seize, Grasp." Louisiana State, 1966. *DA*, XXVII, 203-A.

31. 17. Gordon, Alan Martin. Verb-Creation in the Works of José Martí: Method and Function. Harvard, 1956.

31. 18. Gordon, Calvin Gustav. The Subjunctive Mood in Representative Spanish Works from the 12th to the 18th Century. Nebraska, 1964. *DA*, XXV, 4134.

31. 19. Gould, William Elford. The Subjunctive Mood in *Don Quijote de la Mancha*. Johns Hopkins, 1903. Baltimore, 1905. LC 6-37895.

31. 20. Hatheway, Joel. An Historical Study of *Hubiera* and *Hubiese*. Boston University, 1926.

31. 21. Keys, George Robert, Jr. The Present Tense in the Romance Languages with Special Reference to French and Italian. North Carolina, 1948. North Carolina *Record*, No. 464, p. 362.

31. 22. Leuschel, Donald Ardell. Spanish Verb Morphology. Indiana, 1960. *DA*, XXI, 2708.

31. 23. Markley, James G. The Verbal Categories of Substandard Spanish. Illinois, 1954. *DA*, XV, 118.

31. 24. McDowell, David Franklin. The Nature of Old Spanish Vocabulary as Determined by an Etymological and Semantic Analysis of the Verbs in the *Primera parte* of the *General estoria* of Alfonso el Sabio. North Carolina, 1943. North Carolina *Record*, No. 429, p. 231.

31. 25. Meyer, Christine Louise. A Semantic Survey of

Certain Verbs Indicating Departure and Arrival in the Romance Languages. Ohio State, 1941. Ohio State *Abstracts,* No. 35, p. 201.

31. 26. Moorefield, Allen S. The Infinitive as Accusative in Modern Spanish. Southern California, 1958. Southern California *Abstracts,* 1958, p. 85.

31. 27. Paratore, Angela. Spanish Verb Phrase and Clause Structure. Cornell, 1950.

31. 28. Rallides, Charles. The Tense-Aspect System of the Spanish Verb. Columbia, 1965. *DA, XXVI,* 2738.

31. 29. Reed, Frank Otis. The History of the Spanish Past Participle Compounded with *Haber.* Harvard, 1905.

31. 30. Reid, James Richard. The Expression of Future Time: From Indo-European to Romance. Harvard, 1943. Harvard *Summaries,* 1943-45, p. 161.

31. 31. Scottron, Edith M. The Development of the Latin Passive Verb in the Romance Languages. Columbia, 1949. Wooster, Ohio, 1950. LC 50-3263.

31. 32. Seymour, Arthur Romeyn. The Development of the Latin Pluperfect Indicative in Spanish. Wisconsin, 1907.

31. 33. Solé, Yolanda Antonia F. Russinovich. *Hacer:* Verbo funcional y lexical. Georgetown, 1966. *DA, XXVII,* 486-A.

31. 34. Spaulding, Robert Kilburn. A Study of the History and Syntax of Progressive Constructions in Spanish. California, 1925. *Berkeley, 1926. LC 27-2367.

31. 35. Strausbaugh, John Anthony. The Use of *auer a* and *auer de* as Auxiliary Verbs in Old Spanish from the Earliest Texts to the End of the Thirteenth Century. Chicago, 1933. Chicago, 1936. LC 36-9733.

31. 36. Sublette, Edith B. The Locative Functions of *ser* and *estar* and Some Auxiliary Functions of *ser* and *haber.* Iowa, 1938. Iowa *Abstracts,* II, 238.

31. 37. Taylor, George Benjamin. Verbal Aspect in Early Romance. Stanford, 1951. Stanford *Abstracts,* XXVII, 375.

31. 38. Wilkins, George W., Jr. Verbal Categories of the *Poema del Cid.* Tulane, 1961. *DA, XXII,* 1169.

31. 39. Winget, Lynn Warren. Auxiliary Verbs in the Prose Works of Alfonso X. Wisconsin, 1960. *DA, XX,* 4104.

31. 40. Wisewell, George Ellas. Finite Moods and Tenses in the *Don Quijote* of Cervantes. Wisconsin, 1919.

31. 41. Wolfe, David Lee. A Generative-Transformational Analysis of Spanish Verb Forms. Michigan, 1966. *DA, XXVIII,* 219-A.

31. 42. Woods, Perry Daniel. The *-ra* Verb Form in Spanish-American Writings. Oregon, 1932. Oregon *Theses,* p. 63.

31. 43. Wright, Leavitt Olds. A Study of the History of the *-ra* Verb-Form in Spain. California, 1929. *Berkeley, 1932. LC A32-1580.

### 32. *Word Order*

32. 1. Brownell, George Griffin. The Position of the Attributive Adjective in the *Don Quixote.* Johns Hopkins, 1904. Paris-New York, 1908. LC 13-22980.

32. 2. Chenery, Winthrop Holt. Object Pronouns in Dependent Clauses: A Study in Old Spanish Word Order. Harvard, 1904.

32. 3. Conway, [Sister] M. Ann C., S.N.J.M. Order Classes of Adjectives in Spanish. Texas, 1964. *DA, XXV,* 6607.

32. 4. Crabb, Daniel M. A Comparative Study of Word Order in Old Spanish and Old French Prose Works. Catholic, 1955. Washington, 1955. NUC A55-4943.

32. 5. Leavitt, Walter David. The Position of the Object Pronouns in Old Spanish: A Contribution to Medieval Syntax. Yale, 1954.

32. 6. Ringo, Elbert W. The Position of the Noun Modifier in Colloquial Mexican Spanish. Illinois, 1950. Urbana, 1950. LC A51-2090.

### II. GENERAL

### 1. *Bibliography*

1. 1. Tucker, Scotti M. H. A Bibliography of Spanish Literary Criticism, 1700-1800. Texas, 1951.

1. 2. Zimmerman, Irene. Latin American Periodicals of the Mid-Twentieth Century as Source Material for Research in the Humanities and the Social Sciences. Michigan, 1956. *DA, XVII,* 3027.

### 2. *Miscellaneous*

2. 1. Arriola, Paul ·Manuel. The *Viage a Jerusalem:* A Contribution to the Study of Spanish Travel Literature. California, 1956.

2. 2. Basdekis, Demetrios. Unamuno and Spanish Literature. Columbia, 1965. *DA, XXVI,* 3324.

2. 3. Bernardete, Mair José. Hispanic Culture and Character of the Sephardic Jews. Columbia, 1950. New York: Hispanic Institute in the United States, 1952.

2. 4. Blanch, Mable. Variations on a Picaresque Theme: A Study of Two Twentieth-Century Treatments of Picaresque Form. Colorado, 1966. *DA, XXVIII,* 1427-A. [*The Adventures of Augie March* (1949) and *The Tin Drum* (1959).]

2. 5. Brooks, Mary Elizabeth. Gabriel de Espinosa,

"el pastelero de Madrigal," in History and Literature. New Mexico, 1960. *DA,* XX, 4394.

2. 6.   Brownstein, Rachel Mayer. *Don Juan:* The Absurd Point of View. Yale, 1963.

2. 7.   Buchwalter, Grace May. The Don Carlos Theme in European Literature. Northwestern, 1931.

2. 8.   Chandler, Arthur Alan. The Role of Literary Tradition in the Novelistic Trajectory of Emilia Pardo Bazán. Ohio State, 1956. *DA,* XVI, 1450.

2. 9.   Compton, Merlin D. Spanish Honor in Ricardo Palma's *Tradiciones peruanas.* U.C.L.A., 1959.

2. 10.   De Wendler-Funaro, Carl. The *Gitano* in Spanish Literature. Columbia, 1958. *DA,* XIX, 523.

2. 11.   Espantoso, Augusta María. The Use of the Occult Arts in the *Comedias* of Juan Ruiz de Alarcón: Together with a Preliminary Survey of the Occult Arts in Dramatic Literature. Pennsylvania, 1962. *DA,* XXIII, 1363.

2. 12.   Eveleth, F. W. *La Novela Picaresca* and Its Influence on Subsequent Literature. New York, 1899.

2. 13.   Eyer, Cortland. A Contribution to the Study of the Dido Theme. Northwestern, 1935. Northwestern *Summaries,* III, 13.

2. 14.   Fitzgerald, [Sister] Mary Christine. The Irish in Spain. Western Reserve, 1955. Western Reserve *Abstracts,* 1954-56, p. 177. [Discussion of the Irish and Irish names in Spanish literature.]

2. 15.   Freyschlag, Elizabeth Kyle. A Consideration of Pelayo in Spanish Literature. Stanford, 1965. *DA,* XXVI, 5411.

2. 16.   Hatzantonis, Emmanuel Stamatios. Circe nelle letterature classiche, medioevali e romanze: da Omero a Calderón. California, 1958.

2. 17.   Jackson, George William. A Study of the Spanish Literary Sources of *Don Quijote de la Mancha.* Harvard, 1961.

2. 18.   Kany, Charles Emil. The Beginning of the Epistolary Novel in Romance Languages. Harvard, 1920. *Berkeley, 1937. LC A38-299.

2. 19.   Knopp, Grace. The Motifs of the "Jason and Medea Myth" in Modern Tradition. A Study of Märchentypus 313. Stanford, 1933. Stanford *Abstracts,* 1932-33, p. 59. [Treatment of Spanish and other versions.]

2. 20.   La Grone, Gregory Gough. The Imitations of *Don Quixote* in the Spanish Drama. Pennsylvania, 1936. Philadelphia, 1937. LC 37-3649.

2. 21.   Marshall, Pauline Maude. An Edition of Alonso de Salas Barbadillo's *El caballero perfecto* (1620), Together with a Study of Previous Spanish Literary Portrayals of the Ideal Gentleman. Northwestern, 1943. *Boulder, Colo., 1949. LC 49-47324.

2. 22.   Martin, John Watson. Objective Criteria of Syntax and the Determination of Authorship in Spanish Literature: A Study of the Method and Its Validity. Washington, Seattle, 1956. *DA,* XVII, 855.

2. 23.   Ruggerio, Michael John. The Evolution of the Go-Between: Eros and Witchcraft. Harvard, 1964. Berkeley, 1966. NUC 66-64908. [Type study through the 17th century.]

2. 24.   Singleton, Mack H. Technique and Idea in Early Spanish Fiction. Wisconsin, 1936. Wisconsin *Summaries,* I, 340.

2. 25.   Trachman, Sadie Edith. Cervantes' Women of Literary Tradition. Columbia, 1932. New York, 1932. LC 33-6930.

2. 26.   Waxman, Samuel Montefiore. Chapters on Magic in Spanish Literature. Harvard, 1912.

2. 27.   Weinstein, Leo. A Critical Study of the Don Juan Legend. Stanford, 1951. *Stanford, Calif., 1959. NUC 59-5050.

2. 28.   Weiss, Arnold H. Chroniclers of the Reyes Católicos: Studies in Politics, Biography, and Literary Style. Wisconsin, 1952. Wisconsin *Summaries,* XIV, 466.

2. 29.   Williams, Ethel M. The Development of the Literary *Tertulia.* Cornell, 1934. Ithaca, 1934. LC 35-84.

2. 30.   Winn, Conchita Hassell. The Historical Tale in Hispanic Literature. Columbia, 1953. *DA,* XIV, 2354.

### 3.   *Ballad and Folksong*

3. 1.   Bryant, Shasta M. Comparative Study of the Spanish Ballad Translations of James Young Gibson. North Carolina, 1958. *DA,* XIX, 2611.

3. 2.   Chandler, Richard Eugene. A Study of Treason in the Spanish Ballads. Missouri, 1940. *MA,* V, No. 1, p. 32.

3. 3.   Emmons, Glenroy. The *Romancero* as an Expression of the Ideology of the Spanish People: An Analysis of Medieval Spanish Ideology as Seen in the Oldest Historical Ballads. New Mexico, 1956. *DA,* XVI, 2456.

3. 4.   Endres, Valerie F. The Aesthetic Treatment of *Romancero* Material in the *Comedias* of Luis Vélez de Guevara. Arizona, 1966. *DA,* XXVII, 2150-A.

3. 5.   Franklin, Albert B., III. The Origins of the Legend and *Romancero* of Bernardo del Carpio. Harvard, 1938. Harvard *Summaries,* 1938, p. 353.

3. 6.   House, Ruth D. A Study of Formulas and Repetition in the Spanish Ballad. California, 1948. See Webber, [Mrs.] Ruth D. *Berkeley, 1951. LC A52-1743.

3. 7.   Madrid, Miguel Angel. The Attitudes of the Spanish American People as Expressed in Their

*Coplas* or Folk Songs. Columbia, 1953. *DA,* XIV, 128.

3. 8. Mejía, Leonor María. An Investigation of Spanish Ballad Origins. Stanford, 1937. Stanford *Abstracts,* 1936-37, p. 52.

3. 9. Moore, Jerome Aaron. The *Romancero* in the Chronicle-Legend Plays of Lope de Vega. Pennsylvania, 1937. Philadelphia, 1940. LC 41-5542.

3. 10. Mortenson, Barbara Jeanne. The Lyrical Elements in Spanish Balladry from 1580 to 1650. California, 1966. *DA,* XXVII, 4260-A.

3. 11. Owens, Robert N. The Historical Ballads of the *Manojuelo* of Gabriel Lobo Lasso de la Vega. Iowa, 1939. Iowa *Abstracts,* III, 403.

3. 12. Paredes, Américo. "El corrido de Gregorio Cortez." A Ballad of Border Conflict. Texas, 1956.

3. 13. Pérez, Elisa. La influencia del *Romancero* en Guillén de Castro. Wisconsin, 1932.

3. 14. Poole, Robert Hawkins. Women in Early Spanish Literature with Special Emphasis on the Women in the Medieval Spanish Ballad. Stanford, 1949. Stanford *Abstracts,* XXV, 235.

3. 15. Renk, Eldred J. The Mexican *Corrido* and the Revolution: A People's-Eye View of Events in War, Religion and Politics. Washington, Seattle, 1951.

3. 16. Rogers, Cornelia Hephzibah Bulkley. Sinalefa, sinéresis é hiato en los romances del Cid. Yale, 1894.

3. 17. Seay, Hugh Nelson, Jr. A Classification of Motifs in the Traditional Ballads of Spain. North Carolina, 1958. *DA,* XIX, 2052.

3. 18. Simmons, Merle Edwin. The Mexican *Corrido* as a Source for Interpretive Study of Modern Mexico (1870-1950): With a Consideration of the Origins and Development of the *Corrido* Tradition. Michigan, 1952. *DA,* XII, 310.

3. 19. Torres, María de Guadalupe. Los romances españoles en América. Stanford, 1951. Stanford *Abstracts,* XXVI, 282.

### 4. *Folklore*

4. 1. Boggs, Ralph Steele. Index of Spanish Folktales. Chicago, 1930. Helsinki, 1930. LC 31-16679.

4. 2. Campa, Arthur Leon. Spanish Folk-Poetry in New Mexico. Columbia, 1946. Albuquerque, 1946. LC A47-2618.

4. 3. Fife, Austin E. The Concept of the Sacredness of Bees, Honey and Wax in Christian Popular Tradition. Stanford, 1939. Stanford *Abstracts,* 1938-39, p. 66.

4. 4. Goodwyn, Frank E. An Interpretation of the Hispanic Folk Hero, Pedro de Urdemalas. Texas, 1945.

4. 5. Hansen, Terrence Leslie. The Types of the Folktale in Cuba, Puerto Rico, the Dominican Republic, and Spanish South America. Stanford, 1951. Stanford *Abstracts,* XXVII, 368.

4. 6. Keller, John E. The Exemplum in Spain. North Carolina, 1946. *Knoxville, Tenn., 1949. LC 49-49515.

4. 7. Paullada, Stephen. A Study of the Influence That Similar Environment Had upon the Life and Folklore of the Gaucho and Cowboy Societies. Southern California, 1953. Southern California *Abstracts,* 1953, p. 61.

4. 8. Rael, Juan Bautista. A Study of the Phonology and Morphology of New Mexican Spanish Based on a Collection of 410 Folk-Tales. Stanford, 1937. Stanford *Abstracts,* 1936-37, p. 55.

4. 9. Robe, Stanley L. A Dialect and Folkloristic Study of Texts Recorded in Los Altos of Jalisco, Mexico. North Carolina, 1949. North Carolina *Record,* No. 478, p. 233.

4. 10. Very, Francis George. The Corpus Christi Procession in Spain: A Literary and Folkloric Study. California, 1956. Valencia, 1962. NUC 67-18120.

### 5. *Galician Literature* (General)

5. 1. Landeira, Ricardo López. La saudade en el renacimiento de la literatura gallega. Colorado, 1965. *DA,* XXVII, 776-A.

5. 2. Reckert, Frederick S. Galician Literature: A Study in Essential Romanticism. Yale, 1950.

### 6. *Legends*

6. 1. Kolker, [Sister] M. Delphine. Spanish Legends in English and American Literature: 1800-1860. Catholic, 1952. Washington, 1952. NUC Micp A53-120.

6. 2. Schons, Emily. New Material on the Dramatic Treatment of Peter the Cruel of Castile and the Diffusion of the Legend in France, Germany, and England. Chicago, 1932. Chicago, 1936. LC 36-18707.

6. 3. Sturdevant, Winifred. The *Misterio de los Reyes Magos*: Its Position in the Development of the Mediaeval Legend of the Three Kings. Johns Hopkins, 1920. Baltimore-Paris, 1927. LC 28-9985.

6. 4. Tyler, Richard W. Lope de Vega's *La corona de Hungría*. A Critical Edition, with an Introductory Study of the Treatment of the *Reina Sevilla* Legend in the Theatre of Lope de Vega. Brown, 1946.

### 7. *Literary History and Criticism*

7. 1. Bernstein, Jerome Straus. Theories of the Modern Novel in Spain. Harvard, 1964. See NUC 65-20486.

7. 2.  Biondi, Raymond Liberty.  Hispanism in Italy: An Appraisal of the Contribution of Benedetto Croce to the Evaluation of Spanish Literature. Stanford, 1955.  *DA,* XV, 1060.

7. 3.  Brancaforte, Benito.  Benedetto Croce as Critic of Spanish Literature: Theory and Practice.  Illinois, 1965.  *DA,* XXVI, 2744.

7. 4.  Campbell, Brenton Kay.  The Literary Theories of Ramón Pérez de Ayala.  California, 1961.  Microfilmed, California Library, 1964.  NUC 65-20642.

7. 5.  Cano, Juan.  La *Poética* de Luzán.  Columbia, 1928.  Toronto, 1928.  LC 30-7183.

7. 6.  Cervone, Anthony Valerius.  An Analysis of the Literary and Aesthetic Ideas in *Dell' origine, dei progressi e dello stato attuale d' ogni letterature* of Juan Andrés.  St. Louis, 1966.  *DA,* XXVII, 3039-A.

7. 7.  Collard-Wéry, Andrée Marie.  Cultismo, conceptismo y categorías afines en la crítica española.  Harvard, 1965.  See NUC 67-81780.

7. 8.  Coutu, [Sister] Albert Cécile, F.S.E.  Hispanism in France from Morel-Fatio to the Present (Circa 1875-1950).  Catholic, 1954.  Washington, 1954.  NUC A54-5209.

7. 9.  Dyson, John P.  La evolución de la crítica literaria en Chile.  Kansas, 1965.  *DA,* XXVI, 3332.

7. 10.  Efron, Arthur.  Satire Denied: A Critical History of English and American *Don Quixote* Criticism.  Washington, Seattle, 1964.  *DA,* XXV, 5274.

7. 11.  Forcadas, Alberto Massó.  El Siglo de Oro en las historias literarias norteamericanas recientes.  Missouri, 1966.  *DA,* XXVIII, 628-A.

7. 12.  Fox, Edward Inman.  Azorín as a Literary Critic. Princeton, 1960.  New York, 1962.  NUC 62-6487.

7. 13.  Gibson, M. Carl.  Xavier Lampillas: His Defense of Spanish Literature and His Contributions to Literary History.  Oregon, 1960.  *DA,* XXI, 2713.

7. 14.  Goodale, Hope K.  Pérez Galdós: Dramatic Critic and Dramatist.  Bryn Mawr, 1965.  *DA,* XXVI, 6041.

7. 15.  Grupp, William J.  Dramatic Theory and Criticism in Spain During the Sixteenth, Seventeenth and Eighteenth Centuries.  Cornell, 1949.

7. 16.  Hart, Thomas R., Jr.  A History of Spanish Literary History, 1800-1850.  Yale, 1952.

7. 17.  Hernández, David.  Alfonso Reyes as a Literary Critic.  Illinois, 1966.  *DA,* XXVII, 775-A.

7. 18.  Hernández, Mary Frances Baker.  Gabriela Mistral and the Standards of American Criticism.  New Mexico, 1963.  *DA,* XXIV, 3324.

7. 19.  Hudson, Herman Cleophus.  The Development of Dramatic Criticism in England and Spain During the Elizabethan Period and the Golden Age.  Michigan, 1962.  *DA,* XXIII, 235.

7. 20.  Hutchings, Chesley M.  The Sentiment of Nationality in Spanish Literary Criticism from 1400 to 1621.  Harvard, 1922.

7. 21.  Johnson, Jerry Lee.  Juan Ramón Jiménez, the Critic.  Virginia, 1966.  *DA,* XXVIII, 1051-A.

7. 22.  Kersten, Raquel.  Cuatro maestros de la crítica literaria en España: Ramón Menéndez Pidal, Américo Castro, José Fernández Montesinos y Dámaso Alonso.  Estudio de sus contribuciones a la *Revista de filología española* desde 1914 hasta 1960.  New York, 1964.  *DA,* XXVI, 355.

7. 23.  Koldewyn, Philip Young.  Alfonso Reyes as a Critic of Peninsular Spanish Literature.  California, 1965.  *DA,* XXVI, 1648.

7. 24.  Laughrin, [Sister] Mary Fidelia, I.H.M.  Juan Pablo Forner as a Literary Critic.  Catholic, 1944.  Washington, 1943.  LC A44-1237.

7. 25.  Mazzeo, Guido E.  The Abate Juan Andrés (1740-1817): Literary Historian and Defender of Spanish and Medieval Hispano-Arab Learning, Literature and Culture.  Columbia, 1961.  *DA,* XXII, 565.

7. 26.  Pegues, Charles Melton.  Spanish Literature as Portrayed in the *Revue des Deux Mondes* (1829-1929).  Illinois, 1931.  Urbana, 1931.  LC 31-25308.

7. 27.  Shearer, James Francis.  The *Poética* and *Apéndices* of Martínez de la Rosa: Their Genesis, Sources and Significance for Spanish Literary History and Criticism.  Princeton, 1939.  Princeton, 1941.  LC 41-17114.

7. 28.  Shuford, William Harris.  Angel Ganivet as a Literary Critic.  North Carolina, 1963.  *DA,* XXIV, 3342.

7. 29.  Siegwart, John Thomas.  The Beginnings of Modern Criticism in Spain: 1750-1800.  Tulane, 1959.  *DA,* XX, 3752.

7. 30.  Tucker, Scotti M. H.  A Bibliography of Spanish Literary Criticism, 1700-1800.  Texas, 1951.

### 8.  *Poetry (General)*

8. 1.  Barta, Robert James.  The Traditional Peninsular Lyric as Reflected by Rosalía de Castro (Affinities of Subject and Form: *Cantares gallegos, Follas novas*).  Minnesota, 1965.  *DA,* XXVII, 765-A.

8. 2.  Fein, John Morton.  Eugênio de Castro and the Development of Cosmopolitanism in Hispanic Poetry.  Harvard, 1950.

8. 3.  Rozen, Eva J.  Renaissance Motifs in Epic Theory and Poetry in the Romance Languages.  New York, 1962.  *DA,* XXVII, 1792-A.

### 9.  *Proverbs-Refranes*

9. 1.  Hayes, Francis C.  The Use of Proverbs in the *Siglo de Oro* Drama: An Introductory Study.  North

Carolina, 1936. North Carolina *Record,* No. 311, p. 89.

9. 2.   Johnson, James Henry. The Proverb in the Medieval Spanish Exempla. North Carolina, 1958. *DA,* XIX, 2084.

9. 3.   Lévy, Isaac Jack. Prolegomena to a Study of the *Refranero sefardí.* Michigan, 1966. *DA,* XXVIII, 198-A.

9. 4.   O'Kane, Eleanor S. A Dictionary of Medieval Spanish Proverbs and Proverbial Phrases. Bryn Mawr, 1947. *Madrid, 1959. *BRAE,* Anejos, 2. NUC 62-28689.

9. 5.   Raymond, Joseph B. Attitudes and Cultural Patterns in Spanish Proverbs. Columbia, 1951. *MA,* XI, No. 4, p. 1029.

### 10.   *Stylistics*

10. 1.   Craddock, [Sister] Clare Eileen. Style Theories as Found in Stylistic Studies of Romance Scholars, 1900-1950. Catholic, 1952. Washington, 1952. LC A52-7015.

### 11.   *Theater*

11. 1.   Oliver, William Irvin. Spanish Theatre: A Study in Dramatic Discipline. Cornell, 1959. *DA,* XX, 2434. [Vol. 2 contains actable translations of 3 Spanish plays: *The Lady Nit-Wit* by Lope de Vega, *Phaedra* by Miguel de Unamuno, *Blood Wedding* by Federico García Lorca.]

### 12.   *Versification*

12. 1.   Bailiff, Lawrence Deane. Synalepha and Hiatus in Spanish Poetry. Stanford, 1923.

12. 2.   Berndt, Robert J. A Qualitative Analysis of the Versification of Selected *Comedias* of Luis Vélez de Guevara. Western Reserve, 1956. Western Reserve *Abstracts,* 1954-56, p. 99.

12. 3.   Clarke, Dorothy Clotelle. *Diversas rimas* de Vicente Espinel, edición crítica, con un estudio del desarrollo de la décima. California, 1934. *New York, 1956. See NUC, 1953-57, vol. 7, p. 354.

12. 4.   Dreps, Joseph Antone. The Metrics of José de Espronceda. Iowa, 1931. Iowa *Program,* Aug. 1931.

12. 5.   Eddy, Nelson W. Villasandino and *Arte Mayor.* Michigan, 1939.

12. 6.   Fitz-Gerald, John Driscoll. Versification of the *Cuaderna Vía,* as Found in Berceo's *Vida de Santo Domingo de Silos.* Columbia, 1905. New York, 1905. LC 7-16238.

12. 7.   Gordon, Arthur. Spanish Verse and Versification in the Sixteenth Century. Cornell, 1909.

12. 8.   Henríquez Ureña, Pedro. La versificación irregular en la poesía castellana. Minnesota, 1918. Madrid, 1920. LC 21-11254.

12. 9.   Kline, Lawton. A Metrical Study of the *Cántigas de Santa María* by Alfonso el Sabio. Stanford, 1950. Stanford *Abstracts,* XXV, 232.

12. 10.   Parker, Jack Horace. *La gitanilla* (Attributed to Juan Pérez de Montalván) by Antonio de Solís y Rivadeneyra, Edited, with Introduction and Notes, Together with a Study of the Versification of the Plays of Solís and Montalván. Toronto, 1941.

12. 11.   Poesse, Walter. The Internal Line-Structure of Twenty-Seven Autograph Plays of Lope de Vega. California, 1940. *Bloomington, Ind., 1949. LC 49-45176.

12. 12.   Pope, Isabel. Sources of the Musical and Metrical Forms of the Mediaeval Lyric in the Hispanic Peninsula. Radcliffe, 1930.

12. 13.   Ramelli, Mattie Mae. The Polimetria of Spanish Romantic Poets. Stanford, 1938. Stanford *Abstracts,* 1938-39, p. 72.

12. 14.   Rogers, Cornelia Hephzibah Bulkley. Sinalefa, sinéresis é hiato en los romances del Cid. Yale, 1894.

12. 15.   Sittler, Richard C. Antecedents and Present Characteristics of the Spanish American Alexandrine. Iowa, 1952. Iowa *Abstracts,* X, 211.

## COMPARATIVE STUDIES: Spanish Relations with Other Literatures.

### 13.   *Arabic*

13. 1.   Cirre, Manuela Manzanares. Los estudios árabes en España en el siglo XIX. Michigan, 1958. *DA,* XIX, 1373.

13. 2.   Irving, Thomas Ballantine. A Textual Comparison of a Section of the Arabic *Kalīlah wa Dimnah* and the Corresponding Section of the Old Spanish *Calila e Digna.* Princeton, 1940. *DA,* XII, 187.

13. 3.   Mazzeo, Guido E. The Abate Juan Andrés (1740-1817): Literary Historian and Defender of Spanish and Medieval Hispano-Arab Learning, Literature and Culture. Columbia, 1961. *DA,* XXII, 565.

13. 4.   Monroe, James Thomas. Main Currents in Spanish Arabism (18th Century to the Present). Harvard, 1964. See NUC 65-111162.

### 14.   *Biblical*

14. 1.   Arkin, Alexander Habib. La influencia de la exégesis hebrea en los comentarios bíblicos de Fray Luis de León. New York, 1963. *DA,* XXIV, 2026.

14. 2.   Gormly, [Sister] Francis, S.N.D. The Use of the Bible in Representative Works of Medieval Spanish Literature, 1250-1300. Catholic, 1962. *DA,* XXIII, 3374.

14. 3.   Ramírez, Alejandro. Cervantes y la Biblia. Washington, St. Louis, 1951.

14. 4.   Sáez, Alfred R.   La influencia de la Biblia en las novelas de Galdós.   Northwestern, 1966.   *DA,* XXVII, 2160-A.

14. 5.   Shervill, Robert Newton.   The Old Testament Drama of the *Siglo de Oro.*   North Carolina, 1958. *DA,* XIX, 2093.

### 15.  *Classical*

15. 1.   Beardsley, Theodore Sterling.   Hispano-Classical Translations Printed Between 1482 and 1699: A Study of the Prologues and a Critical Bibliography. Pennsylvania, 1961.   *DA,* XXII, 1170.

15. 2.   Bourne, Marjorie A.   Classic Themes in Contemporary Spanish Drama.   Indiana, 1961.   *DA,* XXII, 1621.

15. 3.   Hatzantonis, Emmanuel Stamatios.   Circe nelle letterature classiche, medioevali e romanze: da Omero a Calderón.   California, 1958.

15. 4.   Hershberg, David Ralph.   A Critical Study of the Treatment of Classical Sources in Juan de Zavaleta's *Errores celebrados.*   Michigan, 1966.   *DA,* XXVIII, 676-A.

15. 5.   McCrary, William Carlton.   The Classical Tradition in Spanish Dramatic Theory of the Sixteenth and Seventeenth Centuries.   Wisconsin, 1958.   *DA,* XIX, 2092.

15. 6.   Melvin, Miriam V.   Juan Ruiz de Alarcón. Classical and Spanish Influences.   Kansas, 1941.

15. 7.   Staaf, Oscar Emil.   Classical Mythology in Calderón.   Yale, 1907.

15. 8.   Thomson, Somerville.   The Extent and Use of Classical Reference in the Spanish Picaresque Novel. Stanford, 1939.   Stanford *Abstracts,* 1938-39, p. 77.

### 16.  *Dutch*

16. 1.   Longhurst, John Edward.   Erasmus and the Spanish Inquisition. The Case of Juan de Valdés. Michigan, 1949.   *MA,* IX, p. 127.

16. 2.   O'Connor, Norine P.   Juan Arce de Otálora, *Coloquios de Palatino y Pinciano*: An Erasmian Dialogue of the Sixteenth Century; A Critical Analysis of the Unpublished Manuscript.   Texas, 1952.

### 17.  *English*

17. 1.   Brown, Louise Stephens.   The Portrayal of Spanish Characters in Selected Plays of the Elizabethan and Jacobean Eras: 1585-1625.   Duke, 1966.   *DA,* XXVII, 1779-A.

17. 2.   Bryant, Shasta M.   Comparative Study of the Spanish Ballad Translations of James Young Gibson. North Carolina, 1958.   *DA,* XIX, 2611.

17. 3.   Chambers, Dwight O.   *Defensa de poesía,* A Spanish Version of Sir Philip Sidney's *Defence of Poesie.* Kansas, 1956.   *DA,* XVI, 2158.

17. 4.   Churchman, Philip Hudson.   Byron and the Spanish Peninsula.   Harvard, 1908.

17. 5.   Delaney, [Sister] Anne Cyril, S.N.D.   Anagogical Mirrors: Reflections in the Poetry of T. S. Eliot of the Doctrine of Saint John of the Cross.   Boston University, 1954.   Boston University *Abstracts,* 1954, n.p.

17. 6.   Earle, Peter G.   Unamuno and English Literature.   Kansas, 1958.   New York, 1960.   See NUC, 1958-62, vol. 13, p. 90.

17. 7.   Effross, Susi H.   English Influence on Eighteenth-Century Spanish Literature, 1700-1808.   Columbia, 1962.   *DA,* XXIII, 630.

17. 8.   Golden, Bruce.   Elizabethan Revenge and Spanish Honor: Analogues of Action in the Popular Drama of the Renaissance.   Columbia, 1966.

17. 9.   Heald, William F.   A Comparison of Plot Patterns in the Plays of Shakespeare and Lope de Vega. North Carolina, 1954.   North Carolina *Record,* No. 548, p. 51.

17. 10.   Hill, Archibald Anderson.   English Translations from the Spanish and Their Influence on the English Drama, 1610-1630.   Yale, 1927.

17. 11.   Hobbs, Edna Earle.   The Influence of Spanish Drama on the Plays of Beaumont and Fletcher and Their Collaborators.   Florida State, 1963.   *DA,* XXIV, 283.

17. 12.   Hudson, Herman Cleophus.   The Development of Dramatic Criticism in England and Spain During the Elizabethan Period and the Golden Age.   Michigan, 1962.   *DA,* XXIII, 235.

17. 13.   Knowles, Edwin B., Jr.   The Vogue of *Don Quixote* in England from 1605 to 1660.   New York, 1939.   *New York, 1941.   LC A42-2143.

17. 14.   Kolker, [Sister] M. Delphine.   Spanish Legends in English and American Literature: 1800-1860. Catholic, 1952.   Washington, 1952.   NUC Micp A53-120.

17. 15.   Linsalata, Carmine R.   Tobias Smollett and Charles Jarvis: Translators of *Don Quijote.*   Texas, 1949.   *Stanford, 1956.   NUC 56-9984.

17. 16.   Longest, Christopher.   Spanish Sources of Southey.   Chicago, 1915.

17. 17.   Marsh, John O., Jr.   The Spanish Version of Sir John Mandeville's *Travels,* a Critical Edition. Wisconsin, 1951.   Wisconsin *Summaries,* XIII, 398.

17. 18.   Mathews, Ernest Garland.   Studies in Spanish-English Cultural and Literary Relations, 1598-1700. Harvard, 1938.   Harvard *Summaries,* 1938, p. 304.

17. 19.   McCann, Eleanor M.   The Influence of Sixteenth and Seventeenth Century Spanish Mystics and Ascetics on Some Metaphysical Writers.   Stanford, 1953.   *DA,* XIII, 229.

17. 20.   McDonald, William Ulma, Jr.   A Critical Edi-

tion of H. D. Inglis' *Rambles in the Footsteps of Don Quixote.* Northwestern, 1956. *DA,* XVII, 363.

17. 21. Moncada, Ernest Joseph. An Analysis of James Mabbe's Translation of Mateo Alemán's *Guzmán de Alfarache.* Maryland, 1966. *DA,* XXVII, 3056-A.

17. 22. Morgan, Rudolph. Moratín's *Hamlet.* Stanford, 1965. *DA,* XXVI, 6719.

17. 23. Park, John Horace. Fry and Casona: A Comparison. Indiana, 1960. *DA,* XXI, 3459.

17. 24. Penner, Allen Richard. Fielding and Cervantes: The Contribution of *Don Quixote* to *Joseph Andrews* and *Tom Jones.* Colorado, 1965. *DA,* XXVI, 6720.

17. 25. Randall, Dale B. J. Renaissance English Translations of Non-Chivalric Spanish Fiction (With Special Reference to the Period from 1620 to 1657). Pennsylvania, 1958. *DA,* XVIII, 2129.

17. 26. Reese, Lowell Grant. Lope de Vega and Shakespeare: A Comparative Study of Tragicomic Style. Washington, Seattle, 1962. *DA,* XXIV, 285.

17. 27. Schons, Emily. New Material on the Dramatic Treatment of Peter the Cruel of Castile and the Diffusion of the Legend in France, Germany, and England. Chicago, 1932. Chicago, 1936. ʟᴄ 36-18707.

17. 28. Underhill, John Garrett. Spanish Literature in the England of the Tudors. Columbia, 1899. New York, 1899. ʟᴄ 11-994.

17. 29. Villarejo, Oscar Milton. Lope de Vega and the Elizabethan and Jacobean Drama. Columbia, 1953. *DA,* XIII, 816.

17. 30. Watt, Ethel Gladstone. Gauchesque Elements in the Works of William H. Hudson. Southern California, 1954. Southern California *Abstracts,* 1955, p. 104.

17. 31. Watts, LeClair B. The Clown: A Comparison of the Comic Figures of Lope de Vega and William Shakespeare. Connecticut, 1966. *DA,* XXVII, 4270-A.

### 18. *European*

18. 1. Donovan, Richard Bertram. The Medieval Liturgical Drama in the Hispanic Peninsula and Its Relation with That of the Rest of Europe, Especially France. Yale, 1956. *Toronto, 1958. ɴᴜᴄ 59-73.

18. 2. Flint, Weston. The Figure of Christopher Columbus in French, Italian and Spanish Dramas. North Carolina, 1957. North Carolina *Record,* No. 590, p. 266.

18. 3. Hatch, Clarence R. The Miller in the Literatures of Western Europe. Western Reserve, 1939.

18. 4. Kurtz, Leonard P. The Dance of Death and the Macabre Spirit in European Literature. Columbia, 1934. New York, 1934. ʟᴄ 35-1633.

18. 5. Matulka, Barbara. The Novels of Juan de Flores and Their European Diffusion; A Study in Comparative Literature. Columbia, 1931. New York, 1931. ʟᴄ A35-26.

18. 6. Peters, Howard Nevin. Sixteenth Century European Tragicomedy: A Critical Survey of the Genre in Italy, France, England, and Spain. Colorado, 1966. *DA,* XXVIII, 240-A.

18. 7. Randolph, Edward Dale Appleton. Pérez Galdós and the European Novel, 1867-1887: A Study of Galdosian Characters and Their European Contemporaries. Tulane, 1965. *DA,* XXVII, 484-A.

18. 8. Tayler, Neale H. The Influence of the Spanish and Other European Theatres on Tamayo y Baus. Toronto, 1948. *Madrid, 1959. ɴᴜᴄ 61-37403.

### 19. *French*

19. 1. Abbott, James H. Azorín and France. U.C.L.A., 1958.

19. 2. Alder, Esther Romella. The Don Juan Theme in the Contemporary French Theatre. California, 1964. *DA,* XXV, 4139.

19. 3. Brown, Donald F. The Influence of Emile Zola on the Novelistic and Critical Work of Emilia Pardo Bazán. Illinois, 1935. Urbana, 1935. ʟᴄ 35-20878.

19. 4. Burnie, William R. Contrast of Sixteenth-Century Christian Attitudes in Cervantes and Montaigne. Wisconsin, 1952. Wisconsin *Summaries,* XIII, 397.

19. 5. Corbière, Anthony Sylvain. Juan Eugenio Hartzenbusch and the French Theatre. Pennsylvania, 1927. Philadelphia, 1927. ʟᴄ 27-24888.

19. 6. Crooks, Esther Josephine. The Influence of Cervantes in France During the First Half of the Seventeenth Century, with Special Reference to Guérin de Bouscal and a Critical Edition of His *Gouvernement de Sanche Pansa.* Johns Hopkins, 1923. *Baltimore, 1931. ʟᴄ 31-13007.

19. 7. Danielson, John David. *Pastorelas and Serranillas,* 1130-1550: A Genre Study. Michigan, 1960. *DA,* XXI, 342.

19. 8. Donovan, Richard Bertram. The Medieval Liturgical Drama in the Hispanic Peninsula and Its Relation with That of the Rest of Europe, Especially France. Yale, 1956. *Toronto, 1958. ɴᴜᴄ 59-73.

19. 9. Dorfman, Eugene. The *Roland* and the *Cid;* A Comparative Structural Analysis. Columbia, 1950. *MA,* X, No. 3, p. 142.

19. 10. Fair, Jeane Delcine. Chateaubriand's Influence upon the Literatures of Spain and Spanish America. Northwestern, 1948. Northwestern *Summaries,* XVI, 53.

19. 11. Gabbert, Thomas Arthur. The Dramas of Du-

mas père in Spain (1834-1850): A Bibliographical Study. California, 1934.

19. 12. Gray, Stanley Everts. Spain Through French Eyes from the Eve of the Peninsular War to the Age of the Realists. Indiana, 1959. *DA*, XX, 1786.

19. 13. Gruber, Vivian M. François Rabelais and Miguel de Cervantes: Novelists of Transition. Florida State, 1960. *DA*, XXI, 2294.

19. 14. Hasbrouck, Francis Mahlon. Spanish and Portuguese Historical Characters in Modern French Drama Before 1830. Johns Hopkins, 1933.

19. 15. Heilman, Walter R., Jr. The *Pastourelle* Theme in the Early Spanish Drama. North Carolina, 1953. North Carolina *Record*, No. 534, p. 249.

19. 16. Janelle, [Sister] Marie Thomas, F.S.E. The Role of Spain in the Works of Alain-René Lesage. Fordham, 1951. Fordham *Abstracts*, XVIII, 72.

19. 17. Jones, Edwin Harvie. Spain in the Works of Victor Hugo. Virginia, 1954. *DA*, XIV, 1723.

19. 18. Kiddle, Lawrence Bayard. *La estoria de Tebas*: The Version of the Siege and Destruction of Thebes Contained in the *General estoria* of Alfonso X. Wisconsin, 1935.

19. 19. Lamond, Marilyn. Eugène Scribe and the Spanish Theater, 1834-1850. North Carolina, 1958. *DA*, XIX, 1385.

19. 20. Luquiens, Frederick Bliss. The *Roman de la Rose* and Medieval Castilian Literature. Yale, 1905.

19. 21. MacDonald, Mary B. The Influence of Emile Zola in the Novels of Benito Pérez Galdós Produced During the Years 1881-1885. Minnesota, 1959. *DA*, XX, 2294.

19. 22. Mazzara, Richard A. Italian and Spanish Influences and Parallels in the Life and Works of Saint-Amant, 1594-1661. Kansas, 1959. *DA*, XX, 1365.

19. 23. Micarelli, Charles Nicholas. Mines and Miners in French and Spanish Literatures of the Nineteenth and Twentieth Centuries. Boston University, 1959. *DA*, XX, 673.

19. 24. Miller, Paul Gerard. The Spanish Version of the Poem of Alexander. Wisconsin, 1914.

19. 25. Morley, Sylvanus Griswold. Spanish Influence on Molière. Harvard, 1902.

19. 26. Mottola, Anthony Clare. The *Amadis de Gaula* in Spain and in France. Fordham, 1962. *DA*, XXIII, 1368.

19. 27. Muller, Leonard R. Voltaire's Interpretation of Spanish History; A Source Study of Some Chapters in the *Essai sur les moeurs et l'esprit des nations*. Harvard, 1951.

19. 28. Niess, Robert Judson. A Study of the Influence of Jean de la Fontaine on the Works of Félix María de Samaniego. Minnesota, 1937. Minnesota *Summaries*, II, 158.

19. 29. Petrizzi, Daniel Joseph. L'Espagne de Barrès et de Montherlant. Middlebury, 1963.

19. 30. Picciotto, Robert S. Dramatic and Lyrical Unity in the *Cid* and the *Roland*. Indiana, 1964. *DA*, XXV, 2966.

19. 31. Qualia, Charles B. The French Neo-Classic Tragedy in Spain in the 18th Century. Texas, 1932.

19. 32. Ramsey, Jerome Alfred. Critical Positions in the Quarrel of the Cid. Chicago, 1962. See NUC 63-53047.

19. 33. Rivet, [Mother] Mary Majella, O.S.U. The Influence of the Spanish Mystics on the Works of Saint Francis de Sales. Catholic, 1941. Washington, 1941. LC 41-11843.

19. 34. Salvador, Graciano. Spanish Traditionalism and French Traditionalistic Ideas of the Nineteenth Century in Spain. Northwestern, 1942. Northwestern *Summaries*, X, 48.

19. 35. Schons, Emily. New Material on the Dramatic Treatment of Peter the Cruel of Castile and the Diffusion of the Legend in France, Germany, and England. Chicago, 1932. Chicago, 1936. LC 36-18707.

19. 36. Segall, Jacob Bernard. Corneille and the Spanish Drama. Columbia, 1902. New York, 1902. LC 2-19594.

19. 37. Seronde, Joseph. A Study of the Relations of Some Leading French Poets of the Fourteenth and Fifteenth Centuries to the Marqués de Santillana. Yale, 1915.

19. 38. Sholod, Barton H. Charlemagne in Spain: The Cultural Legacy of Roncesvalles. Columbia, 1963. *DA*, XXV, 1219.

19. 39. Sorkin, Max. Paul Scarron's Adaptations of Spanish *Comedias*. New York, 1936. *New York, 1938. LC 39-3956.

19. 40. Staubach, Charles Neff. The Influence of French Thought on Feijóo. Michigan, 1937. Iowa City, Iowa, 1941. LC A41-4765.

19. 41. Templin, Ernest Hall. The Carolingian Tradition in the Spanish Drama of the Golden Age (Excluding Lope de Vega). Stanford, 1926. Stanford *Abstracts*, 1926-27, p. 135.

19. 42. Thompson, John Archie. Alexandre Dumas (père) and the Spanish Romantic Drama up to 1850. North Carolina, 1937. University [i.e., Baton Rouge], La., 1938. LC 39-2673.

19. 43. Vaughn, Ethel. *El viage entretenido* by Agustín de Rojas: A Possible Source of *Le Roman comique* by Paul Scarron. Northwestern, 1929.

19. 44. Willis, Raymond S., Jr. The Relationship of the *Libro de Alexandre* to the *Alexandreis* of Gautier de Châtillon. Princeton, 1933. Princeton, 1934. LC 34-1004.

## 20. *Germanic*

20. 1.  Anderson, Vernon Lockwood.  Hugo von Hofmannsthal and Pedro Calderón de la Barca: A Comparative Study.  Stanford, 1954.  *DA,* XIV, 523.

20. 2.  Beckmann, Frederich Ernst.  Spanish Influence on Eichendorff.  Chicago, 1900.

20. 3.  Blanch, Mable.  Variations on a Picaresque Theme: A Study of Two Twentieth-Century Treatments of Picaresque Form.  Colorado, 1966.  *DA,* XXVIII, 1427-A.  [*The Adventures of Augie March* (1949), by Saul Bellow, and *The Tin Drum* (1959), by Günter Grass.]

20. 4.  Crantford, Carey S.  German Lyric Poetry in Spanish Translation Through 1915.  Tulane, 1961.  *DA,* XXII, 3658.

20. 5.  Denslow, Stewart.  Don Juan and Faust: Their Parallel Development and Association in Germany, 1790-1850.  Virginia, 1941.  Virginia *Abstracts,* 1941, p. 23.

20. 6.  Fasel, Oscar A.  Unamuno's Thought and German Philosophy.  Columbia, 1957.  *DA,* XVII, 1336.

20. 7.  Hartsook, John H.  Bécquer and Heine—A Comparison.  Illinois, 1939.  Urbana, 1939.  LC 40-3879.

20. 8.  Iiams, Carlton Laird.  Aegidius Albertinus and Antonio de Guevara.  California, 1956.

20. 9.  Lenz, Harold Frederick H.  Franz Grillparzer's Political Ideas and *Die Jüdin von Toledo.*  New York, 1934.  New York, 1938.  LC 38-39400.

20. 10.  Lyte, Herbert O.  Spanish Literature and Spain in Some of the Leading German Magazines of the Second Half of the Eighteenth Century.  Wisconsin, 1930.  Madison, 1932.  LC 32-27327.

20. 11.  Pfister, Franz Josef.  Die Entwicklung des deutschen Schelmenromans: Motivuntersuchungen.  Washington, Seattle, 1966.  *DA,* XXVII, 4263-A.

20. 12.  Schons, Emily.  New Material on the Dramatic Treatment of Peter the Cruel of Castile and the Diffusion of the Legend in France, Germany, and England.  Chicago, 1932.  Chicago, 1936.  LC 36-18707.

20. 13.  Schweitzer, Christoph Eugen.  Spanien in der deutschen Literatur des 17. Jahrhunderts.  Yale, 1954.  *DA,* XXVIII, 203-A.

20. 14.  Sheets, Jane Millicent.  Landscape in the Poetry of R. M. Rilke and A. Machado.  Indiana, 1965.  *DA,* XXVI, 6725.

## 21. *Greek*

21. 1.  Beach, Robert Mills.  Was Fernando de Herrera a Greek Scholar?  Pennsylvania, 1907.  Philadelphia, 1908.  LC 9-21290.

21. 2.  Howell, Stanley E.  The Use of Lucian by the Author of *El crotalón.*  Ohio State, 1947.  Ohio State *Abstracts,* No. 56, p. 69.

21. 3.  Rothberg, Irving P.  The Greek Anthology in Spanish Poetry, 1500-1700.  Pennsylvania State, 1954.  Pennsylvania State *Abstracts,* XVII, 741.

21. 4.  Shepard, Sanford.  López Pinciano and Aristotelian Literary Criticism in the Spanish Renaissance.  New York, 1960.  *DA,* XXI, 903.

21. 5.  Zimic, Stanislav.  Cervantes, lector de Aquiles Tacio y de Alonso Núñez de Reinoso.  Duke, 1964.  *DA,* XXVI, 379.

## 22. *Italian*

22. 1.  Bourland, Caroline Brown.  Boccaccio and the *Decameron* in Castilian and Catalan Literature.  Bryn Mawr, 1902.  New York-Paris, 1905.  LC 6-7796.

22. 2.  Bricca, John Francis.  Alfonso el Sabio and Niccolò Machiavelli, or the Return to the Pagan Idea of the State.  Harvard, 1943.  Harvard *Summaries,* 1943-45, p. 514.

22. 3.  Del Greco, Arnold Armand.  Giacomo Leopardi in Hispanic Literature.  Columbia, 1950.  New York, 1952.  LC 52-27773.

22. 4.  Falconieri, John Vincent.  A History of Italian Comedians in Spain: A Chapter of the Spanish Renaissance.  Michigan, 1952.  *DA,* XII, 186.

22. 5.  Fucilla, Joseph Guerin.  A Study of Petrarchism in Spain During the Sixteenth Century.  Chicago, 1928.  Chicago *Abstracts,* VII, 471; *RFE,* Anejo 72.  *Madrid, 1960.

22. 6.  Garofalo, Silvano Benito.  The Poetry of Giacomo Leopardi and Miguel de Unamuno.  Minnesota, 1966.  *DA,* XXVII, 2528-A.

22. 7.  Greco, Joseph V.  A Parallel Study of Dante's *Divina commedia* and Imperial's *Dezyr a las syete vertudes.*  Pittsburgh, 1950.  Pittsburgh *Bulletin,* XLVII, No. 5, p. 25.

22. 8.  Lionetti, Harold E.  Ariosto's Influence on the Plays of Lope de Vega.  Northwestern, 1955.  *DA,* XV, 1855.

22. 9.  Mades, Leonard.  A Study of *Don Quixote* in Relation to Castiglione's *Book of the Courtier.*  Columbia, 1965.  *DA,* XXVI, 3305.

22. 10.  Post, Chandler Rathfon.  Castilian Allegory of the Fifteenth Century, with Especial Reference to the Influence of Dante.  Harvard, 1909.  *Cambridge, Mass., 1915.  LC 15-8079.

22. 11.  Ricciardelli, [Rev.] Michele.  Studio estetico-comparativo sul romanzo pastorale: Sannazaro e Lope de Vega.  Oregon, 1961.  *DA,* XXI, 2720.

22. 12.  Rotunda, Dominic P.  The Italian *Novelle* and Their Relation to Literature of Kindred Type in Spanish up to 1615.  California, 1928.

22. 13.  Scungio, Raymond Lewis.  A Study of Lope de Vega's Use of Italian *Novelle* as Source Material for His Plays, Together with a Critical Edition of the

Autograph Manuscript of *La discordia en los casados*. Brown, 1961. *DA,* XXVII, 186-A.

22. 14. Sedwick, B. Frank. Spanish Themes in Italian Opera. Southern California, 1953. Southern California *Abstracts,* 1953, p. 65.

22. 15. Selig, Karl L. Notes on Alciato in Spain. Texas, 1955.

22. 16. Triolo, Alfred Angelo. The Boiardo-Ariosto Tradition in *Las lágrimas de Angélica* of Luis Barahona de Soto (1586). Illinois, 1956. *DA,* XVI, 1909.

22. 17. Wellington, Marie Z. Sannazaro's Influence on the Spanish Pastoral Novel. Northwestern, 1951. Northwestern *Summaries,* XIX, 79.

22. 18. Williams, Robert Haden. Boccalini in Spain: A Study of His Influence on Prose Fiction of the Seventeenth Century. Columbia, 1946. Menasha, Wis., 1946. LC A46-6039.

### 23. *Latin, Classical and Medieval*

23. 1. Ashton, Jon Richard. Ovid's *Heroides* as Translated by Alphonso the Wise: An Experiment in Source Study. Wisconsin, 1944. Wisconsin *Summaries,* IX, 516.

23. 2. Dunstan, Robert T. A Critical Edition of Fernández de Heredia's Translation into Aragonese of Guido delle Colonne's *Crónica troyana.* Wisconsin, 1928.

23. 3. Giulian, Anthony Alphonse. Martial and the Epigram in Spain in the Sixteenth and Seventeenth Centuries. Pennsylvania, 1930. Philadelphia, 1930. LC 31-6631.

23. 4. Grismer, Raymond Leonard. The Influence of Titus Maccius Plautus on the Spanish Theatre Through Juan de Timoneda. California, 1930. *New York, 1944. LC 45-576.

23. 5. Herriott, James Homer. A Spanish Translation of Recension-J² of the *Historia de Preliis.* Wisconsin, 1929.

23. 6. Kniazzeh, Charlotte S. A Critical Edition of a Portion of the Thirteenth Century *Vides de Sants Rosselloneses,* Folios 156-261, Manuscript 44, Paris. Chicago, 1965. See NUC 65-98804. [A Catalan version of the work by Jacobus de Voragine.]

23. 7. Lynch, Theophilus S. *El segundo libro de Eneydas* of Francisco de las Natas. A Critical Edition with Notes. Pennsylvania, 1959. *DA,* XX, 2293.

23. 8. Lynn, Caro. A Life of Lucio Marineo Sículo, with a Determination of the Nature and Extent of His Knowledge of Latin Literature. Cornell, 1927. Ithaca, 1927. LC 34-427 Rev.

23. 9. McManamon, James Edward. Echoes of Virgil and Lucan in the *Araucana.* Illinois, 1955. *DA,* XVI, 966.

23. 10. Neugaard, Edward Joseph. A Critical Edition of a Portion of the 13th Century *Vides de Santz Rosselloneses* with Introduction, Notes, Table of Proper Names, and Glossary. North Carolina, 1964. *DA,* XXVI, 1048.

23. 11. Newman, Richard William. Calderón and Aquinas. Boston University, 1956. Boston University *Abstracts,* 1956, n.p.

23. 12. Norris, Frank Pelletier, II. *La crónica troyana*: A Medieval Spanish Translation of Guido de Colonna's *Historia Destructionis Troiae.* U.C.L.A., 1965. *DA,* XXVI, 7322.

23. 13. Peterson, Holland. *Amphitrión* and *Los Menemnos:* An Edition of the First Two Plays of Juan Timoneda's *Las tres comedias,* with an Introduction on Plautine Influence. Toronto, 1961.

23. 14. Schug, Howard Lesher. Latin Sources of Berceo's *Sacrificio de la misa.* Peabody, 1933. Nashville, Tenn., 1936. LC 36-11493.

23. 15. Stephenson, Robert C. Miguel Sánchez: A Contemporary Terentian Influence upon Lope de Vega. Texas, 1930.

23. 16. Stevens, Charles Henry. *El palacio confuso*: Together with a Study of the Menaechmi Theme in Spanish Literature. New York, 1938. New York, 1939. LC 39-31767.

23. 17. Switzer, Rebecca. The Ciceronian Style in Fray Luis de Granada. Columbia, 1927. New York, 1927. LC 28-7187.

23. 18. Webber, Edwin Jack. Origins of the Spanish Theater as Related to the Classical Latin Drama. California, 1949.

### 24. *Norwegian*

24. 1. Gregersen, Halfdan I. Ibsen and Spain: A Study in Comparative Drama. Columbia, 1936. Cambridge, Mass., 1936. LC 36-10485.

### 25. *Portuguese*

25. 1. Fein, John Morton. Eugênio de Castro and the Development of Cosmopolitanism in Hispanic Poetry. Harvard, 1950.

25. 2. McKenna, James B. A Spaniard in the Portuguese Indies: The Narrative of Martín Fernández de Figueroa. Harvard, 1965. Cambridge, Mass., 1967. NUC 67-27089.

25. 3. Nelson, Jan A. A Critical Edition of the *Livro de citraria.* North Carolina, 1964. *DA,* XXVI, 1653. [15th century Portuguese translation of López de Ayala's *Libro de la caza de las aves.*]

See also Alfonso X, III. 2. 5; III. 2. 9; III. 2. 13; III. 2. 23.

### 26. *Provençal*

26. 1. Danielson, John David. *Pastorelas* and *Serrani-*

*llas*, 1130-1550: A Genre Study. Michigan, 1960. *DA*, XXI, 342.

26. 2.  Horan, William D. A Critical Edition of the Poems of Bonifacio Calvo. Louisiana State, 1963. *DA*, XXIV, 1167. [An Italian troubadour who wrote in Provençal at the court of Alfonso X.]

26. 3.  Pattison, Walter Thomas. A Literary Event in 1170: The Wedding of Alfonso VIII of Castille in Its Relations to Provençal Literature. Harvard, 1931. Harvard *Summaries*, 1931, p. 279.

### 27. *Russian*

27. 1.  Portnoff, George E. La literatura rusa en España. Columbia, 1932. New York, 1932. LC 32-35764.

27. 2.  Turkevich, Ludmilla B. Cervantes in Russia. Columbia, 1950. Princeton, 1950. LC 50-5913.

### 28. *Spanish American*

28. 1.  Andersson, Theodore. The *Españolismo* of Carlos María Ocantos. Yale, 1931. *New Haven-London, 1934. LC 35-1445.

28. 2.  Aponte, Barbara Bockus. The Spanish Friendships of Alfonso Reyes. Texas, 1964. *DA, XXV, 467.

28. 3.  Campa, Arthur Leon. Spanish Folk-Poetry in New Mexico. Columbia, 1946. Albuquerque, 1946. LC A47-2618.

28. 4.  Clinkscales, Orline. Bécquer in Mexico, Central America and the Caribbean Countries. Texas, 1957.

28. 5.  Jaimes-Freyre, Mireya. A Comparison of Modernism and the Generation of '98 with Special Reference to the Works and Theories of Ricardo Jaimes-Freyre. Columbia, 1965.

28. 6.  Metzidakis, Philip. Unamuno e Hispanoamérica. Yale, 1959.

28. 7.  Sarre, Alicia. Spanish Influence on Mexican Lyric Poetry. Stanford, 1945. Stanford *Abstracts*, XX, 44.

28. 8.  Terry, Edward D. The *Academia Española* and the Corresponding Academies in Spanish America, 1870-1956. North Carolina, 1958. *DA*, XIX, 2618.

28. 9.  Torres, María de Guadalupe. Los romances españoles en América. Stanford, 1951. Stanford *Abstracts*, XXVI, 282.

28. 10.  Torres-Ríoseco, Arturo. Rubén Darío and the *Modernista* Movement in Spanish America and Spain. Minnesota, 1931. *Cambridge, Mass.-London, 1931. LC 32-32410.

28. 11.  Turner, Esther Hadassah Scott. Hispanism in the Life and Works of Manuel Gálvez. Washington, Seattle, 1958. *DA*, XIX, 3311.

### 29. *United States*

29. 1.  Blanch, Mable. Variations on a Picaresque Theme: A Study of Two Twentieth-Century Treatments of Picaresque Form. Colorado, 1966. *DA*, XXVIII, 1427-A. [*The Adventures of Augie March* (1949), by Saul Bellow, and *The Tin Drum* (1959), by Günter Grass.]

29. 2.  Englekirk, John E. Edgar Allan Poe in Hispanic Literature. Columbia, 1934. New York, 1934. LC 34-20053.

29. 3.  Farnham, Carrie Evangeline. American Travellers in Spain; The Spanish Inns 1776-1867. Columbia, 1921. New York, 1921. LC 21-10180.

29. 4.  Ferguson, John DeLancey. American Literature in Spain. Columbia, 1916. New York, 1916. LC 17-263.

29. 5.  Gianakos, Perry Edgar. The "Yanko-Spanko War": Our War with Spain in American Fiction. New York, 1961. *DA*, XXVII, 1753-A.

29. 6.  Gleaves, Edwin Sheffield, Jr. The Spanish Influence of Ernest Hemingway's Concepts of Death, *Nada*, and Immortality. Emory, 1964. *DA*, XXV, 2511. [Unamuno.]

29. 7.  González, Louis. Whitman's Hispanic Fame. Columbia, 1960. *DA*, XXI, 195.

29. 8.  Hendrickson, John R. The Influence of *Don Quixote* on *Modern Chivalry*. Florida State, 1959. *DA*, XX, 661. [Brackenridge.]

29. 9.  Hough, Mary E. Santa Teresa in America. Columbia, 1938. New York, 1938. LC 39-3952.

29. 10.  Hyde, Frederic Griswold. American Literature and the Spanish-American War: A Study of the Works of Crane, Norris, Fox, and R. H. Davis. Pennsylvania, 1963. *DA*, XXIV, 2478.

29. 11.  Jackson, William V. Modern Spanish Drama in the American Theatre, 1901-1951. Harvard, 1952.

29. 12.  Klibbe, Lawrence H. The Spanish Experiences of James Russell Lowell. Syracuse, 1954. *DA*, XV, 270.

29. 13.  Kolker, [Sister] M. Delphine. Spanish Legends in English and American Literature: 1800-1860. Catholic, 1952. Washington, 1952. NUC Micp A53-120.

29. 14.  Manchester, Paul Thomas. A Bibliography and Critique of the Spanish Translations from the Poetry of the United States. Peabody, 1927. Nashville, Tenn., 1927. LC 28-2930.

29. 15.  Paullada, Stephen. A Study of the Influence that Similar Environment Had upon the Life and Folklore of the Gaucho and Cowboy Societies. Southern California, 1953. Southern California *Abstracts*, 1953, p. 61.

29. 16.  Stimson, Frederick Sparks. Spanish Themes in Early American Literature in Novels, Drama, and Verse, 1770-1830. Michigan, 1953. *DA*, XIII, 394.

29. 17.   Whitman, Iris Lilian.   Longfellow and Spain. Columbia, 1927.   New York, 1927.   LC 28-7568.

29. 18.   Zardoya, María Concepción.   España en la poesía americana.   Illinois, 1952.   *DA,* XIV, 830.

COMPARATIVE STUDIES: Spanish-American Relations with Other Literatures.

### 30.   *Brazilian*

30. 1.   Flores, Angel.   Three Ecological Patterns in South American Fiction.   Cornell, 1947.   Cornell *Abstracts,* 1947, p. 45.

30. 2.   White, Florence Estella.   *Poesía Negra* in the Works of Jorge de Lima, Nicolás Guillén, and Jacques Roumain, 1927-1947.   Wisconsin, 1952. Wisconsin *Summaries,* XIII, 399.

30. 3.   Woodyard, George William.   The Search for Identity: A Comparative Study in Contemporary Latin American Drama.   Illinois, 1966.   *DA,* XXVII, 2165-A.

### 31.   *Classical*

31. 1.   Kerson, Arnold Lewis.   Rafael Landívar and the Latin Literary Currents of New Spain in the Eighteenth Century.   Yale, 1963.   *DA,* XXVIII, 3187-A.

31. 2.   Schade, George Dewey.   Classical Mythology in the *Modernista* Poetry of Spanish America.   California, 1953.

### 32.   *English*

32. 1.   Cobb, Carl Wesley.   Translations from English and American Lyric Poetry in Colombia.   Tulane, 1961.   *DA,* XXII, 3656.

### 33.   *French*

33. 1.   Bateson, Howard L.   French Influences in the Work of Carlos Reyles, Uruguayan Novelist.   Illinois, 1943.   Urbana, 1943.   LC A44-158.

33. 2.   Conner, Arthur B.   Indications in the Writings of Manuel Gutiérrez Nájera of His Reading of French Literature.   Iowa, 1951.   Iowa *Abstracts,* IX, 710.

33. 3.   Fair, Jeane Delcine.   Chatèaubriand's Influence upon the Literatures of Spain and Spanish America. Northwestern, 1948.   Northwestern *Summaries,* XVI, 53.

33. 4.   Gordon, Bruce R.   French Literary Influence on Mexican Literature (1800-1868).   Syracuse, 1950.

33. 5.   Lowry, Hope.   L'influence française sur les poètes hispano-américains de l'école moderniste.   McGill, 1932.

33. 6.   Luna, José Luis.   La influencia de París en la evolución literaria de Enrique Gómez Carrillo y otros escritores hispano-americanos, 1890-1914.   California, 1940.

33. 7.   Shone, Alice Irwin.   Amado Nervo: A Mexican *Modernista* in the Baudelairian Manner.   California, 1936.

### 34.   *Haiti*

34. 1.   White, Florence Estella.   *Poesía Negra* in the Works of Jorge de Lima, Nicolás Guillén, and Jacques Roumain, 1927-1947.   Wisconsin, 1952.   Wisconsin *Summaries,* XIII, 399.

### 35.   *United States*

35. 1.   Cobb, Carl Wesley.   Translations from English and American Lyric Poetry in Colombia.   Tulane, 1961.   *DA,* XXII, 3656.

35. 2.   Daniel, Elizabeth Rezner.   Spanish American Travelers in the United States Before 1900: A Study in Inter-American Literary Relations.   North Carolina, 1959.   *DA,* XX, 2796.

35. 3.   Miller, Charlotte E.   Florencio Sánchez: The South American Eugene O'Neill.   Washington, Seattle, 1947.

35. 4.   Shuler, Esther Elise.   Poesía y teorías poéticas de José Martí (con especial referencia a su crítica de autores norteamericanos).   Minnesota, 1947.

### III.   LITERATURE TO 1500

### 1.   *Miscellaneous*

1. 1.   Barbera, Raymond Edmond.   The Comic in Early Spanish Literature, 1140-1500.   Wisconsin, 1958. *DA,* XIX, 1738.

1. 2.   Baricevic, Elizabeth Mary.   The Supernatural in Spanish Literature of the Thirteenth and Fourteenth Centuries.   Stanford, 1951.   Stanford *Abstracts,* XXVI, 273.

1. 3.   Buckingham, Elizabeth.   *La perfecta señora*: A Dialogue of the Seventeenth Century Edited from the Original Manuscript with a Survey of the Dialogue in Spanish Literature to 1700.   Texas, 1954.

1. 4.   Callcott, Frank.   The Supernatural in Early Spanish Literature, Studied in the Works of the Court of Alfonso X, el Sabio.   Columbia, 1923.   New York, 1923.   LC 23-11223.

1. 5.   Coleman, Sarah E.   *Cuaderno otorgado a los procuradores en las Cortes de Valladolid de 1351.*   Chicago, 1939.

1. 6.   Crowley, Cornelius Joseph.   Persisting Latinisms in *El poema de Mío Cid* and Other Selected Old Spanish Literary Works.   New York, 1951.   Baltimore, 1952.   NUC A53-1036.

1. 7. Davis, Gifford. Evidences of an Incipient Sentiment of Nationality in Medieval Castilian Literature. Harvard, 1933. Harvard *Summaries, 1933,* p. 308.

1. 8. Deferrari, Harry Austin. The Sentimental Moor in Spanish Literature Before 1600. Pennsylvania, 1926. Philadelphia, 1927. LC 27-16251.

1. 9. Gormly, [Sister] Francis, S.N.D. The Use of the Bible in Representative Works of Medieval Spanish Literature, 1250-1300. Catholic, 1962. *DA,* XXIII, 3374.

1. 10. Lansing, Ruth. Treatment of Woman in Spanish Literature of the Thirteenth, Fourteenth and Fifteenth Centuries. Radcliffe, 1914.

1. 11. Luquiens, Frederick Bliss. The *Roman de la Rose* and Medieval Castilian Literature. Yale, 1905.

1. 12. Mazzeo, Guido E. The Abate Juan Andrés (1740-1817): Literary Historian and Defender of Spanish and Medieval Hispano-Arab Learning, Literature and Culture. Columbia, 1961. *DA,* XXII, 565.

1. 13. McSpadden, George Elbert. The Spanish Prologue Before 1700. Stanford, 1947. Stanford *Abstracts,* XXII, 45.

1. 14. O'Kane, Eleanor S. A Dictionary of Medieval Spanish Proverbs and Proverbial Phrases. Bryn Mawr, 1947. *Madrid, 1959. *BRAE,* Anejos, 2. NUC 62-28689.

1. 15. Palomo, José Roberto. The *Caballero* in Early Spanish Literature. Ohio State, 1938. Ohio State *Abstracts,* No. 29, p. 87.

1. 16. Poole, Robert Hawkins. Women in Early Spanish Literature with Special Emphasis on the Women in the Medieval Spanish Ballad. Stanford, 1949. Stanford *Abstracts,* XXV, 235.

1. 17. Resnick, Seymour. The Jew as Portrayed in Early Spanish Literature (to the End of the Fifteenth Century). New York, 1951.

1. 18. Russell, Billy Maurice. The New World in Spanish Literature Before 1550. North Carolina, 1964. *DA,* XXVIII, 3156-A.

1. 19. Scholberg, Kenneth R. The Attitudes Toward the Moors in Castilian Literature Before 1492. Wisconsin, 1952. Wisconsin *Summaries,* XIV, 464.

## 2. *Alfonso X, el Sabio*

2. 1. Allen, Hazel Dorothy. Christian Doctrine in the *General estoria* of Alfonso X. Wisconsin, 1960. *DA,* XXI, 187.

2. 2. Ashton, Jon Richard. Ovid's *Heroides* as Translated by Alphonso the Wise: An Experiment in Source Study. Wisconsin, 1944. Wisconsin *Summaries,* IX, 516.

2. 3. Brewer, William Benjamin. The Object Pronouns *le* and *lo* in Alphonsine Prose. Tulane, 1966. *DA,* XXVII, 3447-A.

2. 4. Bricca, John Francis. Alfonso el Sabio and Niccolò Machiavelli, or the Return to the Pagan Idea of the State. Harvard, 1943. Harvard *Summaries,* 1943-45, p. 514.

2. 5. Callcott, Frank. The Supernatural in Early Spanish Literature, Studied in the Works of the Court of Alfonso X, el Sabio. Columbia, 1923. New York, 1923. LC 23-11223.

2. 6. Causey, James Young. A Cultural Study of the Agricultural Terms in the Works of Alfonso el Sabio. Wisconsin, 1940. Wisconsin *Summaries,* VI, 321.

2. 7. Darby, George O. S. An Astrological Manuscript of Alfonso X. Harvard, 1932. Harvard *Summaries,* 1932, p. 304.

2. 8. DeLand, Graydon S. An Etymological Vocabulary to the Books of Exodus and Leviticus of the *General estoria* of Alfonso el Sabio. Wisconsin, 1935. Wisconsin *Summaries,* I, 335.

2. 9. Dexter, Elsie Forsythe. Sources of the *Cántigas* of Alfonso el Sabio. Wisconsin, 1926.

2. 10. Duncan, Robert M. An Etymological Vocabulary of Plant Names in the Works of Alfonso el Sabio. Wisconsin, 1936. Wisconsin *Summaries,* I, 333.

2. 11. Edgerly, Clifton T. A Vocabulary of the *Siete partidas,* I and II, of Alfonso X. Yale, 1918.

2. 12. Kiddle, Lawrence Bayard. *La estoria de Tebas*: The Version of the Siege and Destruction of Thebes Contained in the *General estoria* of Alfonso X. Wisconsin, 1935.

2. 13. Kline, Lawton. A Metrical Study of the *Cántigas de Santa María* by Alfonso el Sabio. Stanford, 1950. Stanford *Abstracts,* XXV, 232.

2. 14. London, Gardiner H. Conjunctive Adverbs in the Prose Texts of Alfonso X, the Learned. Wisconsin, 1951. Wisconsin *Summaries,* XII, 464.

2. 15. MacDonald, Robert Alan. Kingship in Medieval Spain: Alfonso X of Castile. Wisconsin, 1957. *DA,* XVIII, 1038.

2. 16. Malone, Carle H. Thirteenth-Century Spain as Seen in the *Siete partidas* of Alfonso el Sabio. Washington, Seattle, 1942. Washington *Abstracts,* VIII, 115.

2. 17. McDowell, David Franklin. The Nature of Old Spanish Vocabulary as Determined by an Etymological and Semantic Analysis of the Verbs in the *Primera parte* of the *General estoria* of Alfonso el Sabio. North Carolina, 1943. North Carolina *Record,* No. 429, p. 231.

2. 18. Munro, Edwin C. An Etymological Vocabulary of Military Terms in the Works of Alfonso X. Wisconsin, 1950. Wisconsin *Summaries,* XI, 373.

2. 19. Newcomer, Charles A. Animal Names in the

Works of Alfonso el Sabio. Wisconsin, 1937. Wisconsin *Summaries,* II, 339.

2. 20.  Nunemaker, John Horace. Index of the Stones in the Lapidary of Alfonso X with Identifications in Other Lapidaries. Wisconsin, 1928.

2. 21.  Shoemaker, Theodore Harvey. Alfonso X as Historian. Wisconsin, 1942. Wisconsin *Summaries,* VII, 324.

2. 22.  Smith, Ruby C. An Edition of the Alphonsine Gospels. Texas, 1931.

2. 23.  Sousa, Thomas Frederic. A Linguistic Analysis of a Portion of the Galician Translation of the *General estoria* by Alfonso X, el Sabio. Wisconsin, 1964. *DA,* XXIV, 5418.

2. 24.  Vanderford, Kenneth H. The *Libro llamado Setenario* of Alfonso el Sabio, Edited from Extant Manuscripts. Chicago, 1940. *Buenos Aires, 1945. LC 47-3957.

2. 25.  Van Scoy, Herbert A. Spanish Words Defined in the Works of Alfonso X. Wisconsin, 1939. Wisconsin *Summaries,* IV, 263.

2. 26.  Winget, Lynn Warren. Auxiliary Verbs in the Prose Works of Alfonso X. Wisconsin, 1960. *DA,* XX, 4104.

### 3.  *Allegory*

3. 1.  Post, Chandler Rathfon. Castilian Allegory of the Fifteenth Century, with Especial Reference to the Influence of Dante. Harvard, 1909. *Cambridge, Mass., 1915. LC 15-8079.

### 4.  *Alvarez de Villasandino, Alfonso*

4. 1.  Eddy, Nelson W. Villasandino and *Arte Mayor.* Michigan, 1939.

### 5.  *Amadis de Gaula*

5. 1.  Fjelstad, Ruth N. Archaisms in *Amadis de Gaula.* Iowa, 1963. *DA,* XXIV, 4687.

5. 2.  Mottola, Anthony Clare. The *Amadís de Gaula* in Spain and in France. Fordham, 1962. *DA,* XXIII, 1368.

5. 3.  Williams, Grace Sara. The *Amadís* Question. Columbia, 1907. New York, 1907. LC A10-451.

### 6.  *Auto de los Reyes Magos*

6. 1.  Sturdevant, Winifred. The *Misterio de los Reyes Magos:* Its Position in the Development of the Mediaeval Legend of the Three Kings. Johns Hopkins, 1920. Baltimore-Paris, 1927. LC 28-9985.

### 7.  *Berceo, Gonzalo de*

7. 1.  DeForest, John Bellows. Old French Borrowed Words in Old Spanish of the Twelfth and Thirteenth Centuries with Special Reference to the *Cid,*

Berceo's Poems, the *Alexandre,* and *Fernán González.* Yale, 1915. New York, 1916. LC 19-16238.

7. 2.  Fitz-Gerald, John Driscoll. Versification of the *Cuaderna Vía,* as Found in Berceo's *Vida de Santo Domingo de Silos.* Columbia, 1905. New York, 1905. LC 7-16238.

7. 3.  Gariano, Carmelo. Análisis estilístico de los *Milagros de Nuestra Señora* de Berceo. Chicago, 1964. Madrid, 1965. NUC 67-25328.

7. 4.  Goode, [Sister] Teresa Clare. Gonzalo de Berceo, *El sacrificio de la misa,* A Study of Its Symbolism and of Its Sources. Catholic, 1933. Washington, 1933. LC 33-35361.

7. 5.  Perry, Theodore Anthony. A Literary Study of Berceo's *Vida de Santa Oria.* Yale, 1966. *DA,* XXVII, 2506-A.

7. 6.  Schug, Howard Lesher. Latin Sources of Berceo's *Sacrificio de la misa.* Peabody, 1933. Nashville, Tenn., 1936. LC 36-11493.

7. 7.  Thomas, Bart E. A Concordance to the Works of Gonzalo de Berceo. Wisconsin, 1937. Wisconsin *Summaries,* II, 344.

### 8.  *Bible*

8. 1.  Brown, Anita Dolores. Linguistic Analysis of St. Paul's Epistle to the Romans and Prologues to the Epistles in MS. I. 1. 2 of the Library of the Escorial. Wisconsin, 1957. *DA,* XVII, 624.

8. 2.  DeLand, Graydon S. An Etymological Vocabulary to the Books of Exodus and Leviticus of the *General estoria* of Alfonso el Sabio. Wisconsin, 1935. Wisconsin *Summaries,* I, 335.

8. 3.  Hauptmann, Oliver Howard. An Edition of the Translation of the Bible (Leviticus and Numbers) with Vocabulary, from the Escorial Manuscript I.J.4. Wisconsin, 1933. *Philadelphia, 1953. NUC 53-12037.

8. 4.  Montgomery, Thomas Andrew. A Linguistic Study of the Book of Matthew in Manuscript I. I. 6. of the Escorial Library. Wisconsin, 1955. *DA,* XVI, 118.

8. 5.  Roybal, [Sister] M. Angelica Ann. Estudio de la traducción castellana de los dos libros de los Macabeos según los manuscritos 87 de la Real Academia de la Historia y I-j-4 del Escorial y edición del texto según el manuscrito 87. Catholic, 1963. *DA,* XXVI, 358.

8. 6.  Smith, Peter Frank, Jr. *Esta es la translación del Psalterio que fizo Maestro Herman el Aleman, segund cuemo esta en el Ebraygo:* Reprint of the Only Extant Manuscript, Esc. I.j.8, with Introduction and Notes. Chicago, 1924. Chicago *Abstracts,* II, 353.

8. 7.  Smith, Ruby C. An Edition of the Alphonsine Gospels. Texas, 1931.

### 9. *Calila y Dimna*

9. 1.  Holmes, Henry Bert. An Etymological Vocabulary of *Calila y Dimna*. Wisconsin, 1935. Wisconsin *Summaries*, I, 338.

9. 2.  Irving, Thomas Ballantine. A Textual Comparison of a Section of the Arabic *Kalīlah wa Dimnah* and the Corresponding Section of the Old Spanish *Calila e Digna*. Princeton, 1940. *DA*, XII, 187.

9. 3.  Pérez, Raoul M. Vocabulario clasificado de *Kalila et Digna*. Chicago, 1942. Chicago, 1943. LC A44-1241.

### 10. *Cancionero de Baena*

10. 1.  Fraker, Charles Frederic, Jr. The Doctrinal Poetry in the *Cancionero de Baena*. Harvard, 1963. *Chapel Hill, N.C., 1966. NUC 67-63054.

### 11. *Cantar de Don Sancho II de Castilla*

11. 1.  Prado, Miguel Angel. Estudio comparado de las derivaciones eruditas y populares del *Cantar de Don Sancho II de Castilla*. Stanford, 1942. Stanford *Abstracts*, 1941-42, p. 68.

### 12. *Cartagena, Alonso de*

12. 1.  Boarino, Gerald Louis. Alonso de Cartagena's *Doctrinal de los caballeros*: Text, Tradition and Sources. California, 1964. *DA*, XXVI, 2723.

### 13. *Cartagena, Teresa de*

13. 1.  Hutton, [Rev.] Joseph Louis. Teresa de Cartagena: *Arboleda de los enfermos. Admiraçion operum Dey.* Introductory Study and Text. Princeton, 1950. *DA*, XV, 585.

### 14. *Castigos e documentos*

14. 1.  Weaver, Billy Rupert. The Forms and Usage of the Personal Pronouns in *Castigos e documentos para bien vivir ordenados por el Rey don Sancho IV*. Wisconsin, 1964. *DA*, XXIV, 3743.

### 15. *Celestina*

15. 1.  Ayllón, Cándido. Pessimism in the *Celestina*. Wisconsin, 1956. *DA*, XVI, 2454.

15. 2.  Berndt, Erna Ruth. Tratamiento de algunos temas humanísticos en *La Celestina*. Wisconsin, 1959. *DA*, XX, 2275.

15. 3.  Davis, Ruth. New Data on the Authorship of Act I of the *Comedia de Calisto y Melibea*. Iowa, 1928. Iowa City, 1928. LC 29-27025.

15. 4.  Hillard, Ernest H. K. Spanish Imitations of the *Celestina*. Illinois, 1957. *DA*, XVIII, 588.

15. 5.  Palmer, Margaret Eva. An Interpretation of *La Celestina*. Washington, Seattle, 1955. *DA*, XV, 2528.

15. 6.  Poston, Lawrence S., Jr. An Etymological Vocabulary to the *Celestina*, A-E. Chicago, 1938. Chicago, 1940. LC 42-2786.

15. 7.  Schiel, [Rev.] Nicholas E. A Theological Interpretation of *La Celestina*. St. Louis, 1965. *DA*, XXVI, 4675.

### 16. *Criticism*

16. 1.  Hutchings, Chesley M. The Sentiment of Nationality in Spanish Literary Criticism from 1400 to 1621. Harvard, 1922.

### 17. *Crónica de once reyes*

17. 1.  Babbitt, Theodore. La *Crónica de once reyes*. Yale, 1932. New Haven, 1936. LC 36-24953.

### 18. *Crónica troyana*

18. 1.  Dunstan, Robert T. A Critical Edition of Fernández de Heredia's Translation into Aragonese of Guido Delle Colonne's *Crónica troyana*. Wisconsin, 1928.

18. 2.  Jaffé, Erwin. A Treatment of Certain Aspects of Galician as Found in the *Crónica troyana*. Harvard, 1939. Harvard *Summaries*, 1939, p. 268.

18. 3.  Norris, Frank Pelletier, II. *La crónica troyana*: A Medieval Spanish Translation of Guido de Colonna's *Historia Destructionis Troiae*. U.C.L.A., 1965. *DA*, XXVI, 7322.

18. 4.  Parker, Kelvin M. A Classified Vocabulary of the *Crónica troyana*. Chicago, 1953. *Salamanca, 1958. NUC 60-26925.

### 19. *Cronicón villarense*

19. 1.  Cooper, Louis. A Linguistic Study of the *Liber regum* of the *Cronicón villarense*. Chicago, 1952. *Zaragoza, 1960. See NUC, 1958-62, vol. 10, p. 417.

### 20. *Cuento de Otas de Roma*

20. 1.  Baird, Herbert Leroy, Jr. Un análisis lingüístico y filológico de *El cuento muy fermoso del enperador Otas de Roma*. Chicago, 1955. Microfilmed, Chicago Library, 1955. NUC, 1952-55 Imprints, vol. 19, p. 204.

### 21. *Dança de la muerte*

21. 1.  Kurtz, Leonard P. The Dance of Death and the Macabre Spirit in European Literature. Columbia, 1934. New York, 1934. LC 35-1633.

21. 2.  Whyte, Florence. The Dance of Death in Spain and Catalonia. Bryn Mawr, 1930. Baltimore, 1931. LC 32-18422.

### 22. *Drama, General, Miscellaneous*

22. 1.  Corbató, Hermenegildo. *Los misterios del Cor-*

*pus de Valencia.* Edición diplomática, notas y estudio. California, 1930. Berkeley, 1932. LC A32-2742.

22. 2. Donovan, Richard Bertram. The Medieval Liturgical Drama in the Hispanic Peninsula and Its Relation with That of the Rest of Europe, Especially France. Yale, 1956. *Toronto, 1958. NUC 59-73.

22. 3. Heilman, Walter R., Jr. The *Pastourelle* Theme in the Early Spanish Drama. North Carolina, 1953. North Carolina *Record*, No. 534, p. 249.

22. 4. Hendrix, William Samuel. Some Native Comic Types in the Early Spanish Drama. Chicago, 1922. Columbus, Ohio, 1924. LC 25-9436.

22. 5. Lovett, Gabriel H. The Churchman and Related Characters in the Spanish Drama Before Lope de Vega. New York, 1951.

22. 6. Martin, Charles Basil. The Survivals of Medieval Religious Drama in New Mexico. Missouri, 1959. *DA,* XX, 3298.

22. 7. Patt, Beatrice Penelope. The Development of the Christmas Play in Spain from the Origins to Lope de Vega. Bryn Mawr, 1945. *MA,* VIII, No. 1, p. 100.

### 23. *Exempla*

23. 1. Johnson, David Donovan. A Study of the Moralizations as They Appear in Thirteenth and Fourteenth Century Spanish Exempla. North Carolina, 1964. *DA,* XXVI, 1647.

23. 2. Johnson, James Henry. The Proverb in the Medieval Spanish Exempla. North Carolina, 1958. *DA,* XIX, 2084.

23. 3. Keller, John E. The Exemplum in Spain. North Carolina, 1946. *Knoxville, Tenn., 1949. LC 49-49515.

23. 4. Nelson, Charles Leslie. Elements of Humor in Medieval Spanish Exempla. North Carolina, 1966. *DA,* XXVII, 3847-A.

### 24. *Fernández de Heredia, Juan*

24. 1. Dunstan, Robert T. A Critical Edition of Fernández de Heredia's Translation into Aragonese of Guido Delle Colonne's *Crónica troyana.* Wisconsin, 1928.

24. 2. Kasten, Lloyd August William. *Secreto de los secretos,* Translated by Juan Fernández de Heredia: An Edition of the Unique Aragonese Manuscript, with Literary Introduction and Glossary. Wisconsin, 1931.

### 25. *Fiction, General*

25. 1. Horne, Ruth Nutt. Lope de Vega's *Peregrino en su patria* and the Romance of Adventure in Spain Before 1604. Brown, 1946.

25. 2. Singleton, Mack H. Technique and Idea in Early Spanish Fiction. Wisconsin, 1936. Wisconsin *Summaries,* I, 340.

### 26. *Flores, Juan de*

26. 1. Matulka, Barbara. The Novels of Juan de Flores and Their European Diffusion; A Study in Comparative Literature. Columbia, 1931. New York, 1931. LC A35-26.

### 27. *Fueros*

27. 1. Cooper, Paul Joel. The Language of the *Forum judicum.* Columbia, 1953. *DA,* XIV, 138.

27. 2. Pardo, Aristóbulo V. Esquema morfológico del leonés antiguo en el *Fuero de Zamora.* Ohio State, 1966. *DA,* XXVII, 3031-A.

27. 3. Petersen, Phillip Burns. A Linguistic Study of the Old Leonese *Fuero de Ledesma.* California, 1955.

### 28. *La gran conquista de Ultramar*

28. 1. Bershas, Henry N. A Critical Edition of *La gran conquista de Ultramar,* Book IV, Chapters 194-288. Michigan, 1946.

28. 2. Calbick, Gladys Stanley. A Critical Text of *La gran conquista de Ultramar,* Chapters CCLXIV-CCC. Chicago, 1939. Chicago, 1940. LC 40-12895.

28. 3. Harrison, Gordon W. A Study of the Range and Frequency of Constructions Involving Pronouns and Pronominal Adjectives in Manuscript J-1, Biblioteca Nacional, of the *Gran conquista de Ultramar.* Chicago, 1940. Chicago, 1940. LC 41-9655.

28. 4. Honsa, Vladimír Jiří Jaroslav. *La gran conquista de Ultramar,* Book IV, Chapters 126-193: Critical Edition, Grammatical Analysis, and Glossary. Michigan, 1957. *DA,* XVIII, 1420.

### 99. *Hayton, Prince of Gorigos*

29. 1. Long, Wesley Robertson. *La flor de las ystorias de orient* by Hayton, Prince of Gorigos. Chicago, 1929. Chicago, 1934. LC 34-7572.

### 30. *Historia troyana*

30. 1. Whitted, Joseph Willard. An Etymological Lexicon to the *Historia troyana.* North Carolina, 1963. *DA,* XXIV, 3346.

### 31. *Imperial, Francisco*

31. 1. Greco, Joseph V. A Parallel Study of Dante's *Divina commedia* and Imperial's *Dezyr a las syete vertudes.* Pittsburgh, 1950. Pittsburgh *Bulletin,* XLVII, No. 5, p. 25.

### 32. *Leomarte*

32. 1. Rey, Agapito. Leomarte: *Sumas de historia troyana;* edición, prólogo, notas y vocabulario. Wiscon-

sin, 1929. *RFE*, Anejo XV. Madrid, 1932. LC 33-5364.

### 33. *Leyenda de Yuçuf*

33. 1. Lincoln, Joseph Newhall. *La leyenda de Yuçuf.* Harvard, 1931. Harvard *Summaries*, 1931, p. 276.

### 34. *Libro de Alexandre*

34. 1. DeForest, John Bellows. Old French Borrowed Words in Old Spanish of the Twelfth and Thirteenth Centuries with Special Reference to the *Cid*, Berceo's Poems, the *Alexandre*, and *Fernán González.* Yale, 1915. New York, 1916. LC 19-16238.
34. 2. Miller, Paul Gerard. The Spanish Version of the Poem of Alexander. Wisconsin, 1914.
34. 3. Nelson, Dana Arthur. Toward a Definitive Edition of *El libro de Alexandre.* Stanford, 1964. *DA*, XXV, 5934.
34. 4. Thalmann, Betty Cheney. *El libro de Alexandre:* A Stylistic Approach. Ohio State, 1966. *DA*, XXVII, 3883-A.
34. 5. Willis, Raymond S., Jr. The Relationship of the *Libro de Alexandre* to the *Alexandreis* of Gautier de Châtillon. Princeton, 1933. Princeton, 1934. LC 34-1004.

### 35. *Libro de los doce sabios*

35. 1. Bird, James Pyper. *El libro de los doce savios— Tractado de nobleza y lealtad.* Michigan, 1918. [Not available in Michigan library.]

36. *Libro de los gatos.* [By Odo, of Cheriton.]

36. 1. Northup, George Tyler. *El libro de los gatos*: A Text with Introduction and Notes. Chicago, 1906. Chicago, 1908. LC 9-5999.

### 37. *Libro del cavallero Cifar*

37. 1. Burke, James Franklin. A Critical and Artistic Study of the *Libro del cavallero Cifar.* North Carolina, 1966. *DA*, XXVII, 2525-A.
37. 2. Wagner, Charles Philip. The Sources of *El cavallero Cifar.* Yale, 1902.

### 38. *López de Ayala, Pero*

38. 1. Bachmann, Ann Opalak. An Etymological and Partial Syntactical Analysis of the *Rimado de palaçio* of Pero López de Ayala. Florida State, 1958. *DA*, XIX, 526.
38. 2. Holman, William Lee. An Edition and Glossary of the *Crónica del Rey D. Enrique Segundo de Castilla* by Pero López de Ayala from Manuscript A-14 of the Academia de la Historia. Wisconsin, 1965. *DA*, XXVI, 5425.
38. 3. Kuersteiner, Albert Frederick. The Use of the Relative Pronoun in the *Rimado de palacio.* Johns Hopkins, 1904. Paris, 1911. LC 13-14242.
38. 4. Nelson, Jan A. A Critical Edition of the *Livro de citraria.* North Carolina, 1964. *DA*, XXVI, 1653. [15th century Portuguese translation of López de Ayala's *Libro de la caza de las aves.*]
38. 5. Zeitlin, Marion Albert. A Vocabulary to the *Rimado de palacio* of López de Ayala. California, 1931.

### 39. *Lucena, Luis de*

39. 1. Ornstein, Jacob. A Critical Study of Luis de Lucena and His *Repetición de amores.* Wisconsin, 1940. Wisconsin *Summaries*, V, 282. *Chapel Hill, N.C., 1954. NUC 54-62328.

### 40. *Lucidarios*

40. 1. Kinkade, Richard Paisley. Los lucidarios españoles. Yale, 1965. *DA*, XXVI, 4633. Madrid: Gredos, 1968.

### 41. *Lull, Ramón*

41. 1. Frost, Francis LeJau. The *Art de contemplacio* of Ramón Lull, Published with an Introduction and a Study of the Language of the Author. Johns Hopkins, 1901. Baltimore, 1903. LC 3-29045.
41. 2. Olabarrieta, [Sister] Miriam Thérèse, S.C.N. The Influence of Ramón Lull on the Style of the Spanish Mystics and Santa Teresa. Catholic, 1963. Washington, 1963. NUC 64-1172.
41. 3. Stone, Herbert Reynolds. A Critical Edition of the *Libro del gentil e de los tres sabios.* North Carolina, 1965. *DA*, XXVI, 4650. [By Lull; transcribed into Castilian in 1378 by Sanches de Uzeda.]

### 42. *Manuel, Juan*

42. 1. Compton, James Donald. A Linguistic Study of the *Libro del cavallero et del escudero* of Don Juan Manuel in Manuscript 6376 of the National Library of Madrid, Spain. Wisconsin, 1965. *DA*, XXV, 6620.
42. 2. Mignani, Rigo. Don Juan Manuel, *El Conde Lucanor*: An Edition According to Ms. E of the Academia de la Historia. Washington, Seattle, 1957. *DA*, XVIII, 1435.
42. 3. Rockwood, Robert Everett. Don Juan Manuel, His Conception and Consideration of Women. Harvard, 1924.
42. 4. Romeo, Andrew L. An Etymological Vocabulary for Ms. S. 34 of Don Juan Manuel's *Los enxiemplos del Conde Lucanor et de Patronio* Together with a Total Word-Frequency Concordance. Tulane, 1950. Tulane *Abstracts*, Series 51, No. 13, p. 63.
42. 5. Selbert, Louis. A Glossary of Juan Manuel's *El libro de los enxiemplos del Conde Lucanor et de Patronio.* Yale, 1916. *DA*, XXVIII, 1409-A [sic].

### 43. *March, Auzias*

43. 1. Flam, Bernard Paul. A Concordance to the Works of Auzias March. Wisconsin, 1962. *DA,* XXIII, 2127.

### 44. *Marineo Sículo, Lucio*

44. 1. Lynn, Caro. A Life of Lucio Marineo Sículo, with a Determination of the Nature and Extent of His Knowledge of Latin Literature. Cornell, 1927. Ithaca, 1927. LC 34-427 Rev.

### 45. *Martínez de Toledo, Alfonso, Arcipreste de Talavera*

45. 1. Billingsley, Allie Ward. The Arcipreste de Talavera: Author and Masterpiece. Illinois, 1959. *DA,* XX, 2794.

45. 2. Marsh, George Bonner. The Diplomatic Edition of the *Arcipreste de Talavera,* with an Introduction. California, 1928.

### 46. *Mena, Juan de*

46. 1. Xupulos, James J. Juan de Mena and His Works. A Study in Fifteenth-Century Spanish Poetry. New York, 1950.

### 47. *Mocedades de Rodrigo*

47. 1. Armistead, Samuel Gordon. *La gesta de las mocedades de Rodrigo;* Reflections of a Lost Epic Poem in the *Crónica de los reyes de Castilla* and the *Crónica general de 1344.* Princeton, 1955. *DA,* XV, 2198.

### 48. *Moner, Francisco de*

48. 1. Cocozzella, Peter. The Two Major Prose Works of Francisco de Moner: A Critical Edition and Translation. St. Louis, 1966. *DA,* XXVII, 3834-A.

### 49. *Novela sentimental*

49. 1. Krause, Anna. La novela sentimental, 1440-1513. Chicago, 1928. Chicago *Abstracts,* VI, 317.

### 50. *Pedro, Maestre*

50. 1. Zapata y Torres, Miguel. *El libro del consejo e los consejeros por Maestre Pedro.* Cornell, 1926.

### 51. *Poema de Alfonso Onceno*

51. 1. DeMent, Russell Duke. An Etymological Lexicon of *El poema de Alfonso Onceno.* North Carolina, 1961. *DA,* XXII, 3653.

51. 2. Poland, George W. *El poema de Alfonso Onceno,* a Critical Edition and Vocabulary. North Carolina, 1953. North Carolina *Record,* No. 534, p. 253.

### 52. *Poema de Fernán González*

52. 1. DeForest, John Bellows. Old French Borrowed Words in Old Spanish of the Twelfth and Thirteenth Centuries with Special Reference to the *Cid,* Berceo's Poems, the *Alexandre,* and *Fernán González.* Yale, 1915. New York, 1916. LC 19-16238.

52. 2. Owre, Jacob R. The *Poema de Fernán Gonçalez:* A Paleographic Edition of the Escorial Manuscript IV-B-21, with Notes and Etymologic Vocabulary. Minnesota, 1934. Minnesota *Summaries,* I, 174.

52. 3. Tappan, Robert L. Estudio lexicográfico del *Poema de Fernán González* con un índice completo de las frecuencias de los vocablos. Tulane, 1954. Tulane *Abstracts,* Series 55, No. 14, p. 103.

### 53. *Poema del Cid*

53. 1. Bandera-Gómez, Cesáreo. La realidad poética en *El poema de Mío Cid.* Cornell, 1965. *DA,* XXVI, 5427.

53. 2. Coester, Alfred Lester. Compression in the *Poema del Cid.* Harvard, 1906. New York-Paris, 1906. LC 30-29224.

53. 3. Crowley, Cornelius Joseph. Persisting Latinisms in *El poema de Mío Cid* and Other Selected Old Spanish Literary Works. New York, 1951. Baltimore, 1952. NUC A53-1036.

53. 4. DeForest, John Bellows. Old French Borrowed Words in Old Spanish of the Twelfth and Thirteenth Centuries with Special Reference to the *Cid,* Berceo's Poems, the *Alexandre,* and *Fernán González.* Yale, 1915. New York, 1916. LC 19-16238.

53. 5. Dorfman, Eugene. The *Roland* and the *Cid;* A Comparative Structural Analysis. Columbia, 1950. *MA,* X, No. 3, p. 142.

53. 6. Flaten, Nils. *Poema del Cid.* Minnesota, 1900.

53. 7. Picciotto, Robert S. Dramatic and Lyrical Unity in the *Cid* and the *Roland.* Indiana, 1964. *DA,* XXV, 2966.

53. 8. Wester, Louise Hatch. A Structural Analysis of the Epic Style of the *Cid.* Illinois, 1954. *DA,* XV, 120.

53. 9. Wilkins, George W., Jr. Verbal Categories of the *Poema del Cid.* Tulane, 1961. *DA,* XXII, 1169.

### 54. *Poetry, General*

54. 1. Danielson, John David. *Pastorelas* and *Serranillas,* 1130-1550. A Genre Study. Michigan, 1960. *DA,* XXI, 342.

54. 2. Eddy, Nelson W. Villasandino and *Arte Mayor.* Michigan, 1939.

54. 3. Mann, Albert, Jr. Spanish Satiric Verse from the Earliest Times to the End of the Sixteenth Century. Harvard, 1923.

54. 4. Michalski, André Stanislaw. Description in Mediaeval Spanish Poetry. Princeton, 1964. *DA,* XXV, 5933.

54. 5. Pope, Isabel. Sources of the Musical and Metrical Forms of the Mediaeval Lyric in the Hispanic Peninsula. Radcliffe, 1930.

54. 6. St. Amour, [Sister] M. Paulina, S.S.N.D. A Study of the *Villancico* up to Lope de Vega: Its Evolution from Profane to Sacred Themes, and Specifically to the Christmas Carol. Catholic, 1940. Washington, 1940. LC 41-681.

54. 7. Sánchez-Romeralo, Antonio. El villancico popular tradicional en los siglos XV y XVI. Wisconsin, 1961. *DA,* XXII, 2005.

54. 8. Xupulos, James J. Juan de Mena and His Works. A Study in Fifteenth-Century Spanish Poetry. New York, 1950.

### 55. *Razón de amor*

55. 1. Jacob, Alfred Bennis. *Razón de amor.* Edition and Evaluation. Pennsylvania, 1956. *DA,* XVI, 1683.

### 56. *Rrekotamiento del rrey Alisandere*

56. 1. Nykl, Alois Richard. *Rrekotamiento del rrey Alisandere,* An *Aljamiado* Text, with Introduction and Notes. Chicago, 1921. Chicago *Abstracts,* II, 347.

### 57. *Rocabertí, Fra*

57. 1. Heaton, Harry Clifton. The *Gloria d' amor* of Fra Rocabertí, a Catalan Vision-Poem of the 15th Century. Edited with Introduction, Notes and Glossary. Columbia, 1916. New York, 1916. LC 17-6377.

### 58. *Rodríguez de la Cámara* [or del Padrón], *Juan*

58. 1. Dudley, Edward Joseph. Structure and Meaning in the Novel of Juan Rodríguez: *Siervo libre de amor.* Minnesota, 1963. *DA,* XXVI, 1038.

### 59. *Rodríguez de Lena, Pero*

59. 1. Evans, Percy Griffith. A Critical Annotated Edition of *El passo honroso de Suero de Quiñones,* by Pero Rodríguez Delena. Illinois, 1929.

### 60. *Romances*

60. 1. Bryant, Shasta M. Comparative Study of the Spanish Ballad Translations of James Young Gibson. North Carolina, 1958. *DA,* XIX, 2611.

60. 2. Chandler, Richard Eugene. A Study of Treason in the Spanish Ballads. Missouri, 1940. *MA,* V, No. 1, p. 32.

60. 3. Emmons, Glenroy. The *Romancero* as an Expression of the Ideology of the Spanish People: An Analysis of Medieval Spanish Ideology as Seen in the Oldest Historical Ballads. New Mexico, 1956. *DA,* XVI, 2456.

60. 4. Franklin, Albert B., III. The Origins of the Legend and *Romancero* of Bernardo del Carpio. Harvard, 1938. Harvard *Summaries,* 1938, p. 353.

60. 5. Levey, Arthur E. The Sources of the Ballads by Lorenzo de Sepúlveda. Chicago, 1937. Chicago, 1939. LC 40-8283.

60. 6. Mejía, Leonor María. An Investigation of Spanish Ballad Origins. Stanford, 1937. Stanford *Abstracts,* 1936-37, p. 52.

60. 7. Poole, Robert Hawkins. Women in Early Spanish Literature with Special Emphasis on the Women in the Medieval Spanish Ballad. Stanford, 1949. Stanford *Abstracts,* XXV, 235.

### 61. *Ruiz, Juan, Arcipreste de Hita*

61. 1. Forsyth, John. The Phonemic Structure of Medieval Spanish as Reflected in the *Libro de buen amor.* New Mexico, 1961. *DA,* XXII, 2792.

61. 2. Frey, Herschel Jerome. A Comparative Phonology of Medieval and Modern Spanish: *El libro de buen amor.* North Carolina, 1963. *DA,* XXIV, 3331.

61. 3. Guzmán, Jorge. El sentido didáctico del *Libro de buen amor.* Iowa, 1961. *DA,* XXII, 1625.

61. 4. Naylor, Eric Woodfin. *El libro de buen amor*: The Gayoso and Toledo Manuscripts. Wisconsin, 1963. *DA,* XXIV, 285.

61. 5. Richardson, Henry Brush. A Vocabulary to the *Libro de buen amor* of Juan Ruiz, Arcipreste de Hita. Yale, 1923. New Haven, 1930. LC 30-25445.

61. 6. Walsh, James L. Some Aspects of Medieval Spanish Sibilants as Reflected in Ms. S. of the *Libro de buen amor.* Illinois, 1963. *DA,* XXIV, 4186.

61. 7. Whittem, Arthur Fisher. The Sources of the Fables in Juan Ruiz's *Libro de buen amor.* Harvard, 1908.

61. 8. Zahareas, Anthony Nicholas. The Art of Juan Ruiz, Archpriest of Hita. Ohio State, 1962. *DA,* XXIV, 289.

### 62. *Sanches de Uzeda, Gonzalo*

62. 1. Stone, Herbert Reynolds. A Critical Edition of the *Libro del gentil e de los tres sabios.* North Carolina, 1965. *DA,* XXVI, 4650. [Transcribed into Castilian in 1378 by Gonzalo Sanches de Uzeda.]

### 63. *Sánchez Vercial, Clemente*

63. 1. Zahn, Louis J. An Etymological Lexicon of *El libro de los exenplos por a.b.c.* North Carolina, 1957. *Madrid, 1961. NUC 62-42136.

### 64. *Santillana, Marqués de*

64. 1. Seronde, Joseph. A Study of the Relations of Some Leading French Poets of the Fourteenth and

Fifteenth Centuries to the Marqués de Santillana. Yale, 1915.

### 65. *Secreto de los secretos*

65. 1.  Kasten, Lloyd August William. *Secreto de los secretos*, Translated by Juan Fernández de Heredia: An Edition of the Unique Aragonese Manuscript, with Literary Introduction and Glossary. Wisconsin, 1931.

### 66. *Sepúlveda, Lorenzo de*

66. 1.  Levey, Arthur E. The Sources of the Ballads by Lorenzo de Sepúlveda. Chicago, 1937. Chicago, 1939. LC 40-8283.

### 67. *Short Story, General*

67. 1.  Baldwin, Spurgeon Whitfield, Jr. Brief Narrative Prose of the Fifteenth and Sixteenth Centuries. North Carolina, 1962. *DA*, XXIII, 4673.

67. 2.  Henning, Eugene A. The Framework of the Spanish Short Story Collections Before 1700. New Mexico, 1950.

### 68. *Talavera, Fray Hernando de*

68. 1.  Nyholm, Hannah Marie. An Edition of Fray Hernando de Talavera's *Tractado prouechoso que demuestra commo en el uestir y calçar comunmente se cometen muchos peccados y aun tanbien en el comer y beuer.* Wisconsin, 1955. *DA*, XVI, 339.

### 69. *Theater, General*

69. 1.  Shoemaker, William Hutchinson. The Multiple Stage in Spain and Catalonia During the Fifteenth and Sixteenth Centuries. Princeton, 1933. *Princeton, 1935. LC 35-31969.

69. 2.  Webber, Edwin Jack. Origins of the Spanish Theater as Related to the Classical Latin Drama. California, 1949.

69. 3.  Williams, Ronald B. The Staging of Plays in the Spanish Peninsula Prior to 1555. Iowa, 1930. Iowa City, 1935. LC 35-27901.

### 70. *Tirant lo Blanch*

70. 1.  Vaeth, Joseph Anthony. *Tirant lo Blanch*: A Study of Its Authorship, Principal Sources and Historical Setting. Columbia, 1918. New York, 1918. LC 19-6030.

### 71. *Toledo, Alfonso de*

71. 1.  Gericke, Philip Otto. The *Invencionario* of Alfonso de Toledo: Edition, with Introductory Study and Notes. California, 1965. *DA*, XXVI, 3952.

### 72. *Torre, Alfonso de la*

72. 1.  Morsello, Casper Joseph. An Edition of the

*Visión delectable de la vida bienaventurada* of Alfonso de la Torre. Wisconsin, 1965. *DA*, XXVI, 3306.

### 73. *Torroella, Pere*

73. 1.  Bach y Rita, Pedro. The Works of Pere Torroella, a Catalan Writer of the Fifteenth Century. New York, 1930. New York, 1930. LC 32-14013.

### 74. *Valera, Diego de*

74. 1.  Vásquez, Burney L. Mosén Diego de Valera, *Doctrinal de príncipes*: edición crítica. Kansas, 1964. *DA*, XXV, 5946.

### 75. *Vidal de Basalú, Raimón*

75. 1.  Field, William Hugh. A Critical Edition of Part of the Works of Raimón Vidal de Basalú, with Linguistic and Literary Commentary. Chicago, 1965. See NUC 67-17704.

### 76. *Vidas de Santa María Medalena y Santa Marta*

76. 1.  Michel, [Sister] Eleanore. *Vidas de Santa María Medalena y Santa Marta*: An Edition of the Old Spanish Text. Chicago, 1930. Chicago *Abstracts*, VIII, 393.

### 77. *Vides de Santz Rosselloneses*

77. 1.  Kniazzeh, Charlotte S. A Critical Edition of a Portion of the Thirteenth Century *Vides de Sants Rosselloneses*, Folios 156-261, Manuscript 44, Paris. Chicago, 1965. See NUC 65-98804. [A Catalan version of the work by Jacobus de Voragine.]

77. 2.  Neugaard, Edward Joseph. A Critical Edition of a Portion of the 13th Century *Vides de Santz Rosselloneses* with Introduction, Notes, Table of Proper Names, and Glossary. North Carolina, 1964. *DA*, XXVI, 1048.

### 78. *Ximénez, Francisco*

78. 1.  Naccarato, Frank. *Lo libre de les dones.* Chicago, 1965. See NUC 65-102094.

### 79. *Ysopete hystoriado*

79. 1.  Pincus, Michael Stern. An Etymological Lexicon of *Ysopete hystoriado.* North Carolina, 1961. *DA*, XXII, 3671.

## IV.  LITERATURE 1500-1700

### 1. *Bibliography*

1. 1.  Beardsley, Theodore Sterling. Hispano-Classical Translations Printed Between 1482 and 1699: A Study of the Prologues and a Critical Bibliography. Pennsylvania, 1961. *DA*, XXII, 1170.

1. 2.  Ricapito, Joseph Virgil.  Toward a Definition of the Picaresque: A Study of the Evolution of the Genre, Together with a Critical and Annotated Bibliography of *La vida de Lazarillo de Tormes*, *Vida de Guzmán de Alfarache*, and *Vida del buscón*. U.C.L.A., 1966.  *DA*, XXVII, 2542-A.

## 2.  *Miscellaneous*

2. 1.  Buckingham, Elizabeth.  *La perfecta señora*: A Dialogue of the Seventeenth Century Edited from the Original Manuscript with a Survey of the Dialogue in Spanish Literature to 1700.  Texas, 1954.

2. 2.  Butterfield, Marvin E.  The Interpreters of Fernando Cortés, Doña Marina and Jerónimo de Aguilar.  Illinois, 1937.  Urbana, 1936.  LC 37-40.

2. 3.  Deferrari, Harry Austin.  The Sentimental Moor in Spanish Literature Before 1600.  Pennsylvania, 1926.  Philadelphia, 1927.  LC 27-16251.

2. 4.  Dillingham, Mary Julia Wall.  *El martirio de Sant Lorencio, comedia y auto*: An Edition of a Sixteenth-Century Spanish Manuscript.  Chicago, 1932. Chicago *Abstracts*, IX, 413.

2. 5.  Donald, Dorothy.  Spanish Autobiography in the Sixteenth Century.  Wisconsin, 1941.  Wisconsin *Summaries*, VII, 323.

2. 6.  Engerrand, Gabriel Horace.  A Diplomatic Edition of the *Comedia de la vida y muerte de San Augustín*, and of the *Comedia de la vida y muerte del Santo Fray Diego* (from MS. 14767 in the Biblioteca Nacional, Madrid).  Iowa, 1941.  Iowa *Abstracts*, III, 367.

2. 7.  Forcadas, Alberto Massó.  El Siglo de Oro en las historias literarias norteamericanas recientes.  Missouri, 1966.  *DA*, XXVIII, 628-A.

2. 8.  Fucilla, Joseph Guerin.  A Study of Petrarchism in Spain During the Sixteenth Century.  Chicago, 1928.  Chicago *Abstracts*, VII, 471.  *RFE*, Anejo 72.  Madrid, 1960.

2. 9.  Giulian, Anthony Alphonse.  Martial and the Epigram in Spain in the Sixteenth and Seventeenth Centuries.  Pennsylvania, 1930.  Philadelphia, 1930. LC 31-6631.

2. 10.  Hatzantonis, Emmanuel Stamatios.  Circe nelle letterature classiche, medioevali e romanze: da Omero a Calderón.  California, 1958.

2. 11.  Hawley, Don C.  A Critical Edition of *Las hazañas del Cid, y su muerte, con la tomada de Valencia*. Iowa, 1961.  *DA*, XXII, 2793.  [Attributed to Lope de Vega.]

2. 12.  Hillard, Ernest H. K.  Spanish Imitations of the *Celestina*.  Illinois, 1957.  *DA*, XVIII, 588.  [Study of 25 works, 1499-1650, derived from *La Celestina*.]

2. 13.  Huff, [Sister] Mary Cyria.  The Sonnet "No me mueve, mi Dios"—Its Theme in Spanish Tradition: A Representative Literary Expression of Traditional Spanish Emphasis on Perfect Love of God.  Catholic, 1948.  Washington, 1948.  LC A48-8665.

2. 14.  Jackson, William R., Jr.  Florida in Early Spanish Colonial Literature.  Illinois, 1952.  Coral Gables, Fla., 1954.  NUC 54-14500.

2. 15.  La Prade, John Harry.  Golden Age Authors in Nineteenth-Century Spanish Plays.  North Carolina, 1963.  *DA*, XXIV, 3750.

2. 16.  Lott, Robert Eugene.  *Siglo de Oro* Tradition and Modern Adolescent Psychology in *Pepita Jiménez*: A Stylistic Study.  Catholic, 1958.  Washington, 1958.  NUC 59-1769.

2. 17.  Luenow, Paul Ferdinand, Jr.  An Edition of *Don Gil de la Mancha*.  New Mexico, 1955.  *DA*, XV, 1846.

2. 18.  Lynch, John Francis.  Concepts of the Indian and Colonial Society in Spanish Writers on Guatemala: 1520-1620.  Washington, Seattle, 1953.  *DA*, XIV, 674.

2. 19.  Mathews, Ernest Garland.  Studies in Spanish-English Cultural and Literary Relations, 1598-1700. Harvard, 1938.  Harvard *Summaries*, 1938, p. 304.

2. 20.  McCready, Warren Thomas.  La heráldica en las obras de Lope de Vega y sus contemporáneos.  Chicago, 1961.  Toronto, 1962.  NUC 64-44808.

2. 21.  McSpadden, George Elbert.  The Spanish Prologue Before 1700.  Stanford, 1947.  Stanford *Abstracts*, XXII, 45.

2. 22.  Molinaro, Julius A. R.  Angélica and Medoro: The Development of a Motif from the Renaissance to the Baroque.  Toronto, 1954.  *See Cañizares, José de.  NUC, 1958-62, vol. 8, p. 96.

2. 23.  Morley, Sylvanus Griswold.  Spanish Influence on Molière.  Harvard, 1902.

2. 24.  Murillo, Louis Andrew.  The Spanish Prose Dialogue of the Sixteenth Century.  Harvard, 1953.

2. 25.  Palomo, José Roberto.  The *Caballero* in Early Spanish Literature.  Ohio State, 1938.  Ohio State *Abstracts*, No. 29, p. 87.

2. 26.  Pavia, Mario N.  Magic and Witchcraft in the Literature of the *Siglo de Oro*, Especially in Drama. Chicago, 1947.  *New York, 1959.  NUC A60-5302.

2. 27.  Peebles, Waldo Cutler.  Democratic Tendencies in the Spanish Literature of the Golden Age.  Harvard, 1932.  Harvard *Summaries*, 1932, p. 313.

2. 28.  Russell, Billy Maurice.  The New World in Spanish Literature Before 1550.  North Carolina, 1964.  *DA*, XXVIII, 3156-A.

2. 29.  Ryan, James J.  The Concept of Nature in the Works of the Moralists of Sixteenth-Century Spain. Wisconsin, 1952.  Wisconsin *Summaries*, XIV, 461.

2. 30.  Sánchez-Barbudo, Angela.  Algunos aspectos de la vida religiosa en la España del siglo XVI: Los alumbrados de Toledo.  Wisconsin, 1953.  Wisconsin *Summaries*, XIV, 463.

2. 31. Schuster, Edward James. "Yo, el rey"—A Study of the Development of Monarchical Absolutism in the Spanish Golden Age, and Its Influence on the Literature of the Period. Minnesota, 1950.

### 3. *Alcalá Yáñez y Rivera, Jerónimo de*

3. 1. Childers, James Wesley. A Study of Sources and Analogues of the *Cuentos* in Alcalá Yáñez' *Alonso, mozo de muchos amos.* Chicago, 1939. Chicago, 1941. LC A42-1485.

3. 2. Utley, John H. Jerónimo de Alcalá Yáñez y Rivera: *Alonso, mozo de muchos amos,* A Critical Edition. Illinois, 1938. Urbana, 1938. LC 38-39401.

### 4. *Aldana, Francisco de*

4. 1. Rivers, Elias Lynch. The Life and Works of Francisco de Aldana. Yale, 1952. *Badajoz, 1955. NUC A57-7135.

### 5. *Alemán, Mateo*

5. 1. Moncada, Ernest Joseph. An Analysis of James Mabbe's Translations of Mateo Alemán's *Guzmán de Alfarache.* Maryland, 1966. *DA,* XXVII, 3056-A.

5. 2. Ricapito, Joseph Virgil. Toward a Definition of the Picaresque: A Study of the Evolution of the Genre, Together with a Critical and Annotated Bibliography of *La vida de Lazarillo de Tormes, Vida de Guzmán de Alfarache,* and *Vida del buscón.* U.C.L.A., 1966. *DA,* XXVII, 2542-A.

### 6. *Arce de Otálora, Juan*

6. 1. O'Connor, Norine P. Juan Arce de Otálora, *Coloquios de Palatino y Pinciano*: An Erasmian Dialogue of the Sixteenth Century; A Critical Analysis of the Unpublished Manuscript. Texas, 1952.

### 7. *Argensola, Lupercio Leonardo de*

7. 1. Green, Otis Howard. The Life and Works of Lupercio Leonardo de Argensola. Pennsylvania, 1927. Philadelphia, 1927. LC 28-3043.

### 8. *Arguijo, Juan de*

8. 1. Vranich, Stanko B. Don Juan de Arguijo (1567-1622): Su vida. California, 1965. *DA,* XXVI, 3965.

### 9. *Auto sacramental*

9. 1. Buck, Vera H. Four *Autos Sacramentales* from Manuscript 14864, Biblioteca Nacional, Madrid, Edited with Preface, Introductions, and Notes. Iowa, 1933. Iowa City, 1937. LC 37-27920. [MS of 1590.]

9. 2. Dorsey, Viola Marie. *Autos Sacramentales* of Calderón de la Barca: An Expression of the Culture of Spain's Golden Age. Stanford, 1941. Stanford *Abstracts,* 1940-41, p. 105.

9. 3. Fleet, Anita K. Prefiguration and Deliberate Anachronism in the Spanish Sacramental *Auto* Based on the Old Testament. Florida State, 1961. *DA,* XXII, 2787.

9. 4. Hunter, William A. An Edition and Translation of a Nahuatl Version of the Calderonian *Auto Sacramental: El gran teatro del mundo.* Tulane, 1954. Tulane *Abstracts,* Series 55, No. 14, p. 94.

9. 5. Kemp, Alice B. Critical Text and Study of Three *Autos Sacramentales* from Manuscript 14864, Biblioteca Nacional, Madrid. Iowa, 1933. Toronto, 1936. LC 36-18704. [MS of 1590.]

9. 6. McGarry, [Sister] Francis de Sales. The Allegorical and Metaphorical Language in the *Autos Sacramentales* of Calderón. Catholic, 1937. Washington, 1937. LC 38-7907.

9. 7. Tyre, Carl A. Three *Autos Sacramentales* from Manuscript 14864, Biblioteca Nacional, Madrid, Edited with Preface, Introduction, and Notes. Iowa, 1935. *Iowa City, 1938. LC 38-28518. [Religious plays of 1590: *Comedia de la historia y adoración de los tres Reyes Magos; Comedia de buena y santa doctrina; Comedia del nacimiento y vida de Judas.*]

9. 8. Wardropper, Bruce Wear. The Growth of the *Auto Sacramental* Before Calderón. Pennsylvania, 1949. *Madrid, 1953. NUC A54-2533.

9. 9. Young, [Sister] Margaret Pauline. The Liturgical Element in the *Autos Sacramentales* of Calderón. Boston University, 1947. Boston University *Abstracts,* 1947, n.p.

### 10. *Barahona de Soto, Luis*

10. 1. Lodge, Louise F. Angélica in *El Bernardo* and *Las lágrimas de Angélica.* Illinois, 1937. Urbana, 1937. LC 37-29897.

10. 2. Triolo, Alfred Angelo. The Boiardo-Ariosto Tradition in *Las lágrimas de Angélica* of Luis Barahona de Soto (1586). Illinois, 1956. *DA,* XVI, 1909.

### 11. *Baroque*

11. 1. Claydon, Ellen Easton. Juan Ruiz de Alarcón: Baroque Dramatist. Colorado, 1965. *DA,* XXVIII, 2203-A.

11. 2. Freund, Markéta Lily. Baroque Technique, Thought and Feeling in Certain Representative *Comedias* of Calderón. Colorado, 1966. *DA,* XXVIII, 1433-A.

11. 3. Iventosch, Herman. Five Types of Onomastic Invention in Spanish Baroque Fiction, 1616-1657. Harvard, 1959.

11. 4. Jones, Ruth Elizabeth. A Study of the Baroque

Elements in the *Persiles y Sigismunda* of Miguel de Cervantes Saavedra. Minnesota, 1965. *DA,* XXVII, 1787-A.

11. 5.  Kane, Elisha Kent. Gongorism and the Artistic Culture of the Golden Age. Harvard, 1926. *Chapel Hill, 1928. LC 28-14921.

11. 6.  Kirk, Susanne Brooke. Relaciones entre la poesía de Sor Juana Inés de la Cruz y la de los poetas del Renacimiento y Barroco en España. Missouri, 1963. *DA,* XXIV, 3338.

11. 7.  Miller, Gustavus Hindman. A Comparison of Late Renaissance and Early Baroque Aesthetics as Seen Through Two Dramatic Interpretations of the Inés de Castro Story. Michigan, 1956. *DA,* XVII, 144.

11. 8.  Molinaro, Julius A. R. Angélica and Medoro: The Development of a Motif from the Renaissance to the Baroque. Toronto, 1954. *See Cañizares, José de. NUC, 1958-62, vol. 8, p. 96.

11. 9.  Roaten, Darnell Higgins. An Explanation of the Forms of Three Serious Spanish Baroque Dramas According to Wölfflin's Principles of Art History. Michigan, 1951. *MA,* XI, No. 3, p. 687.

11. 10.  Uhrhan, Evelyn E. Linguistic Analysis of Góngora's Baroque Style. Illinois, 1950. Urbana, 1950. LC A52-365.

### 12. *Barrionuevo, Jerónimo de*

12. 1.  Fallis, Charles G. A Critical Edition of Selected Poems of D. Jerónimo de Barrionuevo. California, 1940.

### 13. *Barrios, Miguel de*

13. 1.  Moolick, Charles James. The Poetic Styles of Miguel de Barrios. Southern California, 1964. *DA,* XXV, 3578.

### 14. *Belmonte Bermúdez, Luis de*

14. 1.  Kincaid, William Abraham. Life and Works of Luis de Belmonte Bermúdez. California, 1928.

### 15. *Benavides, Luis de*

15. 1.  Babcock, James C. A Critical Edition of *El çerco y libertad de Sevilla por el rey don Fernando el Santo* (MS. of 1595). Iowa, 1934. Iowa *Program,* July, 1934.

### 16. *Bermúdez, Jerónimo*

16. 1.  Miller, Gustavus Hindman. A Comparison of Late Renaissance and Early Baroque Aesthetics as Seen Through Two Dramatic Interpretations of the Inés de Castro Story. Michigan, 1956. *DA,* XVII, 144. [*Nise lastimosa.*]

16. 2.  Triwedi, Mitchell David. The *Nise lastimosa* of' Jerónimo Bermúdez: A Critical Edition Together

with an Introductory Study and Notes. Southern California, 1958. Southern California *Abstracts,* 1958, p. 88.

### 17. *Calderón de la Barca, Pedro*

17. 1.  Anderson, Vernon Lockwood. Hugo von Hofmannsthal and Pedro Calderón de la Barca: A Comparative Study. Stanford, 1954. *DA,* XIV, 523.

17. 2.  Boring, Omen Konn. Structural Balance in Calderón's Dramas. Chicago, 1929. Chicago *Abstracts,* VIII, 369.

17. 3.  Castillo, Carlos. *En la vida todo es verdad y todo mentira* by D. Pedro Calderón de la Barca: An Edition from the Autograph with Introduction and Notes. Chicago, 1923. Chicago *Abstracts,* I, 305.

17. 4.  Connor, Patricia Josephine. The Music in the Spanish Baroque Theatre of Don Pedro Calderón de la Barca. Boston University, 1964.

17. 5.  Cummings, Dorothy Porter. *El secreto a voces* of Don Pedro Calderón de la Barca: An Edition with Introduction and Notes of the Autograph Manuscript of 1642. Ohio State, 1933. Ohio State *Abstracts,* No. 12, p. 41.

17. 6.  Dorsey, Viola Marie. *Autos Sacramentales* of Calderón de la Barca: An Expression of the Culture of Spain's Golden Age. Stanford, 1941. Stanford *Abstracts,* 1940-41, p. 105.

17. 7.  Dreney, Sara Bernadine. Calderón, the Poet of the Eucharist. Boston College, 1939.

17. 8.  Freund, Markéta Lily. Baroque Technique, Thought and Feeling in Certain Representative *Comedias* of Calderón. Colorado, 1966. *DA,* XXVIII, 1433-A.

17. 9.  Hatzantonis, Emmanuel Stamatios. Circe nelle letterature classiche, medioevali e romanze: da Omero a Calderón. California, 1958.

17. 10.  Hesse, Everett Wesley. Vera Tassis' Text of Calderón's Plays. New York, 1941. Mexico, 1941. LC A42-4023.

17. 11.  Hilborn, Harry W. A Chronology of the Plays of Don Pedro Calderón de la Barca. Toronto, 1935. Toronto, 1938. LC 39-31553.

17. 12.  Hunter, William A. An Edition and Translation of a Nahuatl Version of the Calderonian *Auto Sacramental: El gran teatro del mundo.* Tulane, 1954. Tulane *Abstracts,* Series 55, No. 14, p. 94.

17. 13.  Kressin, Hugo Maximilian. Calderón as a Champion of Feminism. New York, 1927.

17. 14.  McGarry, [Sister] Francis de Sales. The Allegorical and Metaphorical Language in the *Autos Sacramentales* of Calderón. Catholic, 1937. Washington, 1937. LC 38-7907.

17. 15.  Newman, Richard William. Calderón and Aquinas. Boston University, 1956. Boston University *Abstracts,* 1956, n.p.

17. 16.  Norton, Richard W.  Causality in *La vida es sueño*.  Illinois, 1960.  *DA*, XXI, 1569.

17. 17.  Oppenheimer, Max, Jr.  Don Pedro Calderón de la Barca's *Comedia del astrólogo fingido*.  Southern California, 1947.  Southern California *Abstracts*, 1947, p. 30.

17. 18.  Roaten, Darnell Higgins.  An Explanation of the Forms of Three Serious Spanish Baroque Dramas According to Wölfflin's Principles of Art History.  Michigan, 1951.  *MA*, XI, No. 3, p. 687.  [*La vida es sueño.*]

17. 19.  Rosenberg, Solomon Leopold Millard.  *La española de Florencia (O burlas veras, y amor invencionero), comedia famosa de Calderón de la Barca*.  Edited with Introduction and Notes.  Pennsylvania, 1909.  Philadelphia, 1911.  LC 11-26765.

17. 20.  Staaf, Oscar Emil.  Classical Mythology in Calderón.  Yale, 1907.

17. 21.  ter Horst, Robert Max.  *La vida es sueño*: The Role of Conflict.  Johns Hopkins, 1963.

17. 22.  Wardropper, Bruce Wear.  The Growth of the *Auto Sacramental* Before Calderón.  Pennsylvania, 1949.  *Madrid, 1953.  NUC A54-2533.

17. 23.  Warenreich, Edward David.  The *Comedias de Capa y Espada* of Calderón.  New York, 1933.

17. 24.  Wexler, Sidney Frederick.  Comedia famosa de *La devoción de la cruz* de D. Pedro Calderón de la Barca (Madrid, 1636).  New York, 1952.

17. 25.  Whitby, William Melcher.  Structural Symbolism in Two Plays of Pedro Calderón de la Barca.  Yale, 1954.

17. 26.  Young, [Sister] Margaret Pauline.  The Liturgical Element in the *Autos Sacramentales* of Calderón.  Boston University, 1947.  Boston University *Abstracts*, 1947, n.p.

### 18.  *Cancioneros*

18. 1.  Askins, Arthur Lee.  A Critical Edition and Study of the *Cancioneiro de Évora,* in Manuscript CXIV/1-17 of the Public Library of Évora, Portugal.  California, 1963.  *DA*, XXIV, 5403.

18. 2.  Schwartz, Rosalind Judith.  El cancionero manuscrito 3168 de la Biblioteca Nacional (Siglo XVI).  California, 1961.

### 19.  *Castillejo, Cristóbal de*

19. 1.  Nicolay, Clara Leonora.  The Life and Works of Cristóbal de Castillejo, the Last of the Nationalists in Castilian Poetry.  Pennsylvania, 1907.  Philadelphia, 1910.  LC 11-26764.

### 20.  *Castillo Solórzano, Alonso*

20. 1.  Nemtzow, Sarah.  Alonso de Castillo Solórzano; An Analysis of His Novelistic Production.  U.C.L.A., 1952.

### 21.  *Castro, Guillén de*

21. 1.  Alpern, Hyman.  *La tragedia por los celos,* comedia famosa de Don Guillén de Castro y Bellvís.  New York, 1925.  Paris, 1926.  LC 27-2221.

21. 2.  Krogh, Richard Neal.  The Growth of Guillén de Castro's Dramatic Technique as Shown by Eight Selected Plays.  Washington, Seattle, 1956.  *DA*, XVI, 2166.

21. 3.  LaDu, Robert Richard.  Honor in the Theater of Guillén de Castro.  Washington, Seattle, 1960.  *DA*, XX, 4660.

21. 4.  Pérez, Elisa.  La influencia del *Romancero* en Guillén de Castro.  Wisconsin, 1932.

21. 5.  Powers, Dorothea Thompson.  The Dramatic Art of Guillén de Castro.  New Mexico, 1958.  *DA*, XIX, 1366.

21. 6.  Roaten, Darnell Higgins.  An Explanation of the Forms of Three Serious Spanish Baroque Dramas According to Wölfflin's Principles of Art History.  Michigan, 1951.  *MA*, XI, No. 3, p. 687.  [*Las mocedades del Cid.*]

### 22.  *Cervantes, Miguel de*

22. 1.  Allen, John Jay.  An Analysis of the Language and Style of Cervantes' *Las dos doncellas* and *El casamiento engañoso*.  Wisconsin, 1960.  *DA*, XXI, 618.

22. 2.  Bates, Margaret Jane.  *Discreción* in the Works of Cervantes: A Semantic Study.  Catholic, 1945.  Washington, 1945.  LC A45-4644.

22. 3.  Bodensieck, Anne Marie.  The Linguistic Comic in Cervantes' *Don Quixote de la Mancha*.  Wisconsin, 1928.

22. 4.  Brenes, Dalai.  The Sanity of Don Quixote: A Study in Cervantine Deception.  Cornell, 1957.  *DA*, XVIII, 580.

22. 5.  Brownell, George Griffin.  The Position of the Attributive Adjective in the *Don Quixote*.  Johns Hopkins, 1904.  Paris-New York, 1908.  LC 13-22980.

22. 6.  Burnie, William R.  Contrast of Sixteenth-Century Christian Attitudes in Cervantes and Montaigne.  Wisconsin, 1952.  Wisconsin *Summaries*, XIII, 397.

22. 7.  Cain, [Sister] Mariano.  The Idea of a Theater in the *Entremeses* of Cervantes.  Wisconsin, 1964.  *DA*, XXV, 2507.

22. 8.  Chaves-García, José M.  Intergroup Relations in the Works of Cervantes.  Columbia, 1953.

22. 9.  Corley, Ames Haven.  A Study in the Word-Play in Cervantes' *Don Quixote*.  Yale, 1914.  New York, 1917.  LC 18-6681.

22. 10.  Crooks, Esther Josephine.  The Influence of Cervantes in France During the First Half of the Seventeenth Century, with Special Reference to Guérin de Bouscal and a Critical Edition of His

*Gouvernement de Sanche Pansa.* Johns Hopkins, 1923. \*Baltimore, 1931. LC 31-13007.

22. 11. Davies, Marian Ruth Loehlin. The Individual and the Bases of an Ideal Society in Cervantes. Stanford, 1964. *DA,* XXV, 1904.

22. 12. Descouzis, Paul Marcel. Don Quixote y la Generación del 98. Maryland, 1959. *DA,* XX, 3290.

22. 13. Efron, Arthur. Satire Denied: A Critical History of English and American *Don Quixote* Criticism. Washington, Seattle, 1964. *DA,* XXV, 5274.

22. 14. El Saffar, Ruth Ann. Distance and Control in *Don Quixote:* A Study of Narrative Technique. Johns Hopkins, 1966. *DA,* XXVII, 3425-A.

22. 15. Escudero, María Julieta. Contemplación del Quijote. Cornell, 1947. Cornell *Abstracts,* 1947, p. 41.

22. 16. Gould, William Elford. The Subjunctive Mood in *Don Quijote de la Mancha.* Johns Hopkins, 1903. Baltimore, 1905. LC 6-37895.

22. 17. Griffiths, Janet. Las ideas literarias de Cervantes. Middlebury, 1949.

22. 18. Gruber, Vivian M. François Rabelais and Miguel de Cervantes: Novelists of Transition. Florida State, 1960. *DA,* XXI, 2294.

22. 19. Haynes, Randolph Arnold. Negation in *Don Quijote.* Chicago, 1931. Chicago, 1933. LC 34-2463.

22. 20. Hendrickson, John R. The Influence of *Don Quixote on Modern Chivalry.* Florida State, 1959. *DA,* XX, 661.

22. 21. Herman, Jack Chalmers. *Don Quijote* and the Novels of Pérez Galdós. Kansas, 1950. Ada, Oklahoma, 1955. NUC 56-62594.

22. 22. Jackson, George William. A Study of the Spanish Literary Sources of *Don Quijote de la Mancha.* Harvard, 1961.

22. 23. Jones, Ruth Elizabeth. A Study of the Baroque Elements in the *Persiles y Sigismunda* of Miguel de Cervantes Saavedra. Minnesota, 1965. *DA,* XXVII, 1787-A.

22. 24. Knowles, Edwin B., Jr. The Vogue of *Don Quixote* in England from 1605 to 1660. New York, 1939. \*New York, 1941. LC A42-2143.

22. 25. La Grone, Gregory Gough. The Imitations of *Don Quixote* in the Spanish Drama. Pennsylvania, 1936. Philadelphia, 1937. LC 37-3649.

22. 26. Linsalata, Carmine R. Tobias Smollett and Charles Jarvis: Translators of *Don Quijote.* Texas, 1949. \*Stanford, 1956. NUC 56-9984.

22. 27. Mades, Leonard. A Study of *Don Quixote* in Relation to Castiglione's *Book of the Courtier.* Columbia, 1965. *DA,* XXVI, 3305.

22. 28. Martínez y Quintana, Fernando. Cervantes, su teatro y sus críticos. Virginia, 1930.

22. 29. McDonald, William Ulma, Jr. A Critical Edition of H. D. Inglis' *Rambles in the Footsteps of Don Quixote.* Northwestern, 1956. *DA,* XVII, 363.

22. 30. Meacham, Barbara Dell. Time in *Don Quixote.* Wisconsin, 1966. *DA,* XXVIII, 685-A.

22. 31. Obaid, Antonio Hadad. El *Quijote* en los *Episodios nacionales* de Pérez Galdós. Minnesota, 1953. *DA,* XIII, 1186.

22. 32. Penner, Allen Richard. Fielding and Cervantes: The Contribution of *Don Quixote* to *Joseph Andrews* and *Tom Jones.* Colorado, 1965. *DA,* XXVI, 6720.

22. 33. Piluso, Robert Vincent. La actitud de Cervantes frente al problema del matrimonio según se desprende de sus obras. New York, 1965. *DA,* XXVII, 1792-A.

22. 34. Quilter, Daniel E. The Image of the *Quijote* in the 17th Century. Illinois, 1962. *DA,* XXIII, 4363.

22. 35. Ramírez, Alejandro. Cervantes y la Biblia. Washington, St. Louis, 1951.

22. 36. Riegner, Helene Irmgard. Humanitas Cervantina. Radcliffe, 1943.

22. 37. Rodríguez-Luis, Julio. Estructura y personaje en el arte narrativo de las *Novelas ejemplares.* Princeton, 1966. *DA,* XXVII, 1383-A.

22. 38. Trachman, Sadie Edith. Cervantes' Women of Literary Tradition. Columbia, 1932. New York, 1932. LC 33-6930.

22. 39. Turkevich, Ludmilla B. Cervantes in Russia. Columbia, 1950. Princeton, 1950. LC 50-5913.

22. 40. Wisewell, George Ellas. Finite Moods and Tenses in the *Don Quijote* of Cervantes. Wisconsin, 1919.

22. 41. Zeidner, Betty Jean. Cervantine Aspects of the Novelistic Art of Benito Pérez Galdós. California, 1957. Microfilmed. See NUC 67-8017.

22. 42. Zimic, Stanislav. Cervantes, lector de Aquiles Tacio y de Alonso Núñez de Reinoso. Duke, 1964. *DA,* XXVI, 379.

### 23. *Cetina, Gutierre de*

23. 1. Withers, Alfred Miles. The Sources of the Poetry of Gutierre de Cetina. Pennsylvania, 1923. Philadelphia, 1923. LC 24-4890.

### 24. *Comedia de figurón*

24. 1. White, Ralph E. *La Comedia de Figurón* of Rojas Zorrilla and Moreto. Texas, 1949.

### 25. *Conceptismo*

25. 1. Collard-Wéry, Andrée Marie. Cultismo, conceptismo y categorías afines en la crítica española. Harvard, 1965. See NUC 67-81780.

25. 2. Fränkel, Hans Hermann. Figurative Language

in the Serious Poetry of Quevedo: A Contribution to the Study of *Conceptismo*. California, 1942.

### 26. *Cortés, Hernán*

26. 1. Reynolds, Winston A. Hernán Cortés in Heroic Poetry of the Spanish Golden Age. Southern California, 1957. Southern California *Abstracts*, 1957, p. 144.

26. 2. Sensing, Welton J. The Policies of Hernán Cortés, as Described in His Letters. Illinois, 1954. *DA*, XV, 126.

### 27. *Criticism*

27. 1. Hudson, Herman Cleophus. The Development of Dramatic Criticism in England and Spain During the Elizabethan Period and the Golden Age. Michigan, 1962. *DA*, XXIII, 235.

27. 2. Hutchings, Chesley M. The Sentiment of Nationality in Spanish Literary Criticism from 1400 to 1621. Harvard, 1922.

27. 3. Shepard, Sanford. López Pinciano and Aristotelian Literary Criticism in the Spanish Renaissance. New York, 1960. *DA*, XXI, 903.

### 28. *El crotalón*

28. 1. Howell, Stanley E. The Use of Lucian by the Author of *El crotalón*. Ohio State, 1947. Ohio State *Abstracts*, No. 56, p. 69.

28. 2. Sharp, John McCarty. A Study of *El crotalón*: Its Sources, Its Ideology, and the Problem of Its Authorship. Chicago, 1949.

### 29. *Cruz, San Juan de la*

29. 1. Delaney, [Sister] Anne Cyril, S.N.D. Anagogical Mirrors: Reflections in the Poetry of T. S. Eliot of the Doctrine of Saint John of the Cross. Boston University, 1954. Boston University *Abstracts*, 1954, n.p.

29. 2. Icaza, [Sister] Rosa María. The Stylistic Relationship Between Poetry and Prose in the "Cántico espiritual" of San Juan de la Cruz. Catholic, 1957. Washington, 1957. NUC 57-4917.

29. 3. Marlay, Peter Clymer. The Theme of Transformation Through Love in the Poetry of San Juan de la Cruz. Harvard, 1966. See NUC 68-6385.

29. 4. Vega, José de Jesús. La afinidad ontológica entre San Juan de la Cruz, Juan Ramón Jiménez, Pedro Salinas y Jorge Guillén. Arizona, 1962. *DA*, XXIV, 782.

### 30. *Cubillo de Aragón, Alvaro*

30. 1. Whitaker, Shirley Blue. The Dramatic Works of Alvaro Cubillo de Aragón. North Carolina, 1965. *DA*, XXVII, 217-A.

### 31. *Cueto y Mena, Juan de*

31. 1. Woodford, Archer. An Edition of the Works of Juan de Cueto y Mena with an Introduction and Notes. Northwestern, 1949. Northwestern *Summaries*, XVII, 73.

### 32. *Cueva, Juan de la*

32. 1. Morby, Edwin Seth. The Plays of Juan de la Cueva. California, 1936.

32. 2. Shields, Robert Lawrence. A General Study of the Transition Period of Spanish Drama Following Juan de la Cueva. Iowa, 1941. Iowa *Abstracts*, III, 411.

### 33. *Cultismo*

33. 1. Collard-Wéry, Andrée Marie. Cultismo, conceptismo y categorías afines en la crítica española. Harvard, 1965. See NUC 67-81780.

### 34. *Delicado, Francisco*

34. 1. Mocas, Christo T. Aspectos lexicográficos de *La lozana andaluza*. Tulane, 1954. Tulane *Abstracts*, Series 55, No. 14, p. 99.

### 35. *Díaz del Castillo, Bernal*

35. 1. Turner, Elbert D., Jr. The Vocabulary of Bernal Díaz del Castillo's *Historia verdadera de la conquista de la Nueva España*. North Carolina, 1949. North Carolina *Record*, No. 478, p. 234.

### 36. *Drama, General, Miscellaneous*

36. 1. Asturias, [Sister] Rosario María, S.N.J.M. A Critical Edition and Study of the Play *El rey don Pedro en Madrid y el infanzón de Illescas*. Southern California, 1963. *DA*, XXIV, 5378.

36. 2. Barclay, Thomas B. The Rôle of the Dance and Dance Lyrics in the Spanish *Comedia* to the Early 18th Century. Toronto, 1957.

36. 3. Barrett, Linton L. The Supernatural in the Spanish Non-Religious *Comedia* of the Golden Age. North Carolina, 1938. North Carolina *Record*, No. 335, p. 126.

36. 4. Barton, Donald K. A Diplomatic Edition of *La vida y muerte de San Gerónimo*. Iowa, 1943. Iowa *Abstracts*, VII, 939.

36. 5. Buckingham, Elizabeth. *La perfecta señora*: A Dialogue of the Seventeenth Century Edited from the Original Manuscript with a Survey of the Dialogue in Spanish Literature to 1700. Texas, 1954.

36. 6. Cauvin, [Sister] Mary Austin, O.P. The *Comedia de Privanza* in the Seventeenth Century. Pennsylvania, 1957. *DA*, XVIII, 229.

36. 7. Coughlin, Edward Vincent. Neo-Classical *Re-*

*fundiciones* of Golden Age *Comedias* (1772-1831). Michigan, 1965. *DA,* XXVI, 2746.

36. 8.   Dale, George Irving.   The Moors in the Spanish Drama of the Golden Age.   Cornell, 1918.

36. 9.   Dillingham, Mary Julia Wall. *El martirio de Sant Lorencio, comedia y auto*: An Edition of a Sixteenth-Century Spanish Manuscript.   Chicago, 1932.   Chicago *Abstracts,* IX, 413.

36. 10.   Douglass, Philip Earle.   The *Comedia Ypólita,* Edited with Introduction and Notes.   Pennsylvania, 1929.   Philadelphia, 1929.   LC 29-24239.

36. 11.   Engerrand, Gabriel Horace.   A Diplomatic Edition of the *Comedia de la vida y muerte de San Augustín,* and of the *Comedia de la vida y muerte del Santo Fray Diego* (from MS. 14767 in the Biblioteca Nacional, Madrid).   Iowa, 1941.   Iowa *Abstracts,* III, 367.

36. 12.   Gillespie, Ruth Caroline.   A Study of the Authorship and Sources of *Nuestra Señora de la peña de Francia* and Its Relation to *La peña de Francia* of Tirso de Molina.   Yale, 1929.

36. 13.   Golden, Bruce.   Elizabethan Revenge and Spanish Honor: Analogues of Action in the Popular Drama of the Renaissance.   Columbia, 1966.

36. 14.   Grismer, Raymond Leonard.   The Influence of Titus Maccius Plautus on the Spanish Theatre Through Juan de Timoneda.   California, 1930.   *New York, 1944.   LC 45-576.

36. 15.   Grupp, William J.   Dramatic Theory and Criticism in Spain During the Sixteenth, Seventeenth and Eighteenth Centuries.   Cornell, 1949.

36. 16.   Hawley, Don C.   A Critical Edition of *Las hazañas del Cid, y su muerte, con la tomada de Valencia.*   Iowa, 1961.   *DA,* XXII, 2793.   [Attributed to Lope de Vega.]

36. 17.   Hayes, Francis C.   The Use of Proverbs in the *Siglo de Oro* Drama: An Introductory Study.   North Carolina, 1936.   North Carolina *Record,* No. 311, p. 89.

36. 18.   Heilman, Walter R., Jr.   The *Pastourelle* Theme in the Early Spanish Drama.   North Carolina, 1953.   North Carolina *Record,* No. 534, p. 249.

36. 19.   Hendrix, William Samuel.   Some Native Comic Types in the Early Spanish Drama.   Chicago, 1922.   Columbus, Ohio, 1924.   LC 25-9436.

36. 20.   Hudson, Herman Cleophus.   The Development of Dramatic Criticism in England and Spain During the Elizabethan Period and the Golden Age.   Michigan, 1962.   *DA,* XXIII, 235.

36. 21.   Kobbervig, Karl Irving.   A System for Classifying Motif Elements in the Drama of the Golden Age and Its Application to the *Comedias* of Juan Ruiz de Alarcón y Mendoza.   Washington, Seattle, 1955.   *DA,* XV, 2210.

36. 22.   Laas, Ilse Gertrud Probst. *Comedia yntitulada del tirano Rey Corbanto,* with Introduction and Notes.   Iowa, 1928.   Iowa City, 1931.   LC 32-27707.   [Biblioteca Nacional, MS 15594, dated 1585.]

36. 23.   Lovett, Gabriel H.   The Churchman and Related Characters in the Spanish Drama Before Lope de Vega.   New York, 1951.

36. 24.   Luenow, Paul Ferdinand, Jr.   An Edition of *Don Gil de la Mancha.*   New Mexico, 1955.

36. 25.   Manson, William R.   Attitudes toward Authority as Expressed in Typical Spanish Plays of the Golden Age.   North Carolina, 1963.   *DA,* XXV, 4703.

36. 26.   Mazur, Oleh.   The Wild Man in Spanish Renáissance and Golden Age Theater.   Pennsylvania, 1966.   *DA,* XXVII, 1341-A.

36. 27.   McCrary, William Carlton.   The Classical Tradition in Spanish Dramatic Theory of the Sixteenth and Seventeenth Centuries.   Wisconsin, 1958.   *DA,* XIX, 2092.

36. 28.   Meredith, Joseph Arthur.   The Development of the *Loa* in Sixteenth-Century Spanish Drama.   Pennsylvania, 1925.   *Philadelphia, 1925.   LC 29-29559.

36. 29.   Morrison, Robert R.   Sainthood in the Golden Age Drama of Spain.   Florida, 1963.   *DA,* XXV, 481.

36. 30.   Mousolite, Peter S.   A Diplomatic Edition of the *Comedia de Nuestra Señora de Lapa y un milagro que hiço.*   Iowa, 1948.   Iowa *Abstracts,* VII, 957.   [Biblioteca Nacional, MS 14767.]

36. 31.   Neale-Silva, Eduardo.   The New World in the Spanish *Comedia*: A Preliminary Study.   Wisconsin, 1935.

36. 32.   Patt, Beatrice Penelope.   The Development of the Christmas Play in Spain from the Origins to Lope de Vega.   Bryn Mawr, 1945.   *MA,* VIII, No. 1, p. 100.

36. 33.   Pavia, Mario N.   Magic and Witchcraft in the Literature of the *Siglo de Oro,* Especially in Drama.   Chicago, 1947.   *New York, 1959.   NUC A60-5302.

36. 34.   Peters, Howard Nevin.   Sixteenth Century European Tragicomedy: A Critical Survey of the Genre in Italy, France, England, and Spain.   Colorado, 1966.   *DA,* XXVIII, 240-A.

36. 35.   Ruffner, Sydney J.   The American Theme in Selected Dramas of the Golden Age.   Southern California, 1954.   Southern California *Abstracts,* 1954, p. 109.

36. 36.   Shervill, Robert Newton.   The Old Testament Drama of the *Siglo de Oro.*   North Carolina, 1958.   *DA,* XIX, 2093.

36. 37.   Shields, Robert Lawrence.   A General Study of the Transition Period of Spanish Drama Following

Juan de la Cueva. Iowa, 1941. Iowa *Abstracts,* III, 411.

36.38. Stafford, Lorna Lavery. The Soliloquy in the Spanish Drama Before Lope de Vega. Johns Hopkins, 1936.

36.39. Stern, Charlotte Daniels. Studies on the *Sayagués* of Early Spanish Drama. Pennsylvania, 1960. *DA,* XXI, 1195.

36.40. Templin, Ernest Hall. The Carolingian Tradition in the Spanish Drama of the Golden Age (Excluding Lope de Vega). Stanford, 1926. Stanford *Abstracts,* 1926-27, p. 135.

36.41. Torreyson, Dorothy. Woman in the Spanish *Comedia* of the Golden Age. Pittsburgh, 1934. Pittsburgh *Abstracts,* X, 372.

36.42. Weiger, John G. The Relationship of Honor, *Fama,* and Death in the Valencian Drama of the Golden Age. Indiana, 1966. *DA,* XXVII, 2165-A.

36.43. Whitehouse, Victor. The Theory of the Divine Right of Kings in the Spanish Drama of the Golden Age. Harvard, 1929. Harvard *Summaries,* 1929, p. 192.

36.44. Yudin, Florence L. Genre Identity in the Golden Age: The Post-Cervantine *Novela Corta* and the *Comedia.* Illinois, 1964. *DA,* XXV, 1223.

### 37. *Encina, Juan del*

37.1. Myers, Oliver T. Phonology, Morphology and Vocabulary in the Language of Juan del Encina. Columbia, 1961. *DA,* XXII, 569.

37.2. Scherr, Elliott B. A Study of the 1496 *Cancionero* of Juan del Encina. Iowa, 1934. Iowa *Program,* August, 1934.

37.3. Turk, Laurel Herbert. Juan del Encina and the Spanish Renaissance. Stanford, 1933. Stanford *Abstracts,* 1933-34, p. 69.

### 38. *Entremés*

38.1. Cain, [Sister] Mariano. The Idea of a Theater in the *Entremeses* of Cervantes. Wisconsin, 1964. *DA,* XXV, 2507.

38.2. Carner, Robert Jordan. The *Loas, Entremeses* and *Bailes* of D. Agustín Moreto. Harvard, 1940. Harvard *Summaries,* 1940, p. 399.

38.3. Jack, William Shaffer. The Early *Entremés* in Spain: The Rise of a Dramatic Form. Pennsylvania, 1923. Philadelphia, 1923. LC 23-17338.

### 39. *Ercilla, Alonso de*

39.1. McManamon, James Edward. Echoes of Virgil and Lucan in the *Araucana.* Illinois, 1955. *DA,* XVI, 966.

39.2. Petty, McKendree. Some Epic Imitations of Ercilla's *La araucana.* Illinois, 1930. Urbana, 1932. LC 34-252.

### 40. *Espinel, Vicente*

40.1. Clarke, Dorothy Clotelle. *Diversas rimas* de Vicente Espinel, edición crítica, con un estudio del desarrollo de la décima. California, 1934. *New York, 1956. See NUC, 1953-57, vol. 7, p. 354.

40.2. Haley, George. The Life of Vicente Espinel and Its Reflection in His Work. Brown, 1956. *DA,* XVII, 137.

40.3. McConnell, Vance Y. Antithetical Expression and Subconscious Conflict in Vicente Espinel's *Vida de Marcos de Obregón.* Arizona, 1966. *DA,* XXVII, 1060-A.

### 41. *Espinosa, Pedro*

41.1. Kouvel, Audrey L. Pedro Espinosa: Desarrollo de su sintaxis, vocabulario, estructuras formales e imágenes. Harvard, 1965.

### 42. *Estebanillo González*

42.1. Jones, Willis Knapp. *Estevanillo González*: A Study with Introduction and Commentary. Chicago, 1927. Chicago *Abstracts,* V, 411.

### 43. *Estella, Fray Diego de*

43.1. Fernández, Xavier A. Fray Diego de Estella. Columbia, 1952. *DA,* XII, 629.

### 44. *Fernández, Lucas*

44.1. Bryant, William C. Lucas Fernández and the Early Spanish Drama. California, 1964. *DA,* XXV, 6616.

44.2. Lihani, John. Glossary of the *Farsas y églogas* of Lucas Fernández. Texas, 1954.

### 45. *Fernández de Avellaneda, Alonso*

45.1. Gilman, Stephen. A Critical Study of the *Quijote apócrifo* of Alonso Fernández de Avellaneda. Princeton, 1943. *Mexico, 1951. NUC 54-20960.

### 46. *Fernández de Figueroa, Martín*

46.1. McKenna, James B. A Spaniard in the Portuguese Indies: The Narrative of Martín Fernández de Figueroa. Harvard, 1965. Cambridge, Mass., 1967. NUC 67-27089.

### 47. *Fiction, General*

47.1. Beeson, Margaret Ellen. The Role of the Hermit in the Seventeenth-Century Spanish Novel. Texas, 1957.

47.2. Gerding, Jess Lee. Spanish Travel Fiction in the *Siglo de Oro.* Texas, 1957. *DA,* XVII, 2608.

47.3. Horne, Ruth Nutt. Lope de Vega's *Peregrino en su patria* and the Romance of Adventure in Spain Before 1604. Brown, 1946.

47.4. King, Willard F. Literary Academies and Prose Fiction in Seventeenth-Century Spain. Brown, 1957. *DA,* XVIII, 590.

47.5. Lopes, Albert Richard. Aspects of the Language of the Realistic Novel of the Seventeenth Century. California, 1935.

47.6. Randall, Dale B. J. Renaissance English Translations of Non-Chivalric Spanish Fiction (With Special Reference to the Period from 1620 to 1657). Pennsylvania, 1958. *DA,* XVIII, 2129.

47.7. Rotunda, Dominic P. The Italian *Novelle* and Their Relation to Literature of Kindred Type in Spanish up to 1615. California, 1928.

47.8. Singleton, Mack H. Technique and Idea in Early Spanish Fiction. Wisconsin, 1936. Wisconsin *Summaries,* I, 340.

47.9. Williams, Robert Haden. Boccalini in Spain: A Study of His Influence on Prose Fiction of the Seventeenth Century. Columbia, 1946. Menasha, Wis., 1946. LC A46-6039.

47.10. Yudin, Florence L. Genre Identity in the Golden Age: The Post-Cervantine *Novela Corta* and the *Comedia.* Illinois, 1964. *DA,* XXV, 1223.

### 48. *Furió Ceriol, Fadrique*

48.1. Bleznick, Donald W. Fadrique Furió Ceriol, Political Thinker of Sixteenth Century Spain. Columbia, 1954. *DA,* XIV, 1212.

### 49. *Garcilaso de la Vega*

49.1. Keniston, Ralph Hayward. Garcilaso de la Vega: A Critical Edition of His Works Together with a Life of the Poet. Harvard, 1911. *New York, 1922. LC 22-10021. *New York, 1925. LC 25-25023.

### 50. *Gómez de Toledo, Gaspar*

50.1. Barrick, Mac Eugene. A Critical Edition of Gaspar Gómez de Toledo's *Tercera parte de la tragicomedia de Celestina.* Pennsylvania, 1966. *DA,* XXVI, 7308.

### 51. *Góngora y Argote, Luis de*

51.1. Gates, Eunice Joiner. The Metaphors of Luis de Góngora. Pennsylvania, 1933. Philadelphia, 1933. LC 34-39.

51.2. Kane, Elisha Kent. Gongorism and the Artistic Culture of the Golden Age. Harvard, 1926. *Chapel Hill, N.C., 1928. LC 28-14921.

51.3. Pérez, Carlos Alberto. Juegos de palabras y formas de engaño en la poesía de don Luis de Góngora. Ohio State, 1961. *DA,* XXII, 2385.

51.4. Uhrhan, Evelyn E. Linguistic Analysis of Góngora's Baroque Style. Illinois, 1950. Urbana, 1950. LC A52-365.

### 52. *Gracián, Baltasar*

52.1. Chambers, Leland Hugh. Baltasar Gracián's *The Mind's Wit and Art.* Michigan, 1962. *DA,* XXIII, 1684.

52.2. Gallardo, José Miguel. The Individuality of Baltasar Gracián. North Carolina, 1933. North Carolina *Record,* No. 286, p. 70.

52.3. Hafter, Monroe Zelig. The Prince in Quevedo, Saavedra Fajardo and Gracián: A Study of Prose Writings on the Formation of the Pre-Eminent Man in Seventeenth-Century Spain. Harvard, 1956. *Cambridge, Mass., 1966. NUC 66-21337.

52.4. Hammond, John H. Francisco Santos' Debt to Gracián. Texas, 1948. Austin, 1950. LC A51-9504.

52.5. Ortiz, Geraldine. La Compañía de Jesús en la vida y en las obras de Baltasar Gracián. Florida State, 1960. *DA,* XXI, 2297.

52.6. Ramos, Virginia María. Literary Ideas of Baltasar Gracián. Missouri, 1966. *DA,* XXVII, 3060-A.

### 53. *Gracioso*

53.1. Bradford, Marjorie Esther Campbell. The "Gracioso" of Lope de Vega. Radcliffe, 1930.

53.2. Hendrix, William Samuel. Some Native Comic Types in the Early Spanish Drama. Chicago, 1922. Columbus, Ohio, 1924. LC 25-9436.

53.3. O'Neal, Robert D. An Interpretation and Extension of the *Gracioso* Idea in the Plays of Lope de Vega. Florida State, 1966. *DA,* XXVII, 3058-A.

53.4. Pollin, Alice M. The *Gracioso* of Significant Name in the Theatre of Juan Ruiz de Alarcón y Mendoza. New York, 1955. *DA,* XVI, 340.

53.5. Watts, LeClaire B. The Clown: A Comparison of the Comic Figures of Lope de Vega and William Shakespeare. Connecticut, 1966. *DA,* XXVII, 4270-A.

### 54. *Granada, Fray Luis de*

54.1. Brentano, [Sister] Mary Bernarda. Nature in the Works of Fray Luis de Granada. Catholic, 1936. Washington, 1936. LC 36-22938.

54.2. Moore, John A. The *Imitation of Christ* and Fray Luis de Granada. A Broadening of Perspective. North Carolina, 1954. North Carolina *Record,* No. 548, p. 278.

54.3. Schuyler, [Sister] John Emmanuel. The Biographies of Fr. Luis de Granada. A Study of His Life, Doctrine, and Literary Genius Revealed in His Biographies and Related Documents. Western Reserve, 1956. Western Reserve *Abstracts,* 1954-56, p. 362.

54.4. Switzer, Rebecca. The Ciceronian Style in Fray Luis de Granada. Columbia, 1927. New York, 1927. LC 28-7187.

## 55. *Guevara, Antonio de*

55. 1. Grey, Ernest. Guevara Across the Centuries. Harvard, 1966. See NUC 67-93425.
55. 2. Iiams, Carlton Laird. Aegidius Albertinus and Antonio de Guevara. California, 1956.
55. 3. Jones, Joseph Ramon, II. Antonio de Guevara's *Una década de Césares*. Wisconsin, 1962. *DA,* XXIII, 2136.

## 56. *Hermosilla, Diego de*

56. 1. Mackenzie, Donald Alexander. *Diálogo de la vida de los pajes de palacio,* Edited with Introduction and Notes. Pennsylvania, 1910. Valladolid, 1916. LC 21-21589.

## 57. *Herrera, Fernando de*

57. 1. Almeida, Joe A. Las ideas literarias de Fernando de Herrera. Missouri, 1966. *DA,* XXVIII, 3135-A.
57. 2. Beach, Robert Mills. Was Fernando de Herrera a Greek Scholar? Pennsylvania, 1907. Philadelphia, 1908. LC 9-21290.
57. 3. Kossoff, Aron David. The Poetic Vocabulary of Fernando de Herrera. Brown, 1954. *DA,* XIV, 2348.

## 58. *Hojeda, Fray Diego de*

58. 1. Corcoran, [Sister] Mary Helen Patricia. *La Christiada,* Fray Diego de Hojeda, O.P.—Introduction and Text. Catholic, 1935. Washington, 1935. LC 35-9384.
58. 2. Meyer, [Sister] Mary Edgar. Sources of *La Cristiada*. Michigan, 1948. Ann Arbor, 1953. NUC 54-62137.

## 59. *Huarte de San Juan, Juan*

59. 1. Schneer, Richard James. Juan Huarte de San Juan and His *Examen de ingenios*. A Sixteenth-Century Contribution to Education. New York, 1961. *DA,* XXII, 567.

## 60. *Humanism*

60. 1. Sánchez y Escribano, Federico. Apuntes para una edición de *La philosophía vulgar* de Juan de Mal Lara (Contribución al estudio del humanismo en España). California, 1933. *New York, 1941. LC 42-19064.

## 61. *Hurtado de Mendoza, Diego*

61. 1. Batchelor, Courtenay Malcolm. The Poetry of Don Diego Hurtado de Mendoza. Yale, 1945. La Habana, 1959. See NUC, 1958-62, vol. 21, p. 254.
61. 2. Vázquez y Medina, Alberto. El fracaso de don Diego Hurtado de Mendoza en Tóscana. Yale, 1935.

## 62. *Jiménez de Cisneros, García*

62. 1. Mapa, Marina Vargas. García Jiménez de Cisneros: A Precursor of Spanish Classical Mysticism. Stanford, 1960. *DA,* XXI, 2717.

## 63. *Lazarillo de Tormes*

63. 1. Asensio, Manuel José. El *Lazarillo de Tormes*: Problemas, Crítica y valoración. Pennsylvania, 1955. *DA,* XV, 2199.
63. 2. Macaya Lahmann, Enrique. El *Lazarillo de Tormes*: Ensayo bibliográfico, precedido de algunas observaciones sobre la misma obra. Cornell, 1933. Ithaca, 1933. LC 34-10262 Rev. *San José, Costa Rica, 1935. LC 37-37237.
63. 3. Ricapito, Joseph Virgil. Toward a Definition of the Picaresque: A Study of the Evolution of the Genre, Together with a Critical and Annotated Bibliography of *La vida de Lazarillo de Tormes, Vida de Guzmán de Alfarache,* and *Vida del buscón*. U.C.L.A., 1966. *DA,* XXVII, 2542-A.

## 64. *León, Fray Luis de*

64. 1. Arkin, Alexander Habib. La influencia de la exégesis hebrea en los comentarios bíblicos de Fray Luis de León. New York, 1963. *DA,* XXIV, 2026.
64. 2. Goode, Helen Dill. The Rhetorical Prose of Fray Luis de León in *Los nombres de Cristo*. Kansas, 1962. *DA,* XXIV, 744.
64. 3. Lusk, Wallace Afton. Fray Luis de León y la Inquisición. Maryland, 1961. *DA,* XXV, 7274.
64. 4. Mazza, Rosario Raphael. A Critical Analysis of the Prose and Poetry of Fray Luis de León. New Mexico, 1956.

## 65. *Literary Academies*

65. 1. King, Willard F. Literary Academies and Prose Fiction in Seventeenth-Century Spain. Brown, 1957. *DA,* XVIII, 590.

## 66. *Lobo Lasso de la Vega, Gabriel*

66. 1. Avilés, Luis. *Mexicana* de Gabriel Lobo Lasso de la Vega. Illinois, 1936. Urbana, 1936. LC 36-33156.
66. 2. Isar, Herbert Eugene. The Tragedies of Gabriel Lobo Lasso de la Vega (1587). Pennsylvania, 1955. *DA,* XV, 1854.
66. 3. Owens, Robert N. The Historical Ballads of the *Manojuelo* of Gabriel Lobo Lasso de la Vega. Iowa, 1939. Iowa *Abstracts,* III, 403.

## 67. *López Pinciano, Alonso*

67. 1. Shepard, Sanford. López Pinciano and Aristotelian Literary Criticism in the Spanish Renaissance. New York, 1960. *DA,* XXI, 903.

### 68. *Loyola, Juan Bautista*

68. 1.   Williams, John D.   *Viage y naufragios del Macedonio* de Juan Baptista de Loyola: A Critical Edition.   Texas, 1949.

### 69. *Lozano, Cristóbal*

69. 1.   García, Barbara M.   An Annotated Edition of Cristóbal Lozano's *Soledades de la vida y desengaños del mundo* (1658).   Chicago, 1949.

### 70. *Luna, Juan de*

70. 1.   Laurenti, Joseph Luciano.   Estudio crítico de la *Segunda parte de la Vida de Lazarillo de Tormes* de Juan de Luna.   Missouri, 1962.   *DA,* XXIII, 3379.

70. 2.   Sims, Elmer Richard.   *La Segunda parte de la Vida de Lazarillo de Tormes Sacada de las Corónicas Antiguas de Toledo por I. de Luna,* castellano intérprete de la lengua española.   Chicago, 1926.   Chicago *Abstracts,* V, 419.

### 71. *Mal Lara, Juan de*

71. 1.   Sánchez y Escribano, Federico.   Apuntes para una edición de *La philosophia vulgar* de Juan de Mal Lara (Contribución al estudio del humanismo en España).   California, 1933.   *New York, 1941. LC 42-19064.

### 72. *Malón de Chaide, Fray Pedro*

72. 1.   Vinci, Joseph.   La predicación de Fray Pedro Malón de Chaide en *La conversión de la Magdalena.*   Middlebury, 1955.

### 73. *Mariana, Juan de*

73. 1.   Laures, John.   The Political Economy of Juan de Mariana.   Columbia, 1928.   New York, 1928. LC 28-24714.

### 74. *Marineo Sículo, Lucio*

74. 1.   Lynn, Caro.   A Life of Lucio Marineo Sículo, with a Determination of the Nature and Extent of His Knowledge of Latin Literature.   Cornell, 1927. Ithaca, 1927.   LC 34-427 Rev.

### 75. *Mesa, Gaspar de*

75. 1.   Basemann, Max L.   A Critical Text of the Dramatic Works Known or Reputed to Be by Gaspar de Mesa.   Iowa, 1940.   Iowa *Abstracts,* III, 361.

### 76. *Mexía, Pero*

76. 1.   Mulroney, Margaret Lois.   *Diálogos o Coloquios* of Pedro Mejía, with Introduction and Notes.   Iowa, 1928.   Iowa City, 1930.   LC 31-27398.

76. 2.   Turner, Philip Allison.   Some Aspects of the Ideology of Pero Mexía.   Harvard, 1949.

### 77. *Mexia de la Cerda*

77. 1.   Miller, Gustavus Hindman.   A Comparison of Late Renaissance and Early Baroque Aesthetics as Seen Through Two Dramatic Interpretations of the Inés de Castro Story.   Michigan, 1956.   *DA,* XVII, 144.   [*Doña Inés de Castro, Reina de Portugal.*]

### 78. *Mira de Amescua, Antonio*

78. 1.   Aníbal, Claude E.   A Critical Text, with Introduction, of *El arpa de David* by Mira de Amescua, Together with a Dissertation on Lisardo, His Pseudonym.   Indiana, 1922.   Columbus, Ohio, 1925. LC 26-27018.

78. 2.   Buchanan, Milton Alexander.   *Comedia famosa del esclavo del demonio compuesta por el doctor Mira de Mesqua.*   Chicago, 1906.   Chicago, 1906. LC 6-45711.

78. 3.   Murray, Donald Alan.   Mira de Amescua's *La desgraciada Raquel.*   Stanford, 1952.   Stanford *Abstracts,* XXVII, 372.

78. 4.   Pickering, Adrian T.   Mira de Amescua, *El conde Alarcos*: A Critical Edition with Introduction and Notes.   Ohio State, 1951.   Ohio State *Abstracts,* No. 67, p. 521.

78. 5.   Stevens, Charles Henry.   *El palacio confuso;* Together with a Study of the Menaechmi Theme in Spanish Literature.   New York, 1938.   New York, 1939.   LC 39-31767.

### 79. *Monroy y Silva, Cristóbal de*

79. 1.   Peters, John William.   The Dramatic Works of Cristóbal de Monroy y Silva: A Preliminary Survey.   Ohio State, 1954.

### 80. *Moreto, Agustín*

80. 1.   Britt, Claude Henry, Jr.   A Variorum Edition of Moreto's *El valiente justiciero.*   Northwestern, 1966. *DA,* XXVII, 3036-A.

80. 2.   Carner, Robert Jordan.   The *Loas, Entremeses* and *Bailes* of D. Agustín Moreto.   Harvard, 1940. Harvard *Summaries,* 1940, p. 399.

80. 3.   Casa, Frank Paul.   The Dramatic Craftsmanship of Moreto.   Michigan, 1963.   *DA,* XXIV, 1611.

80. 4.   Dedrick, Dwain Edward.   A Critical Edition of Moreto's *El poder de la amistad.*   Northwestern, 1964.   *DA,* XXV, 3567.

80. 5.   Kennedy, Ruth Lee.   The Dramatic Art of Moreto.   Pennsylvania, 1931.   Northampton, Mass., 1932.   LC 32-25020.

80. 6.   Lottmann, Anna Marie.   The Comic Elements in Moreto's *Comedias.*   Colorado, 1959.   *DA,* XIX, 2953.

80. 7.   White, Ralph E.   *La Comedia de Figurón* of Rojas Zorrilla and Moreto.   Texas, 1949.

80. 8.  Wofsy, Samuel Abraham.  A Critical Edition of Nine Farces of Moreto.  Wisconsin, 1928.

### 81.  *Mysticism, General*

81. 1.  Mapa, Marina Vargas.  García Jiménez de Cisneros: A Precursor of Spanish Classical Mysticism.  Stanford, 1960.  *DA,* XXI, 2717.

81. 2.  McCann, Eleanor M.  The Influence of Sixteenth and Seventeenth Century Spanish Mystics and Ascetics on Some Metaphysical Writers.  Stanford, 1953.  *DA,* XIII, 229.

81. 3.  Olabarrieta, [Sister] Miriam Thérèse, S.C.N.  The Influence of Ramón Lull on the Style of the Spanish Mystics and Santa Teresa.  Catholic, 1963.  Washington, 1963.  NUC 64-1172.

81. 4.  Rivet, [Mother] Mary Majella, O.S.U.  The Influence of the Spanish Mystics on the Works of Saint Francis de Sales.  Catholic, 1941.  Washington, 1941.  LC 41-11843.

### 82.  *Natas, Francisco de las*

82. 1.  Lynch, Theophilus S.  *El segundo libro de Eneydas* of Francisco de las Natas.  A Critical Edition with Notes.  Pennsylvania, 1959.  *DA,* XX, 2293.

### 83.  *Novela de caballería*

83. 1.  Lapp, Donald.  Archaisms in Four Novels of Chivalry.  Iowa, 1964.  *DA,* XXV, 5270.

83. 2.  Ruiz-de-Conde, Justina.  El amor y el matrimonio secreto en los libros de caballerías.  Radcliffe, 1945.  Madrid, 1948.

### 84.  *Novela pastoril*

84. 1.  Avalle-Arce, Juan B.  La novela pastoril en el Renacimiento español.  Harvard, 1955.  *Madrid, 1959.  NUC A61-5207.

84. 2.  Ricciardelli, [Rev.] Michele.  Studio esteticocomparativo sul romanzo pastorale: Sannazaro e Lope de Vega.  Oregon, 1961.  *DA,* XXI, 2720.

84. 3.  Wellington, Marie Z.  Sannazaro's Influence on the Spanish Pastoral Novel.  Northwestern, 1951.  Northwestern *Summaries,* XIX, 79.

### 85.  *Novela picaresca*

85. 1.  Alter, Robert Bernard.  A Rogue's Progress: Studies in the Picaresque Novel.  Harvard, 1962.  Cambridge, Mass., 1964.  NUC 63-20763.

85. 2.  Cameron, Wallace J.  The Theme of Hunger in the Spanish Picaresque Novel.  Iowa, 1956.  *DA,* XVI, 2157.

85. 3.  Chandler, Frank Wadleigh.  Romances of Roguery.  Part I., The Picaresque Novel in Spain.  Columbia, 1899.  New York, 1899.  LC A11-50.

85. 4.  DeHaan, Fonger.  An Outline of the History of the *Novela Picaresca* in Spain.  Johns Hopkins, 1895.  The Hague-New York, 1903.  LC 4-29849.

85. 5.  Dunstan, Florene J.  Medical Science in the Picaresque Novels, 1550-1650.  Texas, 1936.

85. 6.  Eveleth, F. W.  *La Novela Picaresca* and Its Influence on Subsequent Literature.  New York, 1899.

85. 7.  Guillén, Claudio.  The Anatomies of Roguery: A Comparative Study in the Origins and the Nature of Picaresque Literature.  Harvard, 1953.

85. 8.  Miller, Stuart.  A Genre Definition of the Picaresque Novel.  Yale, 1963.  *Cleveland, 1967.  NUC 67-11489.

85. 9.  Ramon, Michel Robert.  Nueva interpretación del pícaro y de la novela picaresca española hecha a base de un estudio de las tres obras maestras del género.  Northwestern, 1956.  *DA,* XVII, 635.

85. 10.  Ricapito, Joseph Virgil.  Toward a Definition of the Picaresque: A Study of the Evolution of the Genre, Together with a Critical and Annotated Bibliography of *La vida de Lazarillo de Tormes, Vida de Guzmán de Alfarache,* and *Vida del buscón.* U.C.L.A., 1966.  *DA,* XXVII, 2542-A.

85. 11.  Stamm, James Russell.  Didactic and Moral Elements in the Spanish Picaresque Novel.  Stanford, 1959.  *DA,* XX, 676.

85. 12.  Thomson, Somerville.  The Extent and Use of Classical Reference in the Spanish Picaresque Novel.  Stanford, 1939.  Stanford *Abstracts,* 1938-39, p. 77.

### 86.  *Novela sentimental*

86. 1.  Krause, Anna.  La novela sentimental, 1440-1513.  Chicago, 1928.  Chicago *Abstracts,* VI, 317.

### 87.  *Núñez de Reinoso, Alonso*

87. 1.  Zimic, Stanislav.  Cervantes, lector de Aquiles Tacio y de Alonso Núñez de Reinoso.  Duke, 1964.  *DA,* XXVI, 379.

### 88.  *Ortiz, Agustín*

88. 1.  House, Ralph Emerson.  *Comedia Radiana* of Agustín Ortiz.  Chicago, 1909.  Chicago, 1910.  LC A11-1176.

### 89.  *Osuna, Francisco de*

89. 1.  Calvert, Laura De Lashmutt.  Ideas and Style in the *Spiritual Alphabets* of Francisco de Osuna.  Ohio State, 1966.  *DA,* XXVII, 2130-A.

### 90.  *Palau, Bartholomé*

90. 1.  Sweeney, Mary S.  *Victoria de Cristo* by Bartholomé Palau.  Bryn Mawr, 1947.

### 91.  *Pérez, Antonio*

91. 1.  Welch, [Sister] Mary Bernarda, B.V.M.  An-

tonio Pérez: A Study of the *Obras y relaciones.* Illinois, 1931. Urbana, 1930. LC 30-31733.

### 92. *Pérez de Montalván, Juan*

92. 1. Bacon, George William. Life and Dramatic Works of Dr. Juan Pérez de Montalván. Pennsylvania, 1903. *Philadelphia, 1903. LC 3-26667.

92. 2. Hershey, Phares Robert. *Pedro de Vrdemalas,* comedia famosa de Ivan Pérez de Montalván. Northwestern, 1932.

92. 3. Parker, Jack Horace. *La gitanilla* (Attributed to Juan Pérez de Montalván) by Antonio de Solís y Rivadeneyra, Edited, with Introduction and Notes, Together with a Study of the Versification of the Plays of Solís and Montalván. Toronto, 1941.

### 93. *Pérez de Toledo, Juan*

93. 1. Bibb, Elizabeth S. The Published Comedies of Juan Pérez de Toledo. Illinois, 1959. *DA,* XX, 295.

### 94. *Pineda, Fray Juan de*

94. 1. Nelson, Iver Nicholas. A Study of the Language of Fray Juan de Pineda's *Agricultura Christiana.* California, 1934.

### 95. *Poetry, General*

95. 1. Amor y Vázquez, José. Poemas narrativos del siglo XVI, en lengua española, que tratan la empresa cortesiana. Brown, 1957. *DA,* XVIII, 1043.

95. 2. Bryant, Shasta M. Comparative Study of the Spanish Ballad Translations of James Young Gibson. North Carolina, 1958. *DA,* XIX, 2611.

95. 3. Danielson, John David. *Pastorelas* and *Serranillas,* 1130-1550: A Genre Study. Michigan, 1960. *DA,* XXI, 342.

95. 4. Gordon, Arthur. Spanish Verse and Versification in the Sixteenth Century. Cornell, 1909.

95. 5. Kirk, Susanne Brooke. Relaciones entre la poesía de Sor Juana Inés de la Cruz y la de los poetas del Renacimiento y Barroco en España. Missouri, 1963. *DA,* XXIV, 3338.

95. 6. Mann, Albert, Jr. Spanish Satiric Verse from the Earliest Times to the End of the Sixteenth Century. Harvard, 1923.

95. 7. Mortenson, Barbara Jeanne. The Lyrical Elements in Spanish Balladry from 1580 to 1650. California, 1966. *DA,* XXVII, 4260-A.

95. 8. Morton, Frederic Rand. The Spanish Renaissance Epic in America on American Themes: 1530-1630. Harvard, 1958. *Mexico, 1963. NUC 64-42015.

95. 9. Reynolds, Winston A. Hernán Cortés in Heroic Poetry of the Spanish Golden Age. Southern California, 1957. Southern California *Abstracts,* 1957, p. 144.

95. 10. Rothberg, Irving P. The Greek Anthology in Spanish Poetry, 1500-1700. Pennsylvania State, 1954. Pennsylvania State *Abstracts,* XVII, 741.

95. 11. St. Amour, [Sister] M. Paulina, S.S.N.D. A Study of the *Villancico* up to Lope de Vega: Its Evolution from Profane to Sacred Themes, and Specifically to the Christmas Carol. Catholic, 1940. Washington, 1940. LC 41-681.

95. 12. Sánchez Arce, Nellie Esther. Contribución al estudio del tema de la muerte en la poesía española del siglo XVI. Pennsylvania, 1953. *DA,* XIII, 1191.

95. 13. Sánchez-Romeralo, Antonio. El villancico popular tradicional en los siglos XV y XVI. Wisconsin, 1961. *DA,* XXII, 2005.

95. 14. Testa, Daniel Philip. The Pyramus and Thisbe Theme in 16th and 17th Century Spanish Poetry. Michigan, 1963. *DA,* XXIV, 751.

95. 15. Winslow, Mary Isabel. England and Englishmen in Spanish Poetry from 1588 to 1630. Wisconsin, 1935.

### 96. *Proaza, Alonso de*

96. 1. McPheeters, Dean W. Alonso de Proaza, Representative Figure of the Spanish Renaissance. Columbia, 1952. *DA,* XII, 631.

### 97. *Quevedo Villegas, Francisco de*

97. 1. Astiazarán, Gloria Caballero. El humorismo en la obra de Quevedo. Arizona, 1966. *DA,* XXVII, 3024-A.

97. 2. Berumen y Silva, Alfredo. The Satirical Art of Quevedo. Texas, 1949.

97. 3. Birch, William G. The Politico-Religious Philosophy of Francisco de Quevedo. Chicago, 1951.

97. 4. Crosby, James O. Quevedo in Italy: A Satirist in Politics. Yale, 1954.

97. 5. Durán, Manuel. Motivación y valor de la expresión literaria en Quevedo. Princeton, 1953. *DA,* XIV, 123.

97. 6. Fränkel, Hans Hermann. Figurative Language in the Serious Poetry of Quevedo: A Contribution to the Study of *Conceptismo.* California, 1942.

97. 7. Goldenberg, Barbara B. Quevedo's *Sueños:* A Stylistic Analysis. Columbia, 1951. *DA,* XII, 62.

97. 8. Hafter, Monroe Zelig. The Prince in Quevedo, Saavedra Fajardo and Gracián: A Study of Prose Writings on the Formation of the Pre-Eminent Man in Seventeenth-Century Spain. Harvard, 1956. *Cambridge, Mass., 1966. NUC 66-21337.

97. 9. Levisi, Margarita María Adelaida Rosa. Los *Sueños* de Quevedo: El estilo, el humor, el arte. Ohio State, 1964. *DA,* XXV, 6629.

97.10.  Piero, Raúl Alfredo del.  Las fuentes del *Job de Quevedo*.  Harvard, 1958.

97.11.  Ricapito, Joseph Virgil.  Toward a Definition of the Picaresque: A Study of the Evolution of the Genre, Together with a Critical and Annotated Bibliography of *La vida de Lazarillo de Tormes, Vida de Guzmán de Alfarache,* and *Vida del buscón.* U.C.L.A., 1966.  *DA, XXVII*, 2542-A.

97.12.  Rider, Alice Emma.  Forms of Ironic Expression in Quevedo's *Sueños*.  Catholic, 1963.  *DA, XXIV*, 4196.

97.13.  Rose, Robert Selden.  Quevedo and *El buscón.* California, 1915.  *Madrid: Hernando, 1927.

### 98.  *Quiñones de Benavente, Luis*

98.1.  Estermann, Hannah.  Luis Quiñones de Benavente: His Technique of the Interlude.  California, 1953.  See Bergman, [*Mrs.*] Hannah E.  *Madrid, 1965.  NUC 66-37720.

### 99.  *Remón, Fray Alonso*

99.1.  Kaatz, Gerda R.  A Diplomatic Edition of the *Comedia del católico español* and the *Comedia del glorioso San Martín*.  Iowa, 1945.  Iowa *Abstracts,* VII, 947.  [Biblioteca Nacional, MS 14767; *Comedia del católico español,* by Remón; *Comedia del glorioso San Martín,* by Lope?]

99.2.  Serna, Ven.  A Critical Edition of Alonso Remón's *Las tres mujeres en una* (Estudio de la obra teatral de Alonso Remón, seguido de una edición de *Las tres mujeres en una.*)  U.C.L.A., 1966.  *DA, XXVII*, 3018-A.

### 100.  *Reyes, Matías de los*

100.1.  Johnson, Carroll Bernhard.  The Life and Prose Works of Matías de los Reyes.  Harvard, 1966.  See NUC 67-39291.

### 101.  *Roa, Gabriel de*

101.1.  Ewing, Boyd Ross.  *El villano gran señor y gran Tamorlán de Persia* by Rojas, Villanueva and Roa.  Edited with an Introduction and Notes.  Cornell, 1932.  Ithaca, 1932.  LC 33-33919.  [Biblioteca Nacional, MS 14997.]

### 102.  *Rojas Villandrando, Agustín de*

102.1.  Crowell, James White.  Description and Abstract of *El natural desdichado* by Agustín de Rojas Villandrando.  Edited, from an Autograph in the Biblioteca Nacional at Madrid, with an Introduction and Notes.  Cornell, 1929.  *New York, 1939.  LC 39-31449.

102.2.  Vaughn, Ethel.  *El viage entretenido* by Agustín de Rojas: A Possible Source of *Le Roman comique* by Paul Scarron.  Northwestern, 1929.

### 103.  *Rojas Zorrilla, Francisco de*

103.1.  Ewing, Boyd Ross.  *El villano gran señor y gran Tamorlán de Persia* by Rojas, Villanueva and Roa.  Edited with an Introduction and Notes.  Cornell, 1932.  Ithaca, 1932.  LC 33-33919.  [Biblioteca Nacional, MS 14997.]

103.2.  Jeans, Fred Wilson.  An Annotated Critical Edition of Rojas Zorrilla's *Peligrar en los remedios*.  Brown, 1957.  *DA, XVIII*, 589.

103.3.  White, Ralph E.  *La Comedia de Figurón* of Rojas Zorrilla and Moreto.  Texas, 1949.

### 104.  *Rueda, Lope de*

104.1.  Abrams, Frederic.  A Critical Edition of Lope de Rueda's *Comedia Eufemia*.  Iowa, 1960.  *DA, XXI*, 1559.

104.2.  DeChasca, Edmund Villela.  Lope de Rueda's *Comedia de los engañados*: An Edition.  Chicago, 1941.  Chicago, 1941.  LC A42-831.

104.3.  Jablon, Kenneth.  A Critical Edition of Lope de Rueda's Pastoral Colloquies *Camila* and *Tymbria*.  Iowa, 1962.  *DA, XXIII*, 2905.

### 105.  *Ruiz de Alarcón, Juan*

105.1.  Anderson, Carl Dixon.  A Critical Edition of Juan Ruiz de Alarcón's *Examen de maridos*.  Texas, 1965.  *DA, XXVI*, 1035.

105.2.  Brenes, Carmen O.  The Democratic Spirit in the Drama of Juan Ruiz de Alarcón.  Southern California, 1955.  Southern California *Abstracts,* 1955, p. 96.

105.3.  Claydon, Ellen Easton.  Juan Ruiz de Alarcón: Baroque Dramatist.  Colorado, 1965.  *DA, XXVIII*, 2203-A.

105.4.  Ebersole, Alva V., Jr.  El ambiente español visto por Juan Ruiz de Alarcón.  Kansas, 1957.  Valencia, 1959.  NUC 60-30252 Rev.

105.5.  Espantoso, Augusta María.  The Use of the Occult Arts in the *Comedias* of Juan Ruiz de Alarcón; Together with a Preliminary Survey of the Occult Arts in Dramatic Literature.  Pennsylvania, 1962.  *DA, XXIII*, 1363.

105.6.  Hamilton, Thomas Earle.  The Structure of the Alarconian *Comedia*.  Texas, 1940.

105.7.  Kobbervig, Karl Irving.  A System for Classifying Motif Elements in the Drama of the Golden Age and Its Application to the *Comedias* of Juan Ruiz de Alarcón y Mendoza.  Washington, Seattle, 1955.  *DA, XV*, 2210.

105.8.  Melvin, Miriam V.  Juan Ruiz de Alarcón. Classical and Spanish Influences.  Kansas, 1941.

105.9.  Pollin, Alice M.  The *Gracioso* of Significant Name in the Theatre of Juan Ruiz de Alarcón y Mendoza.  New York, 1955.  *DA, XVI*, 340.

105. 10. Schons, Dorothy. Apuntes y documentos nuevos para la biografía de Juan Ruiz de Alarcón y Mendoza. Chicago, 1932. Chicago, 1929. LC 31-13371.

### 106. *Saavedra Fajardo, Diego de*

106. 1. Dowling, John C. The Political Thought of Saavedra Fajardo: A Study of Seventeenth Century Attitudes Towards the Decline of Spain as a World Power. Wisconsin, 1950. Wisconsin *Summaries,* XI, 370.

106. 2. Hafter, Monroe Zelig. The Prince in Quevedo, Saavedra Fajardo and Gracián: A Study of Prose Writings on the Formation of the Pre-Eminent Man in Seventeenth-Century Spain. Harvard, 1956. *Cambridge, Mass., 1966. NUC 66-21337.

### 107. *Salas Barbadillo, Alonso Jerónimo de*

107. 1. Hamlett, Alan Auguste. An Annotated Edition of *El sutil cordobés Pedro de Urdemalas* by Alonso Jerónimo de Salas Barbadillo, Based on the *Princeps* of 1620, with Introduction. Texas, 1940.

107. 2. Marshall, Pauline Maude. An Edition of Alonso de Salas Barbadillo's *El caballero perfecto* (1620), Together with a Study of Previous Spanish Literary Portrayals of the Ideal Gentleman. Northwestern, 1943. *Boulder, Colo., 1949. LC 49-47324.

107. 3. Peyton, Myron Alvin. *Don Diego de noche* de Alonso Gerónimo de Salas Barbadillo: A Critical Edition with Introduction and Notes. Northwestern, 1942. Northwestern *Summaries,* X, 42.

107. 4. Place, Edwin Bray. A Study of the Works of Salas Barbadillo and María de Zayas. Harvard, 1919.

### 108. *Sánchez, Miguel*

108. 1. Stephenson, Robert C. Miguel Sánchez: A Contemporary Terentian Influence upon Lope de Vega. Texas, 1930.

### 109. *Sánchez de Badajoz, Diego*

109. 1. Fluegge, Gladstone R. Four *Farsas* by Diego Sánchez de Badajoz *(Farsa del matrimonio, Farsa de Santa Susana, Farsa de la hechicera, Farsa de la ventera);* Edited with Introduction and Notes. Toronto, 1953.

109. 2. Gustafson, Donna Jean. Tradition and Originality in the *Farsas* of Diego Sánchez de Badajoz. Stanford, 1966. *DA,* XXVII, 4253-A.

### 110. *Santa Teresa de Jesús*

110. 1. Hough, Mary E. Santa Teresa in America. Columbia, 1938. New York, 1938. LC 39-3952.

110. 2. McLoughlin, [Sister] Clara Agnes. A Study of the Letters of Saint Teresa of Avila. Western Reserve, 1955. Western Reserve *Abstracts,* 1954-56, p. 287.

110. 3. Olabarrieta, [Sister] Miriam Thérèse, S.C.N. The Influence of Ramón Lull on the Style of the Spanish Mystics and Santa Teresa. Catholic, 1963. Washington, 1963. NUC 64-1172.

### 111. *Santos, Francisco*

111. 1. Hammond, John H. Francisco Santos' Debt to Gracián. Texas, 1948. Austin, 1950. LC A51-9504.

### 112. *Short Story, General*

112. 1. Baldwin, Spurgeon Whitfield, Jr. Brief Narrative Prose of the Fifteenth and Sixteenth Centuries. North Carolina, 1962. *DA,* XXIII, 4673.

112. 2. Henning, Eugene A. The Framework of the Spanish Short Story Collections Before 1700. New Mexico, 1950.

### 113. *Solís y Rivadeneyra, Antonio de*

113. 1. Martell, Daniel Ernest. Dramas of Don Antonio de Solís y Rivadeneyra. Pennsylvania, 1902. Philadelphia, 1902. LC 3-26500.

113. 2. Parker, Jack Horace. *La gitanilla* (Attributed to Juan Pérez de Montalván) by Antonio de Solís y Rivadeneyra, Edited, with Introduction and Notes, Together with a Study of the Versification of the Plays of Solís and Montalván. Toronto, 1941.

### 114. *Suárez de Figueroa, Cristóbal*

114. 1. Crawford, James Pyle Wickersham. The Life and Works of Cristóbal Suárez de Figueroa. Pennsylvania, 1906. Philadelphia, 1907. LC 8-259.

### 115. *Tarsis y Peralta, Juan de, Conde de Villamediana*

115. 1. Harland, Frances Marguerite. The Sonnets of Villamediana. New York, 1945.

### 116. *Téllez, Fray Gabriel, "Tirso de Molina"*

116. 1. Brown, Sherman William. *La villana de Vallecas* of Tirso de Molina. An Edition with Introduction and Notes. Chicago, 1933. Boston, 1948. LC 48-6991.

116. 2. Chittenden, Jean Stahl. Los nombres de personajes en las comedias de Tirso de Molina. Texas, 1964. *DA,* XXV, 7263.

116. 3. Gillespie, Ruth Caroline. A Study of the Authorship and Sources of *Nuestra Señora de la peña de Francia* and Its Relation to *La peña de Francia* of Tirso de Molina. Yale, 1929.

116. 4. Kennington, Nancy Lou. A Structural Analysis of the Extant Trilogies of Tirso de Molina. North Carolina, 1966. *DA,* XXVII, 2532-A.

116. 5. Miranda, Rafael J. Iberian Geography in the

Plays of Tirso de Molina. North Carolina, 1954. North Carolina *Record,* No. 548, p. 277.

116. 6. Reynolds, John Joseph. A Study and Critical Edition of Tirso de Molina's *El condenado por desconfiado.* California, 1956.

116. 7. Sarre, Dolores. Woman in the Theater of Tirso de Molina. Stanford, 1940. Stanford *Abstracts,* 1939-40, p. 88.

116. 8. Urtiaga, Alfonso. El indiano en la dramática de Tirso de Molina. Louisiana State, 1963. *DA,* XXIV, 4201.

116. 9. Wade, Gerald Edward. Tirso de Molina, *La sancta Juanna. Primera parte.* An Edition with Introduction and Notes. Ohio State, 1936. Ohio State *Abstracts,* No. 22, p. 305.

### 117. *Theater, General*

117. 1. Falconieri, John Vincent. A History of Italian Comedians in Spain: A Chapter of the Spanish Renaissance. Michigan, 1952. *DA,* XII, 186.

117. 2. Shoemaker, William Hutchinson. The Multiple Stage in Spain and Catalonia During the Fifteenth and Sixteenth Centuries. Princeton, 1933. *Princeton, 1935. LC 35-31969.

117. 3. Weaver, William R. An Introductory Study of Stage Devices in the *Siglo de Oro* Drama. North Carolina, 1937. North Carolina *Record,* No. 323, p. 112.

117. 4. Webber, Edwin Jack. Origins of the Spanish Theater as Related to the Classical Latin Drama. California, 1949.

117. 5. Williams, Ronald B. The Staging of Plays in the Spanish Peninsula Prior to 1555. Iowa, 1930. Iowa City, 1935. LC 35-27901.

### 118. *Timoneda, Juan de*

118. 1. Eoff, Sherman Hinkle. The *Patrañuelo* of Juan de Timoneda: An Edition with Introduction and Notes. Chicago, 1929. Chicago *Abstracts,* VII, 457.

118. 2. Grismer, Raymond Leonard. The Influence of Titus Maccius Plautus on the Spanish Theatre Through Juan de Timoneda. California, 1930. *New York, 1944. LC 45-576.

118. 3. Johnson, Mildred E. A Critical Edition of Juan de Timoneda, *Auto del castillo de Emaus* and *Auto de la Iglesia.* Iowa, 1929. *Iowa City, 1933. LC 33-28210.

118. 4. Peterson, Holland. *Amphitrión* and *Los Menemnos:* An Edition of the First Two Plays of Juan Timoneda's *Las tres comedias,* with an Introduction on Plautine Influence. Toronto, 1961.

### 119. *Torquemada, Antonio de*

119. 1. Crow, George D., Jr. *Los coloquios satíricos, con un coloquio pastoril,* por Antonio de Torquemada: A Critical Edition. Texas, 1953.

119. 2. Elsdon, James Harold. Aspects of a Study of the Life and Works of Antonio de Torquemada. California, 1934. Berkeley, 1937. LC A37-942.

### 120. *Valbuena, Bernardo de*

120. 1. Kidder, Margaret. A Critical Edition of *El Bernardo* of Bernardo de Balbuena. Illinois, 1937. Urbana, 1937. LC 37-29895.

120. 2. Lodge, Louise F. Angélica in *El Bernardo* and *Las lágrimas de Angélica.* Illinois, 1937. Urbana, 1937. LC 37-29897.

120. 3. Williams, Sidney James, Jr. A Critical Edition of the *Siglo de oro, en las selvas de Erífile.* North Carolina, 1966. *DA,* XXVII, 3022-A.

### 121. *Valdés, Juan de*

121. 1. Longhurst, John Edward. Erasmus and the Spanish Inquisition. The Case of Juan de Valdés. Michigan, 1949. *MA,* IX, 127.

### 122. *Vega Carpio, Lope Félix de*

122. 1. Aaron, [Sister] M. Audrey. Christological Concepts in the Non-Dramatic Lyric Poetry of Lope de Vega. Johns Hopkins, 1951. *Madrid: Ediciones Cultura Hispánica, 1967.

122. 2. Adam, Francis O., Jr. Some Aspects of Lope de Vega's Dramatic Technique as Observed in His Autograph Plays. Illinois, 1936. Urbana, 1936. LC 36-33151.

122. 3. Adams, Charles Lindsey. Traditional and Novelesque Elements in the Development of Plot in the Dated Plays of Lope de Vega. Stanford, 1954. *DA,* XIV, 706.

122. 4. Arjona, Jaime Homero. El disfraz varonil en Lope de Vega. Brown, 1932. Bordeaux, 1937. LC 38-20957.

122. 5. Artman, Jim P. The Soldier in the Dramatic Works of Lope de Vega. U.C.L.A., 1958.

122. 6. Bradford, Marjorie Esther Campbell. The "Gracioso" of Lope de Vega. Radcliffe, 1930.

122. 7. Breen, Dorothy R. An Edition of *La Dragontea* by Lope Félix de Vega Carpio, with Notes and an Introductory Essay. Illinois, 1936. Urbana, 1941. LC A42-1634.

122. 8. Brooks, John. *La gran comedia del mayor imposible* de Lope de Vega Carpio. Wisconsin, 1924. Tucson, 1934. LC 34-28384.

122. 9. Burner, Jarvis Burr. An Edition of *La hermosura de Angélica* of Lope de Vega Carpio, with Notes and an Introductory Essay. Illinois, 1931.

122. 10. Campiglia, Jeanette. Some Aspects of Nature in the *Comedia* of Lope de Vega. U.C.L.A., 1959.

122. 11. Case, Thomas E. A Critical Edition of Lope

de Vega's *Las almenas de Toro.* Iowa, 1962. *DA,* XXIII, 4673.

122. 12. Castañeda, James A. A Critical Edition of Lope de Vega's *Las paces de los reyes y judía de Toledo.* Yale, 1958. Chapel Hill, 1962. NUC 63-63503.

122. 13. Delano, Lucile K. A Critical Index of Sonnets in the Plays of Lope de Vega. Iowa, 1934. Toronto, 1935. LC 36-6799.

122. 14. Elizondo, Sergio Danilo. A Critical Edition of Lope de Vega's *Si no vieran las mujeres!* North Carolina, 1964. *DA,* XXVIII, 626-A.

122. 15. Erdman, Elmer George. Source, Sense, and Structure in the Poetry of Lope de Vega. Johns Hopkins, 1966. *DA,* XXVII, 177-A.

122. 16. Fernández Cerra, Carmen Pilar. El lirismo en los argumentos históricos de Lope de Vega. Johns Hopkins, 1952.

122. 17. Fichter, William Leopold. Lope de Vega's *El castigo del discreto,* Together with a Study of Conjugal Honor in His Theater. Columbia, 1925. New York, 1925. LC 28-3044.

122. 18. Fox, Arthur M. A Critical Edition of the Autograph Manuscript of *El poder en el discreto* by Lope de Vega Carpio, Together with a Subject Index of Illustrative Anecdotes in His *Comedias Novelescas y Costumbristas.* Toronto, 1961.

122. 19. Halstead, Frank G. The Attitude of Lope de Vega Toward Astrology. Virginia, 1937. Virginia *Abstracts,* 1937, p. 19.

122. 20. Harlan, Mabel Margaret. A Critical Edition of Lope de Vega's *El desdén vengado.* Indiana, 1927. New York, 1930. LC 30-22689.

122. 21. Heald, William F. A Comparison of Plot Patterns in the Plays of Shakespeare and Lope de Vega. North Carolina, 1954. North Carolina *Record,* No. 548, p. 51.

122. 22. Hoge, Henry William. A Critical, Annotated Edition of Lope de Vega's *El príncipe despeñado.* Wisconsin, 1948. Wisconsin *Summaries,* X, 638. Bloomington, 1955. NUC 55-62209.

122. 23. Horne, Ruth Nutt. Lope de Vega's *Peregrino en su patria* and the Romance of Adventure in Spain Before 1604. Brown, 1946.

122. 24. Kaatz, Gerda R. A Diplomatic Edition of the *Comedia del católico español* and the *Comedia del glorioso San Martín.* Iowa, 1945. Iowa *Abstracts,* VII, 947. [Biblioteca Nacional, MS 14767: *Comedia del católico español,* by Remón; *Comedia del glorioso San Martín,* by Lope?]

122. 25. Kaiser, Gunda Sabina. A Critical and Annotated Edition of Lope de Vega's *La villana de Getafe.* Wisconsin, 1958. *DA,* XIX, 2614.

122. 26. Kennedy, Hugh W. Lope de Vega's *La desdichada Estefanía*: A Critical, Annotated Edition of

the Autograph Manuscript. U.C.L.A., 1964. *DA,* XXV, 3575.

122. 27. LeFort, Emilio Carlos. Edición paleográfica de la comedia *Del monte sale (quien el monte quema)* de Lope Félix de Vega Carpio, con un estudio de la misma. Minnesota, 1935. Buenos Aires, 1939. LC 40-4383.

122. 28. Lionetti, Harold E. Ariosto's Influence on the Plays of Lope de Vega. Northwestern, 1955. *DA,* XV, 1855.

122. 29. Lovett, Gabriel H. The Churchman and Related Characters in the Spanish Drama Before Lope de Vega. New York, 1951.

122. 30. Marín, Diego. La intriga secundaria en la técnica dramática de Lope de Vega. Toronto, 1956. Mexico, 1958. NUC 59-48361.

122. 31. McCready, Warren Thomas. La heráldica en las obras de Lope de Vega y sus contemporáneos. Chicago, 1961. Toronto, 1962. NUC 64-44808.

122. 32. Michels, Ralph John. The Dramatic Unities in the Plays of Lope de Vega. Stanford, 1938. Stanford *Abstracts,* 1937-38, p. 58.

122. 33. Moore, Jerome Aaron. The *Romancero* in the Chronicle-Legend Plays of Lope de Vega. Pennsylvania, 1937. Philadelphia, 1940. LC 41-5542.

122. 34. Noble, Beth W. The Function of the Rustic in the Dramatic Technique of Lope de Vega. Yale, 1948.

122. 35. Oliver, William Irvin. Spanish Theatre: A Study in Dramatic Discipline. Cornell, 1959. *DA,* XX, 2434. [Vol. 2 contains actable translations of 3 Spanish plays: *The Lady Nit-Wit* by Lope de Vega, *Phaedra* by Miguel de Unamuno, *Blood Wedding* by Federico García Lorca.]

122. 36. O'Neal, Robert D. An Interpretation and Extension of the *Gracioso* Idea in the Plays of Lope de Vega. Florida State, 1966. *DA,* XXVII, 3058-A.

122. 37. Osuna, Rafael. *La Arcadia* de Lope de Vega: Génesis, estructura y originalidad. Brown, 1966. *DA,* XXVIII, 639-A.

122. 38. Patt, Beatrice Penelope. The Development of the Christmas Play in Spain from the Origins to Lope de Vega. Bryn Mawr, 1945. *MA,* VIII, No. 1, p. 100.

122. 39. Pérez, Louis Celestino. Afirmaciones de Lope de Vega sobre preceptiva dramática a base de cien comedias. Michigan, 1957. *DA,* XVIII, 1438.

122. 40. Phillips, Roy Cleveland. A Critical Edition of *La francesilla,* a Drama by Lope de Vega. Wisconsin, 1924.

122. 41. Pianca, Alvin Hugo. A Paleographic and Annotated Edition of Lope de Vega's *Don Lope de Cardona.* Wisconsin, 1961. *DA,* XXI, 3790.

122. 42. Poesse, Walter. The Internal Line-Structure

of Twenty-Seven Autograph Plays of Lope de Vega. California, 1940. *Bloomington, 1949. LC 49-45176.

122. 43. Powers, Perry John. The Concept of the City-State in the Dramas of Lope de Vega. Johns Hopkins, 1947.

122. 44. Reese, Lowell Grant. Lope de Vega and Shakespeare: A Comparative Study of Tragicomic Style. Washington, Seattle, 1962. *DA*, XXIV, 285.

122. 45. Reid, Charles Gordon, Jr. The Problem of Social Inequality in Love and Marriage as Presented in the Theatre of Lope de Vega. Virginia, 1941. Virginia *Abstracts*, 1941, p. 32.

122. 46. Ricciardelli, [Rev.] Michele. Studio estetico-comparativo sul romanzo pastorale: Sannazaro e Lope de Vega. Oregon, 1961. *DA*, XXI, 2720.

122. 47. Roaten, Darnell Higgins. An Explanation of the Forms of Three Serious Spanish Baroque Dramas According to Wölfflin's Principles of Art History. Michigan, 1951. *MA*, XI, No. 3, p. 687. [*Fuenteovejuna.*]

122. 48. Ross, Cecilia. *La hermosa Ester,* by Lope de Vega. Edited with an Introduction by Cecilia Ross. California, 1952.

122. 49. Rovner, Philip. Lope de Vega on Kingship. Maryland, 1958. *DA,* XX, 307.

122. 50. St. Amour, [Sister] M. Paulina. S.S.N.D. A Study of the *Villancico* up to Lope de Vega: Its Evolution from Profane to Sacred Themes, and Specifically to the Christmas Carol. Catholic, 1940. Washington, 1940. LC 41-681.

122. 51. Scungio, Raymond Lewis. A Study of Lope de Vega's Use of Italian *Novelle* as Source Material for His Plays, Together with a Critical Edition of the Autograph Manuscript of *La discordia en los casados.* Brown, 1961. *DA,* XXVII, 186-A.

122. 52. Sears, Helen L. The Concept of Fortune in Lope de Vega. U.C.L.A., 1950.

122. 53. Seymour, Consuelo Willard. Popular Elements and the Idea of Justice in the *Comedias* of Lope de Vega. Stanford, 1953. *DA,* XIII, 813.

122. 54. Sheppard, Douglas Claire. A Critical and Annotated Edition of Lope de Vega's *El villano en su rincón.* Wisconsin, 1955. *DA,* XVI, 341.

122. 55. Silverman, Joseph H. Lope de Vega's *Figura del Donaire*: Definition and Description. Southern California, 1955. Southern California *Abstracts,* 1955, p. 102.

122. 56. Solenni, Gino de. Lope de Vega's *El Brasil restituido,* Together with a Study of Patriotism in His Theater. Columbia, 1929. New York, 1929. LC 30-15832.

122. 57. Stephenson, Robert C. Miguel Sánchez: A Contemporary Terentian Influence upon Lope de Vega. Texas, 1930.

122. 58. Trueblood, Alan S. Substance and Form in *La Dorotea*: A Study in Lope's Artistic Use of Personal Experience. Harvard, 1951.

122. 59. Tyler, Richard W. Lope de Vega's *La corona de Hungría.* A Critical Edition, with an Introductory Study of the Treatment of the *Reina Sevilla* Legend in the Theatre of Lope de Vega. Brown, 1946.

122. 60. Umpierre, Gustavo. The Dramatic Function of the Songs in the Plays of Lope de Vega. New York, 1966. *DA,* XXVII, 3884-A.

122. 61. Villarejo, Oscar Milton. Lope de Vega and the Elizabethan and Jacobean Drama. Columbia, 1953. *DA,* XIII, 816.

122. 62. Watts, LeClaire B. The Clown: A Comparison of the Comic Figures of Lope de Vega and William Shakespeare. Connecticut, 1966. *DA,* XXVII, 4270-A.

122. 63. Whatley, Frances. The Life of the *Dama* in Lope de Vega. Illinois, 1947. Urbana, 1947. LC A48-4857.

122. 64. Ziomek, Henryk. A Paleographic Edition of Lope de Vega's Autograph Play *La nueva victoria de D. Gonzalo de Cordoua.* Minnesota, 1961. *DA,* XXII, 568.

### 123. *Vélez de Guevara, Luis*

123. 1. Ashcom, Benjamin B. Luis Vélez de Guevara's *El gran Iorge Castrioto y Príncipe Escanderbey,* A Critical Edition, with Introduction and Notes. Michigan, 1938.

123. 2. Berndt, Robert J. A Qualitative Analysis of the Versification of Selected *Comedias* of Luis Vélez de Guevara. Western Reserve, 1956. Western Reserve *Abstracts,* 1954-56, p. 99.

123. 3. Bininger, Robert Jeffers. A Critical Edition, with Introduction and Notes, of Vélez de Guevara's *El conde don Sancho Niño.* Ohio State, 1955. *DA,* XVI, 533.

123. 4. Endres, Valerie F. The Aesthetic Treatment of *Romancero* Material in the *Comedias* of Luis Vélez de Guevara. Arizona, 1966. *DA,* XXVII, 2150-A.

123. 5. Kirk, Charles Frederick. A Critical Edition, with Introduction and Notes, of Vélez de Guevara's *Virtudes vencen señales.* Ohio State, 1957. *DA,* XVII, 2268.

123. 6. Olmsted, Richard Hubbell. A Critical Study of the Autographed Manuscript of the Play *El conde don Pero Vélez y don Sancho el deseado* of Luis Vélez de Guevara. Minnesota, 1934. *Minneapolis, 1944. LC A44-2576.

123. 7. Reichenberger, Arnold G. Luis Vélez de Guevara, *El embuste acreditado y el disparate creído,* A Critical Edition with Introduction and Notes.

Ohio State, 1947. Ohio State *Abstracts,* No. 52, p. 249.

123. 8.  Rosen, Harold Earl. A Critical Edition, with Introduction and Notes, of Vélez de Guevara's *El amor en vizaíno, los celos en francés y torneos de Navarra.* Oregon, 1966. *DA,* XXVII, 3062-A.

123. 9.  Rozzell, Ramon C. Luis Vélez de Guevara, *La niña de Gómez Arias*: A Critical Edition with Introduction and Notes. Ohio State, 1947. Ohio State *Abstracts,* No. 54, p. 313.

123. 10.  Spencer, Forrest Eugene. Luis Vélez de Guevara: A Study in His Life and Dramatic Art. California, 1919.

### 124.  *Vezilla Castellanos, Pedro de la*

124. 1.  Barnett, Esther F. An Edition of *El león de España* by Pedro de la Vezilla Castellanos. Illinois, 1937. Urbana, 1937. LC 37-3651.

### 125.  *Viaje de Turquía*

125. 1.  Markrich, William L. The *Viaje de Turquía*: A Study of Its Sources, Authorship, and Historical Background. California, 1955.

### 126.  *Vicente, Gil*

126. 1.  Andrews, James Richard. The Artistry of the Plays of Gil Vicente. Princeton, 1953. *DA,* XIV, 116.

126. 2.  Joiner, Ida Virginia. The Dramatic Art of Gil Vicente. Texas, 1940.

126. 3.  Lunardini, Peter J. The Poetic Technique of Gil Vicente. New Mexico, 1953.

126. 4.  Moseley, William Whatley. An Etymological Vocabulary of the Spanish in the Works of Gil Vicente. New Mexico, 1954. *DA,* XV, 119.

126. 5.  Tomlins, Jack Edward. The Nature of Gil Vicente's Dramatic Artistry. Princeton, 1957. *DA,* XVIII, 238.

### 127.  *Villalón, Cristóbal de*

127. 1.  Armendáriz, Angel María, S.V.D. Edición y estudio de *El scholástico* de Cristóbal de Villalón. Catholic, 1965. *DA,* XXVII, 1810-A.

### 128.  *Villanueva, Jerónimo de*

128. 1.  Ewing, Boyd Ross. *El villano gran señor y gran Tamorlán de Persia* by Rojas, Villanueva and Roa. Edited with an Introduction and Notes. Cornell, 1932. Ithaca, 1932. LC 33-33919. [Biblioteca Nacional, MS 14997.]

### 129.  *Virués, Cristóbal de*

129. 1.  Sargent, Cecilia Vennard. A Study of the Dramatic Works of Cristóbal de Virués. Columbia, 1930. New York, 1930. LC 31-4415.

### 130.  *Vives, Juan Luis*

130. 1.  Riley, Margaret Anne. Political Ideas of Juan Luis Vives. New Mexico, 1955. *DA,* XV, 1840.

### 131.  *Ximénez de Enciso, Diego*

131. 1.  Platt, Frank Thomas. *El príncipe don Carlos* of Diego Ximénez de Enciso: A Critical Edition with Introduction and Notes (Parts I and II). Ohio State, 1956. *DA,* XVII, 138.

### 132.  *Zabaleta, Juan de*

132. 1.  Doty, George Lewis. Juan de Zabaleta, *El día de fiesta por la mañana.* A Critical Annotated Edition. Illinois, 1925.

132. 2.  Hershberg, David Ralph. A Critical Study of the Treatment of Classical Sources in Juan de Zavaleta's *Errores celebrados.* Michigan, 1966. *DA,* XXVIII, 676-A.

### 133.  *Zárate, Agustín de*

133. 1.  McMahon, Dorothy E. An Edition of Book V of Agustín de Zárate's *Historia del descubrimiento y conquista del Perú.* Southern California, 1947. Southern California *Abstracts,* 1947, p. 38.

### 134.  *Zayas y Sotomayor, María de*

134. 1.  Place, Edwin Bray. A Study of the Works of Salas Barbadillo and María de Zayas. Harvard, 1919.

134. 2.  Sylvania, Lena Evelyn Vincent. Doña María de Zayas y Sotomayor; A Contribution to the Study of Her Works. Columbia, 1922. New York, 1922. LC 22-14303.

## V.  LITERATURE OF THE EIGHTEENTH AND NINETEENTH CENTURIES

### 1.  *Bibliography*

1. 1.  Tucker, Scotti M. H. A Bibliography of Spanish Literary Criticism, 1700-1800. Texas, 1951.

### 2.  *Miscellaneous*

2. 1.  Carrasco, María Soledad. The Moor of Granada in Spanish Literature of the Eighteenth and Nineteenth Centuries. Columbia, 1954. *DA,* XV, 263.

2. 2.  Churchman, Philip Hudson. Byron and the Spanish Peninsula. Harvard, 1908.

2. 3.  Cirre, Manuela Manzanares. Los estudios árabes en España en el siglo XIX. Michigan, 1958. *DA,* XIX, 1373.

2. 4.  Cullen, Arthur J. El periodismo madrileño durante la monarquía constitucional (1820-23). Middlebury, 1956.

2. 5.   Denslow, Stewart.  Don Juan and Faust: Their Parallel Development and Association in Germany, 1790-1850.  Virginia, 1941.  Virginia *Abstracts,* 1941, p. 23.

2. 6.   Effross, Susi H.  English Influence on Eighteenth-Century Spanish Literature, 1700-1808.  Columbia, 1962.  *DA,* XXIII, 630.

2. 7.   Hart, Thomas R., Jr.  A History of Spanish Literary History, 1800-1850.  Yale, 1952.

2. 8.   Hoar, Leo Jerome.  Pérez Galdós and His Critics.  Harvard, 1965.  See NUC 67-39774.

2. 9.   Micarelli, Charles Nicholas.  Mines and Miners in French and Spanish Literatures of the Nineteenth and Twentieth Centuries.  Boston University, 1959.  *DA,* XX, 673.

2. 10.   Salvador, Graciano.  Spanish Traditionalism and French Traditionalistic Ideas of the Nineteenth Century in Spain.  Northwestern, 1942.  Northwestern *Summaries,* X, 48.

2. 11.   Siegwart, John Thomas.  The Beginnings of Modern Criticism in Spain: 1750-1800.  Tulane, 1959.  *DA,* XX, 3752.

2. 12.   Tudisco, Anthony.  America in Eighteenth Century Spanish Literature.  Columbia, 1950.  *MA,* X, No. 4, p. 235.

2. 13.   Tunie, Donald Alvin.  *La Suerte* in the Neo-Classic Drama of Spain.  Pittsburgh, 1958.  *DA,* XIX, 1369.

2. 14.   Worthington, Mabel P.  Don Juan: Theme and Development in the Nineteenth Century.  Columbia, 1953.  *DA,* XIII, 399.

### 3.   *Alarcón, Pedro Antonio de*

3. 1.   Chew, Jeanne Maurer.  The Portrayal of Feminine Life in the Novels of Fernán Caballero, Alarcón, Pereda, and Valera, Viewed Against the Background of Woman's Position in Nineteenth-Century Spain.  Pennsylvania State, 1958.  *DA,* XIX, 1379.

3. 2.   McClendon, Barnett Addison.  The Life and Works of Pedro Antonio de Alarcón.  Nebraska, 1963.  *DA,* XXIV, 3340.

3. 3.   Winslow, Richard Walter.  The Contribution of Pedro Antonio de Alarcón to the Development of the Short Story.  Minnesota, 1961.  *DA,* XXII, 2802.

### 4.   *Alas, Leopoldo, "Clarín"*

4. 1.   Brent, William Albert.  Leopoldo Alas and the Novel from 1875-1885 (A Critical Analysis of *La regenta.*)  Princeton, 1949.  *Columbia, Mo., 1951.  LC A51-7041.

4. 2.   Bull, William Emerson.  Clarín: An Analytical Study of a Literary Critic.  Wisconsin, 1940.  Wisconsin *Summaries,* VI, 318.

4. 3.   Durand, Frank.  A Critical Analysis of Leopoldo Alas's *La regenta.*  Michigan, 1962.  *DA,* XXIII, 3896.

4. 4.   García-Lorca, Laura de.  Los cuentos de Clarín: Proyección de una vida.  Columbia, 1958.  *DA,* XIX, 1381.

4. 5.   Gramberg, Eduard Johannes.  El humorismo de Leopoldo Alas, Clarín.  California, 1957.  *Oviedo, 1958.  NUC A60-501.

4. 6.   Kronik, John William.  The Short Stories of Leopoldo Alas (Clarín): An Analysis and Census of the Characters.  Wisconsin, 1960.  *DA,* XXI, 1566.

4. 7.   Matlack, Charles William.  Leopoldo Alas and Naturalism in the Spanish Novel, 1881-1892.  New Mexico, 1954.  *DA,* XV, 124.

4. 8.   Thompson, Clifford Ray.  A Thematic Study of the Short Stories of Leopoldo Alas.  Harvard, 1965.  Microfilmed.  See NUC 67-10994.

### 5.   *Andrés, Juan*

5. 1.   Cervone, Anthony Valerius.  An Analysis of the Literary and Aesthetic Ideas in *Dell' origine, dei progressi e dello stato attuale d'ogni letterature* of Juan Andrés.  St. Louis, 1966.  *DA,* XXVII, 3039-A.

5. 2.   Mazzeo, Guido E.  The Abate Juan Andrés (1740-1817): Literary Historian and Defender of Spanish and Medieval Hispano-Arab Learning, Literature and Culture.  Columbia, 1961.  *DA,* XXII, 565.

### 6.   *Arenal, Concepción*

6. 1.   Terhune, Mary.  Concepción Arenal y sus ideas sobre la mujer.  Middlebury, 1931.

6. 2.   Vaillant, René Eugene Gabriel.  Concepción Arenal.  Columbia, 1926.  New York, 1926.  LC 27-3384.

### 7.   *Bécquer, Gustavo Adolfo*

7. 1.   Clinkscales, Orline.  Bécquer in Mexico, Central America and the Caribbean Countries.  Texas, 1957.

7. 2.   Harter, Hugh Anthony.  Gustavo Adolfo Bécquer's Significance for Twentieth-Century Spanish Poetry.  Ohio State, 1958.  *DA,* XIX, 811.

7. 3.   Hartsook, John H.  Bécquer and Heine—A Comparison.  Illinois, 1939.  Urbana, 1939.  LC 40-3879.

7. 4.   King, Edmund L.  Gustavo Adolfo Bécquer: From Painter to Poet.  Texas, 1949.  *Mexico, 1953.  NUC 54-40264.

7. 5.   Young, Robert James, Jr.  Estudios estilísticos de las *Rimas* de Gustavo Adolfo Bécquer.  Wisconsin, 1959.  *DA,* XX, 2818.

### 8.   *Böhl de Faber, Cecilia, "Fernán Caballero"*

8. 1.   Chew, Jeanne Maurer.  The Portrayal of Feminine Life in the Novels of Fernán Caballero, Alarcón, Pereda, and Valera, Viewed Against the Background of Woman's Position in Nineteenth-Century

Spain. Pennsylvania State, 1958. *DA,* XIX, 1379.

8. 2. Farnsworth, Howard Merle. The Social Philosophy of Fernán Caballero. Missouri, 1942. *MA,* V, No. 1, p. 37.

8. 3. Hespelt, Ernest Herman. Fernán Caballero, a Study of Her Life and Letters. Cornell, 1925. Ithaca, 1925. LC 33-31097.

8. 4. Minor, Ainslie Burke. A Critical Analysis of the Novels of Fernán Caballero. Princeton, 1943. *MA,* VI, No. 2, p. 56.

### 9. *Burgos, Javier de*

9. 1. McKnight, William A. The Vogue of the *Sainete* on the Madrid Stage: Ramón de la Cruz, Tomás Luceño, Javier de Burgos. North Carolina, 1950. North Carolina *Record,* No. 506, p. 243.

### 10. *Cadalso, José*

10. 1. Hughes, John Brassington. Vital and Artistic Dimensions of the *Cartas marruecas* of José Cadalso. Princeton, 1953. *DA,* XIV, 358.

10. 2. Tucker, Donald Webb. The Patriotic Role of José Cadalso in Eighteenth-Century Spain. North Carolina, 1961. *DA,* XXII, 3210.

### 11. *Castro, Rosalía de*

11. 1. Barta, Robert James. The Traditional Peninsular Lyric as Reflected by Rosalía de Castro (Affinities of Subject and Form: *Cantares gallegos, Follas novas*). Minnesota, 1965. *DA,* XXVII, 765-A.

11. 2. Contreras, Matilda. Two Interpreters of Galicia: Rosalía de Castro and Emilia Pardo Bazán. Pittsburgh, 1960. *DA,* XXI, 2703.

11. 3. Da Rosa, Alberto Machado. Rosalía de Castro. A mulher e o poeta. Wisconsin, 1953. Wisconsin *Summaries,* XIV, 460.

11. 4. Kulp, Kathleen Karen. Manner and Mood in Rosalía de Castro: A Study of Themes and Style. New Mexico, 1966. *DA,* XXVIII, 3675-A.

11. 5. Pierce, Vaudau P. Rosalía de Castro. Kansas, 1961. *DA,* XXII, 2385.

### 12. *Costa, Joaquín*

12. 1. Pérez de la Dehesa, Rafael. El pensamiento de Costa y su repercusión en la Generación del 98. Brown, 1963. *DA,* XXIV, 3755.

### 13. *Costumbrismo*

13. 1. Berkowitz, Hyman C. Ramón de Mesonero Romanos: A Study of His *Costumbrista* Essays. Cornell, 1924. Ithaca, 1924. LC 34-356.

13. 2. Da Cal, Margarita Ucelay. Los españoles pintados por sí mismos (1843-1844); Estudio de un género costumbrista. Columbia, 1950. Mexico, 1951. LC A52-2067 rev.

13. 3. Fonseca, James Francis. Techniques for Depicting the Social Environment in Literature as Illustrated in the Nineteenth-Century Spanish *Cuadro de Costumbres.* U.C.L.A., 1957.

13. 4. Lyon, Albert Eddy. The *Artículo de Costumbres* in the Periodicals of Madrid, 1700-1808. Wisconsin, 1929.

13. 5. Moellering, William DeRochebrune. The Elements of *Costumbrismo* in Pereda's *Escenas montañesas.* Stanford, 1943. Stanford *Abstracts,* XVIII, 56.

13. 6. Montgomery, Clifford Marvin. Early Costumbrista Writers in Spain, 1750-1830. Pennsylvania, 1929. Philadelphia, 1931. LC 31-11945.

### 14. *Cruz, Ramón de la*

14. 1. McKnight, William A. The Vogue of the *Sainete* on the Madrid Stage: Ramón de la Cruz, Tomás Luceño, Javier de Burgos. North Carolina, 1950. North Carolina *Record,* No. 506, p. 243.

14. 2. Moreno, Ernesto E. Influencia de los sainetes de don Ramón de la Cruz en las primeras obras de Benito Pérez Galdós. Minnesota, 1966. *DA,* XXVIII, 2215-A.

### 15. *Drama, General*

15. 1. Browne, James R. An Aspect of Realism in Modern Spanish Drama: The Concept of Society. Chicago, 1940. Chicago, 1941. LC A42-913.

15. 2. Coughlin, Edward Vincent. Neo-Classical *Refundiciones* of Golden Age *Comedias* (1772-1831). Michigan, 1965. *DA,* XXVI, 2746.

15. 3. Grupp, William J. Dramatic Theory and Criticism in Spain During the Sixteenth, Seventeenth and Eighteenth Centuries. Cornell, 1949.

15. 4. Lamond, Marilyn. Eugène Scribe and the Spanish Theater, 1834-1850. North Carolina, 1958. *DA,* XIX, 1385.

15. 5. La Prade, John Harry. Golden Age Authors in Nineteenth-Century Spanish Plays. North Carolina, 1963. *DA,* XXIV, 3750.

15. 6. Matthews, Hester P. Historical Drama in Spain, 1850-1900. North Carolina, 1957. North Carolina *Record,* No. 590, p. 267.

15. 7. McKnight, William A. The Vogue of the *Sainete* on the Madrid Stage: Ramón de la Cruz, Tomás Luceño, Javier de Burgos. North Carolina, 1950. North Carolina *Record,* No. 506, p. 243.

15. 8. Peak, John H. Social Drama in Spain in the Nineteenth Century. North Carolina, 1955. *Chapel Hill, 1964. NUC 65-63589.

15. 9. Rogers, Paul Patrick. The Pre-Romantic Drama of Spain, an Introductory Study. Cornell, 1928. New York, 1930. LC 36-9910.

15. 10. Salley, William C. The Attitude of the Spanish

Romantic Dramatists Toward History. North Carolina, 1930. North Carolina *Record,* No. 268, p. 66.

15. 11. Sparks, Amy James. The Honor Code in Representative Spanish Romantic Dramas. Louisiana State, 1964. *DA,* XXV, 1220.

15. 12. Thompson, John Archie. Alexandre Dumas (père) and the Spanish Romantic Drama up to 1850. North Carolina, 1937. University [i.e., Baton Rouge], La., 1938. LC 39-2673.

15. 13. Tunie, Donald Alvin. *La Suerte* in the Neo-Classic Drama of Spain. Pittsburgh, 1958. *DA,* XIX, 1369.

### 16. *Echegaray, José*

16. 1. Goldberg, Isaac. Don José Echegaray: A Study in Modern Spanish Drama. Harvard, 1912. Microfilmed. See NUC Mic 56-4892.

16. 2. Reindorp, Reginald C. Romanticism in the Drama of José Echegaray. Texas, 1949.

16. 3. Young, John R. José Echegaray: A Study of His Dramatic Technique. Illinois, 1938. Urbana, 1938. LC 38-35964.

### 17. *Escalante, Amós de*

17. 1. Nicholson, Helen Schenck. A *Montañés* Poet: Amós de Escalante (1831-1902). Stanford, 1934. Stanford *Abstracts,* 1934-35, p. 53.

### 18. *Espronceda, José de*

18. 1. Dreps, Joseph Antone. The Metrics of José de Espronceda. Iowa, 1931. Iowa *Program,* August, 1931.

### 19. *Essay*

19. 1. Marichal, Juan Augusto López. Feijóo y el ensayismo hispánico. Princeton, 1949. *DA,* XV, 586.

### 20. *Feijóo, Fray Benito Jerónimo*

20. 1. Marichal, Juan Augusto López. Feijóo y el ensayismo hispánico. Princeton, 1949. *DA,* XV, 586.

20. 2. Rubio, Antonio. La crítica del galicismo desde Feijóo hasta Mesonero (1726-1832). Chicago, 1934. *Mexico, 1937. LC 39-31646.

20. 3. Staubach, Charles Neff. The Influence of French Thought on Feijóo. Michigan, 1937. Iowa City, Iowa, 1941. LC A41-4765.

### 21. *Fernández de Moratín, Leandro*

21. 1. Kerson, Pilar Regalado. Don Leandro Fernández de Moratín y la polémica del teatro de su tiempo. Yale, 1965. *DA,* XXVII, 210-A.

21. 2. Morgan, Rudolph. Moratín's *Hamlet.* Stanford, 1965. *DA,* XXVI, 6719.

21. 3. Redick, Patricia Coughenour. An Interpretation of Leandro Fernández de Moratín—The Man. Pittsburgh, 1959. *DA,* XX, 1793.

21. 4. Rooney, [Sister] St. Dominic, C.S.J. Realism in the Original Comedies of Leandro Fernández de Moratín. Minnesota, 1963. *DA,* XXIV, 2040.

### 22. *Forner, Juan Pablo*

22. 1. Laughrin, [Sister] Mary Fidelia, I.H.M. Juan Pablo Forner as a Literary Critic. Catholic, 1944. Washington, 1943. LC A44-1237.

### 23. *Gabriel y Galán, José María*

23. 1. Hisrich, [Sister] María Thecla. José María Gabriel y Galán, Spanish Folk Poet. Pittsburgh, 1949. Pittsburgh *Bulletin,* XLVI, No. 10, p. 36.

### 24. *Ganivet, Angel*

24. 1. Amner, Floyd Dewey. Ideology of Angel Ganivet. Ohio State, 1938. Ohio State *Abstracts,* No. 27, p. 7.

24. 2. García Lorca, Francisco. Angel Ganivet: Su idea del hombre. Columbia, 1952. Buenos Aires, 1952. NUC 53-20264.

24. 3. Shuford, William Harris. Angel Ganivet as a Literary Critic. North Carolina, 1963. *DA,* XXIV, 3342.

### 25. *García Gutiérrez, Antonio*

25. 1. Adams, Nicholson B. The Romantic Dramas of García Gutiérrez. Columbia, 1922. New York, 1922. LC 22-14456.

### 26. *Gaspar, Enrique*

26. 1. Kirschenbaum, Leo. Enrique Gaspar and the Social Drama in Spain. California, 1936. Berkeley, 1944. LC A44-921.

### 27. *Gil y Carrasco, Enrique*

27. 1. Samuels, Daniel G. Enrique Gil y Carrasco: A Study in Spanish Romanticism. Columbia, 1939. New York, 1939. LC 40-8968.

### 28. *Gil y Zárate, Antonio*

28. 1. Stoudemire, Sterling A. The Dramatic Works of Antonio Gil y Zárate. North Carolina, 1930. North Carolina *Record,* No. 268, p. 66.

### 29. *González del Castillo, Juan Ignacio*

29. 1. Hannan, Dennis. Tradition and Originality in the Dramatic Works of Juan Ignacio González del Castillo. Oregon, 1961. *DA,* XXII, 260.

### 30. *Hartzenbusch, Juan Eugenio*

30. 1. Corbière, Anthony Sylvain. Juan Eugenio Hart-

zenbusch and the French Theatre. Pennsylvania, 1927. Philadelphia, 1927. LC 27-24888.

### 31. *Hurtado, Antonio*

31. 1.   Chart, Ira. Antonio Hurtado: Symbol of the Transition Movement in Spanish Literature. Harvard, 1941. Harvard *Summaries*, 1941, p. 359.

### 32. *Isla, José Francisco de*

32. 1.   Sebold, Russell Perry. José Francisco de Isla, Jesuit Satirist of Pulpiteers in Eighteenth-Century Spain. Princeton, 1953. *DA*, XIV, 360.

### 33. *Jovellanos, Gaspar Melchor de*

33. 1.   Dowdle, Harold Lowe. The Humanitarianism of Gaspar Melchor de Jovellanos. Stanford, 1954. *DA*, XIV, 1718.

### 34. *Lampillas, Xavier*

34. 1.   Gibson, M. Carl. Xavier Lampillas: His Defense of Spanish Literature and His Contributions to Literary History. Oregon, 1960. *DA*, XXI, 2713.

### 35. *Larra, Mariano José de*

35. 1.   Ullman, Pierre Lioni. Larra's Satire of Parliamentary Oratory During the Ministry of Martínez de la Rosa. A Historical and Stylistic Analysis. Princeton, 1962. *DA*, XXIII, 3388.

### 36. *Luceño, Tomás*

36. 1.   McKnight, William A. The Vogue of the *Sainete* on the Madrid Stage: Ramón de la Cruz, Tomás Luceño, Javier de Burgos. North Carolina, 1950. North Carolina *Record*, No. 506, p. 243.

### 37. *Luzán, Ignacio de*

37. 1.   Cano, Juan. La *Poética* de Luzán. Columbia, 1928. Toronto, 1928. LC 30-7183.

*Maragall, Joan* (See VI, Maragall)

### 38. *Martínez de la Rosa, Francisco*

38. 1.   Alfaro, Arsenio. Francisco Martínez de la Rosa (1787-1862): A Study in the Transition from Neo-Classicism to Romanticism and Eclecticism in Spanish Literature. Columbia, 1964. *DA*, XXVI, 3293.
38. 2.   Shearer, James Francis. The *Poética* and *Apéndices* of Martínez de la Rosa: Their Genesis, Sources and Significance for Spanish Literary History and Criticism. Princeton, 1939. Princeton, 1941. LC 41-17114.

### 39. *Meléndez Valdés, Juan*

39. 1.   Colford, William E. Juan Meléndez Valdés: A Study in the Transition from Neo-Classicism to

Romanticism in Spanish Poetry. Columbia, 1942. New York, 1942. LC 43-6230.

### 40. *Mesonero Romanos, Ramón de*

40. 1.   Berkowitz, Hyman C. Ramón de Mesonero Romanos: A Study of His *Costumbrista* Essays. Cornell, 1924. Ithaca, 1924. LC 34-356.
40. 2.   Rubio, Antonio. La crítica del galicismo desde Feijóo hasta Mesonero (1726-1832). Chicago, 1934. *Mexico, 1937. LC 39-31646.

### 41. *Mora, José Joaquín de*

41. 1.   Trease, B. David. José Joaquín de Mora: A Spaniard Abroad. Michigan, 1953. *DA*, XIII, 394.

### 42. *Naturalism*

42. 1.   Dannelly, Henry. Realistic and Naturalistic Elements in Emilia Pardo Bazán's Novels. Texas, 1932.
42. 2.   Lewald, Herald Ernest. The Aristocrat in the Spanish Novel of the Naturalistic Period. Minnesota, 1961. *DA*, XXII, 262.
42. 3.   Matlack, Charles William. Leopoldo Alas and Naturalism in the Spanish Novel, 1881-1892. New Mexico, 1954. *DA*, XV, 124.
42. 4.   Paolini, Gilberto. An Aspect of Spiritualistic Naturalism in the Novels of B. P. Galdós: Charity. Minnesota, 1965. *DA*, XXVII, 1832-A.
42. 5.   Sylvia, Esther B. El primer período de la manera naturalista de Benito Pérez Galdós. Middlebury, 1946.

### 43. *Navarro Ledesma, Francisco*

43. 1.   Greenebaum, Carmen de Zulueta. Navarro Ledesma, el hombre y su tiempo. New York, 1966. *DA*, XXVII, 3047-A.

### 44. *Navarro Villoslada, Francisco*

44. 1.   Cornish, Beatrice Quijada. Francisco Navarro Villoslada. California, 1925. *Berkeley, 1918 [*sic*]. LC A18-2144.

### 45. *Neo-Classicism*

45. 1.   Alfaro, Arsenio. Francisco Martínez de la Rosa (1787-1862): A Study in the Transition from Neo-Classicism to Romanticism and Eclecticism in Spanish Literature. Columbia, 1964. *DA*, XXVI, 3293.
45. 2.   Burks, William Green. The Neo-Classic Tragedy in Spain During the Nineteenth Century. North Carolina, 1948. North Carolina *Record*, No. 464, p. 356.
45. 3.   Colford, William E. Juan Meléndez Valdés: A Study in the Transition from Neo-Classicism to Romanticism in Spanish Poetry. Columbia, 1942. New York, 1942. LC 43-6230.
45. 4.   Cook, John Alfred. The Spanish Neo-Classic

Comedy in Theory and Practice. Texas, 1940. *Dallas, 1959. NUC 59-5737.

45. 5.   Coughlin, Edward Vincent. Neo-Classical *Refundiciones* of Golden Age *Comedias* (1772-1831). Michigan, 1965. *DA,* XXVI, 2746.

45. 6.   Murphy, [Brother] Denis Richard. The Neo-Classic Tragedy in Spain. New York, 1963. *DA,* XXVIII, 238-A.

45. 7.   Pellissier, Robert Edouard. The Neo-Classic Movement in Spain During the Eighteenth Century. Harvard, 1913. Stanford, 1918. LC 18-9764.

45. 8.   Qualia, Charles B. The French Neo-Classic Tragedy in Spain in the 18th Century. Texas, 1932.

45. 9.   Thompson, Frank Reginald. The Classicism of Don Juan Valera. Wisconsin, 1941. Wisconsin *Summaries,* VII, 327.

45. 10.  Tunie, Donald Alvin. *La Suerte* in the Neo-Classic Drama of Spain. Pittsburgh, 1958. *DA,* XIX, 1369.

### 46.   *Novel, General*

46. 1.   Dendle, Brian J. The Novel of Religious Thesis in Spain, 1875-1936. Princeton, 1966. *DA,* XXVII, 1053-A.

46. 2.   Fletcher, Madeleine de Gororza. The Spanish Historical Novel (1870-1965). Harvard, 1966. See NUC 67-83353.

46. 3.   Regalado, Antonio, Jr. Benito Pérez Galdós y la novela histórica en España, 1868-1912. Yale, 1965. *DA,* XXVI, 4638.

46. 4.   Savaiano, Eugene. A Study of the Clergymen in Selected Modern Spanish Novels. Chicago, 1948. *Wichita, Kans., 1952. NUC 53-146.

46. 5.   Zellars, William Cook. Some Aspects of the Historical Novel in Spain Between 1830 and 1850. New York, 1930. *Albuquerque, 1930. LC 30-27425.

### 47.   *Núñez de Arce, Gaspar*

47. 1.   Knowlton, John F. Gaspar Núñez de Arce: His Poetry and the Critics. Oregon, 1965. *DA,* XXVI, 4662.

### 48.   *Ochoa, Eugenio de*

48. 1.   Randolph, Donald Allen. Eugenio de Ochoa y el romanticismo español. California, 1963. *DA,* XXIV, 5415.

### 49.   *Ortega Munilla, José*

49. 1.   Schmidt, Ruth A. José Ortega Munilla and His Novels. Illinois, 1962. *DA,* XXIII, 3385.

### 50.   *Palacio Valdés, Armando*

50. 1.   Bieghler, Edward W. The Social Microcosm of Palacio Valdés: A Register and Consideration of National, Regional, and Certain Social and Professional Types in His Fiction. Ohio State, 1940. Ohio State *Abstracts,* No. 33, p. 23.

50. 2.   MacDonald, [Sister] M. Eileen. Satire in the Novels of Armando Palacio Valdés. Southern California, 1942. Southern California *Abstracts,* 1942, p. 39.

50. 3.   Ríos Ríos, Maximiano. Armando Palacio Valdés (Crítica de su obra novelística del siglo XIX). New York, 1944. *New York, 1947. LC 47-29182.

### 51.   *Pardo Bazán, Emilia*

51. 1.   Brown, Donald F. The Influence of Emile Zola on the Novelistic and Critical Work of Emilia Pardo Bazán. Illinois, 1935. Urbana, 1935. LC 35-20878.

51. 2.   Chandler, Arthur Alan. The Role of Literary Tradition in the Novelistic Trajectory of Emilia Pardo Bazán. Ohio State, 1956. *DA,* XVI, 1450.

51. 3.   Contreras, Matilda. Two Interpreters of Galicia: Rosalía de Castro and Emilia Pardo Bazán. Pittsburgh, 1960. *DA,* XXI, 2703.

51. 4.   Dannelly, Henry. Realistic and Naturalistic Elements in Emilia Pardo Bazán's Novels. Texas, 1932.

51. 5.   Giles, Mary Elizabeth Gottenberg. Descriptive Artistry in the Novels of Emilia Pardo Bazán. California, 1961. Microfilmed. See NUC 67-31160.

51. 6.   Kirby, Harry L., Jr. Evolution of Thought in the Critical Writings and Novels of Emilia Pardo Bazán. Illinois, 1963. *DA,* XXIV, 299.

51. 7.   McLean, Edward F. Objectivity and Change in Pardo Bazán's Treatment of Priests, Agnostics, Protestants and Jews. Duke, 1961. *DA,* XXII, 873.

51.8.   Osborne, Robert Edward. The Critical Ideas of Emilia Pardo Bazán. Brown, 1948.

51. 9.   Richards, Henry Joseph. True and Perverted Idealism in the Works of Emilia Pardo Bazán. Minnesota, 1964. *DA,* XXVI, 4672.

51. 10.  Sánchez, Porfirio. Emilia Pardo Bazán: From Novel to Short Story. A Study in Contrasts. U.C.L.A., 1964. *DA,* XXV, 1924.

51. 11.  Scone, Elizabeth Louise. Cosmopolitan Attitudes in the Works of Emilia Pardo Bazán. New Mexico, 1959. *DA,* XX, 2809.

### 52.   *Pereda, José María de*

52. 1.   Bradley, Henry Addy. Pereda and Galdós: A Comparison of Their Political, Religious, and Social Ideas. Southern California, 1966. *DA,* XXVII, 2145-A.

52. 2.   Chew, Jeanne Maurer. The Portrayal of Feminine Life in the Novels of Fernán Caballero, Alarcón, Pereda, and Valera, Viewed Against the Background of Woman's Position in Nineteenth-Century Spain. Pennsylvania State, 1958. *DA,* XIX, 1379.

52. 3.  Moellering, William DeRochebrune.  The Elements of *Costumbrismo* in Pereda's *Escenas montañesas*. Stanford, 1943. Stanford *Abstracts,* XVIII, 56.

52. 4.  Sánchez, Joseph.  Ideological Index of the Works of José María de Pereda.  Wisconsin, 1940.  Wisconsin *Summaries,* V, 283.

52. 5.  Weiss, Gerard M.  The Novelistic World of Pereda as Seen in His Themes and Characters.  New York, 1964.  *DA,* XXVI, 3355.

52. 6.  Williams, Florence I.  Humor in the Works of Pereda.  Cincinnati, 1961.  *DA,* XXII, 3190.

### 53.   *Pérez Galdós, Benito*

53. 1.  Alfieri, John J.  The Miser in the Novels of Pérez Galdós.  Iowa, 1957.  *DA,* XVII, 1079.

53. 2.  Andrade, Graciela.  Las expresiones del lenguaje familiar de Pérez Galdós en *Fortunata y Jacinta*. Iowa, 1957.  *DA,* XVII, 3008.

53. 3.  Barr, Glenn R.  A Census of the Characters in the *Episodios nacionales* of Benito Pérez Galdós. Wisconsin, 1937.  Wisconsin *Summaries,* III, 347.

53. 4.  Bell, Wendolyn Y.  Galdós' Use of Nomenclature in Characterization.  Iowa, 1964.  *DA,* XXV, 5272.

53. 5.  Belt, William T.  Social Pathology in the Novels of Galdós.  Kansas, 1954.

53. 6.  Bradley, Henry Addy.  Pereda and Galdós: A Comparison of Their Political, Religious, and Social Ideas.  Southern California, 1966.  *DA,* XXVII, 2145-A.

53. 7.  Braun, Lucille Virginia.  Problems of Literary Creation in Five Characters of Galdós' *Fortunata y Jacinta*.  Wisconsin, 1962.  *DA,* XXII, 4011.

53. 8.  Carney, Hal.  The Dramatic Technique of Benito Pérez Galdós.  Nebraska, 1957.  *DA,* XVII, 1081.

53. 9.  Carranza, Matilde.  El pueblo visto a través de los *Episodios nacionales*.  Wisconsin, 1940.  Wisconsin *Summaries,* V, 280.

53. 10.  Chamberlin, Vernon A.  The Blind and Other Physically Handicapped Characters in the Novels of Benito Pérez Galdós.  Kansas, 1957.

53. 11.  Cobb, Edna H.  Children in the Novels of Benito Pérez Galdós.  Kansas, 1952.

53. 12.  Davis, John Frank.  The Proletarian Element in the Works of Pérez Galdós.  Missouri, 1939. *MA,* V, No. 1, p. 34.

53. 13.  Dawson, Thomas L. C.  Religion and Anticlericalism in the Novels of Benito Pérez Galdós. Toronto, 1957.

53. 14.  Dennis, Ward H.  Characterization in the First Series of the *Episodios nacionales* of Benito Pérez Galdós.  Columbia, 1965.  *DA,* XXVI, 4655.

53. 15.  Fedorchek, Robert M.  The Theme of Poverty in the *Novelas españolas contemporáneas* of Pérez Galdós.  Connecticut, 1966.  *DA,* XXVII, 3450-A.

53. 16.  Fite, Shirley R.  The Literary Origins of *Realidad* by Benito Pérez Galdós.  Minnesota, 1958.  *DA,* XIX, 2088.

53. 17.  Flores, Joseph S.  El sacerdote en la novela social de Benito Pérez Galdós.  Illinois, 1941.  Urbana, 1941.  LC A42-1635.

53. 18.  Fry, Gloria Manalo y Mendoza.  Dramatic Structure in the Novels of Pérez Galdós: His Use of the *Scène à faire*.  Washington, Seattle, 1965.  *DA,* XXVI, 4657.

53. 19.  Garwood, Ruth E.  The Ethical Aspect of Human Behavior as Interpreted by Galdós: A Study in Spanish Social Values.  Wisconsin, 1935.

53. 20.  González Araúzo, Angel.  Patología finisecular: La sociedad doliente en la novela galdosiana.  Johns Hopkins, 1966.  *DA,* XXVII, 3455-A.

53. 21.  Goodale, Hope K.  Pérez Galdós: Dramatic Critic and Dramatist.  Bryn Mawr, 1965.  *DA,* XXVI, 6041.

53. 22.  Heironimus, Dorothy H.  Indexes to the *Episodios nacionales* of Pérez Galdós.  Colorado, 1938.  Colorado *Abstracts,* 1938, p. 64.

53. 23.  Herman, Jack Chalmers.  *Don Quijote* and the Novels of Pérez Galdós.  Kansas, 1950.  Ada, Okla., 1955.  NUC 56-62594.

53. 24.  Hoar, Leo Jerome.  Pérez Galdós and His Critics.  Harvard, 1965.  See NUC 67-39774.

53. 25.  Iwanik, John.  A Study of the Abnormal Characters in the Novels of Benito Pérez Galdós.  Cornell, 1949.

53. 26.  Kercheville, Frank Monroe.  Benito Pérez Galdós: A Study in Spanish Liberalism.  Wisconsin, 1930.

53. 27.  Kerr, David R.  A Study of the Literary Treatment of Military Matters by the Spanish Author Benito Pérez Galdós in Ten of His Novels Known as the *Tercera serie, Episodios nacionales*.  George Washington, 1958.  George Washington *Bulletin,* LVIII, No. 3, p. 33.

53. 28.  Kirsner, Robert.  The Role of Spain in Representative Novels of Galdós.  Princeton, 1949.  *DA,* XV, 416.

53. 29.  MacDonald, Mary B.  The Influence of Emile Zola in the Novels of Benito Pérez Galdós Produced During the Years 1881-1885.  Minnesota, 1959.  *DA,* XX, 2294.

53. 30.  Meehan, Thomas Clarke.  A Formal Analysis of *Fortunata y Jacinta* (A Study in the Long Novel Form).  Michigan, 1965.  *DA,* XXVI, 7321.

53. 31.  Mikulski, Richard Michael.  The Carlist Wars in the Serial Novels of Galdós, Baroja and Valle-Inclán.  Kansas, 1956.

53. 32.  Moreno, Ernesto E.  Influencia de los sainetes de don Ramón de la Cruz en las primeras obras

de Benito Pérez Galdós. Minnesota, 1966. *DA*, XXVIII, 2215-A.

53. 33.   Netherton, John P.   The *Novelas españolas contemporáneas* of Pérez Galdós: A Study of Method. Chicago, 1951.

53. 34.   Nimetz, Michael Gerson.   Humor in the *Novelas contemporáneas* of Galdós.   Yale, 1966.   *DA*, XXVII, 2539-A.

53. 35.   Obaid, Antonio Hadad.   El *Quijote* en los *Episodios nacionales* de Pérez Galdós.   Minnesota, 1953. *DA*, XIII, 1186.

53. 36.   Paolini, Gilberto.   An Aspect of Spiritualistic Naturalism in the Novels of B. P. Galdós: Charity. Minnesota, 1965.   *DA*, XXVII, 1832-A.

53. 37.   Pettit, John A.   Las ideas morales en las *Novelas españolas contemporáneas* de Galdós.   Illinois, 1955. *DA*, XV, 827.

53. 38.   Randolph, Edward Dale Appleton.   Pérez Galdós and the European Novel, 1867-1887: A Study of Galdosian Characters and Their European Contemporaries.   Tulane, 1965.   *DA*, XXVII, 484-A.

53. 39.   Regalado, Antonio, Jr.   Benito Pérez Galdós y la novela histórica en España, 1868-1912. Yale, 1965.   *DA*, XXVI, 4638.

53. 40.   Rodríguez, Alfred.   Introduction to the *Episodios nacionales* of Benito Pérez Galdós.   Brown, 1963.   *DA*, XXIV, 3757.

53. 41.   Russell, Robert Hilton.   The *Figura Evangélica* in Three Novels of Pérez Galdós: *Nazarín, Halma*, and *Misericordia*.   Harvard, 1963.

53. 42.   Sackett, Theodore A.   The Crisis in the Novel of Benito Pérez Galdós.   Arizona, 1966.   *DA*, XXVII, 1384-A.

53. 43.   Sáenz y Sáenz, Hilario.   Aspectos de la vida española a través de las obras de don Benito Pérez Galdós.   Illinois, 1931.   Urbana, 1931.   LC 33-33920.

53. 44.   Sáez, Alfred R.   La influencia de la Biblia en las novelas de Galdós.   Northwestern, 1966.   *DA*, XXVII, 2160-A.

53. 45.   Schraibman, Joseph.   Dreams in the Novels of Galdós.   Illinois, 1959.   *DA*, XX, 1795.

53. 46.   Steele, Charles William.   The Literary Expression of Educational Attitudes and Ideas in the Novels of Pérez Galdós.   Ohio State, 1957.   *DA*, XVIII, 2150.

53. 47.   Stout, Elizabeth T.   Women in the Novels of Benito Pérez Galdós.   New Mexico, 1951.

53. 48.   Swett, Douglas B.   A Study of the Carlist Wars as a Literary Theme in the *Episodios nacionales* of Benito Pérez Galdós.   Southern California, 1948. Southern California *Abstracts*, 1948, p. 42.

53. 49.   Sylvia, Esther B.   El primer período de la manera naturalista de Benito Pérez Galdós.   Middlebury, 1946.

53. 50.   Tarr, Frederick Courtney.   Prepositional Complementary Clauses in Spanish, with Special Reference to the Works of Pérez Galdós.   Princeton, 1921. New York-Paris, 1922.   LC 24-14623.

53. 51.   Treat, Jasper W.   Characterization in the Contemporary Novels of Benito Pérez Galdós.   Texas, 1948.

53. 52.   Vázquez-Arjona, Carlos.   Cotejo histórico de cinco *Episodios nacionales* de Galdós.   Johns Hopkins, 1925.   Tours, 1927.   LC 27-14910.

53. 53.   Weber, Robert James.   A Critical Study of the *Miau* Manuscript of Benito Pérez Galdós.   Princeton, 1962.   *DA*, XXIII, 3904.

53. 54.   Zeidner, Betty Jean.   Cervantine Aspects of the Novelistic Art of Benito Pérez Galdós.   California, 1957.   Microfilmed.   See NUC 67-8017.

## 54.   *Poetry, General*

54. 1.   Ramelli, Mattie Mae.   The Polimetria of Spanish Romantic Poets.   Stanford, 1938.   Stanford *Abstracts*, 1938-39, p. 72.

54. 2.   Roberts, Graves B.   The Epithet in Spanish Poetry of the Romantic Period.   Iowa, 1934.   Iowa City, 1936.   LC 36-27994.

## 55.   *Realism*

55. 1.   Browne, James R.   An Aspect of Realism in Modern Spanish Drama: The Concept of Society. Chicago, 1940.   Chicago, 1940.   LC A42-913.

55. 2.   Dannelly, Henry.   Realistic and Naturalistic Elements in Emilia Pardo Bazán's Novels.   Texas, 1932.

55. 3.   Fischbach, Jacob.   Antonio de Trueba: A Study in the Transition from Romanticism to Realism in the Spanish Tales.   Columbia, 1966.   *DA*, XXVII, 1819-A.

55. 4.   Rooney, [Sister] St. Dominic, C.S.J.   Realism in the Original Comedies of Leandro Fernández de Moratín.   Minnesota, 1963.   *DA*, XXIV, 2040.

## 56.   *Rivas, Duque de*

56. 1.   Fitzgerald, Thomas A.   National Feeling in the Narrative Poems of the Duque de Rivas.   Johns Hopkins, 1940.

## 57.   *Rodríguez Rubí, Tomás*

57. 1.   Smith, William Francis.   Tomás Rodríguez Rubí and the Spanish Theatre of the Nineteenth Century. Texas, 1940.

## 58.   *Romanticism*

58. 1.   Adams, Nicholson B.   The Romantic Dramas of García Gutiérrez.   Columbia, 1922.   New York, 1922.   LC 22-14456.

58. 2.   Alfaro, Arsenio.   Francisco Martínez de la Rosa

(1787-1862): A Study in the Transition from Neo-Classicism to Romanticism and Eclecticism in Spanish Literature. Columbia, 1964. *DA,* XXVI, 3293.

58. 3.  Colford, William E.  Juan Meléndez Valdés: A Study in the Transition from Neo-Classicism to Romanticism in Spanish Poetry. Columbia, 1942. New York, 1942. LC 43-6230.

58. 4.  Fischbach, Jacob.  Antonio de Trueba: A Study in the Transition from Romanticism to Realism in the Spanish Tales. Columbia, 1966. *DA,* XXVII, 1819-A.

58. 5.  Jeffers, Coleman R.  Medievalisms in the Writings of the Spanish Romanticists. Iowa. 1954. *DA,* XIV, 1723.

58. 6.  Ramelli, Mattie Mae.  The Polimetria of Spanish Romantic Poets. Stanford, 1938. Stanford *Abstracts,* 1938-39, p. 72.

58. 7.  Randolph, Donald Allen.  Eugenio de Ochoa y el romanticismo español. California, 1963. *DA,* XXIV, 5415.

58. 8.  Reindorp, Reginald C.  Romanticism in the Drama of José Echegaray. Texas, 1949.

58. 9.  Roberts, Graves B.  The Epithet in Spanish Poetry of the Romantic Period. Iowa, 1934. Iowa City, 1936. LC 36-27994.

58. 10.  Salley, William C.  The Attitude of the Spanish Romantic Dramatists Toward History. North Carolina, 1930. North Carolina *Record,* No. 268, p. 66.

58. 11.  Samuels, Daniel G.  Enrique Gil y Carrasco: A Study in Spanish Romanticism. Columbia, 1939. New York, 1939. LC 40-8968.

58. 12.  Sparks, Amy James.  The Honor Code in Representative Spanish Romantic Dramas. Louisiana State, 1964. *DA,* XXV, 1220.

58. 13.  Thompson, John Archie.  Alexandre Dumas (père) and the Spanish Romantic Drama up to 1850. North Carolina, 1937. University [i.e., Baton Rouge], La., 1938. LC 39-2673.

### 59.  *Samaniego, Félix María de*

59. 1.  Burks, Margie Nickelson.  *Fábulas en verso castellano* (1781) por D. Félix María de Samaniego. Books I-II, Critical, Annotated Edition. Illinois, 1929. Urbana, 1933. LC 33-6102.

59. 2.  Niess, Robert Judson.  A Study of the Influence of Jean de la Fontaine on the Works of Félix María de Samaniego. Minnesota, 1937. Minnesota *Summaries,* II, 158.

### 60.  *Serrano, Tomás*

60. 1.  Boyer, Mildred V.  A Critical Edition of Tomás Serrano's *Viaje del Parnaso.* Texas, 1956.

### 61.  *Short Story, General*

61. 1.  Winslow, Richard Walter.  The Contribution of

Pedro Antonio de Alarcón to the Development of the Short Story. Minnesota, 1961. *DA,* XXII, 2802.

### 62.  *Solís, Dionisio* (pseudonym of Dionisio Villanueva y Ochoa)

62. 1.  Ballew, Hal L.  The Life and Works of Dionisio Solís. North Carolina, 1957. North Carolina *Record,* No. 590, p. 264.

### 63.  *Taboada, Luis*

63. 1.  Caliendo, Eugene Louis.  Life and Works of Luis Taboada. Pittsburgh, 1957. *DA,* XVII, 1071.

### 64.  *Tamayo y Baus, Manuel*

64. 1.  Goodell, Blanche E.  Manuel Tamayo y Baus: Sources and Aesthetics. Wisconsin, 1950. Wisconsin *Summaries,* XI, 371.

64. 2.  Tayler, Neale H.  The Influence of the Spanish and Other European Theatres on Tamayo y Baus. Toronto, 1948. *Madrid, 1959. NUC 61-37403.

### 65.  *Theater, General*

65. 1.  Kerson, Pilar Regalado.  Don Leandro Fernández de Moratín y la polémica del teatro de su tiempo. Yale, 1965. *DA,* XXVII, 210-A.

65. 2.  Leslie, John Kenneth.  Trends and Currents in the Spanish Theatre (1820-1865) as Reflected in the Works of Ventura de la Vega. Princeton, 1938. *Princeton, 1940. LC 40-10049.

65. 3.  Lorenz, Charlotte M.  El teatro madrileño, 1808 a 1818. Middlebury, 1932.

65. 4.  Shields, Archibald Kenneth.  The Madrid Stage, 1820-1833. North Carolina, 1933. North Carolina *Record,* No. 286, p. 71.

65. 5.  Smith, William Francis.  Tomás Rodríguez Rubí and the Spanish Theatre of the Nineteenth Century. Texas, 1940.

### 66.  *Torres Villarroel, Diego de*

66. 1.  Hallonquist, Sarina Bono.  Diego de Torres Villarroel, Spanish Eighteenth Century Universal Satirist. New York, 1949. New York, 1949. LC 51-35038.

66. 2.  Schevill, Karl Erwin.  The Moral and Didactic Prose Works of Diego de Torres y Villarroel (1696?-1770). California, 1949.

### 67.  *Trueba, Antonio de*

67. 1.  Fischbach, Jacob.  Antonio de Trueba: A Study in the Transition from Romanticism to Realism in the Spanish Tales. Columbia, 1966. *DA,* XXVII, 1819-A.

### 68.  *Valera, Juan*

68. 1.  Chew, Jeanne Maurer.  The Portrayal of Femi-

nine Life in the Novels of Fernán Caballero, Alarcón, Pereda, and Valera, Viewed Against the Background of Woman's Position in Nineteenth-Century Spain. Pennsylvania State, 1958. *DA,* XIX, 1379.

68. 2. DeCoster, Cyrus C. The Theory and Practice of the Novels of Juan Valera: A Study in Techniques. Chicago, 1951.

68. 3. Fishtine, Edith. Don Juan Valera, the Critic. Bryn Mawr, 1933. Bryn Mawr, Pa., 1933. LC 34-6978.

68. 4. Lott, Robert Eugene. *Siglo de Oro* Tradition and Modern Adolescent Psychology in *Pepita Jiménez*: A Stylistic Study. Catholic, 1958. Washington, 1958. NUC 59-1769.

68. 5. Rundorff, Dorothy Eileen Sutor. D. Juan Valera and Currents of Nineteenth Century Thought Reflected in *Las ilusiones del doctor Faustino*. Minnesota, 1962. *DA,* XXIII, 635.

68. 6. Seamans, Theodore Eugene. An Author-Theme Index to the Works of Juan Valera. California, 1952.

68. 7. Thompson, Frank Reginald. The Classicism of Don Juan Valera. Wisconsin, 1941. Wisconsin *Summaries,* VII, 327.

68. 8. Vorrath, John Charles, Jr. Literary and Social Aspects of Valera's Novels. Yale, 1956. *DA,* XXVIII, 3202-A.

### 69. *Valladares y Saavedra, Ramón de*

69. 1. Amor, Edward. A Formal Analysis of the Melodramas of Ramón de Valladares y Saavedra. Indiana, 1966. *DA,* XXVIII, 220-A.

### 70. *Vega, Ventura de la*

70. 1. Leslie, John Kenneth. Trends and Currents in the Spanish Theatre (1820-1865) as Reflected in the Works of Ventura de la Vega. Princeton, 1938. *Princeton, 1940. LC 40-10049.

### 71. *Zavala y Zamora, Gaspar de*

71. 1. Martin, Frederick C. The Dramatic Works of Gaspar de Zavala y Zamora. North Carolina, 1959. *DA,* XX, 3746.

### 72. *Zorrilla, José*

72. 1. Mansour, George P. The *Don Juan Tenorio, Zarzuela* of Zorrilla: The Progression and Modulation of a Theme. Michigan State, 1965. *DA,* XXVI, 4666.

## VI. LITERATURE OF THE TWENTIETH CENTURY

### 1. *Miscellaneous*

1. 1. Ciplijauskaité, Biruté. Aspectos de la soledad en la poesía española contemporánea. Bryn Mawr, 1960. *Madrid, 1962. NUC 63-3566.

1. 2. Devlin, John J., Jr. Anticlericalism in Spanish Literature, Particularly in the Twentieth Century. Boston University, 1956. Boston University *Abstracts,* 1956, n.p.

1. 3. King, Catherine Doris. *La Voluntad* and *Abulia* in Contemporary Spanish Ideology. Chicago, 1927. Chicago *Abstracts,* V, 415.

1. 4. Lance, Betty Rita Gómez. La actitud picaresca en la novela española del siglo XX. Washington, St. Louis, 1959. *DA,* XX, 2805.

1. 5. Micarelli, Charles Nicholas. Mines and Miners in French and Spanish Literatures of the Nineteenth and Twentieth Centuries. Boston University, 1959. *DA,* XX, 673.

1. 6. Nozick, Martin. The Don Juan Theme in the Twentieth Century. Columbia, 1953. *DA,* XIV, 1417.

1. 7. Wonder, John Paul. Literary and Intellectual Trends in Contemporary Spain. Stanford, 1953. *DA,* XIII, 556.

### 2. *Alberti, Rafael*

2. 1. Marcone, Rose Marie. The Poetic Trajectory of Rafael Alberti. Johns Hopkins, 1964.

2. 2. Marichal, Solita Salinas. "En el principio eran las alas." La primera fase (1924-1929) de la lírica de Rafael Alberti. Bryn Mawr, 1966.

### 3. *Alonso, Dámaso*

3. 1. Kersten, Raquel. Cuatro maestros de la crítica literaria en España: Ramón Menéndez Pidal, Américo Castro, José Fernández Montesinos y Dámaso Alonso. Estudio de sus contribuciones a la *Revista de filología española* desde 1914 hasta 1960. New York, 1964. *DA,* XXVI, 355.

### 4. *Altamira, Rafael*

4. 1. Curtis, Robert Elmer. The Nonhistorical Works of Rafael Altamira. Southern California, 1966. *DA,* XXVII, 2148-A.

### 5. *Alvarez Quintero, Serafín y Joaquín*

5. 1. Mooney, Patricia Ann. Serious Content in the Alvarez Quintero Comedies. Cornell, 1946. Cornell *Abstracts,* 1946, p. 30.

5. 2. Smith, Harriet Louisa. A Critical Study of the Life and Works of the Brothers Serafín and Joaquín Alvarez Quintero. Minnesota, 1946.

### 6.  *Arniches y Barrera, Carlos*

6. 1.  Conis, James Norman.  The Grotesque Tragedies of Carlos Arniches y Barrera.  Virginia, 1965.  *DA,* XXVI, 6035.

### 7.  *Aub, Max*

7. 1.  Ponce de León, Luis Sierra.  Cuatro novelistas de la guerra civil de España (1936-1939).  Stanford, 1966.  *DA,* XXVII, 3467-A.  [Max Aub, Francisco Ayala, Arturo Barea, Ramón Sender.]

### 8.  *Ayala, Francisco*

8. 1.  Ellis, Keith Audley Alexander.  The Narrative Art of Francisco Ayala.  Washington, Seattle, 1962.  *DA,* XXVI, 6038.
8. 2.  Ponce de León, Luis Sierra.  Cuatro novelistas de la guerra civil de España (1936-1939).  Stanford, 1966.  *DA,* XXVII, 3467-A.  [Max Aub, Francisco Ayala, Arturo Barea, Ramón Sender.]

### 9.  *Barea, Arturo*

9. 1.  Ponce de León, Luis Sierra.  Cuatro novelistas de la guerra civil de España (1936-1939).  Stanford, 1966.  *DA,* XXVII, 3467-A.  [Max Aub, Francisco Ayala, Arturo Barea, Ramón Sender.]

### 10.  *Baroja, Pío*

10. 1.  Barrow, Leo.  Negation as a Key to the Novelistic Technique of Pío Baroja.  U.C.L.A., 1961.
10. 2.  Bolinger, Dwight L.  Pío Baroja: A Critique.  Wisconsin, 1936.  Wisconsin *Summaries,* I, 331.
10. 3.  Borenstein, Walter.  Pío Baroja: His Contradictory Philosophy.  Illinois, 1954.  *DA,* XV, 121.
10. 4.  Bowen, Wayne Scott.  Theory and Practice of the Novel in Pío Baroja.  Ohio State, 1958.  *DA,* XIX, 807.
10. 5.  DiBlasi, Daniel.  A Critical Study of the Essays and Other Non-Fiction of Pío Baroja.  Columbia, 1963.  *DA,* XXIV, 3334.
10. 6.  Dismukes, Camillus J.  Les idées dans l' oeuvre du romancier Pío Baroja.  Laval, 1951.
10. 7.  Embeita, María J.  Tema y estilo en Pío Baroja.  Illinois, 1965.  *DA,* XXVI, 1039.
10. 8.  Glascock, Janice Donnell.  The *Héroe Fracasado* in the Novels of Unamuno, Baroja and Azorín.  Louisiana State, 1966.  *DA,* XXVII, 1367-A.
10. 9.  Iglesias, Carmen.  Las ideas de Pío Baroja.  Tulane, 1959.  *DA,* XX, 3743.
10. 10.  Mikulski, Richard Michael.  The Carlist Wars in the Serial Novels of Galdós, Baroja and Valle-Inclán.  Kansas, 1956.
10. 11.  Placer, Eloy L.  Lo vasco en Pío Baroja.  Louisiana State, 1958.  *DA,* XIX, 1745.

10. 12.  Reid, John Turner.  Attitudes Toward Liberalism in the Works of Pío Baroja and Ricardo León.  Stanford, 1936.  Stanford *Abstracts,* 1935-36, p. 77.
10. 13.  Wahl, Rosalie.  The Literary Doctrine of Pío Baroja.  New York, 1959.  *DA,* XX, 3313.
10. 14.  Zimic, Lesley Lee.  The Collective Protagonist in the Historical Novels of Unamuno, Baroja, and Valle-Inclán.  Duke, 1966.  *DA,* XXVII, 1799-A.

### 11.  *Benavente, Jacinto*

11. 1.  Carter, [Sister] Mary R.  The Image of Woman in Selected Plays of Jacinto Benavente.  St. Louis, 1966.  *DA,* XXVI, 4653.
11. 2.  Dash, Anne E.  Un estudio de algunos personajes femeninos en el teatro de Jacinto Benavente y Martínez.  Middlebury, 1963.  See NUC 64-37696.
11. 3.  Dial, John Elbert.  The Dramatic Theories of Benavente: Their Application to Fifty of His Plays.  Missouri, 1966.  *DA,* XXVIII, 672-A.
11. 4.  Molho, Lily S.  The Mother in the Theatre of Jacinto Benavente.  Western Reserve, 1963.  See NUC 65-51311.
11. 5.  Mulvihill, Edward Robert.  Benavente's Dramatic Technique.  Wisconsin, 1942.  Wisconsin *Summaries,* VIII, 217.
11. 6.  Scott, Joseph Reid.  Relativism: The Key to the Dramatic Art of Jacinto Benavente.  California, 1962.  See NUC 63-48709.
11. 7.  Sheehan, Robert Louis.  The Inner Reality in the Dramatic Works of Benavente.  Boston University, 1962.  *DA,* XXIII, 1708.
11. 8.  Tyler, James Austin.  Jacinto Benavente's Plays, 1944-1954.  Indiana, 1966.  *DA,* XXVIII, 218-A.
11. 9.  Woolsey, Arthur W.  The Dramatic Technique of Jacinto Benavente.  Texas, 1945.

### 12.  *Blanco Amor, José*

12. 1.  Vecchio, Frank.  The Theme of Isolation in the Novels of José Blanco Amor.  Washington, Seattle, 1963.  *DA,* XXIV, 4706.

### 13.  *Blasco Ibáñez, Vicente*

13. 1.  Betoret-París, Eduardo.  El costumbrismo regional de Vicente Blasco Ibáñez.  Kansas, 1957.  *Valencia, 1958.  NUC A59-1897.
13. 2.  Curry, Virginia Frances.  Vicente Blasco Ibáñez: Social Reformer and Propagandist.  Indiana, 1956.  *DA,* XVII, 141.
13. 3.  Dalbor, John Bronislaw.  The Short-Stories of Vicente Blasco Ibáñez.  Michigan, 1961.  *DA,* XXII, 2395.
13. 4.  Gilbert, Donald Monroe.  The Personal Accusative in the Works of Blasco Ibáñez.  Wisconsin, 1920.

13.5. Smith, Paul Clarence. Vicente Blasco Ibáñez: A Critical Survey of the Novels from 1894 to 1909. California, 1964. *DA,* XXV, 5943.

13.6. Swain, James O. Vicente Blasco Ibáñez, Exponent of Realism. Illinois, 1932. *Knoxville, Tenn., 1959. NUC 59-15701.

13.7. Vogt, Verne L. Influences of Materialistic Ideas in the Novels of Blasco Ibáñez. Kansas, 1966. *DA,* XXVII, 1841-A.

### 14. *Buero Vallejo, Antonio*

14.1. Halsey, Martha Taliaferro. The Tragedies of Antonio Buero Vallejo. Ohio State, 1964. *DA,* XXV, 5278.

14.2. Machuca-Padín, Arturo H. Three Spanish Plays: A Translation and Adaptation. Denver, 1958. [Plays: *The Mermaid's Tail (La cola de la sirena)* by Conrado Nalé Roxlo; *in Ardent Darkness (En la ardiente obscuridad)* by Antonio Buero Vallejo; *When Five Years Pass (Así que pasen cinco años)* by Federico García Lorca.]

### 15. *Castro, Américo*

15.1. Kersten, Raquel. Cuatro maestros de la crítica literaria en España: Ramón Menéndez Pidal, Américo Castro, José Fernández Montesinos y Dámaso Alonso. Estudio de sus contribuciones a la *Revista de filología española* desde 1914 hasta 1960. New York, 1964. *DA,* XXVI, 355.

### 16. *Cela, Camilo José*

16.1. Foster, David William. Studies on the Contemporary Novel as Experiment: A Technical and Structural Examination of the Novels of Camilo José Cela. Washington, Seattle, 1964. *DA,* XXV, 5275.

16.2. Ilie, Paul. The Novels of Camilo José Cela. Brown, 1959. *DA,* XX, 2291.

16.3. Ortega, José. *La colmena* de Camilo José Cela; Contenido y expresión. Ohio State, 1963. *DA,* XXV, 483.

### 17. *Cernuda, Luis*

17.1. Coleman, John A. The Meditative Poetry of Luis Cernuda. Columbia, 1964. *DA,* XXVIII, 669-A.

17.2. Newman, Robert K. Luis Cernuda: A Neo-Romantic's View of the World. Indiana, 1964. *DA,* XXV, 6632.

17.3. Otero, Carlos Peregrín. La poesía de Luis Cernuda. California, 1960.

17.4. Silver, Philip Warnock. *Et in Arcadia ego*: A Study of the Poetry of Luis Cernuda. Princeton, 1963. *DA,* XXIV, 2042.

### 18. *Costumbrismo*

18.1. Betoret-París, Eduardo. El costumbrismo regional de Vicente Blasco Ibáñez. Kansas, 1957. *Valencia, 1958. NUC A59-1897.

### 19. *D'Ors, Eugenio*

19.1. Sáenz, Pilar González García-Suelto de. Exégesis y crítica de la estética de Eugenio D'Ors. Maryland, 1966. *DA,* XXVIII, 2262-A.

### 20. *Drama, General*

20.1. Boring, Phyllis Z. The Bases of Humor in the Contemporary Spanish Theater. Florida, 1965. *DA,* XXVII, 1812-A.

20.2. Bourne, Marjorie A. Classic Themes in Contemporary Spanish Drama. Indiana, 1961. *DA,* XXII, 1621.

20.3. Browne, James R. An Aspect of Realism in Modern Spanish Drama: The Concept of Society. Chicago, 1940. Chicago, 1941. LC A42-913.

20.4. Jackson, William V. Modern Spanish Drama in the American Theatre, 1901-1951. Harvard, 1952.

20.5. Mueller, [Sister] Grace Marie. The Image of Man in Contemporary Spanish Drama: "Teatro de la Esperanza." Western Reserve, 1962. See NUC 63-44701.

### 21. *Espina, Concha*

21.1. Smith, Charles Wesley. Concha Espina and Her Women Characters. Peabody, 1933. Nashville, Tenn., 1933. LC 34-12873.

### 22. *Essay*

22.1. Rosenthal, William Morris. The Problem of Spain in the Contemporary Spanish Essay. Bryn Mawr, 1966. *DA,* XXVII, 3384-A.

### 23. *Existentialism*

23.1. Chavous, Quentin. The Existential Rhetoric of *Juan de Mairena.* Ohio State, 1966. *DA,* XXVII, 3865-A.

23.2. Winecoff, Janet I. José Ortega y Gasset, Existentialist?: The Major Themes of Existentialism in the Works of José Ortega y Gasset. Duke, 1961. *DA,* XXII, 4357.

### 24. *Felipe, León*

24.1. Elgorriaga, José A. León Felipe: Peculiaridad y sentido de su quehacer poético. U.C.L.A., 1962.

### 25. *Fernández Montesinos, José*

25.1. Kersten, Raquel. Cuatro maestros de la crítica literaria en España: Ramón Menéndez Pidal, Américo Castro, José Fernández Montesinos y Dámaso

Alonso. Estudio de sus contribuciones a la *Revista de filología española* desde 1914 hasta 1960. New York, 1964. *DA,* XXVI, 355.

### 26. *García Lorca, Federico*

26.1. Babín, María T. El mundo poético de Federico García Lorca. Columbia, 1951. *DA,* XII, 58.

26.2. Colecchia, Francesca Maria. The Treatment of Woman in the Theater of Federico García Lorca. Pittsburgh, 1954. *DA,* XIV, 1406.

26.3. Correa, Gustavo. Estudios estilísticos sobre la poesía de Federico García Lorca. Johns Hopkins, 1947.

26.4. Higginbotham, Virginia. The Comic Spirit of Federico García Lorca. Tulane, 1966. *DA,* XXVII, 1368-A.

26.5. Lichtman, Celia Schmukler. Federico García Lorca: A Study in Three Mythologies. New York, 1965. *DA,* XXVII, 777-A.

26.6. Machuca-Padín, Arturo H. Three Spanish Plays: A Translation and Adaptation. Denver, 1958. [Plays: *The Mermaid's Tail (La cola de la sirena)* by Conrado Nalé Roxlo; *In Ardent Darkness (En la ardiente obscuridad)* by Antonio Buero Vallejo; *When Five Years Pass (Así que pasen cinco años)* by Federico García Lorca.]

26.7. Oliver, William Irvin. Spanish Theatre: A Study in Dramatic Discipline. Cornell, 1959. *DA,* XX, 2434. [Vol. 2 contains actable translations of 3 Spanish plays: *The Lady Nit-Wit* by Lope de Vega, *Phaedra* by Miguel de Unamuno, *Blood Wedding* by Federico García Lorca.]

26.8. Sánchez, Roberto Garza. The Theatre of Federico García Lorca. Wisconsin, 1949. Wisconsin *Summaries,* XI, 375. *Madrid, 1950.

26.9. Shamblin, Donald G. Erotic Frustration and Its Causes in the Drama of Federico García Lorca. Minnesota, 1966. *DA,* XXVIII, 2263-A.

### 27. *Generación del '36*

27.1. Lockwood, Alicia María Raffuci de. Cuatro poetas de la "Generación del 36" (Hernández, Serrano Plaja, Rosales y Panero). Wisconsin, 1966. *DA,* XXVIII, 1084-A.

### 28. *Generación del '98*

28.1. Ackerman, Stephen Hamilton. Don Juan in the Generation of '98. Ohio State, 1955. *DA,* XVI, 533.

28.2. Descouzis, Paul Marcel. Don Quijote y la Generación del 98. Maryland, 1959. *DA,* XX, 3290.

28.3. Jaimes-Freyre, Mireya. A Comparison of Modernism and the Generation of '98 with Special Reference to the Works and Theories of Ricardo Jaimes-Freyre. Columbia, 1965.

28.4. Pérez de la Dehesa, Rafael. El pensamiento de Costa y su repercusión en la Generación del 98. Brown, 1963. *DA,* XXIV, 3755.

28.5. Seeleman, Rosa. The Treatment of Landscape in the Novelists of the Generation of 1898. Chicago, 1933. Lancaster, Pa., 1936. LC 36-33155.

### 29. *Gómez de la Serna, Ramón*

29.1. Cardona, Rudolph. Ramón Gómez de la Serna, A Study of His Works and Personality. Washington, Seattle, 1953. *DA,* XIV, 672.

29.2. Jackson, Richard Lawson. The *Greguería* of Ramón Gómez de la Serna: A Study of the Genesis, Composition and Significance of a New Literary Genre. Ohio State, 1963. *DA,* XXIV, 4700.

### 30. *Goytisolo, Juan*

30.1. Larkins, James Edward. Pessimism in the Novels of Juan Goytisolo. Ohio State, 1966. *DA,* XXVII, 3874-A.

### 31. *Grau, Jacinto*

31.1. Fernández, Oscar. Jacinto Grau's Dramatic Technique. Wisconsin, 1953. Wisconsin *Summaries,* XV, 631.

31.2. Giuliano, William Paul. The Life and Works of Jacinto Grau. Michigan, 1950. *MA,* X, No. 4, p. 211.

### 32. *Guillén, Jorge*

32.1. Pleak, Frances Avery. The Poetry of Jorge Guillén. Wisconsin, 1940. Wisconsin *Summaries,* VI, 326.

32.2. Vega, José de Jesús. La afinidad ontológica entre San Juan de la Cruz, Juan Ramón Jiménez, Pedro Salinas y Jorge Guillén. Arizona, 1962. *DA,* XXIV, 782.

### 33. *Hernández, Miguel*

33.1. Lockwood, Alicia Maria Raffuci de. Cuatro poetas de la "Generación del 36" (Hernández, Serrano Plaja, Rosales y Panero). Wisconsin, 1966. *DA,* XXVIII, 1084-A.

### 34. *Hierro, José*

34.1. Rogers, Douglass Marcel. A Study of the Poetry of José Hierro as a Representative Fusion of Major Trends of Contemporary Spanish Poetry. Wisconsin, 1964. *DA,* XXIV, 4198.

### 35. *Jardiel Poncela, Enrique*

35.1. Cebollada Lacosta, Francisco. El humorismo en

las novelas de Enrique Jardiel Poncela. Missouri, 1961. *DA*, XXVII, 1815-A.

35. 2. Hammarstrand, Robert E. The Comic Spirit in the Plays of Enrique Jardiel Poncela. California, 1966. *DA*, XXVII, 2531-A.

### 36. *Jarnés, Benjamín*

36. 1. Fuentes, Víctor Floreal. La obra de Benjamín Jarnés: Un estudio de su novelística y de su estética. New York, 1965. *DA*, XXVI, 1612.

### 37. *Jiménez, Juan Ramón*

37. 1. Johnson, Jerry Lee. Juan Ramón Jiménez, the Critic. Virginia, 1966. *DA*, XXVIII, 1051-A.

37. 2. Johnson, Karen Elizabeth. Juan Ramón Jiménez. Yale, 1958.

37. 3. Kemmerer, Caroline Reinero. The Creative Process of Juan Ramón Jiménez. Bryn Mawr, 1962. *DA*, XXIII, 4359.

37. 4. Nemes, Graciela (Palau). Juan Ramón Jiménez, su vida y su obra. Maryland, 1952. *Madrid, 1957. NUC A58-66.

37. 5. Predmore, Michael Pennock. The Prose of Juan Ramón Jiménez. Wisconsin, 1965. *DA*, XXV, 5939.

37. 6. Salgado, María Antonia. *Españoles de tres mundos*: el arte polifacético de las "caricaturas líricas" de Juan Ramón Jiménez. Maryland, 1966. *DA*, XXVII, 3879-A.

37. 7. Saz-Orozco, Carlos del, S.J. Desarrollo del concepto de Dios en el pensamiento religioso de Juan Ramón Jiménez. Stanford, 1962. *DA*, XXIII, 4763.

37. 8. Ulibarrí, Sabine. Inner Logic in the Poetry of Juan Ramón Jiménez. U.C.L.A., 1959. *Madrid, 1962. NUC 63-61331.

37. 9. Vega, José de Jesús. La afinidad ontológica entre San Juan de la Cruz, Juan Ramón Jiménez, Pedro Salinas y Jorge Guillén. Arizona, 1962. *DA*, XXIV, 782.

### 38. *León, Ricardo*

38. 1. O'Connor, [Sister] Mary Lucilda, B.V.M. The Romanticism of Ricardo León. Minnesota, 1961. *DA*, XXII, 4018.

38. 2. Reid, John Turner. Attitudes Toward Liberalism in the Works of Pío Baroja and Ricardo León. Stanford, 1936. Stanford *Abstracts*, 1935-36, p. 77.

38. 3. Williams, Gladys Louise. The Persistence of Spanish Tradition in the Works of Eduardo Marquina, Ricardo León, and Gregorio Martínez Sierra. Stanford, 1927. Stanford *Abstracts*, 1927-28, p. 82.

### 39. *Linares Rivas, Manuel*

39. 1. Hatcher, Paul Gilliam. The Ideas and Opinions of Manuel Linares Rivas. Michigan, 1956. *DA*, XVI, 2458.

### 40. *López Rubio, José*

40. 1. Holt, Marion P. The Theater of José López Rubio. Illinois, 1964. *DA*, XXV, 4148.

### 41. *Machado, Antonio*

41. 1. Allen, Rupert. Structure in the Poetry of Antonio Machado. California, 1960.

41. 2. Barnstone, Willis Robert. Antonio Machado: The Lyrical Speaker in the Poems and the Forces That Create His Character. Yale, 1960.

41. 3. Chavous, Quentin. The Existential Rhetoric of *Juan de Mairena*. Ohio State, 1966. *DA*, XXVII, 3865-A.

41. 4. Guerra, Manuel Henry. The Theatre of Manuel and Antonio Machado. Michigan, 1957. *DA*, XVIII, 1430.

41. 5. Hutman, Norma Louise. Nature as an Expression of Temporality in the Poetry of Antonio Machado. Pittsburgh, 1961. *DA*, XXII, 3664.

41. 6. Newberry, Wilma Jean. The Dramatic Technique of Manuel and Antonio Machado. Washington, Seattle, 1960. *DA*, XXI, 2296.

41. 7. Predmore, Richard L. La visión de Castilla de Antonio Machado estudiada en sus obras poéticas. Middlebury, 1941.

41. 8. Sheets, Jane Millicent. Landscape in the Poetry of R. M. Rilke and A. Machado. Indiana, 1965. *DA*, XXVI, 6725.

41. 9. Zubiría, Ramón Eduardo de. La poesía de Antonio Machado. Johns Hopkins, 1953. Madrid, 1955. NUC A55-10769.

### 42. *Machado, Manuel*

42. 1. Guerra, Manuel Henry. The Theater of Manuel and Antonio Machado. Michigan, 1957. *DA*, XVIII, 1430.

42. 2. Newberry, Wilma Jean. The Dramatic Technique of Manuel and Antonio Machado. Washington, Seattle, 1960. *DA*, XXI, 2296.

### 43. *Maeztu, Ramiro de*

43. 1. Martínez, Rafael V. La conversión de Ramiro de Maeztu. Northwestern, 1964. *DA*, XXV, 3577.

### 44. *Maragall, Joan*

44. 1. Casas, Rogelio A. Joan Maragall: Catalonian Poet (1860-1911). Columbia, 1954. *DA*, XIV, 1218.

### 45. *Marañón, Gregorio*

45. 1. Hoddie, James Henry. Gregorio Marañón: Historian and Man of Letters. Brown, 1965. *DA*, XXVI, 3339.

### 46. *Marquina, Eduardo*

46. 1. Williams, Gladys Louise. The Persistence of

Spanish Tradition in the Works of Eduardo Marquina, Ricardo León, and Gregorio Martínez Sierra. Stanford, 1927. Stanford *Abstracts,* 1927-1928, p. 82.

### 47. *Martínez Ruiz, José, "Azorín"*

47. 1. Abbott, James H. Azorín and France. U.C.L.A., 1958.

47. 2. Allen, Alma Coppedge. Surrealism and the Prose Fiction of José Martínez Ruiz (Azorín). Boston University, 1960. *DA,* XXI, 887.

47. 3. Fox, Edward Inman. Azorín as a Literary Critic. Princeton, 1960. New York, 1962. NUC 62-6487.

47. 4. Glascock, Janice Donnell. The *Héroe Fracasado* in the Novels of Unamuno, Baroja and Azorín. Louisiana State, 1966. *DA,* XXVII, 1367-A.

47. 5. LaJohn, Lawrence Anthony. Azorín, Dramatist. Indiana, 1958. *DA,* XIX, 1385.

47. 6. Madariaga, Pilar de. Las novelas de Azorín: Estudio de sus temas y de su técnica. Middlebury, 1949.

47. 7. Martin, Charles Edward. Ideas in the Works of Azorín. Tulane, 1965. *DA,* XXVI, 2219.

47. 8. Rand, Marguerite C. The Vision of Castile in the Works of Azorín. Chicago, 1951. *Madrid, 1956. NUC A57-2266.

47. 9. Servodidio, Mirella d'Ambrosio. Azorín as a Short Story Writer. Columbia, 1965. *DA,* XXVI, 4676.

### 48. *Martínez Sierra, Gregorio*

48. 1. Mercer, Lucille Elizabeth. Martínez Sierra's Conception of Woman's Role in Modern Society. Ohio State, 1940. Ohio State *Abstracts,* No. 34, p. 415.

48. 2. O'Connor, Patricia Walker. Women in the Theatre of Gregorio Martínez Sierra. Florida, 1962. *DA,* XXIII, 3899.

48. 3. Williams, Gladys Louise. The Persistence of Spanish Tradition in the Works of Eduardo Marquina, Ricardo León, and Gregorio Martínez Sierra. Stanford, 1927. Stanford *Abstracts,* 1927-28, p. 82.

### 49. *Matute, Ana María*

49. 1. Weitzner, Margaret Elizabeth. The Novelistic World of Ana María Matute: A Pessimistic Vision of Life. Wisconsin, 1963. *DA,* XXIV, 2491.

### 50. *Menéndez Pidal, Ramón*

50. 1. Kersten, Raquel. Cuatro maestros de la crítica literaria en España: Ramón Menéndez Pidal, Américo Castro, José Fernández Montesinos y Dámaso Alonso. Estudio de sus contribuciones a la *Revista de filología española* desde 1914 hasta 1960. New York, 1964. *DA,* XXVI, 355.

### 51. *Mesa, Enrique de*

51. 1. Rivas, Enrique Manuel de. La obra de Enrique de Mesa. California, 1956.

### 52. *Miró, Gabriel*

52. 1. Becker, Alfred Werner. Man and His Circumstance in the Works of Gabriel Miró. Maryland, 1954. *Madrid, 1958. NUC A60-4971.

52. 2. Parr, Marcus. Gabriel Miró: *The Years and the Leagues*: [Translated by the Author], With an Introductory Study, "Vocabulary of Gabriel Miró: Nature and Sources." Utah, 1958. *DA,* XIX, 3307.

52. 3. Schwartz, Henry Charles. Gabriel Miró (1879-1930): A Thematic Analysis of the Secular Works. Michigan, 1954. *DA,* XIV, 1220.

### 53. *Modernismo*

53. 1. Garcia-Girón, Edmundo. The Adjective: A Contribution to the Study of Modernist Poetic Diction. California, 1952.

53. 2. Jaimes-Freyre, Mireya. A Comparison of Modernism and the Generation of '98 with Special Reference to the Works and Theories of Ricardo Jaimes-Freyre. Columbia, 1965.

53. 3. Michel, Joseph. Modernismo y ultraísmo en la obra de Valle-Inclán. New Mexico, 1961. *DA,* XXII, 3668.

53. 4. Torres-Ríoseco, Arturo. Rubén Darío and the *Modernista* Movement in Spanish America and Spain. Minnesota, 1931. *Cambridge, Mass.-London, 1931. LC 32-32410.

### 54. *Nácher, Enrique*

54. 1. Small, Aaron P. Enrique Nácher's *Bed 36:* A Translation. Denver, 1955.

### 55. *Novel, General*

55. 1. Benson, Frederick R. Writers in Arms: A Comparative Study of the Impact of the Spanish Civil War on the Liberal Novelist. New York, 1966. *DA,* XXVII, 1050-A.

55. 2. Bernstein, Jerome Straus. Theories of the Modern Novel in Spain. Harvard, 1964. Microfilmed. See NUC 68-35303.

55. 3. Dendle, Brian J. The Novel of Religious Thesis in Spain, 1875-1936. Princeton, 1966. *DA,* XXVII, 1053.

55. 4. Ferguson, Albert Gordon. Spain Through Her Novel (1940-1960): A Study of Changes in Mores and Attitudes as Reflected in the Contemporary Novel. Nebraska, 1963. *DA,* XXIV, 1615.

55. 5. Fletcher, Madeleine de Gororza. The Spanish Historical Novel (1870-1965). Harvard, 1966. See NUC 67-83353.

55. 6. Lance, Betty Rita Gómez. La actitud picaresca

en la novela española del siglo XX. Washington, St. Louis, 1959. *DA, XX,* 2805.

55. 7.  Lo Ré, Anthony George. The Novel of the Spanish Civil War 1936-1960. North Carolina, 1965. *DA, XXVI,* 3957.

55. 8.  Ponce de León, Luis Sierra. Cuatro novelistas de la guerra civil de España (1936-1939). Stanford, 1966. *DA, XXVII,* 3467-A. [Max Aub, Francisco Ayala, Arturo Barea, Ramón Sender.]

55. 9.  Rust, John B. La novela contemporánea en España (1939-1954). Middlebury, 1955.

55. 10.  Savaiano, Eugene. A Study of the Clergymen in Selected Modern Spanish Novels. Chicago, 1948. *Wichita, 1952. NUC 53-146.

### 56.  *Ortega y Gasset, José*

56. 1.  Baker, Clifford Henry. Reality in the Works of Unamuno and Ortega y Gasset: A Comparative Study. Southern California, 1961. *DA, XXII,* 3226.

56. 2.  Corrigan, Robert. The Pedagogical and Cultural Ideas of Ortega y Gasset. Western Reserve, 1959.

56. 3.  DePuy, Ida Blanche. The Basic Ideology of José Ortega y Gasset: The Conflict of Mission and Vocation. Stanford, 1961. *DA, XXII,* 572.

56. 4.  Duffy, [Sister] Mary Terese Avila, B.V.M. José Ortega y Gasset: The Creation of a Literary Genre for Philosophy. Wisconsin, 1966. *DA, XXVIII,* 674-A.

56. 5.  Livingstone, Leon. José Ortega y Gasset: The Philosophy of Art. Brown, 1947. *Photocopy, Yale Univ. Library, 1965. NUC 66-34964.

56. 6.  Mazlish, Constance Shaw. Ortega and Spain. Columbia, 1957. *DA, XVII,* 1766.

56. 7.  Prescott, Edward Kerrigan. Art and Reality in the Aesthetic Theory of Ortega y Gasset. California, 1965. *DA, XXVII,* 780-A.

56. 8.  Raley, Harold C. José Ortega y Gasset: The Philosophy of European Unity. Alabama, 1966. *DA, XXVII,* 1382-A.

56. 9.  Sesplugues, Juan. La filosofía social de José Ortega y Gasset. Columbia, 1950. *MA,* XI, No. 1, p. 132.

56. 10.  Winecoff, Janet I. José Ortega y Gasset, Existentialist?: The Major Themes of Existentialism in the Works of José Ortega y Gasset. Duke, 1961. *DA, XXII,* 4357.

*Ortega Munilla, José* (See V, Ortega Munilla)
*Palacio Valdés, Armando* (See V, Palacio Valdés)

### 57.  *Panero, Leopoldo*

57. 1.  Lockwood, Alicia María Raffuci de. Cuatro poetas de la "Generación del 36" (Hernández, Serrano Plaja, Rosales y Panero). Wisconsin, 1966. *DA, XXVIII,* 1084-A.

### 58.  *Pérez de Ayala, Ramón*

58. 1.  Bancroft, Robert L. Ramón Pérez de Ayala: A Critical Study of His Works. Columbia, 1957. *DA, XVII,* 1759.

58. 2.  Campbell, Brenton Kay. The Literary Theories of Ramón Pérez de Ayala. California, 1961. Microfilmed, California Library, 1964. NUC 65-20642.

58. 3.  Campbell, Ruth F. Ayala's Vision of Spain. Duke, 1958. *DA, XIX,* 1377.

58. 4.  Dobrian, Walter Anton. The Novelistic Art of Ramón Pérez de Ayala. Wisconsin, 1960. *DA, XXI,* 1563.

58. 5.  Fabian, Donald L. A Critical Analysis of the Novels of Ramón Pérez de Ayala. Chicago, 1950.

58. 6.  Mangold, Frederick Rogers. Ramón Pérez de Ayala: A Critical Study Through His Prose Works. Wisconsin, 1934.

58. 7.  McCall, Mary-Berenice M. An Analysis of Ramón Pérez de Ayala's Novels as a Plea for Freedom. Bryn Mawr, 1959. *DA, XX,* 3747.

58. 8.  Weber, Frances Louise Wyers. The Narrative Perspectivism of Ramón Pérez de Ayala. Michigan, 1962. *DA, XXIII,* 1025.

### 59.  *Poetry, General*

59. 1.  Ciplijauskaité, Biruté. Aspectos de la soledad en la poesía española contemporánea. Bryn Mawr, 1960. *Madrid, 1962. NUC 63-3566.

59. 2.  Harter, Hugh Anthony. Gustavo Adolfo Bécquer's Significance for Twentieth-Century Spanish Poetry. Ohio State, 1958. *DA, XIX,* 811.

### 60.  *Ramón y Cajal, Santiago*

60. 1.  Tzitsikas, Helene. Las obras literarias de Santiago Ramón y Cajal: El tema de la voluntad. Northwestern, 1963. *DA, XXIV,* 3734.

### 61.  *Realism*

61. 1.  Browne, James R. An Aspect of Realism in Modern Spanish Drama: The Concept of Society. Chicago, 1940. Chicago, 1941. LC A42-913.

61. 2.  Swain, James O. Vicente Blasco Ibáñez, Exponent of Realism. Illinois, 1932. *Knoxville, Tenn., 1959. NUC 59-15701.

### 62.  *Rodríguez Alvarez, Alejandro, "Alejandro Casona"*

62. 1.  Leighton, Charles Henry. Alejandro Casona and the New Theater in Spain. Harvard, 1961.

62. 2.  Moon, Harold K. Fantasy and Humor in the Theater of Alejandro Casona. Syracuse, 1963. *DA, XXIV,* 5414.

62. 3.  Park, John Horace. Fry and Casona: A Comparison. Indiana, 1960. *DA, XXI,* 3459.

### 63. *Romanticism*

63.1. O'Connor, [Sister] Mary Lucilda, B.V.M. The Romanticism of Ricardo León. Minnesota, 1961. *DA*, XXII, 4018.

### 64. *Rosales, Luis*

64.1. Lockwood, Alicia María Raffuci. de. Cuatro poetas de la "Generación del 36" (Hernández, Serrano Plaja, Rosales y Panero). Wisconsin, 1966. *DA*, XXVIII, 1084-A.

### 65. *Salaverría, José María*

65.1. Petriz, Beatrice. José María Salaverría: A Biographical and Critical Introduction. U.C.L.A., 1956. *Madrid, 1960. NUC A61-5510.

### 66. *Salinas, Pedro*

66.1. Morello, Martha Eugenia. La realidad poética de Salinas, estudio de una constante temática. Ohio State, 1957. *DA*, XVIII, 1048.

66.2. Palley, Julian Irving. The Idea of Nothingness in the Poetry of Pedro Salinas. New Mexico, 1958. *DA*, XIX, 2957.

66.3. Vega, José de Jesús. La afinidad ontológica entre San Juan de la Cruz, Juan Ramón Jiménez, Pedro Salinas y Jorge Guillén. Arizona, 1962. *DA*, XXIV, 782.

### 67. *Sender, Ramón*

67.1. Jassey, William. A Handbook for Teaching Spanish Civilization Through Ramón Sender's *Requiem por un campesino español* as Selected Literature in the First Term of Fourth-Year Spanish in High School. Columbia, 1962. *DA*, XXIII, 1703.

67.2. King, Charles L. An Exposition of the Synthetic Philosophy of Ramón J. Sender. Southern California, 1953. Southern California *Abstracts*, 1953, p. 57.

67.3. Olstad, Charles Frederick. The Novels of Ramón Sender: Moral Concepts in Development. Wisconsin, 1960. *DA*, XXI, 1570.

67.4. Ponce de León, Luis Sierra. Cuatro novelistas de la guerra civil de España (1936-1939). Stanford, 1966. *DA*, XXVII, 3467-A. [Max Aub, Francisco Ayala, Arturo Barea, Ramón Sender.]

### 68. *Serrano Plaja, Arturo*

68.1. Lockwood, Alicia María Raffuci de. Cuatro poetas de la "Generación del 36" (Hernández, Serrano Plaja, Rosales y Panero). Wisconsin, 1966. *DA*, XXVIII, 1084-A.

### 69. *Surrealism*

69.1. Allen, Alma Coppedge. Surrealism and the Prose Fiction of José Martínez Ruiz (Azorín). Boston University, 1960. *DA*, XXI, 887.

### 70. *Theater, General*

70.1. Holcomb, George Lawrence. The Theater in Spain Since 1939. Texas, 1958. *DA*, XIX, 2406.

70.2. Leighton, Charles Henry. Alejandro Casona and the New Theater in Spain. Harvard, 1961.

70.3. Macías, Manuel Jato. Repertorio de los teatros de Madrid, 1900-1905. Northwestern, 1963. *DA*, XXV, 480.

### 71. *Trigo, Felipe*

71.1. Watkins, Alma T. Eroticism in the Novels of Felipe Trigo. Cornell, 1949. New York, 1954. NUC 54-8091.

### 72. *Ultraísmo*

72.1. Michel, Joseph. Modernismo y ultraísmo en la obra de Valle-Inclán. New Mexico, 1961. *DA*, XXII, 3668.

### 73. *Unamuno, Miguel de*

73.1. Baker, Clifford Henry. Reality in the Works of Unamuno and Ortega y Gasset: A Comparative Study. Southern California, 1961. *DA*, XXII, 3226.

73.2. Basdekis, Demetrios. Unamuno and Spanish Literature. Columbia, 1965. *DA*, XXVI, 3324. Berkeley, 1967. NUC 68-63733.

73.3. Busch, Carolyn Lipshy. Women in the Novels of Unamuno. Maryland, 1965. *DA*, XXVI, 6709.

73.4. Cannon, William C. Miguel de Unamuno's "El Cristo de Velázquez." Tulane, 1958. *DA*, XIX, 2946.

73.5. D'Entremont, Elaine Mary. The *Hogar* as *Intrahistoria* in Unamuno's Life, Thought and Style. Tulane, 1965. *DA*, XXVII, 474-A.

73.6. Earle, Peter G. Unamuno and English Literature. Kansas, 1958. New York, 1960. See NUC, 1958-62, vol. 13, p. 90.

73.7. Fasel, Oscar A. Unamuno's Thought and German Philosophy. Columbia, 1957. *DA*, XVII, 1336.

73.8. Garofalo, Silvano Benito. The Poetry of Giacomo Leopardi and Miguel de Unamuno. Minnesota, 1966. *DA*, XXVII, 2528-A.

73.9. Glascock, Janice Donnell. The *Héroe Fracasado* in the Novels of Unamuno, Baroja and Azorín. Louisiana State, 1966. *DA*, XXVII, 1367-A.

73.10. Gleaves, Edwin Sheffield, Jr. The Spanish Influence of Ernest Hemingway's Concepts of Death, *Nada,* and Immortality. Emory, 1964. *DA*, XXV, 2511. [Unamuno.]

73.11. Joyce, Kathleen Mary. Don Miguel de Unamuno, Poet of Conflict. Wisconsin, 1943. Wisconsin *Summaries*, VIII, 215.

73. 12. Kirby, Kenneth N. Unamuno and Language. Texas, 1953.

73. 13. Luby, Barry Jay. Unamuno in the Light of Contemporary Logical Empiricism. New York, 1966. *DA*, XXIX, 266-A.

73. 14. Metzidakis, Philip. Unamuno e Hispanoamérica. Yale, 1959.

73. 15. Moloney, Raymond L. Unamuno, Creator and Recreator of Books. Colorado, 1954. Colorado *Abstracts*, 1954, p. 94.

73. 16. Oliver, William Irvin. Spanish Theatre: A Study in Dramatic Discipline. Cornell, 1959. *DA*, XX, 2434. [Vol. 2 contains actable translations of 3 Spanish plays: *The Lady Nit-Wit* by Lope de Vega, *Phaedra* by Miguel de Unamuno, *Blood Wedding* by Federico García Lorca.]

73. 17. Paucker, Eleanor Krane. The Short Stories of Unamuno as a Key to His Work. Pennsylvania, 1963. *DA*, XXIII, 3900.

73. 18. Pepperdine, Warren Howard. On *Lucha por la Vida*, the Struggle for Life in Three Plays by Miguel de Unamuno. Minnesota, 1965. *DA*, XXVI, 6238.

73. 19. Romera-Navarro, Miguel. Miguel de Unamuno: novelista, poeta, ensayista. Pennsylvania, 1927. Madrid, 1928. LC 29-3731.

73. 20. Spurlock, Judith C. The Will-to-Be as a Theme in the Novels of Unamuno. Florida, 1966. *DA*, XXVIII, 1829-A.

73. 21. Valdés, Mario J. Death in the Literature of Unamuno. Illinois, 1962. *DA*, XXIII, 2918.

73. 22. Zernickow, Oskar Hans. The *Cancionero* of Unamuno: A Thematic Study. Tulane, 1966. *DA*, XXVII, 3475-A.

73. 23. Zimic, Lesley Lee. The Collective Protagonist in the Historical Novels of Unamuno, Baroja, and Valle-Inclán. Duke, 1966. *DA*, XXVII, 1799-A.

### 74. *Valle-Inclán, Ramón María del*

74. 1. Borelli, Catherine Marshall. Valle-Inclán as Poet (Volumes I and II). Ohio State, 1954. *DA*, XV, 1067.

74. 2. Boudreau, Harold Laverne. Materials Toward an Analysis of Valle-Inclán's *Ruedo ibérico*. Wisconsin, 1966. *DA*, XXVIII, 666-A.

74. 3. Ely, Barbara Fay. The Problem of Spain, as Interpreted in the Works of Don Ramón del Valle-Inclán. Tulane, 1962. *DA*, XXIII, 4355.

74. 4. Greenfield, Sumner Melvin. The Stylistic Development of Valle-Inclán in his *Obras dialogadas*. Harvard, 1957.

74. 5. Lado, María Dolores. España en la obra de Ramón del Valle-Inclán. Florida, 1962. *DA*, XXIX, 902-A.

74. 6. Michel, Joseph. Modernismo y ultraísmo en la obra de Valle-Inclán. New Mexico, 1961. *DA*, XXII, 3668.

74. 7. Mikulski, Richard Michael. The Carlist Wars in the Serial Novels of Galdós, Baroja and Valle-Inclán. Kansas, 1956.

74. 8. Ramírez, Manuel D. A Study of the Style and Vocabulary of the Prose Fiction of Valle-Inclán. North Carolina, 1959. *DA*, XX, 3751.

74. 9. Zimic, Lesley Lee. The Collective Protagonist in the Historical Novels of Unamuno, Baroja, and Valle-Inclán. Duke, 1966. *DA*, XXVII, 1799-A.

### VII. LITERATURE OF SPANISH AMERICA

#### 1. *Bibliography*

1. 1. Ciruti, Joan Estelle. The Guatemalan Novel: A Critical Bibliography. Tulane, 1959. *DA*, XX, 1782.

1. 2. Collins, Pauline P. Bryson. Bibliographers of the Colonial Period in Spanish America. North Carolina, 1955. North Carolina *Record*, No. 562, p. 236.

1. 3. Head, Karolena Barbara. A Bibliography of the Spanish-American Literature in the Collection of Peruvian Serials in the Library of Yale University. Yale, 1939.

1. 4. Kirk, William Wright. The First Literary Periodicals of the Republic of Panama. Illinois, 1955. *DA*, XVI, 121.

1. 5. McNerney, Robert Francis, Jr. A Bibliography of the Venezuelan Literature in the Yale University Library. Yale, 1937.

1. 6. Zimmerman, Irene. Latin American Periodicals of the Mid-Twentieth Century as Source Material for Research in the Humanities and the Social Sciences. Michigan, 1956. *DA*, XVII, 3027.

General Literary Studies by Countries

#### 2. *Argentina*

2. 1. Apstein, Theodore. The Contemporary Argentine Theatre. Texas, 1945.

2. 2. Barcia, Primero. The Argentine Novel of Artistic Design. Southern California, 1951. Southern California *Abstracts*, 1951, p. 89.

2. 3. Carter, Erwin Dale. Magical Realism in Contemporary Argentine Fiction. Southern California, 1966. *DA*, XXVII, 1361-A.

2. 4. Espinosa, José Edmundo. Americanism in Argentine Literature. A Commentary on Critical Opinion. Cornell, 1934. Ithaca, 1934. LC 34-37272.

2. 5. Gibbs, Beverly Jean. A Study of Five Contem-

porary Psychological Novels of Argentina. Wisconsin, 1960. *DA*, XXI, 622.

2.6. Glaser, Edward. Los argentinos vistos por sí mismos. Harvard, 1951.

2.7. Jaén, Didier T. Hispanoamérica como problema a través de la generación romántica en Argentina y Chile. Texas, 1965. *DA*, XXVI, 2215.

2.8. Karnis, Michael V. Social Issues in Argentine Drama Since 1900. Northwestern, 1953. *DA*, XIV, 205.

2.9. King, Harry Lee, Jr. Juan Manuel de Rosas and His Epoch as Portrayed in Argentine Fiction. North Carolina, 1961. *DA*, XXII, 3665.

2.10. Lichtblau, Myron. The Argentine Novel in the Nineteenth Century. Columbia, 1957. *DA*, XVII, 1555.

2.11. Percas, Helena. Women Poets of Argentina (1810-1950). Columbia, 1951. *DA*, XII, 70.

2.12. Polt, John Herman Richard. Eduardo Mallea and the Contemporary Argentine Novel. California, 1956. *Berkeley, 1959. NUC A60-9001.

2.13. Reid, Joseph A. Naturalistic Influences in the Argentine Novel. Michigan, 1946.

2.14. Richardson, Ruth. Florencio Sánchez and the Argentine Theatre. Columbia, 1933. New York, 1933. LC 33-33303.

2.15. Yates, Donald Alfred. The Argentine Detective Story. Michigan, 1961. *DA*, XXII, 578.

### 3. *Bolivia*

3.1. Arana, Oswaldo. La novela de la guerra del Chaco: Bolivia y Paraguay. Colorado, 1963. *DA*, XXIV, 3743.

3.2. MacLeod, Murdo John. Bolivia and Its Social Literature Before and After the Chaco War: A Historical Study of Social and Literary Revolution. Florida, 1962. See NUC 65-29138.

3.3. Ulibarrí, George S. The *Gamonal* in Selected Contemporary Novels of Social Protest in Peru, Bolivia, and Ecuador. Iowa, 1952. Iowa *Abstracts*, X, 217.

### 4. *Chile*

4.1. Alegría, Raúl F. La poesía chilena: Investigación de sus orígenes y desarrollo desde el siglo XVI al siglo XIX. California, 1947. Berkeley, 1954. NUC 54-1229.

4.2. Campbell, Margaret V. Antecedents to the Literary Movement of 1842 in Chile. North Carolina, 1946. North Carolina *Record*, No. 464, p. 357.

4.3. Chapman, George Arnold. Social Types in the Chilean City Novel, 1900-1943. Wisconsin, 1946. Wisconsin *Summaries*, IX, 517.

4.4. Chinchón, Osvaldo. The Sea as a Motif in the Fictional Literature of Chile. Virginia, 1966. *DA*, XXVII, 2495-A.

4.5. Crowley, Cornelius. Costumbrism in Chilean Literary Prose of the Nineteenth Century. California, 1943.

4.6. Dyson, John P. La evolución de la crítica literaria en Chile. Kansas, 1965. *DA*, XXVI, 3332.

4.7. Holton, James Stafford. The Evolution of Attitudes Toward the Social Classes in the Chilean Novel. California, 1958. Microfilm copy. See NUC 67-32584.

4.8. Inostroza, Raúl Armando. El ensayo en Chile desde la colonia hasta 1900. Stanford, 1966. *DA*, XXVII, 3458-A.

4.9. Jaén, Didier T. Hispanoamérica como problema a través de la generación romántica en Argentina y Chile. Texas, 1965. *DA*, XXVI, 2215.

4.10. Ramírez, Adolf. The Chilean Novel of Social Protest. Wisconsin, 1956. *DA*, XVI, 1907.

4.11. Sand, Louise. The Role of Federico Hanssen and Rodolfo Lenz in the Intellectual Life of Chile. North Carolina, 1958. *DA*, XIX, 1391.

4.12. Urbistondo, Vicente. Manifestaciones naturalistas en la novela chilena: D'Halmar, Orrego Luco, y Edwards Bello. California, 1964. *DA*, XXV, 5287.

### 5. *Colombia*

5.1. Duffey, Frank M. The *Cuadro de Costumbres* in Colombia (1838-1880). North Carolina, 1950. North Carolina *Record*, No. 492, p. 265.

5.2. Keller, Jean P. The Indian in the Literature of Colombia. Washington, Seattle, 1949.

5.3. McGrady, Donald Lee. La novela histórica en Colombia, 1844-1959. Indiana, 1961. *DA*, XXII, 1628.

### 6. *Costa Rica*

6.1. Allison, Mary C. A Survey of the Literature and Culture of Costa Rica. Washington, Seattle, 1953.

6.2. Méndez, Margarita Castro de. El costumbrismo en Costa Rica. Columbia, 1964. *DA*, XXVIII, 624-A.

6.3. Solera, Rodrigo. La novela costarricense. Kansas, 1964. *DA*, XXVI, 376.

### 7. *Cuba*

7.1. Arrom, José Juan. Bosquejo histórico del teatro en Cuba (Desde sus orígenes hasta 1868). Yale, 1941. *New Haven-London, 1944. LC A44-1255.

7.2. Boydston, Jo Ann H. The Cuban Novel; A Study of Its Range and Characteristics. Columbia, 1950. *MA*, XI, No. 2, p. 341.

7.3. Lax, Judith H. Themes and Techniques in the

Socially Oriented Cuban Novel, 1933-1952. Syracuse, 1961. *DA,* XXII, 4350.

7.4.   Olivera, Otto H.  Lo nacional en la poesía cubana (1511-1898). Tulane, 1953. Tulane *Abstracts,* Series 54, No. 13, p. 102.

7.5.   Ripoll, Carlos.  La *Revista de avance* (1927-1930): Episodio de la literatura cubana.  New York, 1964. *DA,* XXVI, 373.

### 8.  *Ecuador*

8.1.   Allison, Wayne L.  A Thematic Analysis of the Contemporary Ecuadorian Novel.  New Mexico, 1965.  *DA,* XXV, 6612.

8.2.   Da Silva, Zenia Sachs.  The Contemporary Ecuadorian Novel.  New York, 1955.  *DA,* XV, 2531.

8.3.   Schwartz, Kessel.  The Contemporary Novel of Ecuador.  Columbia, 1953.  *DA,* XIV, 132.

8.4.   Siegel, Reuben.  The Group of Guayaquil: A Study in Contemporary Ecuadorian Fiction.  Wisconsin, 1951.  Wisconsin *Summaries,* XII, 465.

8.5.   Smither, William J.  The Regional and Social Aspects of the Contemporary Ecuadorian Novel (1920-1950).  Tulane, 1952.  Tulane *Abstracts,* Series 53, No. 14, p. 87.

8.6.   Ulibarrí, George S.  The *Gamonal* in Selected Contemporary Novels of Social Protest in Peru, Bolivia, and Ecuador.  Iowa, 1952.  Iowa *Abstracts,* X, 217.

### 9.  *Guatemala*

9.1.   Ciruti, Joan Estelle.  The Guatemalan Novel: A Critical Bibliography.  Tulane, 1959.  *DA,* XX, 1782.

9.2.   Erickson, Martin Elmer.  Guatemalan Literature of the Last Fifty Years.  Washington, Seattle, 1941. Washington *Abstracts,* VII, 225.

9.3.   Lorand de Olazagasti, Adelaida.  El indio en la narrativa guatemalteca.  Puerto Rico, 1966.

9.4.   Nichols, Grace L.  National Elements in the Poetry of Guatemala.  New Mexico, 1951.

9.5.   Pellino, Michael W.  Guatemalan Narrative of the Nineteenth Century.  Cincinnati, 1959.  *DA,* XX, 4399.

### 10.  *Mexico*

10.1.   Anderson, Helene M.  Ignacio Ramírez: Spirit of Nineteenth Century Mexican Culture.  Syracuse, 1961.

10.2.   Avila, Pablo.  The Introduction of Romanticism in Mexico.  Stanford, 1937.  Stanford *Abstracts,* 1936-37, p. 51.

10.3.   Borrowdale, Howard Owen.  Mexican Mirage: A Study of the Belletristic Literature Based upon the Maximilian Empire in Mexico, 1864-1867.  South-

ern California, 1945.  Southern California *Abstracts,* 1945, p. 19.

10.4.   Boyd, Lola Elizabeth.  The Image of Emiliano Zapata in the Art and Literature of the Mexican Revolution.  Columbia, 1965.  *DA,* XXVIII, 4621-A.

10.5.   Bratsas, Dorothy N.  The Prose of the Mexican Modernists.  Missouri, 1963.  *DA,* XXIV, 3320.

10.6.   Brushwood, John Stubbs.  The Romantic Novel in Mexico.  Columbia, 1950.  *MA,* XI, No. 2, p. 342.

10.7.   Campa, David L.  The Mexican Revolution as Interpreted in the Mexican Novel, 1910-1939.  California, 1941.

10.8.   Castagnaro, Rosario A.  J. Rubén Romero and the Novel of the Mexican Revolution.  New York, 1952.

10.9.   Ceide-Echevarría, Gloria.  El *haikai* en la lírica mexicana.  Illinois, 1965.  *DA,* XXVI, 5410.

10.10.   Coll, Edna.  Injerto de temas en las novelistas mexicanas contemporáneas.  Florida, 1963.  San Juan, P.R., 1964.  NUC 65-74850.

10.11.   Ezcurdia, Manuel de.  La aparición del grupo "contemporáneos" en la poesía y en la crítica mexicanas 1920-1931.  California, 1964.  *DA,* XXV, 5273.

10.12.   Fogelquist, Donald Frederick.  The Figure of Pancho Villa in the Literature of the Mexican Revolution.  Wisconsin, 1941.  Wisconsin *Summaries,* VI, 322.

10.13.   Forster, Merlin H.  The *Contemporáneos,* 1915-1932: A Study in Twentieth-Century Mexican Letters.  Illinois, 1960.  *DA,* XXI, 1190.

10.14.   Gordon, Bruce R.  French Literary Influence on Mexican Literature (1800-1868).  Syracuse, 1950.

10.15.   Guzmán, Daniel de.  Aesthetic Currents in Mexico Between 1910-1940: A Cultural Appraisal of the Revolution.  Yale, 1957.  *Mexico, 1962. NUC 63-38812.

10.16.   Hollingsworth, Roberta L.  José Peón Contreras and the Romantic Movement in Mexico. Virginia, 1933.  Virginia *Abstracts,* 1932-33, p. 16.

10.17.   Johnson, Harvey Le Roy.  An Edition of *Triunfo de los santos* with a Consideration of Jesuit School Plays in Mexico Before 1650.  Pennsylvania, 1940.  *Buenos Aires, 1942.  LC 44-21256.

10.18.   Maggipinto, Francis Xavier.  Naturalism in the Mexican Novel.  Stanford, 1953.  *DA,* XIV, 359.

10.19.   McMurray, George Ray.  Recurring Themes and Technical Procedures in the Mexican Short Story of the Twentieth Century.  Nebraska, 1955. *DA,* XV, 1400.

10.20.   Meinhardt, Warren Lee.  The Mexican Indianist Novel: 1910-1960.  California, 1965.  *DA,* XXVI, 3958.

10.21.   Moore, Ernest Richard.  Studies in the Mexican

Novel. Cornell, 1940. Cornell *Abstracts,* 1940, p. 60.

10. 22.  Navarro, Joaquina.  La novela realista mexicana.  Columbia, 1954.  *DA,* XIV, 1416.

10. 23.  Nelle, William H.  Satirical Writings in Mexico, 1860-1870.  Nebraska, 1955.  *DA,* XV, 1401.

10. 24.  Nomland, John B.  Social and Political Aspects in the Contemporary Mexican Theater.  U.C.L.A., 1957.  *Mexico,* 1967.  NUC 68-21302.

10. 25.  Oberdoerffer, Marianne.  Contemporary Mexican Theater, 1923-1959.  Texas, 1960.  *DA,* XXI, 2718.

10. 26.  O'Neill, Samuel Joseph, Jr.  Psychological-Literary Techniques in Representative Contemporary Novels of Mexico.  Maryland, 1965.  *DA,* XXVII, 213-A.

10. 27.  Pleasants, Edwin Hemingway.  The Motivations of the Military Caudillo in Selected Mexican Novels: 1910-37.  Missouri, 1959.  *DA,* XX, 3750.

10. 28.  Read, John L.  The Mexican Historical Novel, 1826-1910.  Columbia, 1939.  New York, 1939.  LC 40-3103.

10. 29.  Renk, Eldred J.  The Mexican *Corrido* and the Revolution: A People's-Eye View of Events in War, Religion and Politics.  Washington, Seattle, 1951.

10. 30.  Rexroat, Ruth.  The *Diario de México,* First Daily of New Spain: Its Literature.  Texas, 1956.

10. 31.  Sarre, Alicia.  Spanish Influence on Mexican Lyric Poetry.  Stanford, 1945.  Stanford *Abstracts,* XX, p. 44.

10. 32.  Simmons, Merle Edwin.  The Mexican *Corrido* as a Source for Interpretive Study of Modern Mexico (1870-1950): With a Consideration of the Origins and Development of the *Corrido* Tradition.  Michigan, 1952.  *DA,* XII, 310.

10. 33.  Sommers, Joseph.  The Contribution of Francisco Rojas González to Mexican Literature.  Wisconsin, 1962.  *DA,* XXIII, 2140.

10. 34.  Stanton, Ellen Ruth.  La novela de la revolución mexicana: estudio relacionado con el movimiento literario y social.  Southern California, 1943.  Southern California *Abstracts,* 1943, p. 23.

10. 35.  Uría-Santos, María R.  El Ateneo de la Juventud: Su influencia en la vida intelectual de México.  Florida, 1965.  *DA,* XXVI, 6727.

10. 36.  Waldorf, Paul Douglass.  The Contemporary Mexican Short Story.  Northwestern, 1949.  Northwestern *Summaries,* XVII, 68.

10. 37.  Wheeler, Howard T.  The Mexican Novel as a Reflection of the National Problems of Mexico.  Stanford, 1934.  Stanford *Abstracts,* 1934-35, p. 57.

10. 38.  Wilson, Irma.  Mexico, A Century of Educational Thought.  Columbia, 1941.  New York, 1941.  LC 41-11488.

10. 39.  Wogan, Daniel Spelman.  The Indian in Mexican Poetry.  North Carolina, 1940.  North Carolina *Record,* No. 359, p. 180.

10. 40.  Worthen, Edward H.  The Reconquest of Mexico: A Panoramic View of Mexican Literary Nationalism.  (Volumes I and II).  Michigan, 1965.  *DA,* XXVII, 464-A.

10. 41.  Yancey, Myra L.  Literary Biographies of Nineteenth Century Mexico.  Colorado, 1939.  Colorado *Abstracts,* 1939, p. 132.

## 11. *Panama*

11. 1.  Kirk, William Wright.  The First Literary Periodicals of the Republic of Panama.  Illinois, 1955.  *DA,* XVI, 121.

## 12. *Paraguay*

12. 1.  Arana, Oswaldo.  La novela de la guerra del Chaco: Bolivia y Paraguay.  Colorado, 1963.  *DA,* XXIV, 3743.

## 13. *Peru*

13. 1.  Aldrich, Earl M., Jr.  Main Trends in the Peruvian Short Story of the Twentieth Century.  Indiana, 1961.  *DA,* XXII, 1619.

13. 2.  Callagham, [Sister] Mary Consuela.  Indianism in Peru—1883-1939.  Pennsylvania, 1951.

13. 3.  Cortés, Louis Joseph.  The Social Novel of Peru, 1920-1952.  Colorado, 1957.  *DA,* XIX, 136.

13. 4.  Dale, William Pratt, II.  The Cultural Revolution in Peru, 1750-1820.  Duke, 1941.

13. 5.  Fox, Lucia U.  La mujer como motivo en ocho poetas representativos del Perú.  Illinois, 1962.  *DA,* XXIII, 2913.

13. 6.  Goodrich, Diane Ruth.  Peruvian Novels of the Nineteenth Century.  Indiana, 1966.  *DA,* XXVII, 2151-A.

13. 7.  Rodríguez, Mario B.  La novela social en el Perú, 1848-1948.  Cornell, 1950.

13. 8.  Ulibarrí, George S.  The *Gamonal* in Selected Contemporary Novels of Social Protest in Peru, Bolivia, and Ecuador.  Iowa, 1952.  Iowa *Abstracts,* X, 217.

## 14. *Puerto Rico*

14. 1.  Rivera-Rivera, Eloísa.  La poesía en Puerto Rico antes de 1843.  Columbia, 1958.  *DA,* XIX, 329.

## 15. *Venezuela*

15. 1.  Chadwick, John Rouse.  Main Currents in the Venezuelan Novel from Romero García to Gallegos.  California, 1955.

15. 2.  McNerney, Robert Francis, Jr.  A Bibliography of the Venezuelan Literature in the Yale University Library.  Yale, 1937.

15. 3.  Ratcliff, Dillwyn.  Venezuelan Prose Fiction.  Columbia, 1933.  New York, 1933.  LC 34-16174.

### 16.  *Miscellaneous*

16. 1.  Bristol, William Baker.  *Hispanidad* in South America, 1936-1945.  Pennsylvania, 1947.  *MA,* XI, No. 2, p. 322.

16. 2.  Burner, Willis Judson.  The Attitudes of Contemporary Spanish-American Authors Towards the United States.  Ohio State, 1930.  Ohio State *Abstracts,* No. 4, p. 26.

16. 3.  Butterfield, Marvin E.  The Interpreters of Fernando Cortés, Doña Marina and Jerónimo de Aguilar.  Illinois, 1937.  Urbana, 1936.  LC 37-40.

16. 4.  Castanien, Donald Garner.  A Seventeenth Century Mexican Library and the Inquisition.  Michigan, 1951.  *MA,* XI, No. 2, p. 344.

16. 5.  Clinkscales, Orline.  Bécquer in Mexico, Central America and the Caribbean Countries.  Texas, 1957.

16. 6.  Daly, Robert W.  An Examination of Manuel Ugarte's Contribution to *Hispanoamericanismo.*  Loyola, Chicago, 1949.

16. 7.  Daniel, Elizabeth Rezner.  Spanish American Travelers in the United States Before 1900: A Study in Inter-American Literary Relations.  North Carolina, 1959.  *DA,* XX, 2796.

16. 8.  Galbán, Julio Suárez.  Apreciaciones contemporáneas hispanoamericanas de los Estados Unidos.  Virginia, 1931.

16. 9.  Groves, John Lawrence.  The Influence of Heidegger in Latin-American Philosophy.  Boston University, 1960.  *DA,* XXI, 926.

16. 10.  Hogan, Margarita B.  Picaresque Literature in Spanish America.  Columbia, 1953.  *DA,* XIV, 126.

16. 11.  Holdsworth, Carole Adele.  A Study of the *Revista moderna* (Mexico, 1898-1903).  Northwestern, 1965.  *DA,* XXVI, 6714.

16. 12.  Jackson, William R., Jr.  Florida in Early Spanish Colonial Literature.  Illinois, 1952.  *Coral Gables, Fla., 1954.  NUC 54-14500.

16. 13.  Leal, Luis.  El cuento y la leyenda en las *Crónicas de la Nueva España.*  Chicago, 1950.

16. 14.  Luna, José Luis.  La influencia de París en la evolución literaria de Enrique Gómez Carrillo y otros escritores hispano-americanos, 1890-1914.  California, 1940.

16. 15.  Metzidakis, Philip.  Unamuno e Hispanoamérica.  Yale, 1959.

16. 16.  Murguía, Theodore Infante.  The Evolution of the Gaucho in Literature.  Washington, Seattle, 1961.  *DA,* XXII, 1630.

16. 17.  Oberhelman, Harley D.  A Study of the *Revista azul.*  Kansas, 1958.

16. 18.  Onis, José M. de.  The United States as Seen by Spanish American Writers (1776-1890).  Columbia, 1951.  New York, 1952.  LC 52-2725.

16. 19.  Rexroat, Ruth.  The *Diario de México,* First Daily of New Spain: Its Literature.  Texas, 1956.

16. 20.  Riccio, Guy John.  *Hispanidad* and the Growth of National Identity in Contemporary Spanish-American Thought.  Maryland, 1963.  *DA,* XXIV, 5416.

16. 21.  Ripoll, Carlos.  La *Revista de avance* (1927-1930): Episodio de la literatura cubana.  New York, 1964.  *DA,* XXVI, 373.

16. 22.  Sibirsky, Saúl Boris.  Proceso y determinación de la cultura y las letras hispanoamericanas durante los siglos de la dominación española.  Pittsburgh, 1964.  *DA,* XXVI, 1050.

16. 23.  Trifilo, Santo Samuel.  Argentina as Seen by British Travelers: 1810-1860.  Michigan, 1957.  *DA,* XVIII, 1440.

16. 24.  Warren, Virgil A.  The Use of Quechua by Contemporary Writers of the Andean Region.  Virginia, 1933.  Virginia *Abstracts,* 1932-33, p. 22.

16. 25.  Wolfe, Mansell Wayne.  Images of the United States in the Hispanic American Press: A Content Analysis of News and Opinions of This Country Appearing in Daily Newspapers from Nineteen Latin American Republics.  Indiana, 1963.  *DA,* XXV, 448.

### 17.  *Acevedo Hernández, Antonio*

17. 1.  Weller, Hubert P.  La obra teatral de Antonio Acevedo Hernández: dramaturgo chileno (1886-1962).  Indiana, 1965.  *DA,* XXVI, 2764.

### 18.  *Agustini, Delmira*

18. 1..  Rosenbaum, Sidonia C.  Modern Women Poets of Spanish America: The Precursors—Delmira Agustini, Gabriela Mistral, Alfonsina Storni, Juana de Ibarbourou.  Columbia, 1945.  New York, 1945.  LC A46-1549.

### 19.  *Altamirano, Ignacio Manuel*

19. 1.  Carrell, Thelma R.  The Role of Ignacio Manuel Altamirano in *El Renacimiento.*  Illinois, 1953.  *DA,* XIII, 387.

19. 2.  Warner, Ralph Emerson.  The Life and Work of Ignacio Manuel Altamirano.  California, 1935.

### 20.  *Alvarez Lleras, Antonio*

20. 1.  Lyday, Leon F., III.  The Dramatic Art of Antonio Alvarez Lleras.  North Carolina, 1966.  *DA,* XXVII, 2534-A.

### 21. *Arguedas, Alcides*

21. 1.  Plevich, Mary.  Alcides Arguedas:Contemporary Bolivian Writer.  Columbia, 1957.  *DA,* XVII, 1557.

### 22. *Asturias, Miguel Angel*

22. 1.  Callan, Richard J.  Fecundity in Two Novels of Miguel Angel Asturias.  St. Louis, 1965.  *DA,* XXVI, 4653.

22. 2.  Donahue, Francis James.  Miguel Angel Asturias: escritor comprometido.  Southern California, 1965.  *DA,* XXVI, 2208.

22. 3.  Verzasconi, Ray Angelo.  Magical Realism and the Literary World of Miguel Angel Asturias.  Washington, Seattle, 1965.  *DA,* XXVI, 2763.

### 23. *Azuela, Mariano*

23. 1.  Dulsey, Bernard M.  The Mexican Revolution as Mirrored in the Novels of Mariano Azuela.  Illinois, 1950.

23. 2.  Luckey, Robert Edmund.  Mariano Azuela as Thinker and Writer.  Stanford, 1951.  Stanford *Abstracts,* XXVI, 279.

### 24. *Ballagas, Emilio*

24. 1.  Cartey, Wilfred G. O.  Three Antillian Poets: Emilio Ballagas, Luis Palés Matos, and Nicolás Guillén.  Literary Development of the Negro Theme in Relation to the Making of Modern Afro-Antillian Poetry and the Historic Evolution of the Negro.  Columbia, 1965.  *DA,* XXVIII, 2203-A.

24. 2.  Rice, Argyll Pryor.  Emilio Ballagas: Poeta o poesía.  Yale, 1961.  Mexico, 1966.  NUC 68-11801.

### 25. *Barrios, Eduardo*

25. 1.  Davison, Ned J.  Psychological Values in the Works of Eduardo Barrios.  U.C.L.A., 1956.  *Albuquerque, 1966.  NUC 67-79139.

25. 2.  Vázquez-Bigi, Angel Manuel.  La verdad sicológica en Eduardo Barrios.  Minnesota, 1962.  *DA,* XXIII, 1371.

### 26. *Batres Montúfar, José de*

26. 1.  Kuhn, Helene G.  The *Tradiciones de Guatemala* of José Batres Montúfar.  Pittsburgh, 1938.  Pittsburgh *Abstracts,* XIV, 191.

### 27. *Blanco, Andrés Eloy*

27. 1.  Moore, Unetta T.  The Poetry of Andrés Eloy Blanco.  Illinois, 1960.  *DA,* XXI, 1192.

### 28. *Blanco-Fombona, Rufino*

28. 1.  Monticone, Charles Ross.  Rufino Blanco-Fombona: The Man and His Work.  Pittsburgh, 1931.  Pittsburgh *Abstracts,* VII, 126.

### 29. *Blest Gana, Alberto*

29. 1.  Phillips, Walter Thomas.  Chilean Customs in the Novels of Alberto Blest Gana.  Southern California, 1943.  Southern California *Abstracts,* 1943, p. 20.

29. 2.  Valenzuela, Víctor M.  Chilean Society as Seen Through the Novelistic World of Alberto Blest Gana.  Columbia, 1965.

29. 3.  Wilson, William Charles Eade.  The Historical Element in the Novels of Alberto Blest Gana.  Washington, Seattle, 1928.  Washington *Digests,* I, 243.

### 30. *Borges, Jorge Luis*

30. 1.  Barrenechea, Ana María V.  La expresión de la irrealidad en la obra de Jorge Luis Borges.  Bryn Mawr, 1956.  Mexico, 1957.  NUC 57-34805.

30. 2.  Capsas, Cleon Wade.  The Poetry of Jorge Luis Borges, 1923-1963.  New Mexico, 1964.  *DA,* XXV, 4697.

30. 3.  Irby, James East.  The Structure of the Stories of Jorge Luis Borges.  Michigan, 1962.  *DA,* XXIII, 3377.

30. 4.  Wheelock, Kinch Carter.  The Myth-Maker: A Study of Motif and Symbol in the Short Stories of Jorge Luis Borges.  Texas, 1966.  *DA,* XXVII, 489-A.

### 31. *Brunet, Marta*

31. 1.  Peel, Roger Martin.  The Narrative Prose of Marta Brunet.  Yale, 1966.  *DA,* XXVII, 2541-A.

### 32. *Bulnes, Francisco*

32. 1.  Lemus, George.  Francisco Bulnes: Su vida y sus obras.  Texas, 1963.  *DA,* XXV, 2515.

### 33. *Bustamante, Carlos María*

33. 1.  Maxwell, Vera R.  The *Diario histórico* of Carlos María Bustamante for 1824.  Edited with Notes, Annotations and a Complete Life of the Author.  Texas, 1947.

### 34. *Campo, Angel del*

34. 1.  McRill, Paul C.  The Life and Works of Angel del Campo.  Colorado, 1955.  *DA,* XVI, 1455.

### 35. *Carballido, Emilio*

35. 1.  Peden, Margaret Sue Sayers.  Emilio Carballido, Dramatic Author: His Work from 1948-1966.  Missouri, 1966.  *DA,* XXVII, 3059-A.

### 36. *Caro, José Eusebio*

36. 1.  Martín, José Luis.  La poesía de José Eusebio Caro: Contribución estilística al estudio del romanticismo hispano-americano.  Columbia, 1965.  *DA,* XXVIII, 5061-A.  Bogotá, 1966.  NUC 67-72155.

37.  *Carpentier, Alejo*

37. 1.  Müller-Bergh, Klaus.   La prosa narrativa de Alejo Carpentier en *Los pasos perdidos*.   Yale, 1966.  *DA, XXVII*, 2537-A.

38.  *Carrasquilla, Tomás*

38. 1.  Levy, Kurt L.   The Life and Works of Tomás Carrasquilla, Pioneer of Spanish American Regionalism.   Toronto, 1951.  *Medellín, 1958.  NUC 59-26856.

39.  *Carrera Andrade, Jorge*

39. 1.  Harth, Dorothy E.   The Poetic World of Jorge Carrera Andrade.   Syracuse, 1958.  *DA, XX*, 669.

40.  *Casal, Julián del*

40. 1.  Nunn, Marshall E.   The Life and Works of Julián del Casal.   Illinois, 1939.   Urbana, 1939.  LC 40-2074.

41.  *Caso, Antonio*

41. 1.  Ahumada, Rodolfo.   The Philosophies of Antonio Caso and José Vasconcelos with Special Emphasis on Their Concepts of Value.   Southern California, 1963.  *DA, XXIV*, 3784.

42.  *Castellanos, Jesús*

42. 1.  Smith, Wilburn P.   Jesús Castellanos, His Life and His Works.   North Carolina, 1935.   North Carolina *Record*, No. 298, p. 75.

42. 2.  Zeigler, Wilbur C.   Las obras literarias de Jesús Castellanos.   Middlebury, 1950.

43.  *Castellanos, Rosario*

43. 1.  Baptiste, Víctor N.   La obra poética de Rosario Castellanos.   Illinois, 1966.  *DA, XXVIII*, 1425-A.

44.  *Chirveches A., Armando*

44. 1.  Soria-Torres, Mario T.   Armando Chirveches A., novelista boliviano.   Western Reserve, 1962.   Hiram, Ohio, 1962.  NUC 65-32083.

45.  *Costumbrismo*

45. 1.  Crowley, Cornelius.  Costumbrism in Chilean Literary Prose of the Nineteenth Century.  California, 1943.

45. 2.  Duffey, Frank M.   The *Cuadro de Costumbres* in Colombia (1838-1880).   North Carolina, 1950.  North Carolina *Record*, No. 492, p. 265.

45. 3.  Glaser, Edward.  Los argentinos vistos por sí mismos.  Harvard, 1951.

45. 4.  Levy, Kurt L.   The Life and Works of Tomás Carrasquilla, Pioneer of Spanish American Regionalism.   Toronto, 1954.  *Medellín, 1958.  NUC 59-26856.

45. 5.  McNeill, Mary L.  *Costumbrismo* in the Social Novel of the Central Andean Region.   Iowa, 1952.  *DA, XII*, 630.

45. 6.  Méndez, Margarita Castro de.   El costumbrismo en Costa Rica.   Columbia, 1964.  *DA, XXVIII*, 624-A.

45. 7.  Phillips, Walter Thomas.   Chilean Customs in the Novels of Alberto Blest Gana.   Southern California, 1943.   Southern California *Abstracts*, 1943, p. 20.

45. 8.  Smither, William J.   The Regional and Social Aspects of the Contemporary Ecuadorian Novel (1920-1950).   Tulane, 1952.   Tulane *Abstracts*, Series 53, No. 14, p. 87.

46.  *Crespo Toral, Remigio*

46. 1.  Terán, Carlos Manuel.   Remigio Crespo Toral: El hombre, su vida y su obra.   California, 1943.

47.  *Cruz, Sor Juana Inés de la*

47. 1.  Flynn, Gerard Cox.   A Revision of the Criticism of Sor Juana Inés de la Cruz.   New York, 1958.  *DA, XXV*, 3568.

47. 2.  Kirk, Susanne Brooke.   Relaciones entre la poesía de Sor Juana Inés de la Cruz y la de los poetas del Renacimiento y Barroco en España.   Missouri, 1963.  *DA, XXIV*, 3338.

48.  *Darío, Rubén*

48. 1.  Fiore, Dolores Ackel.   Greco-Roman Elements in the Vocabulary of Rubén Darío.   Radcliffe, 1958.  *New York, 1963.  NUC 63-3531.

48. 2.  Holm, Lydia.   The Epithet in the Works of Rubén Darío.   Iowa, 1947.   Iowa *Abstracts*, VII, 940.

48. 3.  López-Morillas, Juan.   El vocabulario y la dicción de Rubén Darío.   Iowa, 1940.   Iowa *Abstracts*, III, 384.

48. 4.  Lozano, Carlos.   Rubén Darío in Spain: 1892-1916.   California, 1962.  *DA, XXIV*, 3751.

48. 5.  Thomas, Kathleen Hickey.   *Modernismo* in Poetry and Its Exponents: Manuel Gutiérrez Nájera, Rubén Darío, and Leopoldo Lugones.   Pittsburgh, 1957.  *DA, XVII*, 2273.

48. 6.  Torres-Ríoseco, Arturo.   Rubén Darío and the *Modernista* Movement in Spanish America and Spain.   Minnesota, 1931.  *Cambridge, Mass.-London, 1931.  LC 32-32410.

48. 7.  Watland, Charles D.   The Literary Education of Rubén Darío: An Examination of the Extent and Nature of His Literary Culture to the Period of *Azul* (1888).   Minnesota, 1953.  *DA, XIII*, 1201.

49.  *Degetau, Federico*

49. 1.  Mergal Llera, Angel Manuel.   Federico Degetau,

un orientador de su pueblo. Columbia, 1943. New York, 1944. LC A44-4385.

### 50. *Delgado, Rafael*

50.1. Bickley, James Graham. The Life and Works of Rafael Delgado. California, 1935.

### 51. *Deústua, Alejandro O.*

51.1. Himelblau, Jack. The Aesthetic Ideas of Alejandro O. Deústua. Michigan, 1965. *DA,* XXVI, 3339.

### 52. *D'Halmar, Augusto*

52.1. Bourgeois, Louis C., III. Augusto D'Halmar, Chilean Novelist and Storyteller. U.C.L.A., 1964. *DA,* XXV, 468.

52.2. Smith, George E. Augusto Thomson D'Halmar, Fantasist. Indiana, 1959. *DA,* XX, 1370.

52.3. Urbistondo, Vicente. Manifestaciones naturalistas en la novela chilena: D'Halmar, Orrego Luco, y Edwards Bello. California, 1964. *DA,* XXV, 5287.

### 53. *Díaz Casanueva, Humberto*

53.1. Schweitzer, S. Alan. Two Metaphysical Poets: An Analysis of the Philosophical Poetry of Humberto Díaz Casanueva and Rosamel del Valle. Rutgers, 1966. *DA,* XXVII, 3880-A.

### 54. *Díaz Mirón, Salvador*

54.1. Rojas, Carlos A. Díaz Mirón: Su vida y su época. Washington, Seattle, 1949.

### 55. *Drama, General*

55.1. Mace, Carroll Edward. Three Quiché Dance-Dramas of Rabinal, Guatemala. Tulane, 1966. *DA,* XXVII, 3431-A. [Quiché and Spanish texts.]

55.2. Martin, Charles Basil. The Survivals of Medieval Religious Drama in New Mexico. Missouri, 1959. *DA,* XX, 3298.

55.3. McCrossan, [Sister] Joseph Marie. The Role of the Church and the Folk in the Development of the Early Drama in New Mexico. Pennsylvania, 1945. Philadelphia, 1948. LC 49-5437.

55.4. Pasquariello, Anthony Michael. The *Entremés, Sainete* and *Loa* in the Colonial Theater of Spanish America. Michigan, 1951. *MA,* XI, No. 2, p. 466.

55.5. Woodyard, George W. The Search for Identity: A Comparative Study in Contemporary Latin American Drama. Illinois, 1966. *DA,* XXVII, 2165-A. [Brazilian drama included.]

### 56. *Durand, Luis*

56.1. Decker, Donald M. Luis Durand, Chilean Novelist and Short Story Writer. U.C.L.A., 1961.

### 57. *Edwards Bello, Joaquín*

57.1. Urbistondo, Vicente. Manifestaciones naturalistas en la novela chilena: D'Halmar, Orrego Luco, y Edwards Bello. California,· 1964. *DA,* XXV, 5287.

### 58. *Eichelbaum, Samuel*

58.1. Maloney, Janet Kühner. The Theater of Samuel Eichelbaum. Northwestern, 1962. *DA,* XXIII, 3380.

### 59. *Essay*

59.1. Inostroza, Raúl Armando. El ensayo en Chile desde la colonia hasta 1900. Stanford, 1966. *DA,* XXVII, 3458-A.

59.2. Stabb, Martin Sanford. Racial Theories in Representative Spanish American Essayists of the Contemporary Period. U.C.L.A., 1956.

### 60. *Fernández Juncos, Manuel*

60.1. Carrino, Frank Gaetano. Manuel Fernández Juncos: Pivotal Force in the Insular Movement of Porto Rico Through *El buscapié.* Michigan, 1956. *DA,* XVII, 1335.

### 61. *Fernández de Lizardi, José Joaquín*

61.1. Davis, Jack Emory. Estudio lexicográfico de *El periquillo sarniento.* Tulane, 1956. *DA,* XVI, 1137.

61.2. Spell, Jefferson Rea. The Life and Works of José Joaquín Fernández de Lizardi. Pennsylvania, 1931. Philadelphia, 1931. LC 31-33304.

### 62. *Fernández Moreno, Baldomero*

62.1. Leith, Clara Jean. Baldomero Fernández Moreno: His Life and Works. Michigan, 1957. *DA,* XVIII, 1434.

### 63. *Ferretis, Jorge*

63.1. Holden, Paul Howard. The Creative Writing of Jorge Ferretis: Ideology and Style. Southern California, 1966. *DA,* XXVII, 207-A.

### 64. *Fiction, General*

64.1. Carter, Erwin Dale. Magical Realism in Contemporary Argentine Fiction. Southern California, 1966. *DA,* XXVII, 1361-A.

64.2. Chinchón, Osvaldo. The Sea as a Motif in the Fictional Literature of Chile. Virginia, 1966. *DA,* XXVII, 2495-A.

64.3. Flores, Angel. Three Ecological Patterns in South American Fiction. Cornell, 1947. Cornell *Abstracts,* 1947, p. 45.

64.4. King, Harry Lee, Jr. Juan Manuel de Rosas and

His Epoch as Portrayed in Argentine Fiction. North Carolina, 1961. *DA,* XXII, 3665.

64. 5.  Ratcliff, Dillwyn F. Venezuelan Prose Fiction. Columbia, 1933. New York, 1933. LC 34-16174.

64. 6.  Siegel, Reuben. The Group of Guayaquil: A Study in Contemporary Ecuadorian Fiction. Wisconsin, 1951. Wisconsin *Summaries,* XII, 465.

64. 7.  Smith, Kermit H. The Changing Attitudes Toward the Jungle as Seen in Latin American Prose Fiction. U.C.L.A., 1963. *DA,* XXIV, 749.

64. 8.  Staudinger, Mabel Katharine. The Use of the Supernatural in Modern Spanish-American Fiction. Chicago, 1946. Chicago, 1948. LC Mic A49-108 rev.

64. 9.  Stephenson, Mary E. The Treatment of Religion in Contemporary Spanish-American Fiction. Chicago, 1951.

64. 10.  Thompson, Miriam H. Twentieth Century *Yanqui* Imperialism in the Prose Fiction of Middle America. Tulane, 1955. Tulane *Abstracts,* Series 56, No. 14, p. 101.

### 65.  *Folklore*

65. 1.  Campa, Arthur Leon. Spanish Folk-Poetry in New Mexico. Columbia, 1946. Albuquerque, 1946. LC A47-2618.

65. 2.  Hansen, Terrence Leslie. The Types of the Folktale in Cuba, Puerto Rico, the Dominican Republic, and Spanish South America. Stanford, 1951. Berkeley, 1957. NUC A58-9080.

65. 3.  Madrid, Miguel Angel. The Attitudes of the Spanish American People as Expressed in Their *Coplas* or Folk Songs. Columbia, 1953. *DA,* XIV, 128.

65. 4.  Paullada, Stephen. A Study of the Influence That Similar Environment Had upon the Life and Folklore of the Gaucho and Cowboy Societies. Southern California, 1953. Southern California *Abstracts,* 1953, p. 61.

65. 5.  Robe, Stanley L. A Dialect and Folkloristic Study of Texts Recorded in Los Altos of Jalisco, Mexico. North Carolina, 1949. North Carolina *Record,* No. 478, p. 233.

### 66.  *Gallegos, Rómulo*

66. 1.  Allen, Richard F. Social and Political Thought in the Early Narrative of Rómulo Gallegos. Maryland, 1961. *DA,* XXV, 1901.

66. 2.  Chadwick, John Rouse. Main Currents in the Venezuelan Novel from Romero García to Gallegos. California, 1955.

66. 3.  Dunham, Lowell. Life and Works of Rómulo Gallegos. U.C.L.A., 1954. *Mexico, 1957. NUC A59-141.

66. 4.  Hyde, Jeannine Elizabeth. The Function of

Symbol in the Novels of Rómulo Gallegos. Oklahoma, 1964. *DA,* XXV, 3573.

### 67.  *Gálvez, Manuel*

67. 1.  Messimore, Hazel M. Manuel Gálvez. Colorado, 1950. Colorado *Abstracts,* 1950, p. 25.

67. 2.  Stevens, Leonard E. Feminine Protagonists in Manuel Gálvez' Novels. Indiana, 1964. *DA,* XXVI, 1050.

67. 3.  Turner, Esther Hadassah Scott. Hispanism in the Life and Works of Manuel Gálvez. Washington, Seattle, 1958. *DA,* XIX, 3311.

### 68.  *Gamboa, Federico*

68. 1.  Butler, Charles W. Federico Gamboa, Novelist of Transition. Colorado, 1955. *DA,* XVI, 1449.

68. 2.  Hooker, Alexander C., Jr. La novela de Federico Gamboa. Middlebury, 1954.

68. 3.  Menton, Seymour. The Life and Works of Federico Gamboa. New York, 1952.

### 69.  *Garcilaso de la Vega, "El Inca"*

69. 1.  Crowley, Frances G. A Comparative Study of Garcilaso de la Vega, el Inca, and His Sources in the *Comentarios reales de los Incas, I.* Washington, St. Louis, 1962. *DA,* XXIV, 1613.

### 70.  *Gaucho Literature*

70. 1.  Garganigo, John F. The Gaucho in Some Novels of Argentina and Uruguay. Illinois, 1965. *DA,* XXVI, 367.

70. 2.  Murguía, Theodore Infante. The Evolution of the Gaucho in Literature. Washington, Seattle, 1961. *DA,* XXII, 1630.

70. 3.  Nichols, Madaline Wallis. The Gaucho. California, 1938. *Durham, N.C., 1942. LC 42-10572.

70. 4.  Paullada, Stephen. A Study of the Influence That Similar Environment Had upon the Life and Folklore of the Gaucho and Cowboy Societies. Southern California, 1953. Southern California *Abstracts,* 1953, p. 61.

70. 5.  Wershow, Irving Robert. Aspects of Gaucho Literature. Yale, 1942.

### 71.  *Gautier Benítez, José*

71. 1.  Deily, Myron Bonham. José Gautier Benítez. Cornell, 1931. Ithaca, 1931. LC 33-31303.

### 72.  *Gómez de Avellaneda, Gertrudis*

72. 1.  García, Juan Crisóstomo. L'oeuvre lyrique de la Avellaneda. Laval, 1945.

72. 2.  Williams, Edwin Bucher. The Life and Dramatic Works of Gertrudis Gómez de Avellaneda. Pennsylvania, 1924. Philadelphia, 1924. LC 24-15204.

### 73. *Gómez Carrillo, Enrique*

73. 1. Dárdano, Hersilia Donis de. The Life and Works of Enrique Gómez Carrillo. Pittsburgh, 1936. Pittsburgh *Abstracts*, XII, 72.

73. 2. Luna, José Luis. La influencia de París en la evolución literaria de Enrique Gómez Carrillo y otros escritores hispano-americanos, 1890-1914. California, 1940.

### 74. *González, Joaquín V.*

74. 1. Taylor, Harvey D. Joaquín V. González and Justo Sierra, *Maestros de América*. Illinois, 1956. *DA*, XVI, 1908.

### 75. *González Martínez, Enrique*

75. 1. Bradman, Helen. Lo elegíaco en la poesía de Enrique González Martínez. U.C.L.A., 1964. *DA*, XXV, 1903.

75. 2. Topete, José Manuel. The Poetic World of E. González Martínez. Southern California, 1950. Southern California *Abstracts*, 1950, p. 62.

### 76. *González Obregón, Luis*

76. 1. De Morelos, Leonardo C. Luis González Oberegón (1865-1938); Chronicler of Mexico City. Columbia, 1954. *DA*, XIV, 1371.

### 77. *González Peña, Carlos*

77. 1. Travis, David E. The Life and Works of Carlos González Peña. Texas, 1961. *DA*, XXII, 3674.

### 78. *González Prada, Manuel*

78. 1. Chang-Rodríguez, Eugenio. La literatura política de González Prada, Martiátegui y Haya de la Torre. Washington, Seattle, 1955. *DA*, XVI, 534.

78. 2. Cutler, John H. Manuel González Prada, Precursor of a Modern Peru. Harvard, 1936. Harvard *Summaries*, 1936, p. 377.

78. 3. Mead, Robert G., Jr. Manuel González Prada, prosista. Michigan, 1949. *MA*, IX, No. 3, p. 150.

### 79. *Gorostiza, José*

79. 1. Debicki, Andrew Peter. The Poetry of José Gorostiza. Yale, 1960. Mexico, 1962. NUC 62-58081.

79. 2. Rubin, Mordecai Samuel. *Muerte sin fin* de José Gorostiza—La incorporación de una poética. Maryland, 1961. *DA*, XXII, 4019.

### 80. *Gorostiza, Manuel Eduardo de*

80. 1. Banner, James W. The Dramatic Works of Manuel Eduardo de Gorostiza. North Carolina, 1948. North Carolina *Record*, No. 464, p. 355.

### 81. *Guido y Spano, Carlos*

81. 1. Hulet, Claude Lyle. Carlos Guido y Spano y su tiempo. Michigan, 1954. *DA*, XIV, 1721.

### 82. *Guillén, Nicolás*

82. 1. Cartey, Wilfred G. O. Three Antillian Poets: Emilio Ballagas, Luis Palés Matos, and Nicolás Guillén. Literary Development of the Negro Theme in Relation to the Making of Modern Afro-Antillian Poetry and the Historic Evolution of the Negro. Columbia, 1965. *DA*, XXVIII, 2203-A.

82. 2. Castán de Pontrelli, Mary. The *Criollo* Poetry of Nicolás Guillén. Yale, 1958. *DA*, XXIX, 612-A.

82. 3. White, Florence E. *Poesía Negra* in the Works of Jorge de Lima, Nicolás Guillén, and Jacques Roumain, 1927-1947. Wisconsin, 1952. Wisconsin *Summaries*, XIII, 399.

### 83. *Güiraldes, Ricardo*

83. 1. Previtali, Giovanni. Ricardo Güiraldes and *Don Segundo Sombra*. Yale, 1958. New York, 1963. NUC 63-24139.

83. 2. Rust, Zell Owen. The Prose Style of Ricardo Güiraldes. Southern California, 1957. Southern California *Abstracts*, 1957, p. 147.

83. 3. Weiss, Harry. Ricardo Güiraldes, argentino (1886-1927). Syracuse, 1956. *DA*, XVI, 1143.

### 84. *Gutiérrez Nájera, Manuel*

84. 1. Conner, Arthur B. Indications in the Writings of Manuel Gutiérrez Nájera of His Reading of French Literature. Iowa, 1951. Iowa *Abstracts*, IX, 710.

84. 2. Deuel, Pauline Brandt. The Use of Imagery by Manuel Gutiérrez Nájera. Stanford, 1951. Stanford *Abstracts*, XXVI, 277.

84. 3. Gómez de Baños, Virginia. Manuel Gutiérrez Nájera. Radcliffe, 1938. Radcliffe *Summaries*, 1935-38, p. 178.

84. 4. Kosloff, Alexander. Los cuentos de Manuel Gutiérrez Nájera. Southern California, 1954. Southern California *Abstracts*, 1954, p. 106.

84. 5. Thomas, Kathleen Hickey. *Modernismo* in Poetry and Its Exponents: Manuel Gutiérrez Nájera, Rubén Darío, and Leopoldo Lugones. Pittsburgh, 1957. *DA*, XVII, 2273.

### 85. *Gutiérrez de Santa Clara, Pedro*

85. 1. Knox, Robert Baker. Some Cultural Aspects of the *Quinquenarios* of Pedro Gutiérrez de Santa Clara. Michigan, 1952. *DA*, XII, 188.

### 86. *Hanssen, Federico*

86. 1. Sand, Louise. The Role of Federico Hanssen

and Rodolfo Lenz in the Intellectual Life of Chile. North Carolina, 1958.  *DA*, XIX, 1391.

### 87.  *Haya de la Torre, Víctor Raúl*

87. 1.  Chang-Rodríguez, Eugenio.  La literatura política de González Prada, Mariátegui y Haya de la Torre.  Washington, Seattle, 1955.  *DA*, XVI, 534.

### 88.  *Hernández, José*

88. 1.  Holmes, Henry Alfred.  *Martín Fierro*: An Epic of the Argentine.  Columbia, 1923.  New York, 1923.  LC 23-7818.

### 89.  *Hernández-Catá, Alfonso*

89. 1.  Gardner, Dorothy S.  Psychological Values in the Work of Alfonso Hernández-Catá.  U.C.L.A., 1961.

89. 2.  Trakas, Pedro N.  The Life and Works of Alfonso Hernández-Catá.  North Carolina, 1954.  North Carolina *Record*, No. 548, p. 280.

### 90.  *Herrera, Ernesto*

90. 1.  Schanzer, George O.  Vida y obras de Ernesto Herrera (1889-1917): primer bohemio y segundo dramaturgo del Uruguay.  Iowa, 1950.  Iowa *Abstracts*, IX, 711.

### 91.  *Herrera y Reissig, Julio*

91. 1.  Gicovate, Bernardo.  Julio Herrera y Reissig: A Symbolist Poet.  Harvard, 1952.  *Berkeley, 1957.  NUC 56-11896.

### 92.  *Historical Novel, General*

92. 1.  McGrady, Donald Lee.  La novela histórica en Colombia, 1844-1959.  Indiana, 1961.  *DA*, XXII, 1628.

92. 2.  Read, John L.  The Mexican Historical Novel, 1826-1910.  Columbia, 1939.  New York, 1939.  LC 40-3103.

92. 3.  Soto-Ruiz, Luis.  El tema del pirata en la novela histórica hispanoamericana.  Michigan, 1959.  *DA*, XX, 2280.

### 93.  *Hostos y Bonilla, Eugenio María de*

93. 1.  Parrish, Robert Taylor.  A Study of the Personality and Thought of Eugenio María de Hostos.  Wisconsin, 1940.  Wisconsin *Summaries*, VI, 324.

93. 2.  Sisler, Robert Frank.  Eugenio María de Hostos y Bonilla.  New York, 1963.  *DA*, XXIV, 1346.

93. 3.  Tirado, Moisés.  Hostos, educador.  Middlebury, 1953.

### 94.  *Huidobro, Vicente*

94. 1.  Bary, David Alan.  The Poetry of Vicente Huido-

bro.  California, 1956.  Granada, 1963.  NUC 65-56220.

### 95.  *Ibarbourou, Juana de*

95. 1.  Rosenbaum, Sidonia C.  Modern Women Poets of Spanish America: The Precursors—Delmira Agustini, Gabriela Mistral, Alfonsina Storni, Juana de Ibarbourou.  Columbia, 1945.  New York, 1945.  LC A46-1549.

### 96.  *Icaza, Jorge*

96. 1.  Vetrano, Anthony J.  The Ecuadorian Indian and *Cholo* in the Novels of Jorge Icaza: Their Lot and Language.  Syracuse, 1966.  *DA*, XXVII, 4268-A.

### 97.  *Indianista-Indigenista Literature*

97. 1.  Keller, Jean P.  The Indian in the Literature of Colombia.  Washington, Seattle, 1949.

97. 2.  Lorand de Olazagasti, Adelaida.  El indio en la narrativa guatemalteca.  Puerto Rico, 1966.

97. 3.  Lynch, John Francis.  Concepts of the Indian and Colonial Society in Spanish Writers on Guatemala: 1520-1620.  Washington, Seattle, 1953.  *DA*, XIV, 674.

97. 4.  McIntosh, Clifton Brooke.  *Aves sin nido*, and the Beginning of *Indianismo*.  Virginia, 1932.  Virginia *Abstracts*, 1931-32, p. 9.

97. 5.  Meinhardt, Warren Lee.  The Mexican Indianist Novel: 1910-1960.  California, 1965.  *DA*, XXVI, 3958.

97. 6.  Orlandi, Adorna Agatha.  Characterization and Style in the Indigenist Novel of Spanish America, 1889-1948.  Radcliffe, 1960.  See NUC 65-22701.

97. 7.  Simeone, Anthony Joseph.  The Medicine-Man in the *Novela Indianista*.  Boston University, 1956.  Boston University *Abstracts*, 1956, n.p.

97. 8.  Southard, Gordon D.  La novela indigenista en Hispanoamérica.  Chicago, 1959.

97. 9.  Vetrano, Antony J.  The Ecuadorian Indian and *Cholo* in the Novels of Jorge Icaza: Their Lot and Language.  Syracuse, 1966.  *DA*, XXVII, 4268-A.

97. 10.  Wogan, Daniel Spelman.  The Indian in Mexican Poetry.  North Carolina, 1940.  North Carolina *Record*, No. 359, p. 180.

### 98.  *Jaimes-Freyre, Ricardo*

98. 1.  Jaimes-Freyre, Mireya.  A Comparison of Modernism and the Generation of '98 with Special Reference to the Works and Theories of Ricardo Jaimes-Freyre.  Columbia, 1965.

### 99.  *Landívar, Rafael*

99. 1.  Kerson, Arnold Lewis.  Rafael Landívar and the Latin Literary Currents of New Spain in the Eigh-

teenth Century. Yale, 1963. *DA*, XXVIII, 3187-A.

### 100. *Latorre, Mariano*

100. 1. Castillo, Homero. Mariano Latorre, cuentista y novelista de Chile. Chicago, 1953.

### 101. *Lenz, Rodolfo*

101. 1. Sand, Louise. The Role of Federico Hanssen and Rodolfo Lenz in the Intellectual Life of Chile. North Carolina, 1958. *DA*, XIX, 1391.

### 102. *Lillo, Baldomero*

102. 1. Sedgwick, Ruth. Baldomero Lillo, Chilean Short Story Writer. Yale, 1936.

### 103. *Lira, Miguel N.*

103. 1. Ortiz Morales, Alfredo. Miguel N. Lira: vida y obra. Southern California, 1966. *DA*, XXVII, 482-A.

103. 2. Saunders, John Frederick, The Literary Works of Miguel N. Lira. Missouri, 1965. *DA*, XXVI, 5444.

### 104. *Lloréns Torres, Luis*

104. 1. Duffy, Kenneth J. Luis Lloréns Torres, Poet of Puerto Rico. Pittsburgh, 1940. Pittsburgh *Abstracts*, XVI, 89.

104. 2. Ortiz de Lugo, Nilda S. Vida y obra de Luis Lloréns Torres. Puerto Rico, 1966.

### 105. *López Velarde, Ramón*

105. 1. Phillips, Allen Whitmarsh. Análisis estético de la obra poética de Ramón López Velarde. Michigan, 1954. *DA*, XIV, 676.

### 106. *López y Fuentes, Gregorio*

106. 1. Armitage, Richard H. The Problems of Modern Mexico in the Novels of López y Fuentes. Ohio State, 1946. Ohio State *Abstracts*, No. 49, p. 1.

106. 2. McKegney, James Cuthbert. Female Characters in the Novels of José Rubén Romero and Gregorio López y Fuentes: A Comparative Study. Washington, Seattle, 1959. *DA*, XX, 4115.

### 107. *Lugones, Leopoldo*

107. 1. Scari, Robert Mario. La formación literaria de Lugones. California, 1963. *DA*, XXIV, 4199.

107. 2. Thomas, Kathleen Hickey. *Modernismo* in Poetry and Its Exponents: Manuel Gutiérrez Nájera, Rubén Darío, and Leopoldo Lugones. Pittsburgh, 1957. *DA*, XVII, 2273.

### 108. *Lynch, Benito*

108. 1. Head, Gerald Louis. Characterization in the Works of Benito Lynch. U.C.L.A., 1964. *DA*, XXV, 2512.

108. 2. Nason, Marshall R. Benito Lynch y su creación literaria. Chicago, 1958. Chicago, 1958. NUC Mic 58-6796.

### 109. *Mallea, Eduardo*

109. 1. Armstrong, Argentina Quesada. Eduardo Mallea y la búsqueda de la argentinidad. Missouri, 1965. *DA*, XXVII, 1811-A.

109. 2. Polt, John Herman Richard. Eduardo Mallea and the Contemporary Argentine Novel. California, 1956. *Berkeley, 1959. NUC A60-9001.

109. 3. Rivelli, Carmen. Eduardo Mallea: La continuidad temática de su obra. New York, 1966. *DA*, XXVII, 4229-A.

### 110. *Mariátegui, José Carlos*

110. 1. Chang-Rodríguez, Eugenio. La literatura política de González Prada, Mariátegui y Haya de la Torre. Washington, Seattle, 1955. *DA*, XVI, 534.

### 111. *Mármol, José*

111. 1. Cuthbertson, Stuart. The Poetry of José Mármol and Its Sources. Stanford, 1933. Stanford *Abstracts*, 1932-33, p. 57.

### 112. *Marqués, René*

112. 1. Pilditch, Charles R. A Study of the Literary Works of René Marqués from 1948 to 1962. Rutgers, 1966. *DA*, XXVII, 1833-A.

### 113. *Marroquín, José Manuel*

113. 1. Raab, [Sister] M. Ricarda. José Manuel Marroquín: A Study of His Works. St. Louis, 1964. *DA*, XXVI, 373.

### 114. *Martí, José*

114. 1. Corbitt, Roberta Day. This Colossal Theater: The United States Interpreted by José Martí. Kentucky, 1955. *DA*, XX, 4109.

114. 2. Galindo, Isis. La modalidad impresionista en la obra de José Martí. U.C.L.A., 1966. *DA*, XXVII, 1816-A.

114. 3. Gordon, Alan Martin. Verb-Creation in the Works of José Martí: Method and Function. Harvard, 1956.

114. 4. Gray, Richard Butler. José Martí: His Life, Ideas, Apotheosis, and Significance as a Symbol in Cuban Politics and Selected Social Organizations. Wisconsin, 1957. *DA*, XVII, 2665.

114. 5. Iduarte, Andrés. Martí, escritor. Columbia, 1944. Mexico, 1945. LC A45-4854.

114. 6. Schulman, Ivan A. Symbolism and Color in the

Works of José Martí. U.C.L.A., 1959. *Madrid, 1960. NUC 63-54655.

114. 7. Shuler, Esther Elise. Poesía y teorías poéticas de José Martí (con especial referencia a su crítica de autores norteamericanos). Minnesota, 1947.

114. 8. Sneary, Eugene Chester. José Martí in Translation. Tulane, 1959. *DA*, XX, 1795.

### 115. *Matto de Turner, Clorinda*

115. 1. Crouse, Ruth Compton. Clorinda Matto de Turner: An Analysis of Her Role in Peruvian Literature. Florida State, 1964. *DA*, XXV, 5272.

115. 2. McIntosh, Clifton Brooke. *Aves sin nido*, and the Beginning of *Indianismo*. Virginia, 1932. Virginia *Abstracts*, 1931-32, p. 9.

### 116. *Maya, Rafael*

116. 1. Fahey, [Sister] Miriam Daniel, S.N.J.M. A Study of the Poetry of Rafael Maya. Southern California, 1966. *DA*, XXVII, 1054-A.

### 117. *Milla y Vidaurre, José*

117. 1. Edberg, George J. The Life and Works of José Milla y Vidaurre. Kansas, 1959. *DA*, XX, 2800.

117. 2. Martin, John L. The Literary Works of José Milla. Pittsburgh, 1940. Pittsburgh *Abstracts*, XVI, 211.

### 118. *Mistral, Gabriela*

118. 1. Hernández, Mary Frances Baker. Gabriela Mistral and the Standards of American Criticism. New Mexico, 1963. *DA*, XXIV, 3324.

118. 2. Preston, [Sister] Mary Charles Ann, S.S.N.D. A Study of Significant Variants in the Poetry of Gabriela Mistral. Catholic, 1964. Washington, 1964. NUC 65-2049.

118. 3. Rosenbaum, Sidonia C. Modern Women Poets of Spanish America: The Precursors—Delmira Agustini, Gabriela Mistral, Alfonsina Storni, Juana de Ibarbourou. Columbia, 1945. New York, 1945. LC A46-1549.

118. 4. Taylor, Martin Charles. The Poetic World of Gabriela Mistral. Religious Sensibility in the Life and Poetry of Gabriela Mistral. U.C.L.A., 1964. *DA*, XXV, 3584.

### 119. *Mitre, Bartolomé*

119. 1. Hole, Myra C. Bartolomé Mitre; A Poet in Action. Columbia, 1947. New York, 1947. LC A47-3857.

### 120. *Modernismo*

120. 1. Bratsas, Dorothy N. The Prose of the Mexican Modernists. Missouri, 1963. *DA*, XXIV, 3320.

120. 2. Fraker, Charles Frederic. The Development of Modernism in Spanish-American Poetry. Harvard, 1931. Harvard *Summaries*, 1931, p. 272.

120. 3. García-Girón, Edmundo. The Adjective: A Contribution to the Study of Modernist Poetic Diction. California, 1952.

120. 4. Jaimes-Freyre, Mireya. A Comparison of Modernism and the Generation of '98 with Special Reference to the Works and Theories of Ricardo Jaimes-Freyre. Columbia, 1965.

120. 5. Keller, Daniel Schneck. Early Modernist Literary Theories in Spanish America. California, 1953.

120. 6. Lowry, Hope. L'influence française sur les poètes hispano-américains de l'école moderniste. McGill, 1932.

120. 7. Maule, Mary Eleanor. *Modernismo* in Two Spanish American Novelists: Carlos Reyles and Pedro Prado. Wisconsin, 1957. *DA*, XVII, 633.

120. 8. Oberhelman, Harley D. A Study of the *Revista azul*. Kansas, 1958.

120. 9. Schade, George Dewey. Classical Mythology in the *Modernista* Poetry of Spanish America. California, 1953.

120. 10. Shone, Alice Irwin. Amado Nervo: A Mexican *Modernista* in the Baudelairian Manner. California, 1936.

120. 11. Thomas, Kathleen Hickey. *Modernismo* in Poetry and Its Exponents: Manuel Gutiérrez Nájera, Rubén Darío, and Leopoldo Lugones. Pittsburgh, 1957. *DA*, XVII, 2273.

120. 12. Torres-Ríoseco, Arturo. Rubén Darío and the *Modernista* Movement in Spanish America and Spain. Minnesota, 1931. *Cambridge, Mass.-London, 1931. LC 32-32410.

### 121. *Nalé Roxlo, Conrado*

121. 1. Machuca-Padín, Arturo H. Three Spanish Plays: A Translation and Adaptation. Denver, 1958. [Plays: *The Mermaid's Tail (La cola de la sirena)* by Conrado Nalé Roxlo; *In Ardent Darkness (En la ardiente obscuridad)* by Antonio Buero Vallejo; *When Five Years Pass (Así que pasen cinco años)* by Frederico García Lorca.]

121. 2. Tull, John Frederick, Jr. The Life and Works of Conrado Nalé Roxlo. Yale, 1958.

### 122. *Naturalism*

122. 1. Maggipinto, Francis Xavier. Naturalism in the Mexican Novel. Stanford, 1953. *DA*, XIV, 359.

122. 2. Reid, Joseph A. Naturalistic Influences in the Argentine Novel. Michigan, 1946.

122. 3. Urbistondo, Vicente. Manifestaciones naturalistas en la novela chilena: D'Halmar, Orrego Luco, y Edwards Bello. California, 1964. *DA*, XXV, 5287.

### 123. *Neruda, Pablo*

123. 1. Lozada, Alfredo Ruiz. **Contribución al estudio** crítico de *Residencia en la tierra* de Pablo Neruda. California, 1962. See NUC 63-33192.

### 124. *Nervo, Amado*

124. 1. Shone, Alice Irwin. Amado Nervo: A Mexican *Modernista* in the **Baudelairian Manner. California, 1936.**

124. 2. Wellman, Esther T. Amado Nervo, Mexico's Religious Poet. Columbia, 1936. New York, 1936. LC 36-32952.

### 125. *Novás Calvo, Lino*

125. 1. Souza, Raymond Dale. The Literary World of Lino Novás Calvo. Missouri, 1964. *DA,* XXV, 1926.

### 126. *Novel, General*

126. 1. Anderson, Robert R. A Study of the Theory of the Novel in Representative Spanish American Authors, 1896-1956. California, 1957.

126. 2. Avila, Eneida. Las compañías bananeras en la novesística centroamericana. Tulane, 1959. *DA,* XX, 3740.

126. 3. Corbett, Evelyn D. La influencia de la tierra en la novela contemporánea rioplatense. Minnesota, 1950.

126. 4. Kline, Walter D. The Use of Novelistic Elements in Some Spanish-American Prose Works of the Seventeenth and Eighteenth Centuries. Michigan, 1957. *DA,* XVIII, 1431.

126. 5. Orlandi, Adorna Agatha. Characterization and Style in the Indigenist Novel of Spanish America, 1889-1948. Radcliffe, 1960. See NUC 65-22701.

126. 6. Soto-Ruiz, Luis. El tema del pirata en la novela histórica hispanoamericana. Michigan, 1959. *DA,* XX, 2280.

126. 7. Suárez-Murias, Marguerite. La novela romántica en Hispanoamérica. Columbia, 1957. *DA,* XVII, 2018.

### 127. *Ocantos, Carlos María*

127. 1. Andersson, Theodore. The *Españolismo* of Carlos María Ocantos. Yale, 1931. *New Haven-London, 1934. LC 35-1445.

### 128. *Oña, Pedro de*

128. 1. Dinamarca, Salvador. Estudio del *Arauco domado* de Pedro de Oña. Columbia, 1951. New York, 1952. LC A52-8754.

### 129. *Orrego Luco, Luis*

129. 1. Urbistondo, Vicente. Manifestaciones naturalistas en la novela chilena: D'Halmar, Orrego Luco, y Edwards Bello. California, 1964. *DA,* XXV, 5287.

### 130. *Ortiz Guerrero, Manuel*

130. 1. Roberts, William H. Manuel Ortiz Guerrero, Paraguayan Poet: A Biographical and Critical Study. Wisconsin, 1950. Wisconsin *Summaries,* XI, 373.

### 131. *Othón, Manuel José*

131. 1. Udick, Helen Bernice. Manuel José Othón, Nature Poet of Mexico. Colorado, 1945. Colorado *Abstracts,* 1945, p. 106. Microfilmed, 1945. See LC A46-2496.

### 132. *Palés Matos, Luis*

132. 1. Cartey, Wilfred G. O. Three Antillian Poets: Emilio Ballagas, Luis Palés Matos, and Nicolás Guillén. Literary Development of the Negro Theme in Relation to the Making of Modern Afro-Antillian Poetry and the Historic Evolution of the Negro. Columbia, 1965. *DA,* XXVIII, 2203-A.

### 133. *Palma, Ricardo*

133. 1. Arora, Shirley L. Proverbial Comparisons in Ricardo Palma's *Tradiciones peruanas.* U.C.L.A., 1962. Berkeley, 1966. NUC 66-63986.

133. 2. Compton, Merlin D. Spanish Honor in Ricardo Palma's *Tradiciones peruanas.* U.C.L.A., 1959.

133. 3. Thomas, Ruth S. Sources of the *Tradiciones peruanas* of Ricardo Palma. Washington, Seattle, 1938. Washington *Abstracts,* III, 373.

133. 4. Webb, Kenneth W. Ricardo Palma's Techniques in Recreating Colonial Lima. Pittsburgh, 1951. Pittsburgh *Bulletin,* XLVIII, No. 10, p. 30.

133. 5. Wilder, William R. Romantic Elements in the First Edition of the First Series of the *Tradiciones peruanas* by Ricardo Palma. St. Louis, 1966. *DA,* XXVII, 3068-A.

### 134. *Paz, Octavio*

134. 1. Bernard, Judith Ann. Mexico as Theme, Image, and Contribution to Myth in the Poetry of Octavio Paz. Wisconsin, 1964. *DA,* XXIV, 4187.

134. 2. Panico, Marie Joan. Motifs and Expressions in Octavio Paz: An Explication of His Spoken Anthology. Maryland, 1966. *DA,* XXVII, 3058-A.

134. 3. Wing, George Gordon. Octavio Paz: Poetry, Politics and the Myth of the Mexican. California, 1961. Microfilmed. See NUC 65-9692.

### 135. *Pellicer, Carlos*

135. 1. Schlak, Carolyn Brandt. The Poetry of Carlos Pellicer. Colorado, 1966. *DA,* XXVIII, 2263-A.

### 136. *Peón Contreras, José*

136. 1. Hollingsworth, Roberta L. José Peón Con-

treras and the Romantic Movement in Mexico. Virginia, 1933. Virginia *Abstracts,* 1932-33, p. 16.

### 137.  *Pérez Bonalde, Juan Antonio*

137. 1.  Johnson, Ernest Alfred, Jr.  Juan Antonio Pérez Bonalde, 1846-1892: A Biographical Study.  Harvard, 1950.

### 138.  *Peza, Juan de Dios*

138. 1.  Cobb, Herbert L.  The Life and Works of Juan de Dios Peza. Missouri, 1947. *MA,* IX, No. 2, p. 127.

### 139.  *Picaresque Literature*

139. 1.  Hogan, Margarita B.  Picaresque Literature in Spanish America.  Columbia, 1953.  *DA,* XIV, 126.

### 140.  *Poetry, General*

140. 1.  Brower, Gary Layne.  The *Haiku* in Spanish American Poetry.  Missouri, 1966.  *DA,* XXVII, 3036-A.

140. 2.  Campa, Arthur Leon.  Spanish Folk-Poetry in New Mexico.  Columbia, 1946.  Albuquerque, 1946. LC A47-2618.

140. 3.  Kolb, Glen L.  Some Satirical Poets of the Spanish American Colonial Period.  Michigan, 1953. *DA,* XIII, 811.

140. 4.  Morton, Frederic Rand.  The Spanish Renaissance Epic in America on American Themes: 1530-1630.  Harvard, 1958.

140. 5.  Paredes, Américo.  "El corrido de Gregorio Cortez," A Ballad of Border Conflict.  Texas, 1956. Austin, 1958.  NUC 58-10853 rev.

140. 6.  Petty, McKendree.  Some Epic Imitations of Ercilla's *La araucana.*  Illinois, 1930.  Urbana, 1932. LC 34-252.

140. 7.  Sittler, Richard C.  Antecedents and Present Characteristics of the Spanish American Alexandrine. Iowa, 1952.  Iowa *Abstracts,* X, 211.

140. 8.  Torres, María de Guadalupe.  Los romances españoles en América.  Stanford, 1951.  Stanford *Abstracts,* XXVI, 282.

140. 9.  White, Florence E.  *Poesía Negra* in the Works of Jorge de Lima, Nicolás Guillén, and Jacques Roumain, 1927-1947.  Wisconsin, 1952.  Wisconsin *Summaries,* XIII, 399.

### 141.  *Pombo, Rafael*

141. 1.  Orjuela, Héctor Hugo.  Rafael Pombo: Vida y obras.  Kansas, 1961.  *DA,* XXII, 874.

### 142.  *Prado, Pedro*

142. 1.  Maule, Mary Eleanor.  *Modernismo* in Two Spanish American Novelists: Carlos Reyles and Pedro Prado.  Wisconsin, 1957.  *DA,* XVII, 633.

142. 2.  Petersen, Gerald W.  The Narrative Art of Pedro Prado.  Illinois, 1966.  *DA,* XXVIII, 1444-A.

### 143.  *Prieto, Guillermo*

143. 1.  McLean, Malcolm D.  The Life and Works of Guillermo Prieto (1818-1897).  Texas, 1951.  *Mexico, 1960.  NUC 61-36623.

### 144.  *Quiroga, Horacio*

144. 1.  Coons, Dix Scott.  Horacio Quiroga—The Master Storyteller.  A Study of the Creative Processes. Texas, 1964.  *DA,* XXV, 2978.

144. 2.  Floripe, Rodolfo.  Horacio Quiroga: Novelistic Materials and Technique.  Wisconsin, 1951.  Wisconsin *Summaries,* XII, 463.

### 145.  *Ramírez, Ignacio*

145. 1.  Anderson, Helene M.  Ignacio Ramírez: Spirit of Nineteenth Century Mexican Culture.  Syracuse, 1961.

### 146.  *Realism, General*

146. 1.  Carter, Erwin Dale.  Magical Realism in Contemporary Argentine Fiction.  Southern California, 1966.  *DA,* XXVII, 1361-A.

146. 2.  Navarro, Joaquina.  La novela realista mexicana.  Columbia, 1954.  *DA,* XIV, 1416.

### 147.  *Reyes, Alfonso*

147. 1.  Aponte, Barbara Bockus.  The Spanish Friendships of Alfonso Reyes.  Texas, 1964.  *DA,* XXV, 467.

147. 2.  Hernández, David.  Alfonso Reyes as a Literary Critic.  Illinois, 1966.  *DA,* XXVII, 775-A.

147. 3.  Koldewyn, Philip Young.  Alfonso Reyes as a Critic of Peninsular Spanish Literature.  California, 1965.  *DA,* XXVI, 1648.

147. 4.  Mata, Elba Teresa.  La cultura en Alfonso Reyes. Florida State, 1964.  *DA,* XXV, 7247.

147. 5.  Robb, James Willis.  Patterns of Image and Structure in the Essays of Alfonso Reyes.  Catholic, 1958.  Washington, 1958.  NUC 61-4359.

### 148.  *Reyles, Carlos*

148. 1.  Bateson, Howard L.  French Influences in the Work of Carlos Reyles, Uruguayan Novelist.  Illinois, 1943.  Urbana, 1943.  LC A44-158.

148. 2.  Mattiace, Vincenza Ann.  Carlos Reyles and His Social Consciousness of the Uruguayan Scene.  New York, 1958.  *DA,* XIX, 2954.

148. 3.  Maule, Mary Eleanor.  *Modernismo* in Two Spanish American Novelists: Carlos Reyles and Pedro Prado.  Wisconsin, 1957.  *DA,* XVII, 633.

148. 4.  Montgomery, Hugh.  The Genesis and Trajectory of the Ideology of Force in the Works of Carlos Reyles.  Harvard, 1952.

148. 5.  Sisto, David T.   Character Analysis in the Works of Carlos Reyles.   Iowa, 1952.   Iowa *Abstracts*, X, 203.

### 149.  *Riva Palacio, Vicente*

149. 1.  Slavens, Marjorie.  Mexican Identity in the Prose Works of Vicente Riva Palacio.  St. Louis, 1966.  *DA*, XXVIII, 3198-A.

### 150.  *Rizal, José* (Philippine author)

150. 1.  Del-Pan, José Felipe.  Educación, nacionalismo y propaganda en la literatura del Dr. José Rizal.  Southern California, 1961.  *DA*, XXII, 257.

### 151.  *Roa Bárcena, José María*

151. 1.  Rosaldo y Hernández, Renato.  D. José María Roa Bárcena, vida y obras.  Illinois, 1942.  Urbana, 1942.  LC A43-1015.

### 152.  *Robles, Vito Alessio*

152. 1.  de Vette, Robert O.  Vito Alessio Robles: Biographer of Mexican Cities.  Florida State, 1953.  *DA*, XIII, 805.

### 153.  *Rodó, José Enrique*

153. 1.  Bacheller, Cecil Clifton.  José Enrique Rodó: His Ideas on Aesthetics.  Michigan, 1961.  *DA*, XXII, 571.

153. 2.  Berrien, William Joseph.  Rodó: Biografía y estudio crítico.  California, 1937.

153. 3.  Pereda, Clemente.  Rodó's Main Sources.  Columbia, 1948.  San Juan, P.R.-Venezuela, 1948.  LC A48-10111.

153. 4.  Pereyra-Suárez, Ester Enríquez Sarano.  La selección en la democracia: Rodó y el novecientos hispanoamericano.  Stanford, 1965.  *DA*, XXVI, 6721.

153. 5.  Rice, William Francis.  The Ideology of José Enrique Rodó.  Northwestern, 1930.

153. 6.  Scroggins, Daniel Coy.  *Motivos de Proteo* by José Enrique Rodó.  A Stylistic Study.  Michigan, 1966.  *DA*, XXVII, 2161-A.

### 154.  *Rojas, Ricardo*

154. 1.  Glauert, Earl Theodore.  Ricardo Rojas and the Emergence of Argentine Nationalism (1903-1933).  Pennsylvania, 1962.  *DA*, XXIII, 1340.

### 155.  *Rojas González, Francisco*

155. 1.  Sommers, Joseph.  The Contribution of Francisco Rojas González to Mexican Literature.  Wisconsin, 1962.  *DA*, XXIII, 2140.

### 156.  *Romanticism*

156. 1.  Avila, Pablo.  The Introduction of Romanticism in Mexico.  Stanford, 1937.  Stanford *Abstracts*, 1936-37, p. 51.

156. 2.  Brushwood, John Stubbs.  The Romantic Novel in Mexico.  Columbia, 1950.  *MA*, XI, No. 2, p. 342.

156. 3.  Hollingsworth, Roberta L.  José Peón Contreras and the Romantic Movement in Mexico.  Virginia, 1933.  Virginia *Abstracts*, 1932-33, p. 16.

156. 4.  Jaén, Didier T.  Hispanoamérica como problema a través de la generación romántica en Argentina y Chile.  Texas, 1965.  *DA*, XXVI, 2215.

156. 5.  Martín, José Luis.  La poesía de José Eusebio Caro: Contribución estilística al estudio del romanticismo hispano-americano.  Columbia, 1965.  *DA*, XXVIII, 5061-A.  Bogotá, 1966.  NUC 67-72155.

156. 6.  Norman, Isabel Hernández.  La novela romántica en las Antillas.  Yale, 1966.  *DA*, XXVII, 2539-A.

156. 7.  Suárez-Murias, Marguerite.  La novela romántica en Hispanoamérica.  Columbia, 1957.  *DA*, XVII, 2018.

156. 8.  Wilder, William R.  Romantic Elements in the First Edition of the First Series of the *Tradiciones peruanas* by Ricardo Palma.  St. Louis, 1966.  *DA*, XXVII, 3068-A.

### 157.  *Romero, Francisco*

157. 1.  Rodríguez-Alcalá, Hugo R.  Francisco Romero, el pensador de la Argentina moderna.  Wisconsin, 1953.  Wisconsin *Summaries*, XV, 633.

### 158.  *Romero, José Rubén*

158. 1.  Castagnaro, Rosario A.  J. Rubén Romero and the Novel of the Mexican Revolution.  New York, 1952.

158. 2.  Cord, William Owen.  José Rubén Romero: The Voice of Mexico.  Colorado, 1960.  *DA*, XXI, 3456.

158. 3.  Eason, Sarah Martin.  José Rubén Romero: His Ideology with Some Observations on His Style.  Ohio State, 1942.  Ohio State *Abstracts*, No. 40, p. 77.

158. 4.  McKegney, James Cuthbert.  Female Characters in the Novels of José Rubén Romero and Gregorio López y Fuentes: A Comparative Study.  Washington, Seattle, 1959.  *DA*, XX, 4115.

### 159.  *Romero García, Manuel*

159. 1.  Chadwick, John Rouse.  Main Currents in the Venezuelan Novel from Romero García to Gallegos.  California, 1955.

### 160.  *Rubín, Ramón*

160. 1.  Brown, Carol Paul.  Major Themes in the Works of Ramón Rubín.  Oklahoma, 1966.  *DA*, XXVII, 1052-A.

### 161. *Sábato, Ernesto*

161. 1. Petersen, John Fred. Ernesto Sábato: Essayist and Novelist. Washington, Seattle, 1963. *DA*, XXIV, 2910.

### 162. *Sánchez, Florencio*

162. 1. Miller, Charlotte E. Florencio Sánchez: The South American Eugene O'Neill. Washington, Seattle, 1947.

162. 2. Richardson, Ruth. Florencio Sánchez and the Argentine Theatre. Columbia, 1933. New York, 1933. LC 33-22810.

162. 3. Shedd, Karl Eastman. Florencio Sánchez. Yale, 1933. *Chapel Hill, N.C., 1936. LC 42-6429.

### 163. *Santa Cruz y Espejo, Francisco Javier Eugenio de*

163. 1. Astuto, Philip L. Francisco Javier Eugenio de Santa Cruz y Espejo, a Man of the Enlightenment in Ecuador. Columbia, 1956. *DA*, XVII, 626.

### 164. *Sarmiento, Domingo Faustino*

164. 1. Barager, Joseph R. Sarmiento and the United States. Pennsylvania, 1951.

164. 2. Bunkley, Allison Williams. Titan of the Andes: The Life of Domingo Faustino Sarmiento. Princeton, 1949. Princeton, 1952. LC 52-8763.

164. 3. Nepper, Dorothy Nicole. Sarmiento in the United States. Bryn Mawr, 1944.

### 165. *Segura, Manuel Ascensio*

165. 1. Tessen, Howard William. Manuel Ascensio Segura: His Life and Works. Yale, 1947.

### 166. *Short Story, General*

166. 1. Aldrich, Earl M., Jr. Main Trends in the Peruvian Short Story of the Twentieth Century. Indiana, 1961. *DA*, XXII, 1619.

166. 2. McMurray, George Ray. Recurring Themes and Technical Procedures in the Mexican Short Story of the Twentieth Century. Nebraska, 1955. *DA*, XV, 1400.

166. 3. Waldorf, Paul Douglass. The Contemporary Mexican Short Story. Northwestern, 1949. Northwestern *Summaries*, XVII, 68.

### 167. *Sierra, Justo*

167. 1. Davis, Joe E. The Development of Justo Sierra's Educational Thought. Texas, 1951.

167. 2. Taylor, Harvey D. Joaquín V. González and Justo Sierra, *Maestros de América*. Illinois, 1956. *DA*, XVI, 1908.

### 168. *Sigüenza y Góngora, Carlos*

168. 1. Leonard, Irving Albert. Don Carlos de Sigüenza y Góngora: His Life and Works, 1645-1700. California, 1928. *Berkeley, 1929. LC A29-798.

### 169. *Silva, José Asunción*

169. 1. Osiek, Betty T. A Stylistic Study of the Poetry of José Asunción Silva. Washington, St. Louis, 1966. *DA*, XXVII, 4262-A.

### 170. *Solana, Rafael*

170. 1. Smith, John David. Humor in the Short Stories and Plays of Rafael Solana. Southern California, 1966. *DA*, XXVII, 216-A.

### 171. *Storni, Alfonsina*

171. 1. Rosenbaum, Sidonia C. Modern Women Poets of Spanish America: The Precursors—Delmira Agustini, Gabriela Mistral, Alfonsina Storni, Juana de Ibarbourou. Columbia, 1945. New York, 1945. LC 46-4895.

### 172. *Tablada, José Juan*

172. 1. Young, Howard T. José Juan Tablada, Mexican Poet (1871-1945). Columbia, 1956. *DA*, XVI, 1458.

### 173. *Trinidad Reyes, José*

173. 1. Hoffman, Edward Lewis. The *Pastorelas* of José Trinidad Reyes: A Critical Study. George Washington, 1960. George Washington *Bulletin*, LX, No. 2, p. 49.

### 174. *Unánue, Hipólito*

174. 1. Woodham, John Edward. Hipólito Unánue and the Enlightenment in Peru. Duke, 1964. *DA*, XXVI, 2174.

### 175. *Urbina, Luis G.*

175. 1. Sáenz, Gerardo. El "Viejecito": Vida del poeta Luis G. Urbina. Texas, 1959. *DA*, XX, 2303.

### 176. *Usigli, Rodolfo*

176. 1. Rosenberg, Donald Louis. The Dramatic Theory of Rodolfo Usigli: The Poetry of Selective Realism. Iowa, 1962. *DA*, XXIII, 1827.

### 177. *Valdés, Gabriel de la Concepción, "Plácido"*

177. 1. Carruthers, Ben F. The Life Work and Death of Plácido. Illinois, 1941. Urbana, 1941. LC 41-24501.

### 178. *Valencia, Guillermo*

178. 1. Glickman, Robert J. Guillermo Valencia and the Poetic World of *Ritos*: Interpretations Based upon the Use of a Concordance. U.C.L.A., 1963. *DA*, XXIV, 1169.

178. 2. Karsen, Sonja P. Guillermo Valencia, Colombian Poet, 1873-1943. Columbia, 1950. New York, 1951. LC 52-1200.

### 179. *Valle, José Cecilio del*

179. 1. Bumgartner, Louis E. José Cecilio del Valle: Central American Savant. Duke, 1956. Durham, 1963. NUC 63-9007.

### 180. *Valle, Rosamel del*

180. 1. Schweitzer, S. Alan. Two Metaphysical Poets: An Analysis of the Philosophical Poetry of Humberto Díaz Casanueva and Rosamel del Valle. Rutgers, 1966. *DA,* XXVII, 3880-A.

### 181. *Valle y Caviedes, Juan del*

181. 1. Reedy, Daniel R. The Poetic Art of Juan del Valle Caviedes. Illinois, 1962. *DA,* XXIII, 2917.

### 182. *Varela, Félix*

182. 1. Del Ducca, [Sister] Gemma Marie. Félix Varela, Christian Liberal (1788-1853). New Mexico, 1966. *DA,* XXVII, 1751-A.

### 183. *Vargas Valdés, José Joaquín*

183. 1. Vargas-Barón, Aníbal. José Joaquín Vargas Valdés y su contribución a la democracia colombiana. Washington, Seattle, 1943. Washington *Abstracts,* VIII, 119.

### 184. *Vasconcelos, José*

184. 1. Ahumada, Rodolfo. The Philosophies of Antonio Caso and José Vasconcelos with Special Emphasis on Their Concepts of Value. Southern California, 1963. *DA,* XXIV, 3784.

184. 2. Crowley, Florence Joseph. The Conservative Thought of José Vasconcelos. Florida, 1963. *DA,* XXIV, 1994.

184. 3. DeBeer, Gabriella. José Vasconcelos and His Social Thought. Columbia, 1965. *DA,* XXVI, 7313.

184. 4. Phillips, Richard B. José Vasconcelos and the Mexican Revolution of 1910. Stanford, 1953. *DA,* XIV, 347.

### 185. *Viana, Javier de*

185. 1. Redmond, Emily. Javier de Viana, The Man and His Work. Pittsburgh, 1939. Pittsburgh *Abstracts,* XV, 291.

### 186. *Villaurrutia, Xavier*

186. 1. Dauster, Francis Nicholas, Jr. The Literary Art of Xavier Villaurrutia. Yale, 1953.

186. 2. Moreno, Anthony W. Xavier Villaurrutia: The Man and His Dramas. Pittsburgh, 1954. Pittsburgh *Bulletin,* L, No. 13, p. 22.

### 187. *Yáñez, Agustín*

187. 1. Evans, Gilbert Edward. El mundo novelístico de Agustín Yáñez. Yale, 1965. *DA,* XXVII, 1819-A.

187. 2. Haddad, Elaine. Agustín Yáñez: From Intuition to Intellectualism. Wisconsin, 1962. DA, XXIII, 2526.

### 188. *Zarco, Francisco*

188. 1. Pierce, Lester Charles. Satire in the Prose of Francisco Zarco. Southern California, 1964. *DA,* XXV, 3580.

188. 2. Wheat, Raymond Curtis. Francisco Zarco, the Liberal Spokesman of *La Reforma.* Texas, 1957. *DA,* XVII, 1745.

# PART TWO

# Portugal and Brazil

## VIII. LINGUISTICS

### 1. Bibliography

1.1. Rutherford, Phillip Roland. Linguistic Research in American Universities: Dissertations and Influences from 1900 to 1964. East Texas State, 1966. *DA*, XXVII, 2517-A.

1.2. Zimmerman, Irene. Latin American Periodicals of the Mid-Twentieth Century as Source Materials for Research in the Humanities and the Social Sciences. Michigan, 1956. *DA*, XVII, 3027.

### 2. Miscellaneous

2.1. Da Cal, Ernesto Guerra. Lengua y estilo de Eça de Queiroz. Columbia, 1950. Coimbra, 1954. NUC A55-1899.

2.2. Puglisi, Elizabeth A. The Bio-Psychological Determination of the Adequacy of Informants in American English and Brazilian Portuguese. Michigan, 1954. *DA*, XIV, 721.

2.3. Richman, Stephen Herbert. A Comparative Study of Spanish and Portuguese. Pennsylvania, 1965. *DA*, XXVI, 3319.

2.4. Schappelle, Benjamin Franklin. The German Element in Brazil, Colonies and Dialect. Pennsylvania, 1917. Philadelphia, 1917. LC 17-21802.

### 3. Adjective

3.1. Avelino, Leonidas Querubim, S.J. The Adjective and the Verb in *The Lusiads* of Camões: A Critical Analysis and Interpretation Preceded by a Survey of Camonean Criticism. Harvard, 1965. See NUC 67-79915.

### 4. Dialects

4.1. Head, Brian Franklin. A Comparison of the Segmental Phonology of Lisbon and Rio de Janeiro. Texas, 1964. *DA*, XXV, 5268.

4.2. Rogers, Francis Millet. The Pronunciation of the Madeira and Azores Dialects as Compared with Standard Portuguese. Harvard, 1940. Harvard *Summaries*, 1940, p. 414.

4.3. Thomas, Earl W. The Pronunciation of the Portuguese of Central Minas Gerais. Michigan, 1947.

See also I. 12. *Galician*

### 5. Lexicography-Lexicology

5.1. Allen, Joseph Heatly Dulles, Jr. Portuguese Word Formation with Suffixes. Pennsylvania, 1940. Philadelphia, 1941. LC 41-12537.

5.2. Clemens, George Beaver. A Tentative Portuguese Dictionary of Dated First Occurrences to the Year 1350. Pennsylvania, 1949. *DA*, XIII, 817.

5.3. Parker, Kelvin M. A Classified Vocabulary of the *Crónica troyana*. Chicago, 1953. *Salamanca, 1958. NUC 60-26925. [Galician.]

5.4. Pratola, Daniel J. Portuguese Words of Italian Origin. California, 1952.

5.5. Roberts, Kimberley Sidney. Orthography, Phonology, and Word Study of the *Leal conselheiro*. Pennsylvania, 1940. Philadelphia, 1940. LC A42-4263.

5.6. Ruiz y Ruiz, Lina Antonia. A Tentative Portuguese Dictionary of Dated First Occurrences in Certain Documents Between 1351-1450. Pennsylvania, 1964. *DA*, XXV, 5285.

5.7. Sacks, Norman Paul. The Latinity of Dated Documents in the Portuguese Territory. Pennsylvania, 1940. Philadelphia, 1941. LC A42-185.

5.8. Sharpe, Lawrence Allbright. A Critical Edition of the Old Portuguese *Vida de S. Bernardo*, with Introduction, Notes and Glossary. North Carolina, 1956. North Carolina *Record*, No. 576, p. 288.

### 6. Linguistic Analysis

6.1. Abraham, Richard D. A Portuguese Version of the *Life of Barlaam and Josaphat*. Paleographical Edition and Linguistic Study. Pennsylvania, 1937. Philadelphia, 1938. LC 39-7230.

6.2. Carter, Henry Hare. Paleographical Edition and Study of the Language of a Portion of Codex Alcobacensis 200. Pennsylvania, 1937. Philadelphia, 1938. LC 38-11959. [A dialogue on Christian doctrine and confession.]

6.3. Daniel, Mary Lou. Guimarães Rosa: A Linguistic Study. Wisconsin, 1965. *DA*, XXVI, 3331.

6.4. Jaffé, Erwin. A Treatment of Certain Aspects of Galician as Found in the *Crónica troyana*. Harvard, 1939. Harvard *Summaries*, 1939, p. 268.

6.5. Pap, Leo. Portuguese-American Speech: An Outline of Speech Conditions Among Portuguese Immigrants in New England and Elsewhere in the United States. Columbia, 1948. New York, 1949. LC 49-9387.

6. 6. Sousa, Thomas Frederic. A Linguistic Analysis of a Portion of the Galician Translation of the *General estoria* by Alfonso X, el Sabio. Wisconsin, 1964. *DA,* XXIV, 5418.

### 7. *Morphology*

7. 1. Eastlack, Charles Leonard. The Morphology of the Verb in Portuguese. Texas, 1964. *DA,* XXV, 2973.

7. 2. Russo, Harold J. Morphology and Syntax of the *Leal conselheiro.* Pennsylvania, 1939. Philadelphia, 1942. LC A43-1274.

### 8. *Orthography*

8. 1. Domincovich, Ruth. Portuguese Orthography to 1500. Pennsylvania, 1947. Philadelphia, 1948. LC A50-505.

8. 2. Freeman, Ludmila Cermak. A History of Portuguese Orthography Since 1500. Pennsylvania, 1965. *DA,* XXVI, 3335.

8. 3. Learned, Erma R. Old Portuguese Vocalic Finals (Phonology and Orthography of Accented -ou, -eu, -iu and -ao, -eo, -io). Pennsylvania, 1948. Philadelphia, 1950. LC A50-7435.

8. 4. Roberts, Kimberley Sidney. Orthography, Phonology, and Word Study of the *Leal conselheiro.* Pennsylvania, 1940. Philadelphia, 1940. LC A42-4263.

### 9. *Phonetics-Phonology*

9. 1. Head, Brian Franklin. A Comparison of the Segmental Phonology of Lisbon and Rio de Janeiro. Texas, 1964. *DA,* XXV, 5268.

9. 2. Learned, Erma R. Old Portuguese Vocalic Finals (Phonology and Orthography of Accented -ou, -eu, -iu and -ao, -eo, -io). Pennsylvania, 1948. Philadelphia, 1950. LC A50-7435.

9. 3. Pap, Leo. Portuguese-American Speech: An Outline of Speech Conditions Among Portuguese Immigrants in New England and Elsewhere in the United States. Columbia, 1948. New York, 1949. LC 49-9387.

9. 4. Roberts, Kimberley Sidney. Orthography, Phonology, and Word Study of the *Leal conselheiro.* Pennsylvania, 1940. Philadelphia, 1940. LC A42-4263.

9. 5. Rogers, Francis Millet. The Pronunciation of the Madeira and Azores Dialects as Compared with Standard Portuguese. Harvard, 1940. Harvard *Summaries,* 1940, p. 414.

9. 6. Thomas, Earl W. The Pronunciation of the Portuguese of Central Minas Gerais. Michigan, 1947.

*Romance Languages, Comparative, General.* See I. 26.

### 10. *Suffix*

10. 1. Allen, Joseph Heatly Dulles, Jr. Portuguese Word Formation with Suffixes. Pennsylvania, 1940. Philadelphia, 1941. LC 41-12537.

### 11. *Syntax*

11. 1. Russo, Harold J. Morphology and Syntax of the *Leal conselheiro.* Pennsylvania, 1939. Philadelphia, 1942. LC A43-1274.

11. 2. Schnerr, Walter J. Modern Portuguese Uses of *Ser* and *Estar.* Pennsylvania, 1947. *MA,* X, No. 2, p. 106.

### 12. *Transformational Grammar*

12. 1. Wyatt, James L. An Automated Portuguese to English Transformational Grammar. Texas, 1965. *DA,* XXVII, 195-A.

### 13. *Verb*

13. 1. Avelino, Leonidas Querubim, S.J. The Adjective and the Verb in *The Lusiads* of Camões: A Critical Analysis and Interpretation Preceded by a Survey of Camonean Criticism. Harvard, 1965. See NUC 67-79915.

13. 2. Eastlack, Charles Leonard. The Morphology of the Verb in Portuguese. Texas, 1964. *DA,* XXV, 2973.

13. 3. Schnerr, Walter J. Modern Portuguese Uses of *Ser* and *Estar.* Pennsylvania, 1947. *MA,* X, No. 2, p. 106.

### IX.   LITERATURE OF PORTUGAL

### 1. *Miscellaneous*

1. 1. Carter, Henry Hare. Paleographical Edition and Study of the Language of a Portion of Codex Alcobacensis 200. Pennsylvania, 1937. Philadelphia, 1938. LC 38-11959. [A dialogue on Christian doctrine and confession.]

1. 2. Duffy, James Edward. Portuguese Narratives of Shipwreck, 1552-1649. Harvard, 1952. *Cambridge, Mass., 1955. NUC 54-9774.

1. 3. Hower, Alfred. Hipólito da Costa and Luso-Brazilian Journalism in Exile: London, 1808-1822. Harvard, 1954.

1. 4. Newman, Elizabeth Thompson. A Critical Edition of an Early Portuguese Cookbook. North Carolina, 1964. *DA,* XXVI, 1641.

### 2. *Alfonso X, King of Castile*

2. 1.   Callcott, Frank.   The Supernatural in Early Spanish Literature, Studied in the Works of the Court of Alfonso X, el Sabio.   Columbia, 1923.   New York, 1923.   LC 23-11223.   [Treatment of the *Cántigas de Santa María.*]

2. 2.   Dexter, Elsie Forsythe.   Sources of the *Cántigas* of Alfonso el Sabio.   Wisconsin, 1926.

2. 3.   Kline, Lawton.   A Metrical Study of the *Cántigas de Santa María* by Alfonso el Sabio.   Stanford, 1950.   Stanford *Abstracts*, XXV, 232.

2. 4.   Sousa, Thomas Frederic.   A Linguistic Analysis of a Portion of the Galician Translation of the *General estoria* by Alfonso X, el Sabio.   Wisconsin, 1964.   *DA*, XXIV, 5418.

*Amadís de Gaula.*   See III. 5.

### 3. *Barlaam and Josaphat*

3. 1.   Abraham, Richard D.   A Portuguese Version of the *Life of Barlaam and Josaphat.*   Paleographical Edition and Linguistic Study.   Pennsylvania, 1937.   Philadelphia, 1938.   LC 39-7230.

### 4. *Barros, João de*

4. 1.   Hernández, Gustavo Augusto.   João de Barros: First Great Portuguese Prose Writer.   North Carolina, 1952.   North Carolina *Record*, No. 520, p. 250.

### 5. *Camões, Luiz de*

5. 1.   Avelino, Leonidas Querubim, S.J.   The Adjective and the Verb in *The Lusiads* of Camões: A Critical Analysis and Interpretation Preceded by a Survey of Camonean Criticism.   Harvard, 1965.   See NUC 67-79915.

5. 2.   Freitas, William John.   An Historic and Geographic Commentary on *The Lusiads* of Camões.   Stanford, 1958.   *DA*, XIX, 327.

5. 3.   Giamatti, Angelo Bartlett.   The Earthly Paradise in the Renaissance Epic.   Yale, 1964.   Princeton, 1966.   NUC 66-10554.   [Treatment of Camões.]

5. 4.   Letzring, Madonna Marie.   The Influence of Camoens in English Literature.   Maryland, 1962.   *DA*, XXV, 1915.

5. 5.   Rozen, Eva J.   Renaissance Motifs in Epic Theory and Poetry in the Romance Languages.   New York, 1962.   *DA*, XXVII, 1792-A.   [Treatment of Camões.]

### 6. *Cancioneiros*

6. 1.   Askins, Arthur Lee.   A Critical Edition and Study of the *Cancioneiro de Évora*, in Manuscript CXIV/ 1-17 of the Public Library of Évora, Portugal.   California, 1963.   *DA*, XXIV, 5403.

6. 2.   Fraker, Charles Frederic, Jr.   The Doctrinal Poetry in the *Cancionero de Baena.*   Harvard, 1963.   *Chapel Hill, N.C., 1966.   NUC 67-63054.

### 7. *Cantigas d'escarnho e de maldizer*

7. 1.   Phillips, Florence Virginia.   An Edition of Some of the *Cantigas d'escarnho e de maldizer.*   Ohio State, 1955.   *DA*, XVI, 529.

### 8. *Cape Verdean Literature*

8. 1.   Araujo, Norman.   From Classicism to Clarity: A Study of Cape Verdean Literature.   Harvard, 1962.   *Chestnut Hill, Mass., 1966.   NUC 67-7522.

### 9. *Castro, Eugênio de*

9. 1.   Fein, John Morton.   Eugênio de Castro and the Development of Cosmopolitanism in Hispanic Poetry.   Harvard, 1950.

*Castro, Rosalía de.*   See V. 11.

### 10. *Crónica troyana*

10. 1.   Jaffé, Erwin.   A Treatment of Certain Aspects of Galician as Found in the *Crónica troyana.*   Harvard, 1939.   Harvard *Summaries*, 1939, p. 268.

10. 2.   Parker, Kelvin M.   A Classified Vocabulary of the *Crónica troyana.*   Chicago, 1953.   *Salamanca, 1958.   NUC 60-26925.

### 11. *Duarte, King of Portugal*

11. 1.   Roberts, Kimberley Sidney.   Orthography, Phonology, and Word Study of the *Leal conselheiro.*   Pennsylvania, 1940.   Philadelphia, 1940.   LC A42-4263.

11. 2.   Russo, Harold J.   Morphology and Syntax of the *Leal conselheiro.*   Pennsylvania, 1939.   Philadelphia, 1942.   LC A43-1274.

### 12. *Eça de Queiroz, José Maria de*

12. 1.   Da Cal, Ernesto Guerra.   Lengua y estilo de Eça de Queiroz.   Columbia, 1950.   Coimbra, 1954.   NUC A55-1899.

12. 2.   Hill, Emma May.   Irony in the Novels of Eça de Queiroz.   Wisconsin, 1954.   *DA*, XVII, 2610.

### 13. *Ferreira de Vasconcellos, Jorge*

13. 1.   Piper, Anson Conant.   The Portuguese Court of the Sixteenth Century as Reflected in the Dramatic Novels of Jorge Ferreira de Vasconcellos.   Wisconsin, 1953.   Wisconsin *Summaries*, XV, 629.

*Galician Literature, General.*   See II. 5.

#### 14. *Livro de citraria*

14. 1.  Nelson, Jan A.  A Critical Edition of the *Livro de citraria*. North Carolina, 1964. *DA*, XXVI, 1653.  [15th century Portuguese translation of López de Ayala's *Libro de la caza de las aves*.]

#### 15. *Lobo, Jeronymo*

15. 1.  Gold, Joel Jay.  Samuel Johnson's "Epitomizing" of Lobo's *Voyage to Abyssinia*. Indiana, 1962. *DA*, XXIII, 4357.

15. 2.  Lockhart, Donald Merritt.  Father Jeronymo Lobo's Writings Concerning Ethiopia, Including Hitherto Unpublished Manuscripts in the Palmella Library.  Harvard, 1959.

#### 16. *Machado, Francisco*

16. 1.  Dordick, Mildred E.  An Edition of the Sixteenth-Century Portuguese Manuscript *Espelho de christãos novos* by Francisco Machado.  Wisconsin, 1965. *DA*, XXVIII, 625-A.

#### 17. *Poetry*

17. 1.  Pope, Isabel.  Sources of the Musical and Metrical Forms of the Mediaeval Lyric in the Hispanic Peninsula.  Radcliffe, 1930.

#### 18. *Rodrigues Lobo, Francisco*

18. 1.  Preto-Rodas, Richard A.  Structure and Theme in Rodrigues Lobo's *Corte na aldeia e noites de inverno*.  Michigan, 1966. *DA*, XXVII, 3467-A.

#### 19. *Stylistics*

19. 1.  Craddock, [Sister] Clare Eileen.  Style Theories as Found in Stylistic Studies of Romance Scholars, 1900-1950.  Catholic, 1952.  Washington, 1952. LC A52-7015.

19. 2.  Da Cal, Ernesto Guerra.  Lengua y estilo de Eça de Queiroz.  Columbia, 1950.  Coimbra, 1954. NUC A55-1899.

#### 20. *Tales*

20. 1.  Martínez, Quino E.  Motif-Index of Portuguese Tales.  North Carolina, 1955.  North Carolina *Record*, No. 562, p. 237.

#### 21. *Versification*

21. 1.  Pope, Isabel.  Sources of the Musical and Metrical Forms of the Mediaeval Lyric in the Hispanic Peninsula.  Radcliffe, 1930.

#### 22. *Vicente, Gil*

22. 1.  Andrews, James Richard.  The Artistry of the Plays of Gil Vicente.  Princeton, 1953. *DA*, XIV, 116.

22. 2.  Joiner, Ida Virginia.  The Dramatic Art of Gil Vicente.  Texas, 1940.

22. 3.  Lunardini, Peter J.  The Poetic Technique of Gil Vicente.  New Mexico, 1953.

22. 4.  Moseley, William Whatley.  An Etymological Vocabulary of the Spanish in the Works of Gil Vicente.  New Mexico, 1954. *DA*, XV, 119.

22. 5.  Tomlins, Jack Edward.  The Nature of Gil Vicente's Dramatic Artistry.  Princeton, 1954. *DA*, XVIII, 238.

#### 23. *Vida de S. Bernardo*

23. 1.  Sharpe, Lawrence Allbright.  A Critical Edition of the Old Portuguese *Vida de S. Bernardo*, with Introduction, Notes and Glossary.  North Carolina, 1956.  North Carolina *Record*, No. 576, p. 288.

#### 24. *Vieira, Antônio*

24. 1.  Gotaas, Mary C.  Bossuet and Vieira, A Study in National, Epochal and Individual Style.  Catholic, 1953.  Washington, 1953. NUC A53-5211.

COMPARATIVE STUDIES: Portuguese Relations with Other Literatures.

#### 25. *English*

25. 1.  Gold, Joel Jay.  Samuel Johnson's "Epitomizing" of Lobo's *Voyage to Abyssinia*. Indiana, 1962. *DA*, XXIII, 4357.

25. 2.  Letzring, Madonna Marie.  The Influence of Camoens in English Literature.  Maryland, 1962. *DA*, XXV, 1915.

#### 26. *European*

26. 1.  Giamatti, Angelo Bartlett.  The Earthly Paradise in the Renaissance Epic.  Yale, 1964.  Princeton, 1966. NUC 66-10554.  [Treatment of Camões.]

26. 2.  Rozen, Eva J.  Renaissance Motifs in Epic Theory and Poetry in the Romance Languages.  New York, 1962. *DA*, XXVII, 1792-A.  [Treatment of Camões.]

#### 27. *French*

27. 1.  Gotaas, Mary C.  Bossuet and Vieira, A Study in National, Epochal and Individual Style.  Catholic, 1953.  Washington, 1953. NUC A53-5211.

27. 2.  Hasbrouck, Francis Mahlon.  Spanish and Portuguese Historical Characters in Modern French Drama Before 1830.  Johns Hopkins, 1933.

#### 28. *Latin, Medieval*

28. 1.  Jaffé, Erwin.  A Treatment of Certain Aspects of Galician as Found in the *Crónica troyana*.  Harvard, 1939.  Harvard *Summaries*, 1939, p. 268.

28. 2.   Parker, Kelvin M.   A Classified Vocabulary of the *Crónica troyana*.   Chicago, 1953.   \*Salamanca, 1958.   NUC 60-26925.

### 29. *Spanish*

29. 1.   Fein, John Morton.   Eugênio de Castro and the Development of Cosmopolitanism in Hispanic Poetry.   Harvard, 1950.

29. 2.   McKenna, James B.   A Spaniard in the Portuguese Indies: The Narrative of Martín Fernández de Figueroa.   Harvard, 1965.   Cambridge, Mass., 1967.   NUC 67-27089.

29. 3.   Nelson, Jan A.   A Critical Edition of the *Livro de citraria*.   North Carolina, 1964.   *DA,* XXVI, 1653.   [15th century Portuguese translation of López de Ayala's *Libro de la caza de las aves.*]

See also *Alfonso X, King of Castile,* IX. 2.

## X.   LITERATURE OF BRAZIL

### 1. *Bibliography*

1. 1.   Zimmerman, Irene.   Latin American Periodicals of the Mid-Twentieth Century as Source Materials for Research in the Humanities and Social Sciences.   Michigan, 1956.   *DA,* XVII, 3027.

### 2. *Miscellaneous*

2. 1.   Driver, David Miller.   The Indian in Brazilian Literature.   Columbia, 1942.   New York, 1942.   LC 43-11332.

2. 2.   Hower, Alfred.   Hipólito da Costa and Luso-Brazilian Journalism in Exile: London, 1808-1822.   Harvard, 1954.

2. 3.   Sayers, Raymond Samuel.   The Negro in Brazilian Literature Until 1888.   Columbia, 1952.   \*New York, 1956.   NUC 56-2175.

### 3. *Alencar, José de*

3. 1.   Winkler, Norman.   The *Sertão* in the *Romances* of Four Brazilian Writers: José Alencar, Bernardo de Guimarães, Franklin Távora, and Alfredo d'Escragnolle Taunay.   Pittsburgh, 1960.   *DA,* XXI, 3794.

### 4. *Amado, Jorge*

4. 1.   Ellison, Fred P.   The Novel of Brazil's Northeast.   California, 1952.   \*Berkeley, 1954.   NUC 54-11314.   [José Lins do Rego, Jorge Amado, Graciliano Ramos, Rachel de Queiroz.]

4. 2.   Turner, Doris Jean.   The Poor and Social Symbolism in Three Novels of Jorge Amado.   St. Louis, 1966.   *DA,* XXVIII, 3201-A.

### 5. *Delfino dos Santos, Luís*

5. 1.   Haberly, David Tristam.   Luís Delfino dos Santos, Prince of Brazilian Lyric Poets, 1834-1910.   Harvard, 1966.   See NUC 67-94010.

### 6. *Drama, General*

6. 1.   Woodyard, George William.   The Search for Identity: A Comparative Study in Contemporary Latin American Drama.   Illinois, 1966.   *DA,* XXVII, 2165-A.   [Spanish-American and Brazilian drama.]

### 7. *Escragnolle Taunay, Alfredo de*

7. 1.   Mate, Hubert E.   Alfredo d'Escragnolle Taunay— Writer, Soldier, and Political Figure of the Brazilian Empire.   Northwestern, 1949.   Northwestern *Summaries,* XVII, 64.

7. 2.   Winkler, Norman.   The *Sertão* in the *Romances* of Four Brazilian Writers: José Alencar, Bernardo de Guimarães, Franklin Távora, and Alfredo d'Escragnolle Taunay.   Pittsburgh, 1960.   *DA,* XXI, 3794.

### 8. *Fiction, General*

8. 1.   Flores, Angel.   Three Ecological Patterns in South American Fiction.   Cornell, 1947.   Cornell *Abstracts,* 1947, p. 45.   [Spanish-American and Brazilian fiction.]

8. 2.   Rabassa, Gregory.   The Negro in Brazilian Fiction Since 1888.   Columbia, 1954.   *DA,* XIV, 2072.

8. 3.   Walther, Don H.   Brazilian Prose Fiction—The Amazon Region.   North Carolina, 1948.   North Carolina *Record,* No. 464, p. 362.

### 9. *Guimarães, Bernardo*

9. 1.   Andrews, Norwood H., Jr.   Bernardo Guimarães and the Brazilian Novel of Transition.   Wisconsin, 1964.   *DA,* XXV, 4140.

9. 2.   Winkler, Norman.   The *Sertão* in the *Romances* of Four Brazilian Writers: José Alencar, Bernardo de Guimarães, Franklin Távora, and Alfredo d'Escragnolle Taunay.   Pittsburgh, 1960.   *DA,* XXI, 3794.

### 10. *Lima, Jorge de*

10. 1.   White, Florence Estella.   *Poesía Negra* in the Works of Jorge de Lima, Nicolás Guillén, and Jacques Roumain, 1927-1947.   Wisconsin, 1952.   Wisconsin *Summaries,* XIII, 399.

### 11. *Lins do Rego, José*

11. 1.   Ellison, Fred P.   The Novel of Brazil's Northeast.   California, 1952.   \*Berkeley, 1954.   NUC 54-11314.   [José Lins do Rego, Jorge Amado, Graciliano Ramos, Rachel de Queiroz.]

11. 2.   Maxwell, Henry James.   The Sociological Novels of José Lins do Rego.   Wisconsin, 1955.   Wisconsin *Summaries*, XVI, 570.

11. 3.   Rose, Theodore Everett.   An Historical Survey of the Development of the Regional Novel of Northeastern Brazil and More Especially to the Works of José Lins do Rego.   New York, 1959.   *DA*, XX, 4662.

### 12.   *Lisboa, Henriqueta*

12. 1.   Lobo Filho, Blanca.   The Poetry of Henriqueta Lisboa.   New York, 1965.   *DA*, XXV, 7274.   *Belo Horizonte, 1966.

### 13.   *Machado de Assis, Joaquim Maria*

13. 1.   Kocher, [Sister] John.   Machado de Assis and the Book of Ecclesiastes: Influences, Reminiscences and Parallels.   Wisconsin, 1957.   *DA*, XVII, 1555.

13. 2.   Virgillo, Carmelo.   Some Themes in Machado de Assis' Short Stories.   Indiana, 1963.   *DA*, XXV, 488.

13. 3.   Woodbridge, Benjamin M., Jr.   Pessimism in the Writings of Machado de Assis: A Study in the Development of an Attitude and Its Expression.   Harvard, 1949.

### 14.   *Monteiro Lobato, José Bento*

14. 1.   Brown, Timothy.   Monteiro Lobato: A Critique.   Wisconsin, 1955.   *DA*, XVI, 961.

### 15.   *Novel, General*

15. 1.   Andrews, Norwood H., Jr.   Bernardo Guimarães and the Brazilian Novel of Transition.   Wisconsin, 1964.   *DA*, XXV, 4140.

15. 2.   Bailey, Dale S.   Slavery in the Novels of Brazil and the United States: A Comparison.   Indiana, 1961.   *DA*, XXII, 1620.

15. 3.   Ellison, Fred P.   The Novel of Brazil's Northeast.   California, 1952.   *Berkeley, 1954.   NUC 54-11314.   [José Lins do Rego, Jorge Amado, Graciliano Ramos, Rachel de Queiroz.]

15. 4.   Loos, Dorothy Scott.   The Naturalistic Novel of Brazil.   Columbia, 1950.   *MA*, X, No. 4, p. 217.

15. 5.   Rose, Theodore Everett.   An Historical Survey of the Development of the Regional Novel of Northeastern Brazil and More Especially of the Works of José Lins do Rego.   New York, 1959.   *DA*, XX, 4662.

15. 6.   Slutzkin, Herman Bernard.   The Immigrant and Other Foreign Characters in the Brazilian Novel.   Columbia, 1957.   *DA*, XVIII, 1439.

15. 7.   Winkler, Norman.   The *Sertão* in the *Romances* of Four Brazilian Writers: José Alencar, Bernardo de Guimarães, Franklin Távora, and Alfredo d'Escragnolle Taunay.   Pittsburgh, 1960.   *DA*, XXI, 3794.

### 16.   *Poetry, General*

16. 1.   Wallis, Marie P.   Modern Women Poets of Brazil.   New Mexico, 1947.

### 17.   *Queiroz, Rachel de*

17. 1.   Ellison, Fred P.   The Novel of Brazil's Northeast.   California, 1952.   *Berkeley, 1954.   NUC 54-11314.   [José Lins do Rego, Jorge Amado, Graciliano Ramos, Rachel de Queiroz.]

### 18.   *Ramos, Graciliano*

18. 1.   Ellison, Fred P.   The Novel of Brazil's Northeast.   California, 1952.   *Berkeley, 1954.   NUC 54-11314.   [José Lins do Rego, Jorge Amado, Graciliano Ramos, Rachel de Queiroz.]

18. 2.   Hamilton, Russell George, Jr.   A arte de ficção de Graciliano Ramos: A apresentação de personagens.   Yale, 1965.   *DA*, XXVI, 2211.

### 19.   *Rosa, João Guimarães*

19. 1.   Daniel, Mary Lou.   Guimarães Rosa: A Linguistic Study.   Wisconsin, 1965.   *DA*, XXVI, 3331.

### 20.   *Stylistics*

20. 1.   Craddock, [Sister] Clare Eileen.   Style Theories as Found in Stylistic Studies of Romance Scholars, 1900-1950.   Catholic, 1952.   Washington, 1952.   LC A52-7015.

### 21.   *Távora, Franklin*

21. 1.   Winkler, Norman.   The *Sertão* in the *Romances* of Four Brazilian Writers: José Alencar, Bernardo de Guimarães, Franklin Távora, and Alfredo d'Escragnolle Taunay.   Pittsburgh, 1960.   *DA*, XXI, 3794.

COMPARATIVE STUDIES: Brazilian Relations with Other Literatures.

### 22.   *Biblical*

22. 1.   Kocher, [Sister] John.   Machado de Assis and the Book of Ecclesiastes: Influences, Reminiscences and Parallels.   Wisconsin, 1957.   *DA*, XVII, 1555.

### 23.   *Haiti*

23. 1.   White, Florence Estella.   *Poesía Negra* in the Works of Jorge de Lima, Nicolás Guillén, and Jacques Roumain, 1927-1947.   Wisconsin, 1952.   Wisconsin *Summaries*, XIII, 399.

### 24. *Spanish-American*

24. 1. Flores, Angel. Three Ecological Patterns in South American Fiction. Cornell, 1947. Cornell *Abstracts*, 1947, p. 45.

24. 2. White, Florence Estella. *Poesia Negra* in the Works of Jorge de Lima, Nicolás Guillén, and Jacques Roumain, 1927-1947. Wisconsin, 1952. Wisconsin *Summaries*, XIII, 399.

24. 3. Woodyard, George William. The Search for Identity: A Comparative Study in Contemporary Latin American Drama. Illinois, 1966. *DA*, XXVII, 2165-A.

### 25. *United States*

25. 1. Bailey, Dale S. Slavery in the Novels of Brazil and the United States: A Comparison. Indiana, 1961. *DA*, XXII, 1620.

# General Index

Berndt, Erna R., III.15.2.
Berndt, Robert J., II.12.2.
Bernstein, Jerome S., II.7.1.
Berrien, William J., VII.153.2.
Bershas, Henry N., III.28.1.
Berumen y Silva, Alfredo, IV.97.2.
Betoret-París, Eduardo, VI.13.1.
Beym, Richard, I.2.3.
Bibb, Elizabeth S., IV.93.1.
Bible, II.14, V.53.44.
—Medieval Spanish, III.8; Epistles, prologue,
  III.8.1; etymology, III.8.2; Exodus, III.8.2;
  Gospels, III.8.7; Herman the German,
  III.8.6; Leviticus, III.8.2, III.8.3; linguistic
  analysis, III.8.1, III.8.4; Maccabees, III.8.5;
  Matthew, III.8.4; Numbers, III.8.3; Psalter,
  III.8.6; Romans, III.8.1; vocabulary, III.8.
  3.
Biblical influence in Spanish literature,
  II.14.
Bibliography, I.1, II.1, IV.1, V.1, VII.1;
  bibliographers of Spanish Colonial period,
  VII.1.2; criticism, Spanish, 1700-1800, V.
  1.1.; Guatemalan novel, VII.1.1; Hispano-
  Classical translations, 1482-1699, IV.1.1;
  Latin-American periodicals, humanities
  and social sciences, 20th century, VII.1.6;
  linguistics, articles in serials, 1887-1947,
  I.1.1., linguistics, research in American
  universities, I.1.2; picaresque novel, IV.1.2;
  Spanish-American literature in Peruvian
  serials, Yale Library, VII.1.3; Venezuelan
  literature, Yale Library, VII.1.5.
Bickley, James G., VII.50.1.
Bieghler, Edward W., V.50.1.
Bilingualism, I.2.16.
Billingsley, Allie W., III.45.1.
Bininger, Robert J., IV.123.3.
Biographical studies, Alarcón, Pedro Anto-
  nio de, V.3.2; Aldana, Francisco de, IV.4.1;
  Altamirano, Ignacio Manuel, VII.19.2;
  Alvarez Quintero, Serafín y Joaquín, VI.
  5.2; Argensola, Lupercio Leonardo de,
  IV.7.1; Arguijo, Juan de, IV.8.1; Belmonte
  Bermúdez, Luis de, IV.14.1; Blanco-
  Fombona, Rufino, VII.28.1; Böhl de
  Faber, Cecilia, V.8.3; Bulnes, Francisco,
  VII.32.1; Bustamante, Carlos, VII.33.1;
  Campo, Angel del, VII.34.1; Carrasquilla,
  Tomás, VII.38.1; Casal, Julián del, VII.
  40.1; Castellanos, Jesús, VII.42.1; Castillejo,
  Cristóbal de, IV.19.1; Castro, Rosalía de,
  V.11.3· Crespo Toral, Remigio, VII.46.1;
  Delgado, Rafael, VII.50.1; Díaz Mirón,
  Salvador, VII.54.1; Fernández de Lizardi,
  José Joaquín, VII.61.2; Fernández de
  Moratín, Leandro, V.21.3; Fernández Mo-
  reno, Baldomero, VII.62.1; Gallegos, Ró-
  mulo, VII.66.3; Gálvez, Manuel, VII.67.3;
  Gamboa, Federico, VII.68.3· Gómez de la
  Serna, Ramón, VI.29.1; González Peña,
  Carlos, VII.77.1; Grau, Jacinto, VI.31.2;
  Hernández Catá, VII.89.2; Herrera, Ernes-
  to, VII.90.1; Jiménez, Juan Ramón, VI.
  37.4; Lira, Miguel N., VII.103.1; Lloréns
  Torres, Luis, VII.104.2; Marineo Sículo,
  Lucio, IV.74.1; Martí, José, VII.114.4; Milla
  y Vidaurre, José, VII.117.1; Nalé Roxlo,
  Conrado, VII.121.2; Navarro Ledesma,
  Francisco, V.43.1; Ortiz Guerrero, Manuel,
  VII.130.1; Pérez Bonalde, Juan Antonio,
  VII.137.1; Pérez de Montalván, Juan, IV.

92.1; Peza, Juan de Dios, VII.138.1; Prieto,
  Guillermo, VII.143.1; Reyes, Matías de
  los, IV.100.1; Roa Bárcena, José María,
  VII.151.1; Rodó, José Enrique, VII.153.2;
  Ruiz de Alarcón, IV.105.10; Sarmiento,
  Domingo Faustino, VII.164.2; Segura,
  Manuel Ascensio, VII.165.1; Sigüenza y
  Góngora, Carlos, VII.168.1; Solís, Dionisio,
  V.62.1; Suárez de Figueroa, Cristóbal, IV.
  114.1; Taboada, Luis, V.63.1; Torque-
  mada, Antonio de, IV.119.2; Unamuno,
  Miguel de, VI.73.5; Urbina, Luis G., VII.
  175.1; Vélez de Guevara, Luis, IV.123.
  10.
Biography, IV.54.3, VII.10.41.
Biondi, Raymond L., II.7.2.
Birch, William G., IV.97.3.
Bird, James P., III.35.1.
Blanch, Mable, II.2.4.
Blanco, Andrés Eloy, poetry, VII.27.1.
Blanco Amor, José, theme of isolation in
  novels, VI.12.1.
Blanco-Fombona, Rufino, man and work,
  VII.28.1.
Blansitt, Edward L., Jr., I.24.1.
Blasco Ibáñez, Vicente, VI.13; accusative,
  personal, in works, VI.13.4; costumbrismo,
  VI.13.1; materialistic ideas, VI.13.7; novels,
  1894-1909, survey, VI.13.5; propagandist,
  social, VI.13.2; realism, exponent of, VI.
  13.6; reformer, social, VI.13.2; short stories,
  VI.13.3.
Blaylock, William C., I.23.4.
Blest Gana, Alberto, VII.29; Chilean cus-
  toms, VII.29.1; historical element, VII.29.
  3; novels, VII.29.1, VII.29.2, VII.29.3; so-
  ciety, Chilean, VII.29.2.
Bleznick, Donald W., IV.48.1.
Blind, V.53.10.
Boarino, Gerald L., III.12.1.
Boccaccio, Giovanni, II.22.1.
Boccalini, II.22.18.
Bodensieck, Anne M., I.2.4.
Boggs, Ralph S., II.4.1.
Böhl de Faber, Cecilia, "Fernán Caballero,"
  V.8; feminine life, V.8.1; life and letters,
  V.8.3; novels, V.8.1, V.8.4; social philoso-
  phy, V.8.2.
Bolinger, Dwight L., VI.10.2.
Bolivian literature, VII.3; contemporary,
  social protest, VII.3.3; gamonal, VII.3.3;
  Guerra del Chaco, VII.3.1, VII.3.2; social
  literature, VII.3.2.
Borelli, Catherine M., VI.74.1.
Borenstein, Walter, VII.10.3.
Borges, Jorge Luis, VII.30; poetry, VII.30.2;
  stories, structure, VII.30.3; symbol and
  motif, VII.30.4; unreality, expression in
  works, VII.30.1.
Boring, Omen K., IV.17.2.
Boring, Phyllis Z., VI.20.1.
Borrowdale, Howard O., VII.10.3.
Boudreau, Harold L., VI.74.2.
Bourgeois, Louis C., VII.52.1.
Bourland, Caroline B., II.22.1.
Bourne, Marjorie A., II.15.2.
Bouscal, Guérin de, II.19.6.
Bowen, Benjamin L., I.26.4.
Bowen, Jean D., I.9.1.
Bowen, Wayne S., VII.10.4.
Boyd, Lola E., VII.10.4.
Boyd-Bowman, Peter M., I.9.2.

Boydston, Jo Ann H., VII.7.2.
Boyer, Mildred V., V.60.1.
Brackenridge, II.29.8.
Bradford, Marjorie E., IV.53.1.
Bradley, Henry A., V.52.1.
Bradman, Helen, VII.75.1.
Brancaforte, Benito, II.7.3.
Bratsas, Dorothy N., VII.10.5.
Braun, Lucille V., V.53.7.
Brazilian-Biblical literary relations, X.22.1.
Brazilian-Haiti literary relations, X.23.1.
Brazilian-Spanish American literary
  relations, II.30.
Brazilian-United States literary relations,
  X.25.1.
Breen, Dorothy R., IV.122.7.
Brend, Ruth M., I.8.1.
Brenes, Carmen O., IV.105.2.
Brenes, Dalai, IV.22.4.
Brent, William A., V.4.1.
Brentano, Sr. Mary B., IV.54.1.
Brewer, William B., I.18.2.
Bricca, John F., II.22.2.
Bristol, William B., VII.16.1.
Britt, Claude H., Jr., IV.80.1.
Brooks, John, IV.122.8.
Brooks, Mary E., II.2.5.
Brosman, Margaret C., I.27.3.
Brower, Gary L., VII.140.1.
Brown, Anita D., I.16.3.
Brown, Carol P., VII.160.1.
Brown, Charles B., I.29.8.
Brown, Donald F., II.19.3.
Brown, Leslie P., I.15.3.
Brown, Louise S., II.17.1.
Brown, Sherman W., IV.116.1.
Brown, Timothy, X.14.1.
Browne, James R., V.15.1.
Brownell, George G., I.3.1.
Brownstein, Rachel M., II.2.6.
Brunet, Marta, narrative prose, VII.31.1.
Brushwood, John S., VII.10.6.
Bryant, Shasta M., II.3.1.
Bryant, William C., IV.44.1.
Buchanan, Milton A., IV.78.2.
Buchwalter, Grace M., II.2.7.
Buck, Vera H., IV.9.1.
Buckingham, Elizabeth, III.1.3.
Buckingham, Lucius H., I.23.5.
Bucklin, Lincoln B., I.2.5.
Buero Vallejo, Antonio, VI.14; *En la
  ardiente oscuridad*, translation, VI.14.2;
  tragedies, VI.14.1.
Bulatkin, Eleanor Webster, I.15.4.
Bull, William E., V.4.2.
Bulnes, Francisco, life and works, VII.32.1.
Bumgartner, Louis E., VII.179.1.
Bunkley, Allison W., VII.164.2.
Burgos, Javier de, sainete, V.9.1.
Burke, James F., III.37.1.
Burks, Margie N., V.59.1.
Burks, William G., V.45.2.
Burner, Jarvis B., IV.122.9.
Burner, Willis J., VII.16.2.
Burnie, William R., II.19.4.
Busch, Carolyn L., VI.73.3.
*El buscapié*, VII.60.1.
Bustamante, Carlos, *Diario histórico*, edited,
  with life of author, VII.33.1.
Butler, Charles W., VII.68.1.
Butterfield, Marvin E., IV.2.2.
Byron, II.17.4.

Caballero, II.2.21; III.1.15.

Cadalso, José, V.10; *Cartas marruecas,* vital and artistic dimensions, V.10.1; patriotic role, V.10.2.

Cain, Sr. Mariano, IV.22.7.

Calbick, Gladys S., III.28.2.

Calderón de la Barca, Pedro, IV.17; and Aquinas, IV.17.15; auto sacramental, expression of culture, IV.17.6; Baroque, IV.17.8; causality, IV.17.16; chronology of plays, IV.17.11; Circe, IV.17.9; classical mythology, IV.17.20; Comedias de capa y espada, IV.17.23; *La devoción de la cruz,* edition, IV.17.24; *En la vida todo es verdad y todo mentira,* edition, IV.17.3; *La española de Florencia,* edition, IV.17.19; feminism, IV.17.13; form, *La vida es sueño,* IV.17.18; *El gran teatro del mundo,* Nahuatl version, edition, IV.17.12; Hofmannsthal, comparison, IV.17.1; language, IV.17.14; liturgical element, IV.17.26; music, IV.17.4; poet of the Eucharist, IV.17.7; role of conflict, *La vida es sueño,* IV.17.21; *El secreto a voces,* edition, IV.17.5; structure, balance, IV.17.2; symbolism, IV.17.25; Vera Tassis' text, IV.17.10.

Caliendo, Eugene L., V.63.1.

*Calila y Dimna,* III.9; classified vocabulary, III.9.3; comparison, Arabic-Old Spanish versions, III.9.2; etymological vocabulary, III.9.1.

Callagham, Sr. Mary Consuela, VII.13.2.

Callan, Richard J., VII.22.1.

Callcott, Frank, III.1.4.

Calvert, Laura D., V.89.1.

Calvo, Bonifacio, II.26.2.

Cameron, Wallace J., IV.85.2.

Camões, Luiz de, IX.5; adjective, IX.5.1; commentary, historic and geographic, IX.5.2; criticism, IX.5.1; earthly paradise, IX.5.3; influence in English literature, IX.5.4; *Lusiads,* IX.5.1, IX.5.2; Renaissance motifs, IX.5.5; verb, IX.5.1.

Campa, Arthur L., II.4.2.

Campa, David L., VII.10.7.

Campbell, Brenton K., II.7.4.

Campbell, Margaret V., VII.4.2.

Campbell, Richard J., I.23.6.

Campbell, Ruth F., VI.58.3.

Campiglia, Jeanette, IV.122.10.

Campo, Angel del, life and works, VII.34.1.

*Cancioneiro de Évora,* edition, IV.18.1; IX.6.1.

*Cancionero,* MS 3168, Biblioteca Nacional (Siglo XVI), IV.18.2.

*Cancionero de Baena,* doctrinal poetry, III.10.1.

Canfield, Delos L., I.23.7.

Cannon, William C., VI.73.4.

Cano, Juan, II.7.5.

*Cantar de Don Sancho II de Castilla,* derivations, III.11.

*Cantigas d'escarnho e de maldizer,* edition, IX.7.

Capa y espada, comedias de, IV.17.23.

Cape Verdean literature, study, IX.8.1.

Capsas, Cleon W., VII.30.2.

Carballido, Emilio, dramatic work, VII.35.1.

Cárdenas, Daniel N., I.9.3.

Cardona, Rudolph, VI.29.1.

Carner, Robert J., IV.38.2.

Carney, Hal, V.53.8.

Caro, José Eusebio, poetry, VII.36.1.

Carpentier, Alejo, *Los pasos perdidos,* narrative prose of, VII.37.1.

Carranza, Matilde, V.53.9.

Carrasco, María S., V.2.1.

Carrasquilla, Tomás, dialect, I.9.16; life and works, VII.38.1.

Carrell, Thelma R., VII.19.1.

Carrera Andrade, Jorge, poetic world of, VII.39.1.

Carrino, Frank G., VII.60.1.

Carruthers, Ben F., VII.177.1.

Cartagena, Alonso de, *Doctrinal de los caballeros,* text, sources, III.12.1.

Cartagena, Teresa de, *Arboleda de los enfermos. Admiraçion operum Dey,* study and edition, III.13.1.

Carter, Erwin D., VII.2.3.

Carter, Henry Hare, IX.1.1.

Carter, Sr. Mary R., VI.11.1.

Cartey, Wilfred G., VII.24.1.

Casa, Frank P., IV.80.3.

Casal, Julián del, life and works, VII.40.1.

Casas, Rogelio A., VI.44.1.

Case, Thomas E., IV.122.11.

Caso, Antonio, philosophy of, VII.41.1.

Castagnaro, Rosario A., VII.10.8.

Castán de Pontrelli, Mary, VII.82.2.

Castañeda, James A., IV.122.12.

Castanien, Donald G., VII.16.4.

Castellanos, Jesús, VII.42; life and work, VII.42.1; literary works, VII.42.2.

Castellanos, Rosario, poetic work, VII.43.1.

Castiglione, II.22.9.

*Castigos e documentos,* personal pronouns, III.14.1.

Castilla, vision of, VI.41.7, VI.47.8.

Castillejo, Cristóbal de, life and works, IV.19.1.

Castillo, Carlos, IV.17.3.

Castillo, Homero, VII.100.1.

Castillo Solórzano, Alonso, analysis of novelistic production, IV.20.1.

Castro, Américo, criticism in *RFE,* 1914-1960, VI.15.1.

Castro, Eugênio de, cosmopolitanism in Hispanic poetry, IX.9.1.

Castro, Guillén de, IV.21; dramatic art, IV.21.5; dramatic technique, IV.21.2; form, *Las mocedades del Cid,* IV.21.6; honor, IV.21.3; *Romancero,* influence, IV.21.4; *La tragedia por los celos,* IV.21.1.

Castro, Rosalía de, V.11; *Cantares gallegos,* V.11.1; *Follas novas,* V.11.1; interpreter of Galicia, V.11.2; lyric, traditional, V.11.1; manner and mood, V.11.4; poet, V.11.3; study, V.11.5; style, V.11.4; themes, V.11.4.

Catalan, I.7; concordance of Auzias March, I.7.1; *Gloria d'amor,* glossary, I.7.4; historical phonetics, I.7.6; language of Lull, I.7.2; of northern New York, I.7.3; *Vides de Santz Rosselloneses,* glossary, I.7.5.

Caudillo, military, VII.10.27.

Causality, IV.17.16.

Causey, James Y., I.15.5.

Cauvin, Sr. Mary A., IV.36.6.

Cebollada Lacosta, Francisco, VI.35.1.

Cebuano vocabulary of Bible, I.2.7.

Ceide-Echevarría, Gloria, VII.10.9.

Cela, Camilo José, VI.16; *La colmena,* content and expression, VI.16.3; novels, VI.16.2; technical and structural examination, VI.16.1.

*Celestina,* III.15; authorship, III.15.3; etymological vocabulary, III.15.6; humanistic themes, III.15.2; imitations, III.15.4; interpretation, III.15.5, III.15.7; pessimism, III.15.1; theology, III.15.7.

Cerezo de Ponce, Engracia, I.9.4.

Cernuda, Luis, VI.17; meditative poetry, VI.17.1; poetry, VI.17.3, VI.17.4; world view, VI.17.2.

Cervantes, Miguel de, IV.22; bases of society, IV.22.11; Bible, IV.22.35; Bouscal, Guérin de, IV.22.10; *El casamiento engañoso,* language and style, IV.22.1; Christian attitudes, IV.22.6; deception, IV.22.4; discreción, IV.22.2; *Las dos doncellas,* language and style, IV.22.1; entremeses, IV.22.7; Humanitas Cervantina, IV.22.36; idea of the theater, IV.22.7; individual, IV.22.11; influence in France, IV.22.10; intergroup relations, IV.22.8; literary ideas, IV.22.17; matrimony, IV.22.33; *Novelas ejemplares,* narrative art, IV.22.37; novelist of transition, IV.22.18; Núñez de Reinoso, IV.22.42; Pérez Galdós, novels of, IV.22.41; *Persiles y Sigismunda,* Baroque elements, IV.22.23; Rabelais, IV.22.18; Russia, IV.22.39; Tacio, Aquiles, IV.22.42; theater, IV.22.28; women, IV.22.38.

—*Don Quijote,* adjective, position, IV.22.5; Castiglione, IV.22.27; comic, linguistic, IV.22.3; contemplation, IV.22.15; criticism, English and American, IV.22.13; distance and control, IV.22.14; Fielding, IV.22.32; Generation of '98, IV.22.12; image, IV.22.34; imitations, IV.22.25; influence, IV.22.20; Inglis, IV.22.29; moods and tenses, IV.22.40; negation, IV.22.19; Pérez Galdós, novels of, IV.22.21, IV.22.31; sanity, IV.22.4; satire, IV.22.13; sources, IV.22.22; subjunctive, IV.22.16; technique, narrative, IV.22.14; time, IV.22.30; translators, IV.22.26; word-play, IV.22.9.

Cervone, Anthony V., II.7.6.

Cetina, Gutierre de, sources of poetry, IV.23.1.

Chadwick, John R., VII.15.1.

Chamberlain, Mary H., I.20.2.

Chamberlin, Vernon A., V.53.10.

Chambers, Dwight O., II.17.3.

Chambers, Frank M., I.26.8.

Chambers, Leland H., IV.52.1.

Chandler, Arthur A., II.2.8.

Chandler, Frank W., IV.85.3.

Chandler, Richard E., II.3.2.

Chang-Rodríguez, Eugenio, VII.78.1.

Change, V.51.7.

*Chanson de Roland,* II.19.9, II.19.30.

Chapman, George A., VII.4.3.

Characterization, V.53.4, V.53.14, V.53.51, VII.108.1, VII.126.5.

Characters, census, V.4.6, V.53.3; creation, V.53.7; feminine, VI.11.2, VI.21.1, VII.106.2 (*See also* Woman); types, V.50.1, V.52.5, VII.105.2.

Charlemagne, II.19.38.

Chart, Ira, V.31.1.

Chateaubriand, II.19.10, II.33.3.

Chatham, James R., I.8.2.

Châtillon, Gautier de, II.19.44.
Chaves-García, José M., IV.22.8.
Chavous, Quentin, VI.23.1.
Chenery, Winthrop H., I.8.3.
Cheskis, Joseph I., I.9.5.
Chew, Jeanne M., V.3.1.
Childers, James W., IV.3.1.
Chilean literature, VII.4; costumbrismo, VII.
    4.5; criticism, evolution, VII.4.6; essay, to
    1900, VII.4.8; fiction, sea in, VII.4.4; His-
    panoamérica, problem in literature, VII.
    4.9; intellectual life, role of Hanssen and
    Lenz, VII.4.11; literary movement of 1842,
    antecedents, VII.4.2; naturalism, VII.4.12;
    novel, city, 1900-1943, VII.4.3; poetry, de-
    velopment 16th-19th centuries, VII.4.1;
    prose, costumbrismo, VII.4.5; Romantic
    generation, VII.4.9; social classes, VII.4.7;
    social protest, VII.4.10; social types, VII.
    4.3, VII.4.7.
Chilean Spanish, Anglicism, I.5.1; phonetic
    modification, I.5.1.
Chinchón, Osvaldo, VII.4.4.
Chirveches A., Armando, novelist, VII.44.1.
Chittenden, Jean S., I.20.3.
Cholo, VII.96.1.
Christmas carol, IV.122.50.
Christmas play, III.22.7.
Chronicle-legend plays, IV.122.33.
Chronology of plays, IV.17.11.
Churchman (type), III.22.5.
Churchman, Philip H., II.17.4.
Cicero, II.23.17.
Ciplijauskaité, Biruté, VI.1.1.
Circe, II.2.16.
Circumstance of man, VI.52.1.
Cirre, Manuela M., II.13.1.
Ciruti, Joan E., VII.9.1.
Clarke, Dorothy C., II.12.3.
Classical reference, II.15.8.
Classical-Spanish American literary
    relations, II.31.
Classical-Spanish literary relations, II.15.
Clause, I.8; dependent, I.8.2, I.8.3; indirect
    interrogative, I.8.2; prepositional comple-
    mentary, I.8.6; relative, I.8.4; tagmemic
    analysis, I.8.1; verb, structure, I.8.5.
Claydon, Ellen E., IV.11.1.
Clemens, George B., VIII.5.2.
Clergyman, V.46.4, V.51.7, V.53.17.
Clinkscales, Orline, II.28.4.
Clown, IV.53.5.
Cobb, Carl W., II.32.1.
Cobb, Edna H., V.53.11.
Cobb, Herbert L., VII.138.1.
Cocozzella, Peter, III.48.1.
Coester, Alfred L., III.53.2.
Cognates, Spanish-English, I.27.9.
Colecchia, Francesca M., VI.26.2.
Coleman, John A., VI.17.1.
Coleman, Sarah E., III.1.5.
Colford, William E., V.39.1.
Coll, Edna, VII.10.10.
Collard-Wéry, Andrée M., II.7.7.
Collins, Pauline P., VII.1.2.
Colloquial Spanish, adverb, I.4.4; Colom-
    bian, glossary, I.9.30; emphasis, I.2.3.
—Mexican, I.3.6, I.9.13, I.9.31; noun suffixes,
    I.9.31; position of noun modifier, I.9.37;
    syntax of exclamation, I.9.13.
Colombian literature, VII.5; cuadro de cos-

tumbres, VII.5.1; historical novel, 1844-
    1959, VII.5.3; Indian, VII.5.2.
Colombian Spanish, Antioquian Oriente,
    I.9.28; colloquial speech of males, I.9.30;
    spoken styles, I.9.25.
Colonne, Guido delle, II.23.2, II.23.12.
Color, VII.114.6.
Color terms, I.27.6.
Columbus, Christopher, II.18.2.
Comedia de figurón, Rojas Zorrilla and
    Moreto, IV.24.1.
Comedia de la vida y muerte de San
    Augustín, edition, IV.36.11.
Comedia de la vida y muerte del Santo Fray
    Diego, edition, IV.36.11.
Comedia de Nuestra Señora de Lapa y un
    milagro que hiço, edition, IV.36.30.
Comedia del glorioso San Martín, edition,
    IV.99.1.
Comedia yntitulada del tirano Rey
    Corbanto, edition, IV.36.22.
Comedia Ypólita, edition, IV.36.10.
Comedians, Italian, IV.117.1.
Comedy, Neo-Classic, V.45.4.
Comic character, II.17.31, III.1.1, III.22.4,
    IV.22.3.
Comic elements, IV.80.6, VI.26.4, VI.35.2.
Comic, linguistic, I.2.4.
Compañía de Jesús, IV.52.5.
Compañías bananeras, VII.126.2.
Comparative studies, Brazilian relations with
    other literatures, X.22-25; Brazil-Biblical,
    X.22; Brazil-Haiti, X.23; Brazil-Spanish
    America, X.24; Brazil-United States, X.25.
—Portuguese relations with other literatures,
    IX.25-29; Portuguese-English, IX.25; Portu-
    guese-European, IX.26; Portuguese-French,
    IX.27; Portuguese-Latin, IX.28; Portu-
    guese-Spanish, IX.29.
—Spanish American relations with other
    literatures, II.30-35; Spanish American-
    Brazilian, II.30; Spanish American-Classi-
    cal, II.31; Spanish American-English, II.
    32; Spanish American-French, II.33; Span-
    ish American-Haiti, II.34; Spanish Ameri-
    can-United States, II.35.
—Spanish relations with other literatures,
    II.13-29; Spanish-Arabic, II.13; Spanish-
    Biblical, II.14; Spanish-Classical, II.15;
    Spanish-Dutch, II.16; Spanish-English, II.
    17; Spanish-European, II.18; Spanish-
    French, II.19; Spanish-Germanic, II.20;
    Spanish-Greek, II.21; Spanish-Italian, II.
    22; Spanish-Latin (Classical and Medi-
    eval), II.23; Spanish-Norwegian, II.24;
    Spanish-Portuguese, II.25; Spanish-Pro-
    vençal, II.26; Spanish-Russian, II.27; Span-
    ish-Spanish American, II.28; Spanish-
    United States, II.29.
Comparison, phonetic, English-Spanish,
    I.23.20.
Compression, III.53.2.
Compton, James D., I.16.4.
Compton, Merlin D., II.2.9.
Computer processing, I.2.10.
Conceptismo, IV.25; in Spanish criticism,
    IV.25.1; Quevedo, IV.25.2.
Concepts, Christological, IV.122.1; Fortune,
    IV.122.52; God, VI.37.7; moral, VI.67.3;
    society, V.15.1.
Concordances (See also Glossaries): Berceo,

I.15.56; Juan Manuel, El conde Lucanor,
    I.10.13; Auzias March, I.7.1.
Conflict, border, VII.140.5; of mission and
    vocation, VI.56.3; poet of, VI.73.11; role
    of, IV.17.21; subconscious, IV.40.3.
Conis, James N., VI.6.1.
Connell, Chester C., I.23.8.
Conner, Arthur B., II.33.2.
Connor, Patricia J., IV.17.4.
Consonant, alternation of h and f in Old
    Spanish, I.23.13; clusters, intervocalic,
    I.23.2; groups, I.23.3, I.23.31; nasal, I.23.15;
    sibilants, I.23.12, I.23.17, I.23.39; velar,
    I.23.1.
Contemplation, IV.22.15.
"Contemporáneos," VII.10.11.
Content, serious, VI.5.1.
Contreras, Matilda, V.11.2.
Control, IV.22.14.
Conversion, VI.43.1.
Conway, Sr. M. Ann, I.3.2.
Cook, John A., V.45.4.
Coons, Dix S., VII.144.1.
Cooper, Louis, I.16.5.
Cooper, Paul J., I.16.6.
Corbató, Hermenegildo, III.22.1.
Corbett, Evelyn D., VII.126.3.
Corbière, Anthony S., II.19.5.
Corbitt, Roberta D., VII.114.1.
Corcoran, Sr. Mary H., IV.58.1.
Cord, William O., VII.158.2.
Corley, Ames H., I.2.6.
Corneille, Pierre, II.19.32, II.19.36.
Cornish, Beatrice Q., V.44.1.
Corpus Christi Procession, II.4.10.
Correa, Gustavo, VI.26.3.
Corrido, II.3.15, II.3.18.
"Corrido de Gregorio Cortez," VII.140.5.
Corrigan, Robert, VI.56.2.
Cortés, Hernán, IV.26; in poetry, IV.26.1;
    letters, IV.26.2; policies, IV.26.2.
Cortés, Luis J., VII.13.3.
Cosmopolitanism in poetry, II.8.2.
Costa, Joaquín, thought and influence in
    Generation of '98, V.12.1.
Costa Rican literature, VII.6; costumbrismo,
    VII.6.2; culture, VII.6.1; novel, VII.6.3;
    survey, VII.6.1.
Costa Rican Spanish, Anglicism, I.5.4; argot,
    I.9.48.
Costumbrismo, Spanish, V.13, VI.18; Blasco
    Ibáñez, VI.18.1; early writers, 1750-1830,
    V.13.6; genre study, V.13.2; Mesonero
    Romanos, essays, V.13.1; Pereda, Escenas
    montañesas, V.13.5; periodicals of Madrid,
    V.13.4; social environment, V.13.3.
—Spanish America, VII.45; Andean region,
    VII.45.5; Argentina, VII.45.3; Carrasquilla,
    VII.45.4; Chile, VII.45.1, VII.45.7; Co-
    lombia, VII.45.2; Costa Rica, VII.45.6;
    Ecuador, VII.45.8.
Coughlin, Edward V., V.15.2.
Coutu, Sr. Albert C., II.7.8.
Cowboy, II.4.7.
Cowles, Ella N., I.9.6.
Crabb, Daniel M., I.26.10.
Craddock, Sr. Clare E., II.10.1.
Crane, Stephen, II.29.10.
Crantford, Carey S., II.20.4.
Craven, Robert K., I.17.1.
Crawford, James P., IV.114.1.

Rodríguez Rubí, Tomás, theater of the 19th
century, V.57.1.

Rogers, Cornelia H., II.3.16.

Rogers, Douglass M., VI.34.1.

Rogers, Francis M., VIII.4.2.

Rogers, Paul P., V.15.9.

Rogue. *See* Pícaro.

Rojas, Carlos A., VII.54.1.

Rojas, Ricardo, and Argentine nationalism,
VII.154.1.

Rojas González, Francisco, contribution to
Mexican literature, VII.155.1.

Rojas Villandrando, Agùstín de, IV.102; *El
natural desdichado*, edition, IV.102.1; *El
viage entretenido*, possible source of Scarron, IV.102.2.

Rojas Zorrilla, Francisco de, IV.103; comedia
de figurón, IV.103.3; *Peligrar en los remedios*, edition, IV.103.2; *El villano gran
señor y gran Tamorlán de Persia*, edition,
IV.103.1.

Roland, II.19.9.

Roldán, María M., I.29.37.

*Roman de la rose*, II.19.20.

*Romance*, semantic development of the
word, I.27.10.

Romance of adventure, III.25.1.

Romance languages, comparative, general,
I.26; Arabic words, I.26.5; article, I.26.40;
aspect, I.26.39; *-aticus*, I.26.30; auditory
equivalence, I.26.11; auxiliary verbs, I.26.
19; color terms, I.26.15; comparison, Span-
ish-Portuguese, I.26.35; conditional relations, I.26.17; departure and arrival, verbs
of, I.26.29; diphthongization, I.26.36; future
time, I.26.34; gerundial construction, I.26.
20; glide sounds, I.26.2; hiatus groups,
I.26.28; imperatives, I.26.3; indefiniteness,
*(some, any)*, I.26.23; kinship terminology,
I.26.41; Latin passive in Romance, I.26.37;
loan words, I.26.33; nasals, I.26.16; nouns,
I.26.21; participial substantives, *-ata* type,
I.26.1; passive, I.26.37; patterns, linguistic,
I.26.18; periphrasis, I.26.4; phonetic tendency, I.26.26; phonology, I.26.24; Portu-
guese-Spanish, comparison, I.26.35; present tense, I.26.25; redundancy, I.26.38;
semantics, I.26.15, I.26.22, I.26.29; Spanish-
Portuguese, comparison, I.26.35; stringed
instruments, designations, I.26.14; subjunctive, I.26.8; substratum theory, I.26.
24; syncope, I.26.12; verbal formations,
I.26.6; verbs of thinking, I.26.13; vowel,
I.26.9, I.26.16; word order, I.26.10.

Romancero, II.3.3, II.3.4, II.3.5, II.3.9,
II.3.13.

Romances, III.60; Bernardo del Carpio, III.
60.4; Gibson, James Young, translations,
III.60.1; historical, III.60.3; ideology, Spanish, III.60.3; origins, III.60.6; Sepúlveda,
Lorenzo de, sources of ballads, III.60.5;
treason in, III.60.2; women in, III.60.7.
*See also* Ballad and folksong.

Romanticism, V.58, VI.63, VII.156; Argen-
tina, VII.156.4; Chile, VII.156.4; Dumas
père, influence, V.58.13; Echegaray, drama,
V.58.8; epithet, poetry, V.58.9; García
Gutiérrez, V.58.1; Gil y Carrasco, V.58.11;
history, dramatists' attitude toward, V.58.
10; honor code, in drama, V.58.12; León,
Ricardo, VI.63.1; Martínez de la Rosa,
V.58.2; medievalisms, V.58.5; Meléndez
Valdés, V.58.3; Mexico, VII.156.1, VII.156.

2, VII.156.3; novel, VII.156.2, VII.156.6,
VII.156.7; Ochoa, Eugenio de, V.58.7;
polimetria of poets, V.58.6; *Tradiciones
peruanas*, Romantic elements, VII.156.8;
Trueba, Antonio de, V.58.4.

Romeo, Andrew L., I.10.13.

Romeo, Luigi, I.23.32.

Romera-Navarro, Miguel, VI.73.19.

Romero, Francisco, Argentine thinker,
VII.157.1.

Romero, José Rubén, VII.158; female characters, VII.158.4; ideology, VII.158.3; novel
of the revolution, VII.158.1; style, VII.
158.3; voice of Mexico, VII.158.2.

Romero García, Manuel, Venezuelan
novelist, VII.159.1.

Rooney, Sr. St. Dominic, V.55.4.

Rosa, João Guimarães, linguistic study,
X.19.1.

Rosaldo y Hernández, Renato, VII.151.1.

Rosales, Luis, poet of "Generación del '36,"
VI.64.1.

Rose, Robert S., IV.97.13.

Rose, Theodore Everett, X.11.3.

Rosen, Harold E., IV.123.8.

Rosenbaum, Sidonia C., VII.18.1.

Rosenberg, Donald L., VII.176.1.

Rosenberg, Solomon, IV.17.19.

Rosenthal, William M., VI.22.1.

Ross, Cecilia, IV.122.48.

Rossi, Pietro C., I.27.13.

Rothberg, Irving P., II.21.3.

Rotunda, Dominic P., II.22.12.

Rovner, Philip, IV.122.49.

Roybal, Sr. M. Angelica, III.8.5.

Rozen, Eva J., II.8.3.

Rozzell, Ramon C., IV.123.9.

*Rrekotamiento del rrey Alisandere*, edition,
notes, glossary, III.56.1.

Rubin, Joan, I.2.16.

Rubin, Mordecai S., VII.79.2.

Rubín, Ramón, themes in works, VII.160.1.

Rubio, Antonio, I.13.3.

Rueda, Lope de, IV.104; *Camila*, edition,
IV.104.3; *Comedia de los engañados*, edi-
tion, IV.104.2; *Comedia Eufemia*, edition,
IV.104.1; *Tymbria*, edition, IV.104.3.

Ruffner, Sydney J., IV.36.35.

Ruggerio, Michael J., II.2.23.

Ruiz, Juan, Arcipreste de Hita, III.61;
artistry, III.61.8; didactic sense, III.61.3;
fables, sources, III.61.7; *Libro de buen
amor*, III.61.1, III.61.2, III.61.3, III.61.4,
III.61.5, III.61.6, III.61.7; manuscripts,
III.61.4; phonology, III.61.1, III.61.2,
III.61.6; sibilants, III.61.6; vocabulary,
III.61.5.

Ruiz de Alarcón, Juan, IV.105; Baroque
dramatist, IV.105.3; biography, IV.105.10;
classical influences, IV.105.8; democratic
spirit, IV.105.2; *Examen de maridos*, edition, IV.105.1; gracioso, IV.105.9; motif
elements, classification, IV.105.7; occult
arts, IV.105.5; Spanish environment, IV.
105.4; Spanish influences, IV.105.8; structure of comedia, IV.105.6.

Ruiz-de-Conde, Justina, IV.83.2.

Ruiz y Ruiz, Lina A., VIII.5.6.

Rundorff, Dorothy E., V.68.5.

Russell, Billy M., III.1.18.

Russell, Robert H., V.53.41.

Russian-Spanish literary relations, II.27.

Russo, Harold J., IX.11.2.

Rust, John B., VI.55.9.

Rust, Zell O., VII.83.2.

Rustic, IV.122.34.

Rutherford, Phillip R., I.1.2.

Ryan, James J., IV.2.29.

Saavedra Fajardo, Diego de, IV.106; political thought, IV.106.1; the prince, IV.106 2.

Sábato, Ernesto, essayist and novelist,
VII.161.1.

Sackett, Theodore A., V.53.42.

Sacks, Norman P., VIII.5.7.

Sacredness, II.4.3.

Sáenz, Gerardo, VII.175.1.

Sáenz, Pilar G., VI.19.1.

Sáenz y Sáenz, Hilario, V.53.43.

Sáez, Alfred R., II.14.4.

Sáez, Mercedes, I.9.39.

Sainete, V.9.1, VII.55.4.

Saint-Amant, II.19.22.

St. Amour, Sr. M. Paulina, III.54.6.

Sainthood, IV.36.29.

Salas Barbadillo, Alonso Jerónimo de,
IV.107; *El caballero perfecto*, edition, IV.
107.2; *Don Diego de noche*, edition, IV.
107.3; study of works, IV.107.4; *El sutil
cordobés Pedro de Urdemalas*, edition,
IV.107.1.

Salaverría, José María, biographical and
critical study, VI.65.1.

Sales, Saint Francis de, II.19.33.

Salgado, María A., VI.37.6.

Salinas, Pedro, VI.66; nothingness, VI.66.2;
ontological affinity, VI.66.3; poetic reality,
VI.66.1.

Salley, William C., V.15.10.

Salvador, Graciano, II.19.34.

Samaniego, Félix María de, V.59; *Fábulas en
verso castellano*, edition, V.59.1; Fontaine,
Jean de la, influence, V.59.2.

Samuels, Daniel G., V.58.11.

Sanches de Uzeda, Gonzalo, translator, *Libro
del gentil e de los tres sabios*, edition,
III.62.1.

Sánchez, Florencio, VII.162; Argentine theatre, VII.162.2; studies, VII.162.1, VII.
162.3.

Sánchez, Joseph, V.52.4.

Sánchez, Miguel, influence on Lope, IV.108.1.

Sánchez, Porfirio, V.51.10.

Sánchez, Roberto G., VI.26.8.

Sánchez Arce, Nellie E., IV.95.12.

Sánchez de Badajoz, Diego, IV.109; *Farsa de
la hechicera, Farsa del matrimonio, Farsa
de Santa Susana, Farsa de la ventera*,
edition, IV.109.1; tradition and originality in farces, IV.109.2.

Sánchez-Barbudo, Angela, IV.2.30.

Sánchez y Escribano, Federico, IV.60.1.

Sánchez-Romeralo, Antonio, III.54.7.

Sánchez Vercial, Clemente, *El libro de los
exenplos por a.b.c.*, etymological lexicon,
III.63.1.

Sand, Louise, I.2.17.

Sanelo, Manuel Joaquín, *Diccionario
valenciano-castellano*, I.9.12.

Sanity, IV.22.4.

Sannazaro, II.22.11, II.22.17.

Santa Cruz y Espejo, Francisco Javier
Eugenio de, Ecuadorian man of the Enlightenment, VII.163.1.

Santa Teresa de Jesús, IV.110; America,
IV.110.1; letters, IV.110.2; Lull, influence,
IV.110.3.

IV.122.8; *La hermosa Ester*, edition, IV.
122.48; *La hermosura de Angélica*, edition, IV.122.9; historic plots, IV.122.16;
honor, conjugal, IV.122.17; inequality,
social, IV.122.45; justice, IV.122.53; kingship, IV.122.49; *The Lady Nit-Wit*, translation, IV.122.35; line-structure, internal,
IV.122.42; love, IV.122.45; lyricism, IV.
122.16; marriage, IV.122.45; nature, aspects in comedia, IV.122.10; novelesque
elements, IV.122.3; *La nueva victoria de
D. Gonzalo de Cordoua*, edition, IV.122.
64; *Las paces de los reyes y judía de
Toledo*, edition, IV.122.12; pastoral romance, Lope-Sannazaro, IV.122.46; patriotism, IV.122.56; *El peregino en su patria*,
IV.122.23; personal experience, IV.122.58;
plot, patterns, IV.122.21; plot, secondary,
IV.122.30; *El poder en el discreto*, edition,
IV.122.18; poetry, IV.122.1, IV.122.15;
popular elements, IV.122.53; precepts,
dramatic, IV.122.39; *El príncipe despeñado*, edition, IV.122.22; Reina Sevilla
legend, IV.122.59; romance of adventure,
IV.122.23; romancero, IV.122.33; rustic,
IV.122.34; Sánchez, Miguel, Terentian influence, IV.122.57; *Si no vieran las mujeres!*, edition, IV.122.14; soldier, IV.122.5;
songs, dramatic function, IV.122.60; sonnets in plays, critical index, IV.122.13;
sources, Italian novelle, IV.122.51; technique, dramatic, IV.122.2; Terrence, influence, IV.122.57; traditional elements,
IV.122.3; tragicomic style, Lope-Shakespeare, IV.122.44; unities, dramatic, IV.
122.32; *La villana de Getafe*, edition,
IV.122.25; villancico, IV.122.50; *El villano
en su rincón*, edition, IV.122.54.
Velar sounds, I.23.1.
Vélez de Guevara, Luis, IV.123; *El amor en
vizcaino, los celos en francés y torneos
de Navarra*, edition, IV.123.8; comedias,
romancero in, IV.123.4; comedias, versification, IV.123.2; *El conde don Pero Vélez
y don Sancho el deseado*, IV.123.6; *El
conde don Sancho Niño*, edition, IV.123.3;
*El embuste acreditado y el disparate
creido*, edition, IV.123.7; *El gran Iorge
Castrioto y Príncipe Escanderbey*, edition,
IV.123.1; life and dramatic works, IV.123.
10; *La niña de Gómez Arias*, edition, IV.
123.9; romancero material, aesthetic treatment, IV.123.4; versification, qualitative
analysis, IV.123.2; *Virtudes vencen señales*,
edition, IV.123.5.
Venezuelan literature, VII.15; bibliography,
Yale University Library, VII.15.2; fiction,
VII.15.3; novel, currents in, VII.15.1.
Ventura, Miguel, I.7.6.
Verb, I.31; Alfonso X, *General estoria, primera parte*, study, I.31.24; arrival, I.31.25;
aspect, I.31.28, I.31.37; auxiliary, I.31.13,
I.31.35, I.31.39; Camões, *Lusiads*, study,
VIII.13.1; categories, I.31.23, I.31.38; clause
structure, I.31.27; cognate, Indo-European,
I.2.14; compound tenses, I.31.29; departure, I.31.25; *estar*, I.31.36, VIII.13.3;
formation, I.31.9; generative-transformational analysis, I.31.41; gerundial construction, I.31.14; *haber*, I.31.20, I.31.29,
I.31.35, I.31.36; *hacer*, I.31.33; imperatives,
I.31.1; infinitive, I.31.4, I.31.26; modal,
I.31.12, I.31.26; morphology, I.31.22, VIII.

13.2; motion, I.31.7; nouns from past
participles, I.31.15; passive, I.31.8, I.31.31;
past participle, I.31.15, I.31.29; periphrasis, I.31.6; phrase, I.31.5, I.31.12, I.31.27;
progressive, I.31.34; *-ra* form, I.31.42,
I.31.43; reflexives, I.31.2, I.31.8; semantics,
I.31.3, I.31.11, I.31.24, I.31.25; *ser*, I.31.36,
VIII.13.3; subjunctive, I.31.10, I.31.18,
I.31.19; tenses, I.31.3, I.31.21, I.31.28,
I.31.30, I.31.32, I.31.40; thinking, I.31.11;
"to take, seize, grasp," in Spanish, I.31.16;
verb-creation, I.31.17.
Vergil, II.23.7, II.23.9.
Versification, II.12; Alexandrine, II.12.15;
Alfonso X, II.12.9; arte mayor, II.12.5;
Berceo, II.12.6; cuaderna vía, II.12.6;
décima, II.12.3; Espinel, II.12.3; Espronceda, II.12.4; hiatus, II.12.1, II.12.14; irregular, II.12.8; medieval, II.12.12; Pérez
de Montalván, II.12.10; Romantic, II.12.13;
sixteenth century, II.12.7; Solís y Rivadeneyra, Antonio de, II.12.10; synalepha,
II.12.1, II.12.14; syneresis, II.12.14; Vega,
Lope de, II.12.11; Vélez de Guevara,
II.12.2; Villasandino, II.12.5.
Very, Francis G., II.4.10.
Verzasconi, Ray A., VII.22.3.
Vetrano, Anthony J., I.9.47.
Vezilla Castellanos, Pedro de la, *El león de
España*, edition, IV.124.1.
*Viage a Jerusalem*, II.2.1.
*Viaje de Turquia*, sources, authorship,
historical background, IV.125.1.
Viana, Javier de, man and works, VII.185.1.
Vicente, Gil, IV.126, IX.22; artistry, IV.126.1,
IV.126.2, IV.126.5; etymological vocabulary, IV.126.4; poetic technique, IV.126.3.
*Vida de S. Bernardo*, critical edition, IX.23.1.
Vida española, V.53.43.
*La vida y muerte de San Gerónimo*, edition,
IV.36.4.
Vidal de Basalú, Raimón, edition and
commentary, III.75.1.
*Vidas de Santa María Medalena y Santa
Marta*, edition, III.76.1.
*Vides de Santz Rosselloneses*, III.77; glossary,
III.77.2; introduction, III.77.2; partial
edition, III.77.1, III.77.2; proper names,
III.77.2.
Vieira, Antônio, Bossuet and, stylistic
comparison, IX.24.1.
Villa, Pancho, VII.10.12.
Villalón, Cristóbal de, *El scholástico*, edition
and study, IV.127.1.
Villancico, III.54.6, III.54.7.
Villanueva, Jerónimo de, *El villano gran
señor y gran Tamorlán de Persia*, edition,
IV.128.1.
Villarejo, Oscar M., II.17.29.
Villaurrutia, Xavier, VII.186; literary art,
VII.186.1; man and dramas, VII.186.2.
Villegas, Francisco, I.9.48.
Vinci, Joseph, IV.72.1.
Virgillo, Carmelo, X.13.2.
Virués, Cristóbal de, study of dramatic
works, IV.129.1.
Vision, of Castilla, VI.41.7, VI.47.8; of life,
VI.49.1; of Spain, VI.58.3; of the world,
VI.17.2.
Vives, Juan Luis, political ideas, IV.130.1.
Vogt, Verne L., VI.13.7.
Voltaire, II.19.27.
Voluntad, VI.1.3, VI.60.1.

Voragine, Jacobus de, II.23.6, II.23.10.
Vorrath, John C., V.68.8.
Vowel, atonic, I.23.8; nasalization, I.23.15;
spectrographic·analysis, I.23.33.
Vranich, Stanko A., IV.8.1.
Wade, Gerald E., IV.116.9.
Wagner, Charles P., III.37.2.
Wahl, Rosalie, VI.10.13.
Waldorf, Paul D., VII.10.36.
Wallis, Marie P., X.16.1.
Walsh, James L., I.21.3.
Walther, Don H., X.8.3.
War, Carlist, V.53.31, V.53.48, VI.10.10;
Civil, VI.7.1, VI.55.1, VI.55.7, VI.55.8;
Guerra del Chaco, VII.3.1, VII.3.2; people's
view of, VII.10.29; Spanish-American, II.
29.10; "Yanko-Spanko," II.29.5.
Wardropper, Bruce W., IV.9.8.
Warenreich, Edward D., IV.17.23.
Warner, Ralph E., VII.19.2.
Warren, Virgil A., VII.16.24.
Watkins, Alma T., VI.71.1.
Watland, Charles D., VII.48.7.
Watt, Ethel G., II.17.30.
Watts, LeClaire B., II.17.31.
Waxman, Samuel M., II.2.26.
Weaver, Billy R., I.18.17.
Weaver, William R., IV.117.3.
Webb, Kenneth W., VII.133.4.
Webber, Edwin J., II.23.18.
Weber, Frances L., VI.58.8.
Weber, Robert J., V.53.53.
Weiger, John G., IV.36.42.
Weinstein, Leo, II.2.27.
Weiss, Arnold H., II.2.28.
Weiss, Gerard M., V.52.5.
Weiss, Harry, VII.83.3.
Weitzner, Margaret E., VI.49.1.
Welch, Sr. Mary B., IV.91.1.
Weller, Hubert P., VII.17.1.
Wellington, Marie Z., II.22.17.
Wellman, Esther T., VII.124.2.
Wershow, Irving R., VII.70.5.
Wester, Louise H., III.53.8.
Wexler, Sidney F., IV.17.24.
Whatley, Frances, IV.122.63.
Wheat, Raymond Curtis, VII.188.2.
Wheeler, Howard T., VII.10.37.
Wheelock, Kinch D., III.30.4.
Whitaker, Shirley B., IV.30.1.
Whitby, William M., IV.17.25.
White, Florence E., II.30.2.
White, Ralph E., IV.24.1.
Whitehouse, Victor, IV.36.43.
Whitman, Iris L., II.29.17.
Whitman, Walt, II.29.7.
Whitted, Joseph W., I.10.15.
Whittem, Arthur F., III.61.7.
Whyte, Florence, III.21.2.
Wild man, IV.36.26.
Wilder, William R., VII.133.5.
Wilkins, George W., Jr., I.31.38.
Willbern, Glen D., I.15.61.
Williams, Edwin B., VII.72.2.
Williams, Ethel M., II.2.29.
Williams, Florence I., V.52.6.
Williams, Gladys L., VI.38.3.
Williams, Grace S., III.5.3.
Williams, John D., IV.68.1.
Williams, Robert H., II.22.18.
Williams, Ronald B., III.69.3.
Williams, Sidney J., Jr., IV.120.3.
Willis, Raymond S., Jr., II.19.44.